The Economy of the Word

OXFORD STUDIES IN THE HISTORY OF ECONOMICS

Series Editor: Steven G. Medema, University of Colorado, Denver

This series publishes leading-edge scholarship by historians of economics and social science, drawing upon approaches from intellectual history, the history of ideas, and the history of the natural and social sciences. It embraces the history of economic thinking from ancient times to the present, the evolution of the discipline itself, the relationship of economics to other fields of inquiry, and the diffusion of economic ideas within the discipline and to the policy realm and broader publics. This enlarged scope affords the possibility of looking anew at the intellectual, social, and professional forces that have surrounded and conditioned economics' continued development.

The Economy of the Word

Language, History, and Economics

Keith Tribe

OXFORD
UNIVERSITY PRESS

OXFORD
UNIVERSITY PRESS

Oxford University Press is a department of the University of Oxford.
It furthers the University's objective of excellence in research, scholarship,
and education by publishing worldwide.

Oxford New York
Auckland Cape Town Dar es Salaam Hong Kong Karachi
Kuala Lumpur Madrid Melbourne Mexico City Nairobi
New Delhi Shanghai Taipei Toronto

With offices in
Argentina Austria Brazil Chile Czech Republic France Greece
Guatemala Hungary Italy Japan Poland Portugal Singapore
South Korea Switzerland Thailand Turkey Ukraine Vietnam

Oxford is a registered trade mark of Oxford University Press
in the UK and certain other countries.

Published in the United States of America by
Oxford University Press
198 Madison Avenue, New York, NY 10016

Library of Congress Cataloging-in-Publication Data
Tribe, Keith.
The economy of the word : language, history, and economics / Keith Tribe.
p. cm. — (Oxford studies in the history of economics)
Includes bibliographical references and index.
ISBN 978-0-19-021161-5 (alk. paper)
1. Economics literature—History. 2. Economics—History.
3. Economics—Philosophy. I. Title.
HB75.T7147 2015
330.01'4—dc23
2014026933

1 3 5 7 9 8 6 4 2

Printed in the United States of America on acid-free paper

CONTENTS

LIST OF FIGURES

ACKNOWLEDGMENTS

As a postgraduate student in Cambridge, when I first began to think seriously about the historical analysis of economic discourse, I could always rely on the insights and criticism of Terry Counihan, who arrived from Australia with a Shell Scholarship in 1972. Writing this book has reminded me of his early death in 1999, and of what a great loss it was. During the long winter of 2012–2013 I also lost the two friends who have since the early 1980s been my prime sources of intellectual inspiration: Wilhelm Hennis died in November 2012, and Istvan Hont in March 2013.

I completed the draft for most of this book while Guest of the Principal, Björn Wittrock, at the Swedish Collegium for Advanced Study, Uppsala, in the autumn of 2012. With ideal working conditions and congenial company, SCAS is in a scholarly time warp, and I am very grateful to Björn Wittrock and Lars Magnusson for the experience. Thanks are due also to the staff at SCAS: Ulrika Andersson, Bjarne Graff, Martin Grentzelius, Pia Hultgren, Linn Östman, Sandra Recanovic, Sophie Sköld, and Anna Svensson.

I learned a considerable amount from, and very much enjoyed the company of, the resident SCAS fellows: Pietro Bortone, Antti Gronow, Gerhard Jäger, Asifa Majid, Anthoula Malkopoulou, Przemyslaw Marciniak, Stephan Palmié, Na'ama Pat-El, Eric Pederson, Wendelin Reich, Krishnan Srinivasan, and Joost Zwarts. I am especially grateful to Asifa, Na'ama, Eric, Wendelin, and Joost for showing me how much could be learned from modern linguistics.

I have long benefited from the advice and criticism of Roger Backhouse, Greg Claeys, Simon Cook, Ross Emmett, Gilbert Faccarello, Peter Ghosh, Pat Hudson, Béla Kapossy, Gauthier Lanot, Isaac Nakhimovsky, Terry Peach, Mike Sonenscher, Philippe Steiner, Chris Stray, Ryan Walter, Richard Whatmore, Mike White, and John Winckler; I thank them all. Edward Castleton was especially generous in sharing his transcriptions of Proudhon and other materials with me while I was working on chapters 6 and 7. I also owe a great deal to my editors in New York, Scott Parris and Cathryn Vaulman, who have done much to restore a flagging faith in the book trade.

I am very glad to say that I have received no financial support at all from the usual sources while working on this book, other than the opportunity to spend time at SCAS. Instead, I have relied on my own translation company, Klartext, for all the various costs associated with scholarly activity. Trying to explain this to the fellows at SCAS made me realise that I was, after all, a harbinger of the neoliberal dream for the humanities: the self-financing scholar with several part-time jobs. Chief among the latter has been my employment from 2002 to 2013 at King's School Worcester as a rowing coach, the practical demands of which kept me sane and fit, and gave me the privilege of working with a great team of coaches—Jim Chalmers, Jo Wootton, Tom Sharp, Meg Glenn, Bill Needham, Helen Taylor, and Olivia Rothbury—training a succession of talented young people. Among these, James Green and Becky Lane deserve special mention; and my last squad can stand for all those who preceded them: Theo Beever, Jacob Blasdale, Tom Briggs, Henry Campion, Ollie Copeland, Ben Foster, Chris Gregg, Tom Harrison, Nathan Moss, Joe Murcott, Kaushik Rai, Nick Thomas, Laurence Tonks, Matt Underwood, George Watson, and Jack Welch.

My family has, as always, been a great support while I have been working on this book; it is dedicated to Gabs, my first grand-daughter. The future. However it turns out.

SOURCES

Chapter 1 was drafted at SCAS in October 2012 and completed in March 2014.

Chapter 2 was drafted at SCAS in September 2012. It incorporates some material first published as 'German Economics in the Early Nineteenth Century', in Steven Durlauf, Lawrence Blume (eds.) *The New Palgrave Dictionary of Economics*, 2nd edition, Palgrave Macmillan, Basingstoke 2008.

Chapter 3 was published as 'Constructing National Income in Britain, 1907–1941', *The History of Economic Thought* (Japan) Vol. 47 No. 1 (June 2005) pp. 1–17; it has been slightly revised here.

Chapter 4 was originally published as 'Reading Trade in the *Wealth of Nations*', *History of European Ideas* Vol. 32 (2006) pp. 57–89; it was revised during October 2012 at SCAS.

Chapter 5 was originally presented at the annual meeting of the Dogmenhistorischer Auschuss of the Verein für Sozialpolitik, Lüdinghausen June 2007. In places I draw upon material included in my essays on the Smith reception in *A Critical Bibliography of Adam Smith* (edited by Keith Tribe, with Hiroshi Mizuta), Pickering and Chatto, London 2002. It was published in English as '"Das Adam Smith Problem" and the Origins of Modern Smith Scholarship', *History of European Ideas* Vol. 34 (2008) pp. 514–25; minor revisions were made at SCAS in October 2012.

Chapter 6 began as two lectures on the Year 3 History of Economic Thought course at the University of Birmingham in January 2012. Its main arguments were exposed in the lecture 'Karl Marx: Ricardian Socialist?' at the University of Sussex in May 2012. It was then written up during October 2012 at SCAS, and also in part presented at the CAMHIST Seminar, Clare Hall, Cambridge in January 2014.

Sections of Chapter 7 were originally published as '"The Price is Right": Léon Walras and Economic Justice', *Schweizerische Zeitschrift für Geschichte* Vol. 50 (2000) pp. 388–402, but that essay has here become the conclusion to a more extended argument which was drafted in April 2013.

The Economy of the Word

Whether this propensity ['to truck, barter, and exchange one thing for another'] be one of the original principles in human nature, of which no further account can be given; or whether, as it seems more probable, it be the necessary consequence of the faculties of reason and speech, it belongs not to our present subject to enquire. (Adam Smith, *An Inquiry into the Nature and Causes of the Wealth of Nations*, I.ii.2.)

A book like this, a problem like this, cannot be hurried; and we are both friends of *lento*, me and my book. One did not become a philologist for nothing, perhaps we could even say—a teacher of slow reading:—and in the end one also writes slowly. . . . Philology is that honourable art which, for its admirers, means above all turning aside, giving oneself time, becoming calm, becoming slow -, a savouring of the *word* that achieves nothing that is not reached *lento*. (Friedrich Nietzsche, Preface to *Morgenröte*, Karl Schlechta (ed.) *Werke in Sechs Bände*, Bd. 2, Carl Hanser Verlag, Munich 1980 p. 1016.

CHAPTER 1

Introduction: Not a Method, but a Grammar

Here I may notice a discussion that has been raised . . . as to the pretensions of Political Economy to be regarded as a science at all. I certainly think the language sometimes used by economic writers, suggesting as it does that the doctrines they expound are entitled in respect of scientific perfection to rank with those of physics, is liable to be seriously misleading. But I am not disposed to infer from this that we ought deliberately to acquiesce in treating Political Economy unscientifically. My inference would rather be, not that we ought not to aim at being as scientific as we can, but that we ought to take care not to deceive ourselves as to the extent to which we have actually attained our aim: that, for instance, so far as we are treating Political Economy positively, we should avoid mistaking a generalisation from limited experience for a universal law; and so far as we are treating it hypothetically, we should take care not to use words in different meanings without being aware of the difference, nor suppose our notions to be quantitatively precise when they are really indefinite.

—Henry Sidgwick, *The Principles of Political Economy* (1903)[1]

This book has a broadly methodological intent: to argue that the use of economic language is the proper object of the history of economic discourse, and that in understanding economic argument we must pay attention to 'the economy of the word'. As Sidgwick rightly insisted, we should take care in using our words; and George Orwell later added to this the

1. Henry Sidgwick, *The Principles of Political Economy*, 3rd edition, Macmillan, London 1903 pp. 51–52.

sound principle that while our language 'becomes ugly and inaccurate because our thoughts are foolish, . . . the slovenliness of our language makes it easier for us to have foolish thoughts'.[2] Since 1883, when the first edition of Sidgwick's *Principles* was published, economic argument has become increasingly formalised and technical; but this has not always enhanced the precision with which economic language is used. We might bear in mind that Sidgwick's Cambridge near-contemporary Alfred Marshall had graduated with a First in the 1865 mathematical tripos, as did John Maynard Keynes forty years later, in 1905.[3] Both of them, Maynard Keynes especially, shared Sidgwick's concern that an enthusiasm for logic and number might overwhelm the ability to make good judgements, and form clear arguments. Today 'economic' argument prevails everywhere over political or ethical argument, but the sense of 'economy' this implies is a remarkably attenuated and impoverished one: its meaning has been cheapened. As chapter 2 demonstrates, however, such usage is a recent development, for the contemporary assumption that 'economy' associates efficiency and optimality with a logic of choice only gained general acceptance in the second half of the twentieth century. 'Economy' originated with the ancient Greeks, both semantically and etymologically; and if we follow the term back, we encounter a sense that is quite detached from this contemporary meaning. On a historical scale, modern usage is quite possibly as ephemeral as the mayfly. When, for example, Charles Darwin referred to the 'economy of nature' in his first thoughts about the evolution of species,[4] he was using the term in a sense very close to that of the Greeks; a sense reflected today in the term 'ecology', of a self-organising and self-correcting system in which the connections between parts and whole are not immediately evident, nor reducible to any law-like functioning, but where interference with one part could lead to unforeseeable consequences for the whole—or possibly not. This is one sense in which the 'economy of the word' is meant here—as a complex and ever-changing semantic system. But there remains also a sense of parsimony, that the use of a particular word, or set of words, can convey meaning more precisely than rows of equations. Provided, of course, that we choose our words carefully.

2. George Orwell, 'Politics and the English Language', in his *Collected Essays*, Secker and Warburg, London 1961 p. 353.

3. Marshall was placed second overall (Second Wrangler), Keynes twelfth (although the form of the tripos that each sat was different, and so this is not a direct comparison).

4. Charles Darwin, 'Journal of Researches into the Natural History and Geology of the Countries Visited during the Voyage of H.M.S. Beagle Round the World' (1845), in his *Evolutionary Writings*, ed. James A. Secord, Oxford University Press, Oxford 2010 p. 14.

A focus on the use of language requires particular instruments and techniques. The resources upon which I draw here derive broadly from the history of the sciences, literary analysis, linguistics, and philology. No one 'method' is here advocated, simply an orientation to the organisation of word and text; hence the title to this chapter. Even if there were one such 'method', it could at most be exemplified; methodology, like the philosophy of science, is too often thought of as a technique, rather than as a means for reflection. Setting out to determine rules for the formation of argument, it can end up as a self-sustaining argument about rules.[5]

These essays are therefore designed to exemplify a particular approach to the understanding of economic language. In order to clarify what 'economic' here might mean, I begin with a consideration of the various uses which have attached themselves to the word 'economy'—and to the shifting valency of economic allusions and imagery. Until the early modern period, the significance of 'economic activity', of sustaining life, was so obvious that it more or less went unsaid. It consequently attracted little direct attention from writers, and this apparent indifference prevailed well past the invention of movable type and the printed book. It is not until the later sixteenth century that the stream of economic writing begins to flow unchecked. Pamphlets and books appear in western Europe directed to 'economic issues'—to matters of husbandry, trade, money, and population. General treatises upon economic principles first appear in the last third of the eighteenth century: works by two different kinds of Scotsman, Sir James Steuart and Adam Smith, and by the Frenchman Anne Robert Jacques Turgot. During the nineteenth century texts called 'Principles of Political Economy' appear, beginning with Jean-Baptiste Say's *Principes d'économie politique* (1803)[6] and more or less ending with

5. '. . . methodology can only ever be a reflection on means that have in practice *proved* themselves, and this is just as little the precondition of fruitful work as is a knowledge of anatomy to the ability to walk "correctly". Indeed, just as someone who wanted to regulate his way of walking by applying anatomical knowledge would risk stumbling, much the same thing can happen to a scholar who seeks in methodological considerations the aims of his work. If methodological work is to be of any particular use to the practice of a historian, it is by enabling him, once and for all, to resist the attractions of "philosophical" fashion—which is of course *one* of the purposes of methodological work'. Max Weber, 'Kritische Studien auf dem Gebiet der kulturwissenschaftlichen Logik. 1. Zur Auseinandersetzung mit Eduard Meyer', in his *Gesammelte Aufsätze zur Wissenschaftslehre*, 5th edition, J. C. B. Mohr (Paul Siebeck), Tübingen 1982 p. 217.

6. Say's text established the model for the nineteenth century; by contrast, Canard's *Principes d'économie politique* (Paris 1801) seeks (only in part, despite its reputation) a mathematical treatment of exchange and price formation, while Garnier's *Abrégé élémentaire des principes d'économie politique* (Paris 1796) is presented as a critique of Smith's *Wealth of Nations*.

Marshall's *Principles of Economics* (1890). Hereafter, general works of economics are explicitly textbooks written for the use of students, and books written for those who already understand the principles of economics now direct themselves to particular branches of the subject—for example, the works by two of Marshall's students, Pigou's *Economics of Welfare* (1920) and Maynard Keynes's *General Theory of Employment, Interest and Money* (1936). During the 1930s journal articles begin to displace the book, and by the end of the twentieth century economists read hardly any books at all—indeed, modern economists sometimes seem to struggle with the idea.[7] There are many issues here, not least the late emergence of the 'economist' as the reader and/or writer of economic texts.[8] My concern in chapter 2 is however with the slowly shifting meaning of 'economy' as it moves through new textual genres, in an ever-increasing flow of writing.

In tracing the shifts in meaning of 'economy' from Aristotle to late twentieth-century neoclassical economics I recapitulate in a more condensed form positions already advanced in my first book, *Land, Labour and Economic Discourse*. There I argued that mere use of the categories of land, labour, and population was not a sufficient condition for the existence of a systematic consideration of the economy and economic activity; that they were not inherently 'economic categories' whose use signalled the existence of 'economic thought'. Instead, the emergence of such a systematic consideration required that 'the economy' be constituted as an autonomous domain distinct from the polity or the domestic household. This came about through the construction of a particular conceptual structure, not by the presence of individual terms, nor by the adoption of any one 'scientific method', nor by an empirical alignment of 'theory' and 'reality'—for as I then argued, what we treat as 'reality' is constructed in language.[9] Chapter 2 approaches the same idea from another direction, tracing the lengthy process through which this work of

7. See for example George A. Akerlof, Robert J. Shiller, *Animal Spirits: How Human Psychology Drives the Economy, and Why It Matters for Global Capitalism*, Princeton University Press, Princeton (NJ) 2009; taking up an idea originally advanced by Keynes in his *General Theory*, the way in which the authors traduce Keynes suggests a very superficial acquaintance with Keynes's actual writings.

8. Massimo M. Augello, Marco E. L. Guidi (eds.) *The Economic Reader: Textbooks, Manuals and the Dissemination of the Economic Sciences during the Nineteenth and Early Twentieth Centuries*, Routledge, London 2012.

9. Hence the emphasis here on the analysis of economic language, although this should not be taken as a denial of the need to know the material context of language use—see for example my essay 'The Structure of Agrarian Capitalism—the "English Model"', in my *Genealogies of Capitalism*, Macmillan, London 1981 pp. 35–100.

construction occurred,[10] concluding that our modern conception of 'economy' is actually much more modern than usually thought, dating from the mid-twentieth century at the earliest, and fully established even more recently than that. The construction of this chapter clearly owes a great deal to *Begriffsgeschichte*; but at the time that I wrote *Land, Labour and Economic Discourse* I knew nothing of the work of Brunner and Koselleck, drawing instead primarily on the work of Michel Foucault, especially his *Archaeology of Knowledge*.[11]

Chapter 3 shifts gears, both conceptually and chronologically: it considers the manner in which the modern economy was first provided with a metric. When in 1907 Pigou reviewed the fifth edition of Marshall's *Principles*, he directed attention to the concept of 'national dividend', which he described as '*a practical instrument of great power designed for service in the concrete solution of social problems*'.[12] The 'national dividend' was the annual flow of goods and services, what we today know as gross domestic product (GDP). This was an idea that ran back to Adam Smith at least, for whom the origin of the 'wealth of a nation' was 'the annual labour . . . which originally supplies it with all the necessaries and conveniences of life which it annually consumes'.[13] Throughout the nineteenth century, however, this remained simply an idea. As Pigou pointed out, some more exact notion of the number attached to this idea would be of great significance for the framing of social policy, since one needed to know the precise impact of any proposed policy on the 'national dividend'. However, as chapter 3 shows, it took more than fifty years of hard work following Marshall's first usage until British economists and statisticians finally developed a consistent national accounting framework capable of putting a definite number to the concept; and since the mid-twentieth century small armies of statisticians have been employed refining the data used to create this number, and considering alternative sources.

Of course, the seeming positivity of metrics over the ambiguity of words encourages heedless faith in the certainty of the former. Today,

10. Siegfried Landshut's 1932 Habilitation thesis traced a similar history—'Der Begriff des Ökonomischen', in his *Kritik der Soziologie und andere Schriften zur Politik*, Luchterhand, Neuwied am Rhein 1969 pp. 131–75.

11. My attention was first drawn to *Begriffsgeschichte* by Pasquale Pasquino in the summer of 1979, and it was through him that I met Reinhart Koselleck and then began to translate his writings into English.

12. A. C. Pigou, Review of Alfred Marshall, *Principles of Economics*, 5th edition, *Economic Journal* Vol. 17 (1907) pp. 533–4.

13. Adam Smith, *An Inquiry into the Nature and Causes of the Wealth of Nations*, 'Introduction and Plan of the Work' para. 1, Oxford University Press, Oxford 1976.

small variations in the rate of change of GDP play an important role in political rhetoric: political parties promise if elected to 'increase growth', economies are compared on the rate of growth 'achieved', and levels of sovereign debt are expressed as a proportion of GDP—a relationship which it was only possible to formulate subsequent to the first officially published figure for GDP in 1941. During the 1990s levels of sovereign debt as a percentage of GDP formed part of the convergence criteria for currencies adopting the euro, but only became a controversial issue when it emerged in 2009 that Greek government debt had been systematically misreported, resulting in a downgrading of Greek sovereign debt to junk bond status in April 2010. However, reconstructed data now show that during the 1920s and 1930s the debt:GDP ratio for Britain was comparable to that of present-day Greece;[14] but this never became a political issue at the time since there was then no way of putting a number to national output and using it to scale levels of indebtedness. The Great Depression has instead always been talked about in terms of levels of unemployment. By the 1940s there was a method for computing national output, and a number which represented it; but the path from the idea of national dividend to a number for GDP was not a short one. In examining this path, we gain some insight into how misguided a blind faith in metrics over words may be.

Part II pairs two essays addressed to Adam Smith's *Wealth of Nations*, considering first one particular aspect of that text's construction, and then the history of the work's reception in the nineteenth century. While we always read texts in a specific framework, a framework which is just a link in the reception of any one text, we are nonetheless able to become conscious of the specificity of any given framework, and in re-reading a work make use of this consciousness. Of course, there is a considerable body of postmodern criticism that denies this premise, suggesting that the idea of 'a text' is inherently unstable, there being as many versions of a 'text' as readers; but such speculations presume that postulating such difference trumps all consideration of *what* is different. Here I show how we might usefully approach the difference between reading Smith's *Wealth of Nations*, and appreciating the manner in which one particular reading of the text became the 'Adam Smith Problem'.

Chapter 4 examines the manner in which Smith's *Wealth of Nations* exposes an argument about the development of international trade. Modern

14. See Table 4, Fiscal Sustainability Data, 1921–1929, in Nicholas Crafts, 'Walking Wounded: The British Economy in the Aftermath of World War I' (http://www.voxeu.org/article, accessed 31 August 2014).

trade theory builds upon the idea of comparative advantage, usually thought to have originated in chapter 7 of David Ricardo's *On the Principles of Political Economy and Taxation* (1817). Consequently, it has been assumed that the arguments advanced by Smith some forty years earlier must be in some way incomplete, or faulty. Rather than engage directly with this commentary, I present a reading of Smith's text that examines the sequence in which issues related to international trade are actually dealt with, paragraph by paragraph, chapter by chapter. I look at the way that Smith writes about trade, and not the extent to which Smith might or might not have anticipated Ricardo's conception of comparative advantage. This somewhat unorthodox, even simple-minded, approach owes a great deal to Practical Criticism as first elaborated in the 1920s by I. A. Richards, who had observed that students 'read' texts via the context provided by authorship, school of writing or time of composition. Once this canonical orientation was concealed from them students entirely lost their critical bearings, and had very great difficulty in evaluating the literary qualities of pieces of writing; they were compelled to consider how this writing actually worked, and not impose upon it canonical interpretation. While such literary positivism has its limits, I use it to show that Smith does seem to understand the principle of comparative advantage, but that it is not critical to his argument; the consistency of his 'trade theory' instead presumes the importance of conceptions of time and space that Ricardo subsequently ignored. As it happens, Smith's account of the flux of international trade as revealed by this reading turns out to throw more light on the spatial distribution of economic activities in a modern globalised economy than do now-conventional theories of comparative advantage, whether these be based on Heckscher-Ohlin or New Trade Theory.

The following chapter maintains the focus upon Adam Smith's *Wealth of Nations*, but shifts the emphasis to its reception. Drawing here upon the work of Hans Robert Jauß and the idea of literary reception,[15] attention shifts from the structure of a piece of writing to the variant ways in which it is read, the history of its reception. Of course, this history often has a quick ending; the work is after a time simply forgotten, never again read or referred to. This has always been the fate of most books, and it is a phenomenon to which reception theory draws attention: that our perception of the literary past is conditioned by our current concerns, and not by the

15. Hans Robert Jauß, *Literaturgeschichte als Provokation*, Suhrkamp, Frankfurt a.M. 1970. Jauß also emphasises the importance of the Russian Formalists (pp. 164ff.), which I discuss in ch. 8.

empirical history of the printed book.[16] But the *Wealth of Nations* has been constantly in print, in many languages, ever since 1776, and so we can ask how readings of this text have altered over time, and what this might suggest to us about our own approach to the work. In the case of Adam Smith, responding to this question is made easier by the fact that a controversy developed among German scholars in the second half of the nineteenth century about the relationship between Smith's two books, *The Theory of Moral Sentiments* (1759) and *An Inquiry into the Nature and Causes of the Wealth of Nations* (1776). Did the former work advance a conception of human motivation founded upon sympathy, and the latter one founded upon selfishness? If so, how could one reconcile two apparently conflicting approaches from the same author? This was the 'Adam Smith Problem', today understood to be a non-problem. However, in reconstructing this debate I draw attention to the fact that, by the mid-nineteenth century, only German scholars showed any real interest in Smith's writing. While Smith was still in Britain treated as a canonical figure, there is little evidence that *Wealth of Nations*, new editions of which continued to appear more or less annually, was treated as a book that needed careful reading. By the end of the century the work was thought to be of historical interest only, and there was little enough of that. Nonetheless, while today the 'Adam Smith Problem' is usually thought simply to be a mistaken idea, it was discussion among German scholars that laid the foundation for a new understanding of the significance of Smith's work; indeed, modern scholarship takes for granted the idea that his two books are related, and that much can be learned by reading one against the other.

This juxtaposition of a text and its reception also suggests that all discussion of a writer, or a text, or sets of ideas, is part of a reception process, and so guided by concerns that might be quite variant to those prevailing when the text thought to advance such ideas was written. While the existence of this caesura is inevitable and undeniable, the appropriate response is first to acknowledge its existence, and then devise ways in which we might build a path back to an understanding of past texts that does not simply replicate whatever the current view happens to be. The first essay on Adam Smith shows how we might work around this by directly addressing a particular text and considering how it is organised. In that essay I provide the reader with some references to the way in which modern commentary

16. At its limit, all copies of a book that had once demonstrably existed vanish from libraries; see my remarks on the impact of the Allied bombing campaign in Germany on the holdings of university libraries in my 'Locating German Economics: A Biographical Guide to the Study of the History of German Economics', *German History* Vol. 8 (1990) pp.73–81.

treats Smith's account of international trade, but my engagement with the commentary is indirect; while the essay implies a critique of modern readings of Smith on trade, I seek to prevent these readings from dictating how I read Smith and describe what I find in *Wealth of Nations*. I do of course end up going along with the long-established practice of treating *Wealth of Nations* as a canonical text; but in a world in which canonical texts are more often referred to than read, one can do worse than re-read them.[17]

Part III joins together Karl Marx and Léon Walras as writers who turned to political economy to develop an economic theory of industrial society, an essentially Saint-Simonian idea. Central to both writers was the problem of exchange and equality: the mechanics of equal exchange in an unequal society. Of course, they responded to this question in very different ways, and their responses have had very different histories. But they did share a common Saint-Simonian heritage: Marx, reading political economy for the first time in Paris in 1844, drew heavily on contemporary French arguments about socialism, capitalism,[18] and poverty; Léon Walras turned to political economy in the late 1850s at the bidding of his father, Auguste, whose own Saint-Simonian roots went back to the 1820s. During the later 1870s Léon came to realise that his general equilibrium system had a precursor in a book by Gossen published in 1854; but from what little we know of Gossen, he too shared this intellectual lineage. The essay on Léon Walras illuminates his link to contemporary socialist argument by demonstrating how he developed his father's ideas. The long essay on the political economy of Karl Marx turns primarily on a neglected question: upon what sources did Marx draw in constructing his 'critique' of political economy, and in identifying these sources, what conclusions might we draw concerning the construction of his central work, *Das Kapital* Bd. 1?

It has of course long been acknowledged that the political economy of Smith, Malthus, Ricardo, and James Mill was the primary source from which Marx constructed his account of the capitalist mode of production, conceived as a historically specific form in which economic relationships became the dominant forces in social formations. However, this has become one of those things so well known that no one has ever got around to examining just what Marx does take from political economy, what he rejects, what he overlooks, and what he apparently just misunderstands.

17. See the remarks on an older tradition of canonical readings in Quentin Skinner, *Liberty before Liberalism*, Cambridge University Press, Cambridge 1998 pp. 101ff. My point here is that the canonical readings criticised by Skinner did at least aspire to be close readings of a particular text, for which there is much to be said.

18. Indeed, the terms 'capitalist' and 'capitalism' were coined by Louis Blanc, the root then being adopted by Marx.

The writings of Karl Marx have over the years been argued about at great length, but an astonishing analytical naïveté prevails: Marx's own account of what he intended, and what he had achieved, sets the terms in which his writing is evaluated. By contrast, I examine Marx's sources, seeking the use Marx makes of them, first of all identifying the point at which Marx begins to read political economy, and what he makes of what he reads.

I use here the transcriptions of the 1844 notebooks first published in 1932, comparing his notes upon Say, Smith, Ricardo, Mill, and McCulloch with the works he was reading. Coming across these notes for the first time in late 2011, I was struck by the insights into Marx's early development they afforded, and by the fact that since 1932 so little use had been made of them. My essay focuses primarily upon Marx's economic writings before 1850, drawing from that some conclusions regarding the structure of the first (1867) edition of *Das Kapital*. In dealing with his earlier writings I rely almost exclusively upon the original, but incomplete, Ryazanov *Marx Engels Gesamtausgabe*,[19] making the point that the neglect of the textual resources upon which my essay draws has nothing to do with their accessibility, since in this case they have been in the public domain since the early 1930s. The '1844 Manuscripts' were also published in their original language for the first time in 1932, but here again they have almost always been read and discussed in formats that isolate them from the series of notebooks that Marx made. By reading the '1844 Manuscripts' as part of this corpus of writing we gain insight into Marx's working methods; and these insights also illuminate the construction of Marx's later writings, especially the work associated with the composition of *Das Kapital*.

It has from time to time also been suggested that the publication of other manuscript material would reveal hitherto unknown aspects of Marx's thought. So it was with the appearance in 1973 of the first English translation of the notebooks of 1857–58, the so-called *Grundrisse der Kritik der politischen Ökonomie*.[20] More recently, the editors of the new

19. This was a joint Russo-German project terminated by the Soviet authorities in 1935.

20. First published in Moscow 1939/1941, then in East Berlin in 1953, this was first translated into English by Martin Nicolaus in 1973 as *Grundrisse: Foundations of the Critique of Political Economy (Rough Draft)*, Penguin Books, Harmondsworth 1973. See Nicolaus, 'The Unknown Marx', *New Left Review* No. 48 (1968) pp. 41–61: Nicolaus here argues that significant work by Marx remained inaccessible to Anglophone readers. This persuaded me in 1970 that I should learn German, an idea which I then pursued while working as a *Gastarbeiter* for the British Army in West Berlin and the US Army in Fürth during the autumn and winter of 1971–72. Back in Cambridge in the autumn of 1972 the first thing I did as a graduate student was to read through all three volumes of *Das Kapital*, and the three-part *Theorien über den Mehrwert*—unfortunately all of them in the defective Dietz *Werke* editions that I had bought in Berlin.

Gesamtausgabe have doggedly continued to publish reams of notes and drafts, 'revealing' further new material on the basis of which arcane but curiously limited arguments have been elaborated. But there is in fact very little hidden either in the *Grundrisse* or Marx's other unpublished work that cannot be established from an examination of the early notes, drafts, and writings on political economy already published in the 1930s, or from a consideration of the writings which Marx himself read. The problem has always been to read and understand what has long been available. Importantly, placing Marx's early reading of political economy in its context reveals the degree to which he drew upon the contemporary French critique of political economy. Extending this analysis to *Das Kapital* Bd. 1, it can then be shown that the ideas of Proudhon, Blanc, and Sismondi shape much of what has long been considered to be Marx's own work. I consequently suggest that the early parts of *Das Kapital* Bd. 1,[21] long supposed to contain Marx's principal theoretical achievement, should be treated as evidence of Marx's very laborious struggle to move on from the arguments of the 1840s, and his general failure to do so. On the other hand, the analysis of the labour process that follows on from this, his demonstration of how 'surplus value' is realised in a free and equal exchange between labourer and capitalist, does succeed in reorganising and updating an earlier (French) critique of English economic development. Engels's own *Condition of the English Working Class in 1844* was itself also a latecomer to an established body of literature on the 'condition of England' that has generally been overlooked when considering Marx's early intellectual formation. In both cases, to properly appreciate what is new in *Das Kapital* we need to know the arguments with which Marx became acquainted when he moved to Paris in late 1843. This might seem an elementary point, but in the reams of Marx commentary generated in the course of the twentieth century, first by Marxist radicals and revolutionaries, then by academics, it counts as a novel idea. But it is not. In making this rough distinction between the 'two halves' of *Das Kapital* Bd. 1, I do little more than echo a perceptive comment already made by Philip Wicksteed in the closing lines of his 1884 review of the book; although my point here is to demonstrate how and why this distinction came about.[22]

21. The first two chapters of the original six-chapter 1867 edition, which I use here for reasons I explain in ch. 6.

22. 'It appears to me, therefore, that Marx has failed to indicate any immanent law of capitalistic production by which a man who purchases labour-force at its value will extract from its consumption a surplus value. We are simply thrown back on the fact that a man can purchase (not produce) as much labour-force as he likes at the price of bare subsistence. But this fact is the problem we are to investigate, not the solution

Marx drafted and rewrote *Das Kapital* from the later 1850s to the mid-1870s, roughly the same period in which Léon Walras first turned to the study of economics, then became involved in economic journalism, and later published in two parts his *Élements d'économie politique pure* (1874, 1877). On the face of it, these are two quite distinct works: *Das Kapital*, based squarely on the labour theory of value, proposing an analysis of the rise and decline of the capitalist mode of production couched in the language of German philosophy; *Éléments* developing a mathematical theory of the emergence of a general economic equilibrium out of the choices made by large numbers of independent economic agents, a model of the economy that neoclassical economics made its own by the mid-twentieth century. One connection between the two writers lies in their legacy: while socialist command economies of the twentieth century developed out of political movements associated with late nineteenth-century Marxism, their planning mechanisms came to owe more to Walras than to Marx. However, I am here more interested in the fact that Marx and Walras supplied different answers to similar questions concerning the linkage of equal exchange to distributional outcomes. Both worked in terms of a common Saint-Simonian heritage.

In the case of Léon Walras, this was because the source of his economic thinking was his father's own work from the 1830s and 1840s, effectively aligning Léon Walras and Karl Marx within the political culture of pre-1848 France. Marx took from this context the problem that, while the accumulation of capital was founded upon the exploitation of labour, this exploitation ran through the free and equal contract represented by the wage relationship. Walras's system began from material supplied to him by his father—his first book and his prize essay of 1861 were in effect his father's reworked notes. The actual form that his own work took originated in a challenge posed to him in 1860 by the Saint-Simonist Charles-Joseph Lambert, who objected that Walras lacked proof of the optimality of laissez-faire.[23] Walras's solution was to endogenise 'fairness' in an

---

of the problem. . . . Only let me repeat that in the latter portion of the published volume of *Das Kapital* Marx appears to me to have made contributions of extreme importance to the solution of the great problem, though I cannot see that they stand in any logical connection with the abstract reasoning of his early chapters'. Philip Wicksteed, 'Review of *Das Kapital*', reprinted in C. H. Herford, *Philip Henry Wicksteed: His Life and Work*, J. M. Dent and Sons, London 1931 p. 370. Salutary here is also Wicksteed's first footnote: 'I cite from the second German edition (1872), which is probably the one in the hands of most of my readers. References to the French translation are added in square brackets' (p. 356).

23. Albert Jolink, *The Evolutionist Economics of Léon Walras*, Routledge, London 1996 p. 53.

equilibrium system, turning upon a conception of commutative justice. This equilibrium system was developed mathematically, but severely constrained in scope, a constraint that others later ignored.

Both writers, Marx and Walras, therefore sought to show, albeit in different ways, how inequality might be compatible with free and fair exchange, and both writers had roots in French socialist thinking of the 1840s and early 1850s. A consideration of Walras that begins from this premise offers a fresh perspective upon the reasons for his adoption of a formal and mathematical account of exchange and equilibrium, demonstrating that this work went along with a critique of the contemporary French liberal economic emphasis on laissez-faire; for the impetus behind Walrasian general equilibrium, and its strictly limited scope, was as much a 'critique' of contemporary French political economy as was Marx's 'critique' of early English political economy. Walras employed a mathematical formalism because he believed this offered his result the greatest degree of clarity and generality, but he made clear that the set of equations which resulted were quite limited in their application: the universality of the techniques used implied nothing about the universality of the results produced using these techniques.

This book is divided into three parts so that the progression in the argument can be seen more clearly. The first two essays are fairly obviously related as respectively lexical and numerical representations of economic activity, providing some preliminary sense of what we mean when we talk about 'the economy'. Part II contrasts a close reading of Smith's *Wealth of Nations* with an account of its reception. Chapter 4 ignores the contexts in which the work has been read in order to focus upon the internal organisation of the text; chapter 5 reverses this, examining instead the variant ways in which Smith's work has been read. Part III returns to the idea of close reading, for the most part setting aside what has been written about Marx and Walras in order to gain a better understanding of how their works were constructed out of materials that they read. In the case of Karl Marx, this amounts to ignoring the entire 'history of Marxism' in order to gain a clearer perspective on the context in which Marx worked; although appended to chapter 6 there is a brief account which provides some explanation of what 'Marxism' came to mean in the twentieth century.

As already noted, while the analytical method at work in these essays is relatively coherent—an emphasis upon the text as object of both material and linguistic analysis, attention to the internal organisation of texts, the manner in which they generate meaning, their interconnection with sources, and a flexible sense of the context relevant in reaching understanding of the work done by the text—this approach has diverse sources.

In the conclusion I present an account of the path I followed in developing this approach—not as a template that has to be replicated, but as an explanation of the way in which influences have come together in my work, both with respect to its aims, and the means I employ in seeking to realise these aims. Here it is enough to say that I now conceive my work as broadly philological in style and inspiration: seeking to extend our understanding of economic argument by considering the historical construction of this language. The purpose of the following essays is to demonstrate this at work, leaving it to the reader to decide what might be of wider value in this approach.

PART I

Word and Number

Chapter 2 examines how the Greek term *oikonomía* became the root from which the modern concept of 'economy' developed; but in the course of some two thousand years its underlying meaning has diverged from the original Greek sense. My purpose here is to demonstrate how very long this transformation took, and to emphasise the comparative novelty of our modern understanding. The account is by no means comprehensive; indeed, it would amount to a total history of economic writing if it were, and that is an impossible, even undesirable, project. My inspiration comes from *Begriffsgeschichte*, in particular the writings of Otto Brunner and Reinhart Koselleck. Accordingly, I seek to highlight not the diversity of activities associated with economic life, but the manner in which these activities have been classified and ordered; this classification and order shifting in significant ways over time. Our evidence for such changes lies in written texts, not in the evaluation of how these texts, and the concepts they deployed, might or might not have corresponded to contemporary conditions.

The importance of making this distinction can be seen in Moses Finley's *The Ancient Economy*. Like Finley, I begin with Hutcheson's *Short Introduction to Moral Philosophy*, which he describes as standing 'at the end of a tradition stretching back more than 2000 years'.[1] He also draws attention to Xenophon's *Oikonomikos*, and to Otto Brunner's use of *Hausväterliteratur*;

1. Moses I. Finley, *The Ancient Economy*, Chatto and Windus, London 1973 p. 17.

but Finley's purpose in so doing is to make the argument that modern 'economic concepts' have no purchase on the ancient economy:

> I am suggesting . . . that the ancients . . . lacked the concept of 'an economy', and, *a fortiori*, that they lacked the conceptual elements which together constitute what we call 'the economy'.[2]

Finley considers that 'modern economics' emerged with Adam Smith; that is why he begins with Hutcheson, who stands 'at the end' of a continuous tradition. My argument is rather different: that instead of this essentially 'ancient and modern' perspective, we should think in terms of a constant transformation of the conceptualisation of economic activity from ancient Greece right through to the present. Throughout this process, prevailing conceptions of economy have been retrospectively imposed on earlier conceptions and conditions. Current ideas are assumed to be the best ideas, in the light of which previous ideas seem wrong, or incomplete, or faulty in some other way. However, my prime purpose here is not to argue that 'modern' concepts are inapplicable to ancient conditions—although this is an entirely valid argument, and one that seems to need constant repetition.[3] My purpose is rather to draw attention to the process of semantic change; that when we use a word, we are not free to define it in any way that we like.

> 'When *I* use a word', Humpty Dumpty said, in a rather scornful tone, 'it means just what I choose it to mean—neither more nor less'.
>
> 'The question is', said Alice, 'whether you *can* make words mean so many different things'.
>
> 'The question is', said Humpty Dumpty, 'which is to be master—that's all.'[4]

While this might work for symbolic logic, it is a poor precept for the sciences, whether they be the physical, life, or human sciences. All of these have at one time or another drawn upon metaphors in developing their basic terminology, so that this terminology relied semantically on

2. Finley, *Ancient Economy*, op. cit. p. 21.
3. A need exemplified *in extenso* by the *Cambridge History of Capitalism*, 2 vols., ed. Larry Neal and Jeffrey Williamson, Cambridge University Press, Cambridge 2014.
4. Lewis Carroll, *The Annotated Alice*, ed. Martin Gardner, Penguin Books, Harmondsworth 1970 p. 269. See Gardner's marginal note 6 here, quoting Carroll, *Symbolic Logic* (1896) to the effect that 'If I find an author saying, at the beginning of his book, "Let it be understood that by the word '*black*' I shall always mean '*white*', and that by the word '*white*' I shall always mean '*black*'", I meekly accept his ruling, however injudicious I may think it'.

an implicit reference to contemporary language use that escaped mere definition.[5] Indeed, chapter 2 is an extended argument to the effect that we need to pay attention to the use of words, and discount claims that it is enough to define them—that we 'know' what capital, interest, wages, growth, and so on are, that all we need to do is refer to their definition in modern economics. When using economic language, we would do well to pay attention to *which* language we are speaking. And this could well be a basic description of the role that the history of economic thought could play in training modern economists.

Stanley Jevons had a similar point in mind when writing the preface to the English translation of Luigi Cossa's *Guida allo Studio dell'Economia Politica*, originally published in 1876. This translation was a popular book during the 1880s, when a broadly based interest in economics first really developed in Britain. Jevons made the point that economic science might well appear to English readers to be largely an English science. However, he went on to suggest that there had been a marked tendency to overlook the work of French, Italian, and German economists:

> The survey of the foreign literature of the subject given in this *Guide* will enable the English student to fix the bearings of the point of knowledge which he has reached, and to estimate the fraction of the ocean of economic literature which he has been able to traverse.[6]

Jevons was also a keen collector of economic literature, and so this admonition could also be read as applying to the past, as well as the present, state of the ocean. And Cossa's *Guide* begins with a familiar observation—that in common language

> *economy* sometimes means frugality or thrift, sometimes a well-ordered system of things. This is the case, for instance, in such phrases as the economy of the universe, the economy of the human body. The name as thus used always implies the conception of order, proportion, harmony.[7]

5. The idea of a computer 'programming language' in the 1950s was itself a metaphorical usage, which then was adopted by linguists in the 1960s, who took concepts used to study programming language and applied them to natural languages; while biologists adopted the idea of a 'code' to study the structure of DNA—see David Nofre, Mark Priestley, Gerard Alberts, 'When Technology Became Language: The Origins of the Linguistic Conception of Computer Programming, 1950–1960', *Technology and Culture* Vol. 55 (2014) pp. 41–42.

6. William Stanley Jevons, 'Preface' to Luigi Cossa, *Guide to the Study of Political Economy*, Macmillan, London 1880 p. viii.

7. Cossa, *Guide*, op. cit. p. 1.

But he then turns to etymology, the linkage to *oikos*, the connection with the household, and how this relates to *polis*; and then on to the ways in which, out of this, there have developed conceptions of political economy, public economy, social economy, domestic economy, or industrial economy. Cossa confronts the reader not with any one definition, but a range of descriptions that is continued into the second chapter, 'Division of Political Economy', which deals with the various subordinate branches; so that the reader of Cossa's book is confronted, not with an unequivocal definition of an unfamiliar subject, but a description and calibration of its range.

While this is also the purpose of the next chapter, the argument is extended into chapter 3 along a different axis—not how we might conceive economic activity, but rather how we might measure it. In one way or another this had been an issue since the seventeenth century, as evident in the writings of Gregory King, William Petty, Pierre de Boisguilbert, and Johann Peter Süßmilch, for all of whom the starting point was estimation of the size and composition of a population. During the nineteenth century this problem was resolved by the introduction of regular national censuses, joined by the collection of statistical data on employment, wages, and taxation as part of the development of state administrations. Reformist politics in the later nineteenth century favoured the creation of national systems of unemployment and sickness insurance, the financing of which also involved a knowledge of economic activity and mortality. By the early twentieth century Western governments commanded increasing amounts of data relevant to the measurement of national income, but it was the First World War that propelled governments into the active management of national economic activity, for which they however lacked the necessary conceptual, empirical, and administrative resources.[8]

Efforts to remedy some of these problems began in the early 1920s, most notably in the United States with the creation in 1920 of the National Bureau of Economic Research under the leadership of Wesley Mitchell.[9] By the early 1930s there were several competing ways of estimating national income,[10] which had by the later 1940s been resolved into a

8. See the overview provided by John W. Kendrick, 'The Historical Development of National-Income Accounts', *History of Political Economy* Vol.2 (1970) pp. 284–315.

9. For an overview of the background see Robert W. Fogel et al., *Political Arithmetic: Simon Kuznets and the Empirical Tradition in Economics*, University of Chicago Press, Chicago 2013 pp. 24–37.

10. See Josiah Stamp's comprehensive survey, 'Methods Used in Different Countries for Estimating National Income', *Journal of the Royal Statistical Society* Vol. 97 No. 3 (1934) pp. 423–66. He draws primarily on work done in Britain, Australia, France, Austria, Hungary, and Japan.

standardised form based broadly on the British model—national income at factor cost cast up as a system of national accounts.[11] While the direct involvement of the American Department of Commerce from the early 1930s provided powerful institutional support,[12] and the empirical work of Simon Kuznets and his students rapidly developed an extensive and standardised empirical foundation, in Britain the conceptual framework of Keynes, together with the insights of James Meade and Richard Stone,[13] was eventually combined with the existing empirical work of Stamp, Bowley, and Clark within the wartime administration in the development of a system of national accounts. The general methodology developed in Britain was then adopted internationally after the war,[14] so that it was now for the first time possible to compare economies on the basis of a standard measure of gross domestic product and its rate of growth.

Chapter 2 presents a single word, 'economy', and shows how its meanings have to be described, rather than defined. Chapter 3 is primarily addressed to numbers, rather than words; here it turns out that the definition of 'national income' was relatively uncontroversial. Instead, the problem was how one moved from this definition to a set of reliable numbers. The various histories of national income accounting have largely directed their attention to definitions, and overlooked the laborious work of finding reliable numbers and making them fit into a consistent conceptual framework. But there is much to be learned from the process of turning ideas into numbers.

11. Simon Kuznets was closely associated with the early development of American national income calculations, but was hostile to their organisation as accounts, rather than flows—see his 'National Income: A New Version', *Review of Economics and Statistics* Vol. 30 (1948) p. 152.

12. See for a description of American work in the 1930s that paralleled British experience Robert R. Nathan, 'GNP and Military Mobilization', *Journal of Evolutionary Economics* Vol. 4 (1994) pp. 2–5.

13. See Martin Weale's entry on Stone in the *Oxford Dictionary of National Biography* for an emphasis on the distinction between national income and national accounts, the work of Meade and Stone being directed to the latter.

14. United Nations, *Measurement of National Income and the Construction of Social Accounts*, Geneva 1947.

CHAPTER 2

The Word: Economy

The celebrated division of philosophy among the ancients was into the *rational* or *logical*, the *natural*, and the *moral*. Their moral philosophy contained these parts, *ethicks* taken more strictly, teaching the nature of virtue and regulating the internal dispositions; and the knowledge of the *law of nature*. This latter contained, 1. the doctrine of *private rights*, or the laws obtaining in natural liberty. 2. *Oeconomicks*, or the laws and rights of the several members of a family; and 3. *Politicks*, shewing the various plans of civil government, and the rights of states with respect to each other. The following books contain the elements of these several branches of moral philosophy; which if they are carefully studied may give the youth an easier access to the well known and admired works either of the ancients, *Plato, Aristotle, Xenophon, Cicero*; or of the moderns, *Grotius, Cumberland, Puffendorf, Harrington* and others, upon this branch of philosophy.

—Francis Hutcheson, 'To the Students in Universities', in *A Short Introduction to Moral Philosophy, in Three Books; containing the Elements of Ethicks and the Law of Nature* (1747)[1]

Thus Adam Smith's teacher and predecessor in the Glasgow Chair for Moral Philosophy, articulating a conception of polity and economy relating explicitly to Greek and Roman classical texts (the ancients), as reworked by the writings of the moderns. Within a few years a group of French writers would dub themselves the *Économistes*, and in 1776 Adam

1. Francis Hutcheson, 'To the Students in Universities', in *A Short Introduction to Moral Philosophy, in Three Books; containing the Elements of Ethicks and the Law of Nature* [1747], 2nd edition, Robert and Andrew Foulis, Glasgow 1753 p. v.

Smith would entitle Book IV of the *Wealth of Nations* 'Of Systems of Political Oeconomy', bringing together two domains that are here, in Hutcheson, quite separate. Smith's book was not itself a 'system of political œconomy', but by the early 1800s Robert Malthus, James Mill, and David Ricardo would create their own system of 'political economy' out of a critique of Smith, while Jean-Baptiste Say, himself a reader of Smith's text, would argue in his own treatise for a separation of 'political economy' from 'politics'. Say was more or less everywhere a more influential figure than the English political economists,[2] and his own formulations played a major part in the subsequent reshaping of 'political economy' into 'economics' later in the century. Described by Alfred Marshall in 1890 as 'the ordinary business of life', this was nonetheless a conception remote from our understanding today, where economics is thought to be the analysis of choices made by agents under conditions of constrained optimisation. The premises of this latter idea were first clearly articulated in the 1930s, initially by Lionel Robbins in his *Nature and Significance of Economic Science*, but this in turn took a considerable amount of time to be completely absorbed into a neoclassical economic framework that was at this time still under construction.

By drawing attention to this changing usage I hope to make a number of points. There is first of all the principle that the meaning of a word lies in its use, and so in tracing the changing usage of 'economy' and its cognates we are identifying conceptual discontinuities. Second, by demonstrating the existence of these conceptual discontinuities we are alerted to the fact that one should not simply apply present-day conceptions of economic action either to past texts, or to past behaviours. Each age has its 'economics', if we understand by that some form of organising ideas about the basic problems of human need and the meeting of those needs. But we should not assume that what we today think 'economics' is has much, or indeed any, bearing on the way in which actors in the remote past organised their conceptual worlds.[3] Writing a text is a human action like any other, and is thus 'human

2. Ricardo's early reputation in Britain was fleeting, and his influence in the later nineteenth century limited—see the judicious remarks on the latter in Terence Hutchison, 'Some Questions about Ricardo', *Economica* Vol. 19 New Series (1952) pp. 421–22.

3. Carlo Natali's survey of post-Aristotelian 'economic thought' makes this point well in noting how historians of 'Greek economic thought' have homed in on a few statements in a small corpus of texts thought to be 'modern', and ignored the mass of material which has come down to us—Carlo Natali, '*Oikonomia* in Hellenistic Political Thought', in André Laks, Malcolm Schofield (eds.) *Justice and Generosity: Studies in Hellenistic Social and Political Philosophy*, Proceedings of the Sixth Symposium of Hellenisticum, Cambridge University Press, Cambridge 1995 pp. 96–97. What he has in

behaviour linked to a subjective *meaning*',[4] where any understanding of this meaning involves consideration of the material and conceptual contexts of that action. What an '*economic* action' might be therefore depends upon the meaning given to it by that subject, something that might not be immediately accessible to us, but for which an 'objective' explanation always turns out to be *someone else's* subjective meaning. The argument advanced here is that we need to develop practical means for the understanding of past actions and their conceptual contexts; applied to texts, this involves attention to the conceptual field employed, not simply the use of individual terms, or indeed, the lack of such use. 'Economic activity' as we today generally understand it—the exchange of labour, time, goods, and money in the process of sustaining human lives, families, and communities—has certainly existed for much more than two millennia, but its conceptualisation as a discrete domain of human activity dedicated to these ends dates at most from the early nineteenth century, and in its current sense is much less than a century old. By considering the shifting semantics of 'economy' and its cognates we might come to appreciate what is meant by its use, and also understand why it took so long for such an old word to become a new concept.

'Oeconomicks', as Hutcheson has it, derives from the Greek *oikonomía*, household management or thrift, administration, government, arrangement, stewardship. As such, it is made up of two elements: *oîk-os*, a dwelling-place, household, or household goods, the same root in Latin being *vic-us*, a row of houses, a street, hence *vicinus*, neighbour, also Old English *wic* and Old Norse *vik*, as in Norwich and Reykjavik; and *nomós*, pasture, sphere of command, dwelling place; *némos*, wooded pasture, glade; *nómos*, habitual possession or practice, custom, law, convention, law; and *nemesis*, dispensing, dealing out what is due. Further, the verb *némō* covers dispense, deal out, distribute (what is due), afford, administer, manage, maintain, reap the fruits of, possess, occupy, inhabit, graze one's flock over (a place); and a further and more frequent verb, derivative of the noun is *nomízō*, have or adopt as custom, be accustomed or used to, have as part of one's culture, believe, and later simply 'think'.[5]

---

mind can be seen at work in S. Todd Lowry, 'The Economics and Jurisprudential Ideas of the Ancient Greeks: Our Heritage from Hellenic Thought', in S. Todd Lowry, Barry Gordon (eds.) *Ancient and Medieval Ideas and Concepts of Social Justice*, Brill, Leiden 1998 pp. 11–38—on p. 32 he identifies conceptions of diminishing marginal utility and a hierarchy of values which, for him, prefigures Maslow's Hierarchy of Needs.

4. Max Weber, 'Soziologische Grundbegriffe' in Knut Borchardt, Edith Hanke, Wolfgang Schluchter (eds.) *Wirtschaft und Gesellschaft: Soziologie. Unvollendet 1919–1920, Max Weber Gesamtausgabe* vol. I/23, J.C.B. Mohr (Paul Siebeck), Tübingen 2013 p. 149 §1.

5. I am very grateful to Pietro Bortone for providing me with this etymology.

As we shall see, this etymology is sometimes reduced to 'household' and 'law',[6] but from this listing we can see that both elements involve semantic fields that run beyond this simply duality, and in the case of the nom/nem root in a very significant way. For this is not simply 'law' in the sense of prescribed regularity; it involves senses of distribution, of disposition, of commutative justice. Moreover, these various senses did not necessarily coexist, for as in any other language, their use shifted over time. Any more nuanced appreciation of these meanings must therefore take account of the developing literature of antiquity.[7]

And so *oikonomikē technē* is the art of household management,[8] the root *oikos* relating to the house or household.[9] Although it is possible to trace elements of this usage in Plato and Homer, the central source for our purposes begins with Aristotle's *Politics*, in which he identifies *oikonomia* as the care and ordering of a rural agricultural household, and distinguishes this from *politeia*, the ordering of the polis, the domain of the city-state in which decisions are made by citizens.[10] Book I of *Politics* is

6. This is what Rousseau does in his *Encyclopédie* entry, see below.

7. Kurt Singer's 'Oikonomia: An Inquiry into Beginnings of Economic Thought and Language', *Kyklos* Vol. 11 (1958) pp. 29–57 remains the most reliable and comprehensive survey of this kind, despite Finley's view that this is an 'amateur intervention which is best ignored'—*The Ancient Economy*, Chatto and Windus, London 1973 p. 19 n. 3. For a recent review of the ancient scope of *oikonomia* see Dotan Leshem, 'The Ancient Art of Economics', *European Journal of the History of Economic Thought* Vol. 21 (2014) pp. 201–29.

8. As an 'art' it is therefore a practical skill, rather than an episteme, a knowledge or a science. At least this is how the terms are used by Aristotle; in Xenophon's *Oeconomicus* they are in fact employed by Socrates interchangeably. See the illuminating discussion by Richard Parry, '*Episteme* and *Techne*', *Stanford Encyclopedia of Philosophy* (Fall 2008 Edition) ed. Edward N. Zalta: http://plato.stanford.edu/archives/fall2008/entries/episteme-techne/.

9. Peter Spahn, 'Wirtschaft II.1', in Otto Brunner, Werner Conze, Reinhart Koselleck (eds.) *Geschichtliche Grundbegriffe* Bd. 7, Klett-Cotta, Stuttgart 1992 p. 514. See also H. Rabe, 'Ökonomie', in J. Ritter, K. Gründer (eds.) *Historisches Wörterbuch der Philosophie* Bd. 6, Wissenschaftliche Buchgesellschaft, Darmstadt 1984 cols. 1149–53. 'Ecology' also comes from the root *oikos*, first used by Ernst Haeckel, *Generelle Morphologie der Organismen* Bd. 1: *Allgemeine Anatomie der Organismen*, Georg Reimer, Berlin 1866 to refer to the 'science of *Oeconomie*, of the mode of living, of the external vital relationships of organisms to each other'—p. 8, see also pp. 237, 238.

10. There is a substantial literature which seeks to identify and evaluate the presence, or absence, of elements of economic calculation in Aristotle's writings, starting with Finley, 'Aristotle and Economic Analysis', *Past and Present* No. 47 (1970) pp. 3–25, whose approach was criticised by Scott Meikle, 'Aristotle and the Political Economy of the Polis', *Journal of Hellenic Studies* Vol. 99 (1979) pp. 57–73; see also Meikle, *Aristotle's Economic Thought*, Oxford University Press, Oxford 1995. However, what we are concerned with here is the contemporary usage of *oikonomia*, and not whether or not there can be found in Aristotle something that is today recognisable as 'economic analysis'.

nominally dedicated to the household, but begins with a discussion of the polis, making the point in §2 that it was mistaken to believe that a *politikos* was the same as a monarch, or a manager of a household, or a master of a number of slaves, for

> This view abolishes any real difference between a large household and a small polis; and it also reduces the difference between the 'statesman' and the monarch to the one fact that the latter has an uncontrolled and sole authority, while the former exercises his authority in conformity with the rules imposed by the art of statesmanship and as one who rules and is ruled in turn.[11]

While one might therefore make an analogy between the head of a household and the authority of a ruler,[12] it is here made clear that *oikos* and polis were quite different things, since the statesman exercised authority over 'free men and equals'. The polis was an association of free citizens; the *oikos* an association formed of a master with his wife, and their children, servants, slaves, and animals, all of which were part of his property.

As for the acquisition of property, a distinction could be made between the acquisition, through exchange, of objects needed for the upkeep of the household; and the pursuit of wealth through the exchange of money, the latter being considered perverted or unsound. As we can read in the *Nicomachean Ethics*, 'The life of money-making is one undertaken under compulsion, and wealth is evidently not the good we are seeking, for it is merely useful and for the sake of something else'.[13] The virtuous man was liberal in his giving, the degree of his goodness consisting in the right disposition of that which he had, not in its mere possession and accumulation.[14] The sphere of money-getting, *chrēmatismos*, therefore lay outside the household and was consequently not the object of *oikonomikē technē*. Additionally, of course, the work of the household was centred upon agricultural activity, for this was the source of the household's subsistence; in field or in vineyard, ploughing, sowing, and reaping, the annual rhythm of the seasons was the rhythm of the household.[15] Those engaged in agriculture

11. Aristotle, *Politics*, ed. and trans. Ernest Barker, Oxford University Press, London 1958 pp. 1–2 (A 1252a).
12. Ibid. p. 17 (1255b §1).
13. Aristotle, *The Nicomachean Ethics*, trans. D. Ross, revised J. L. Ackrill, Oxford University Press, Oxford 1980 p. 7.
14. Ibid. pp. 85–86.
15. This idea is elaborated at length in Columella, *Res rustica*, 3 vols., Harvard University Press, Cambridge (MA) 1941 (I–IV trans. Harrison Boyd Ash); 1954 (V–IX trans. E. S. Forster, Edward H. Heffner); 1955 (X–XII trans. Forster and Heffner). See also C. Mossé, *The Ancient World at Work*, Chatto and Windus, London 1969 pp. 37–38.

were engaged 'in the most honest of all such occupations; seeing that the wealth it brings is not derived from other men',[16] but directly from nature. This source goes on to state the four qualities that a head of household must possess in dealing with his property:

> Firstly, he must have the faculty of acquiring, and secondly that of preserving what he has acquired, other wise there is no more benefit in acquiring them than in baling with a colander, or in the proverbial wine-jar with a hole in the bottom. Thirdly and fourthly, he must know how to improve his property, and how to make use of it; since these are the ends for which the powers of acquisition and of preservation are sought.[17]

Acquiring, preserving, improving, using—these are the 'economic activities' of classical antiquity, where 'acquisitive' activity is merely the initial condition for the remaining elements, whose end point and purpose is use by the household.

Xenophon[18] and others subsequently elaborated on these ideas, Natali[19] identifying in Hellenistic writing five different senses associated with *oikonomia*. First of all, these writers use the term *oikonomia* to denote household management, that is, the control of the household's internal affairs, which is the province of the wife, rather than of matters external to the household, which is the province of the husband. Second, the term denotes the man's management, as head of the household, of the house and its properties. Third, it denotes the philosopher's management of his own possessions. Fourth, the term was used figuratively where a complex structure can be successfully managed, or the general organisation of one's life or actions—the division of spoils, the proper supply of equipment to an army, the handling of political affairs in a city. This could also be applied to 'the good ordering of the cosmos and of the principles of nature'.[20] Fifth, *oikonomia* was used as a technical term in rhetoric, the organisation of the parts of a discourse, translated into Latin as *dispositio*.

The term *oekonomia* is clearly the root of our modern category 'economy', but it also has a quite idiosyncratic sense in the small number of classical texts in which it figures. Not only does it have a specific meaning,

16. [Pseudo]Aristotle, *Oeconomia*, trans. G. Cyril Armstrong, Harvard University Press, Cambridge (MA) 1935 p. 329.
17. Ibid. p. 339.
18. Xenophon, *Memorabilia and Oeconomicus*, trans. E. C. Marchant, Harvard University Press, Cambridge (MA) 1923.
19. Natali, '*Oikonomia* ', op. cit. pp. 97–99.
20. Ibid. p. 99.

its absence from the bulk of the classical corpus suggests that it was not something thought to require any extended consideration, unlike politics and ethics; it is simply an everyday art that is the precondition for something else, and so mentioned only in passing. This art of householding involves the maintenance and ordering of the objects and people engaged in the production of household needs, ensuring the continued existence of the household as an autarchic entity, hence necessarily presupposing that the household lives largely from its own produce. The rhythms of rural life follow the seasons, Hesiod's *Works and Days* noting for example the manner in which the activities of the household were determined by the seasons:

> Take notice, when you hear the voice of the crane every year calling from above out of the clouds: she brings the sign for plowing and indicates the season of winter rain, and this gnaws at the heart of the man without oxen.[21]

There is no accumulation of capital or of wealth; no growth, but instead the unending agrarian cycle; exchange is limited to transactions with objects in which money plays no necessary role; work is activity that contributes to the ongoing maintenance of the household. Trade and money do exist, but independently of the household as a social unit; commerce is an activity conducted by individuals for their own ends, of no wider consequence for the polis and its constituent households.

While the *oikos* is in Aristotle the basic element of the polis, this relationship survived into medieval Europe only in the relation of the nobility and their 'houses' to their rulers. The wider semantic field of the *oikos* did however survive, identifying 'economy' with the work of (agricultural) subsistence and the social context in which it took place. If we consider usage in Middle English, we find that 'hosbondrie' is derived from *housbond*, and defined as '1. (a) The management of a household, housekeeping; household duties or activities; *stuffe of* - household articles; (b) skilful management, economical use, economy, thrift; *gret*-, a thrift bargain'.[22] Examples of usage include for 1425: 'Iconomia: hosbondrie';[23] for around 1475, 'The grete charge of polycy and husbandry of all this houshold . . . stondyth moste part by his . . . dylygent pourveyaunce';[24] or for 1454,

21. Hesiod, *Works and Days*, trans. Glenn W. Most, Harvard University Press, Cambridge (MA) 2006 pp. 123–5.
22. *Middle English Dictionary* online, University of Michigan: http://quod.lib.umich.edu/m/med/ (accessed 27 March 2014).
23. *Catholicum Anglicum*, British Library Add MS 15562.
24. *Liber Niger Domus Regis Anglia (Edward IV)*, British Library MS Harley 642.

'Prudence is departid into many braunchis . . . and into þilk kunnyng which is called yconomy or hosbondri'.[25] These examples can be supplemented and extended using the *Oxford English Dictionary*, which cites Shakespeare in the *Merchant of Venice* (III.iv.25): 'Lorenso I commit into your hands, The husbandry and mannage of my house' (1600), and with an explicitly agricultural sense, around 1460: 'the new husbondry þat is done þer, namely in grobbyng and stokkyng off treis, busses, and groves'.[26]

Economy, management,[27] prudence, husbandry, householding—these clearly belong together and as far as activity is concerned, generally in an agricultural sense—for this entire conceptual framework turns on the activity of preserving and sustaining, rather than getting and spending. Importantly, unrelated to this field is any conception of commercial activity associated with trade or finance, or even with manufacturing, since of course workshops and smithies were typically attached to a household. Instead, the OED identifies the etymology of 'economy' as deriving from

> Middle French *yconomie*, *economie*, French *économie*, *oeconomie* management of a household or of its expenses or of domestic or familial matters (c1370), order according to which things are administered or organized (15th cent.), good use of a thing (15th cent.), economy or restraint in expenditure (c1510), good order in conduct and administration with regard to production and consumption (17th cent.), harmonious disposition of parts of a whole (17th cent.), harmony in the different parts of an organized body (1671), order of things as established by Providence as regards salvation by Christ (1721) and its etymon classical Latin *oeconomia* (in post-classical Latin also *economia*, *yconomia*, *iconomia*) arrangement of material by an author.

Relating these definitions back to their original agricultural context, we can see these reflected in early English husbandry tracts, beginning with Fitzherbert's *Boke of Husbandrye* (1523). Besides descriptions of the annual round of agricultural labour reminiscent of Hesiod, we find that the husbandman cannot be successful unless he has a wife who can run the household, milk the cows, send the corn to the mill, make butter and cheese, gather eggs, and also make sheets, towels, and shirts among a list of other

25. Reginald Pecock, *The Folewer to the Donet*, British Library MS Royal 17.D.9.

26. Sir John Fortescue, *The Governance of England*, ed. Charles Plummer, Oxford University Press, Oxford 1885 ch. 12, p. 141.

27. Deriving from the Italian, '*maneggiare* to handle (1298–1309), to be able to use skilfully, to manage, to direct or exercise a horse (14th cent., Spanish *manejar* to manage, use, manipulate (1591))'—OED for the verb 'manage'.

chores.[28] The wife also has to keep accounts and accompany her husband to the market, so that she can see how he buys and sells: 'For if one of them shoulde use to deceyve the other, he deceyveth hym-selfe, and he is not lyke to thryve'.[29] Hence this conception of husbandry begins with the 'plowynge and sowyng of theyr cornes'[30], and develops into a conception of prudence and thrift, matching spending to income. The same sentiments are expressed in Thomas Tusser's *Five hundredth pointes of good husbandrie* (1557, 1586). By the time we arrive at Walter Blith's *The English Improver, or a New Survey of Husbandry* (1649) the focus on the household has given way to a discussion of the diverse ways in which land can be improved, and the various obstacles to this—landlords who seek to reap the benefit of tenant's improvements, the conflict between those who wish to float water meadows and the miller, and the problems presented by the intermixing of arable and common land. The classical sources were not however forgotten: Worlidge's *Systema Agriculturae; the Mystery of Husbandry Discovered* (1675) notes in its preface Xenophon's elevation of agriculture as a 'noble' pursuit, and Pliny is cited together with a number of other Roman writers.[31] But quite plainly, by the end of the seventeenth century, 'husbandry' had shifted away from householding towards agricultural improvement—as in the title of Leonard Meager's *The Mystery of Husbandry: or, Arable, Pasture, and Wood-land Improved* (1697).[32] By the early eighteenth century the genre includes gardening and country living, being written by, or for, country gentlemen, and for the most part shedding all direct connection of husbandry to economy.

Nonetheless, that the latter term did retain the sense of 'good order' is also illustrated by the runaway success of a work originally published anonymously in 1750–1751, and which by the end of the century had run

28. Fitzherbert, *The Book of Husbandry*, edited by W. W. Skeat, Trübner, London 1882 pp. 95–97.

29. Ibid. p. 98.

30. Ibid. p. 1.

31. '*Xenophon* in his Elegant Tract of *Oeconomicks* tells you, *That nothing can be of a more Regal* (or Noble) *Estimation and Splendour, than a Judicious* Agriculture'. Worlidge, *Systema Agriculturae*, 2nd edition, 'Prooemium in Laudem Agriculturæ; being the Preface or Introduction to the Work: Shewing the Excellency, Utility, and Necessity of Husbandry'.

32. There is a parallel literature regarding agricultural property, its supervision and assessment: John Norden, *The Svrveyors Dialogve, Very profitable for all men to pervse, but especially for Gentlemen, Farmers and Husbandmen, that shall either haue occasion, or be willing to buy, hire or sell Lands: As in the ready and perfect Surueying of them, with the manner and Method of keeping a Court of Suruey with many necessary rules, and familiar Tables to that purpose*, 3rd edition, London 1618; Charles Calthrope, *The Relation betweene the Lord of a Mannor and the Coppy-holder his Tenant*, London 1635; Sir Edward Coke, *The Compleat Copy-Holder, wherein is contained a Learned Discourse of the Antiquity and Nature of Mannors and Copy-holds*, London 1650.

to some two hundred editions, including translations into Latin, Hebrew, Russian, German, Dutch, French, and Danish: Robert Dodsley's *Oeconomy of Human Life*.[33] Supposedly a translation from the work of an 'Indian brahmin', and quickly being parodied as *Maxims and Cautions for the Ladies. Being a Complete Oeconomy for the Female Sex* (1752), Dodsley's work presented a guide to human conduct, proposing maxims such as: 'As one that runneth in haste, and leapeth over a fence, may fall into a pit which he doth not see; so is the man that plungeth suddenly into any action, before he hath consider'd the consequences thereof'.[34] And when translated into Dutch the title became *De Huishouding de Menschelyken Levens*,[35] demonstrating the continuing linkage between householding, oeconomy, and good order. Francis Hutcheson's usage reflects this too, for Book III of his *Elements of Moral Philosophy*, 'The Principles of Oeconomicks and Politicks', while excluding all reference to household activities, presents Oeconomicks in three chapters concerning the proper conduct of marriage, the duties of parents and children, and the rights of masters and servants. The conception of 'oeconomy' articulated in Hutcheson's teaching of the 1740s has been emptied of the broader senses it had in the seventeenth century, but there is still an explicit relation to 'Politicks', the subsequent chapters of Book III running from the personal moral order to 'The Origin of Civil Government', concluding with 'Of Treaties, Ambassadors, and the dissolution of Civil Societies'. By contrast, from the mid-seventeenth century 'commerce' was consistently used in the context of exchange, trade, intercourse, a transaction entirely neutral with respect to the moral order implicit in conceptions of household and husbandry.[36]

Having arrived back at the point from which I started, it would be logical to move directly on to French and English usage in the mid-eighteenth century, and the significance of the first English treatise using the title

33. Donald D. Eddy, 'Dodsley's "Oeconomy of Human Life", 1750–1751', *Modern Philology* Vol. 85 (1988) p. 460.

34. *The Oeconomy of Human Life. Translated from an Indian Manuscript written by an ancient Bramin*, R. Dodsley, London 1751—Part I Duties That relate to Man, Consider'd as an Individual: Section I Consideration, p. 4.

35. Haarlem 1751—details in Eddy, 'Dodsley's "Oeconomy"', op. cit. p. 469.

36. '*Comercio*, trafficke, intercourse, commerce' (J. Florio, *World of Wordes*, 1598) OED, 'commerce, n.'. McCulloch traced the first appearance of 'the general principles of the science' of political economy to the association of wealth with gold and silver, and hence to the 'extraordinary extension of commerce during the fifteenth and sixteenth centuries', proceeding to expound what he terms the 'mercantile system' in relation to the writings of Mun, Child, Petty, and North. This is one of the very earliest attempts to provide a historical account of the emergence of political economy, but does so by focusing on conceptions of wealth, rather than economy—J. R. McCulloch, *A Discourse on the Rise, Progress, Peculiar Objects, and Importance, of Political Economy*, Archibald Constable, Edinburgh 1824 pp. 21, 23, 37f.

'political economy': Sir James Steuart's *Inquiry into the Principles of Political Oeconomy* published in 1767. But first we need to retrace our steps, for Steuart's text was not the first to present itself as a treatise on political economy, while there is also a substantial seventeenth and eighteenth century German-language history of which we need to take account if we are to understand the specifically German transformation of the concept of 'economy' in the early nineteenth century.

So far I have implied that the connection of 'œconomy' to 'politics' as 'political œconomy' first came about in the mid-eighteenth century. This is not strictly true, although this qualification has no larger significance for the argument being developed here. First, there is a passage in the Pseudo-Aristotelian *Oeconomica* including the term *oikonomia politikē*, referring to the administration of the city revenues.[37] This clearly makes use of the sense of good order implicit in *oikonomia*, as does the more explicit *politikē oikonomia* that we can find used by Dionysius of Halicarnassus to describe public civil administration as distinct from military administration.[38] But in neither case does the conjunction imply the good order of a political body as such, which is what the term came to mean in the second half of the eighteenth century. These are casual metaphors, not the early expression of subsequent concepts.

More problematic is the use of 'économie politique' in the title of a text by Antoyne de Montchrétien in 1615. This is a substantial volume of 370 pages in the modern edition, whose title was originally *Traité économique du trafic*, but which in being dedicated to the king and the queen mother was altered to bear more directly on the king's 'polity', and so became *Traicté de l'économie politique*.[39] It should be said straight away that this is not a text on 'political economy' in the later eighteenth-century sense, nor is it a treatise, but merely a forerunner of what became a common seventeenth-century genre of advice to a ruler regarding the 'strength of the nation'. The work also appears to have quickly sunk into complete obscurity, in that few, if any, subsequent authors even mention Montchrétien.[40] The text is divided into four parts, the first dealing with the mechanical arts, manufactures,

37. [Pseudo]Aristotle, *Oeconomia*, op. cit. Book II pp. 345f.

38. Natali, '*Oikonomia*', op. cit. p. 98.

39. Théophile Funck-Brentano, 'Introduction. L'économie politique patronale', in Antoyne de Montchrétien, *Traicté de l'économie politique*, Plon, Paris 1889 p. xxiii.

40. Joseph Garnier's brief treatment of Montchrétien in his 'De l'origine et de la filiation du mot économie politique et des divers autres noms donnés à la science économique', *Journal des Économistes* t. 32 (May–August 1852) p. 306 raises the question of whether the term 'political economy' was already part of the language in 1615, or whether the book had been mentioned at all for the next 150 years, but then admits that he has no way of knowing. He passes straight from Montchrétien to Rousseau.

village trades, and the like; the second with overseas commerce; the third with navigation; and the fourth with the Prince's orientation to piety, charity, censorship and finances. Book I begins with a discussion of the features of an 'Estat bien reglé' (p. 14), and the art of politics is said to depend upon the model of household rule: 'Car le bon gouvernement domestic, à la bien prendre, est un patron et modelle du public . . .' (p. 17). The dominance of the classical household model is also clear in the argument that 'The wealth of a state depends not only on its great extent, nor on the abundance of its population, but in leaving no land empty and placing everyone, with judgement, in his proper place' (p. 31). Later Montchrétien argues that 'The maintenance of the state is like that of the body, which retains from its nourishment that which is necessary, and rejects the superfluous. . . . Good political order chooses the useful, appropriating and incorporating it, only relinquishing that which is superfluous and unprofitable' (p. 247). Montchrétien's 'economic treatise on traffic' in fact enumerates the various sources of the 'commerce' of France and proposes means for their improvement. It was the dedication to the king that brought about its retitling as 'political economy', a term that does not actually occur in the text itself; while the conception of order implicit in the text as a whole is clearly continuous with the sentiments of classical usage. It cannot be said therefore that Montchrétien's introduction of the term *œconomie politique* has any particular conceptual-historical significance; if anything, it recalls the sense noted above in the Pseudo-Aristotelean *Oeconomica*. The text itself is entirely comparable with English and German literature of the period, presenting assessments of a ruler's national assets and the means for their enhancement, and none of these Continental European writers appear to have thought to have made use of this neologism. The term then disappeared for more than a century, and then re-emerged without any direct reference being made to Montchrétien's treatise.

That Montchrétien's usage is quite coincidental for the time can be reinforced by considering the way in which German literature articulated the classical conceptions of order and structure outlined above. German historians have long accepted the idea that the economic discourse of the seventeenth and early eighteenth centuries was 'neo-Aristotelian', a position first argued at length by Otto Brunner, in his book *Adeliges Landleben*, and also in a much-cited essay from 1958 on the household and its economy.[41] Before dealing with these, however, we first need to clarify an

41. 'Das "Ganze Haus" und die alteuropäische "Ökonomik"' [1958], in his *Neue Wege der Verfassungs- und Sozialgeschichte*, 3rd edition, Vandenhoeck und Ruprecht, Göttingen 1980 pp. 103–27. There is also an extensive history which forms a backstory

etymological issue, since the German terminology relating to 'economy' distinguishes between Germanic and non-Germanic sources. For in German there are two words for 'economy': *Wirtschaft* and *Oekonomie*. Sometimes they have been interchangeable, sometimes not, but they have quite distinct etymologies.

The stem 'Wirt' is recorded as such in Old High German, and its etymology is outlined by Grimm as follows:

> Germ. *werduz* . . . dual meaning as 'wirt' and 'meal', ahd. wirt 'hospitality, innkeeper, husband' [gastfreund, gastwirt, ehemann] as. werd 'host, husband' and ahd. wirtscaft, mhd. wirtschaft 'hospitality, banquet' [bewirtung, gastmahl].[42]

Early northern High German derived from this the term *Wirtschaft*, referring to the 'administration of house and property', and often extended to 'hospitable reception, care';[43] while Zedler has for *Wirtschafft* 'means in general to give and take the necessities of life, or engage in the business of the same'.[44] The parallels with classical usage are plain in the linkage to a household, with the modification that a *Wirt* is not head of a household but rather a host, possibly of an inn, defined by his function of providing the 'necessities of life' to guests. Zedler adds to a listing of the possible variations on the term that some sources claim that use of the term should be confined to arable farming and cattle-rearing, that is, explicitly excluding trade and commerce.[45] Hence the Germanic etymology of *Wirtschaft*, the contemporary substantive equivalent of the English 'economy', is independent of the Graeco-Latin tradition, but by the sixteenth century had ended up in more or less the same place semantically in German usage. The linkage to householding, and specifically to agricultural activities, likewise limited the term to the sense of maintenance and redistribution, and not to acquisitive activity in general.

---

to the neo-Aristotelian perspective upon the seventeenth and eighteenth centuries; this has been discussed in detail by Otto Gerhard Oexle, 'Wirtschaft III. Mittelalter', in Brunner, Conze, Koselleck, *Geschichtliche Grundbegriffe* Bd. 7, op. cit., pp. 526–50.

42. Grimm, *Deutsches Wörterbuch* Bd. 14/2 cols. 229–30. ahd. = althochdeutsch, mhd. = mittelhochdeutsch, as. = altsächsisch.

43. Grimm, *Deutsches Wörterbuch* Bd. 14/2 col. 662.

44. J. H. Zedler, *Grosses Vollständiges Universal-Lexikon*, Bd. 57, p. 1130, Leipzig 1748.

45. Ibid. Bd. 57 p. 1131.

Ökonomie by contrast is a *Fremdwort*, an alien borrowing, first appearing in the sixteenth century.[46] In Zedler again we can read that

> *Oeconomie, Haußhaltungswissenschaft, Haußhaltungskunst, Oeconomia, Disciplina Domestica, Oeconomica Ars, Oeconomia Prudentia,* is a part of Practical Philosophy which teaches how one should gain an honest living and maintain what has been gained, so that shortage and poverty is countered, keeping oneself and one's own honestly from this. Instruction in this is called *Studium Oeconomicum.* Oeconomy is divided into *State Oeconomy* (*Oeconomiam publicam*) and Private Oeconomy (*Oeconomiam privatam*). See householding Bd. 12 p. 902.[47]

And if we follow this reference we find that householding is

> one of the most excellent sciences through which human happiness is principally achieved. It teaches this through the rules of prudence, not only by rational and well-structured Christian direction, how to acquire possessions, how to prudently make use of what has been acquired, storing it with practical thrift and increasing it, which is even a greater art than that of acquisition itself.[48]

Even in the late eighteenth century the agricultural emphasis of œconomy was still evident, Strelin's dictionary defining an '*Oekonom* or *Landwirt* as a person who has either learned agriculture in its widest sense, or pursues it in practice or teaches others the same. . . . An *Oeconomic Society* or *Academy* is an association of such persons who are familiar with agriculture, cattle-raising, forestry and all the disciplines belonging to œconomy'.[49] If we look at the second edition of Zincke's dictionary, we find 'Oeconomy, see householding', and added in the fifth edition, 'Oeconom, see householder'.[50] A later dictionary summarises the meaning of this loan word as it develops from the seventeenth to the nineteenth century:

> To this is then added in the early 17th century *Ökonom*—that likewise occurs in its Latin form right into the 18th century—and in the sense of the economic,

46. Grimm, *Deutsches Wörterbuch* Bd. 7 col. 1268.
47. J. H. Zedler, *Grosses Vollständiges Universal-Lexikon*, Bd. 25, p. 528, Leipzig 1740.
48. Loc. cit.
49. G. G. Strelin, *Realwörterbuch für Kameralisten und Oekonomen*, Bd. 6 pp. 301, 302, Karl Gottlieb Beeke, Nördlingen 1791.
50. G. H. Zincke, *Allgemeines Oeconomisches Lexicon*, col. 2085, Johann Friedrich Gleditsch, Leipzig 1744; 5th ed. 1780.

> proficient *Hausvater.* In the 18th century the connotation of thriftiness, already associated with *oeconomia*, becomes increasingly widespread, and this preponderates in the very many instances during the second half of the century. . . . But in the nineteenth century the agricultural semantic group tends to separate the *Landwirt* from the *Bauer.*[51]

It would be quite possible to write an entire history of German economic thought in the seventeenth and eighteenth centuries by tracing the shifting usage of *Ökonomie* and *Wirtschaft* in the very extensive literature of the period.[52] Here we can do no more than indicate the lexical opportunities that these terms represented, and the manner in which both were centred on the rural household until later in the eighteenth century, the domain in which 'economy' was practised being therefore more or less equivalent to agricultural activity.

This can also be established in the negative: sixteenth- and seventeenth-century writings on finance, taxation, trade, and commerce are not included within the conceptual field centring on *Oeconomie* and *Wirtschaft.* Jochen Hoock has noted that the extensive collection of merchant and commercial literature held in Wolfenbüttel Library, founded in 1572, is not catalogued among the œconomic writings, but is dispersed among Arithmetica, Juridica, Geographica, Politica, and Quodlibetica.[53] By the later seventeenth century such writings did find a unity, but through being understood as so many tracts on *Commercienwesen.* By the early eighteenth century the term *Handelswissenschaft* was also being used, sometimes interchangeably with *Commercienwissenschaft*, mirroring the distinction between German and classic stems that we have already seen at work with *Ökonomie* and *Wirtschaft*, but not interchangeable with this pairing—commerce was about a particular form of exchange, whereas economy was linked to particular kinds of activity, and it would not be until the later nineteenth century that 'economy' and 'exchange' would be firmly yoked to each other. As already noted, *Ökonomie* and *Wirtschaft*—the Germanic root 'wirt' and the later Graeco-Latin *oeconomia*—would become lexical resources providing alternative possibilities for the construction of distinctions in the economic sciences, sometimes confusingly so. When for

51. *Deutsches Fremdwörterbuch* Bd. 2 p. 240, Walter de Gruyter, Berlin 1942.
52. Johannes Burkhardt's entry in GG provides the best overview: 'IV. "Wirtschaft" und "Ökonomie" im Kontext der frühneuzeitlichen Hauslehre (16–18 Jh.)', in Brunner, Conze, Koselleck, *Geschichtliche Grundbegriffe* Bd. 7 pp. 550–94.
53. Cited in Burkhardt, 'V.2 Der Ausbau eines kommerziellen Gegenstands- und Theoriebereichs (16.–18. Jh.)', in Brunner, Conze, Koselleck, *Geschichtliche Grundbegriffe* Bd. 7 pp. 561–62.

example Carl Menger published his *Grundsätze der Volkswirthschaftslehre* (1871) this was an abstract analysis of economically oriented action, of *das Wirtschaften*. But later, responding to Schmoller's attack on his text, he wrote a methodological critique of historical economics which distinguished between a *Nationalökonomie*, a *Volkswirtschaftslehre*, and a *Volkswirtschaftspolitik*, now respectively economic theory, a descriptive account of real economies, and economic policy.[54] This only serves to emphasise the point that the conceptual field defining 'economy' in nineteenth-century German developed out of a conception of economic activity linked to reproduction and household order; the domains of trade, finance, and manufacture were subsequently added to this, but their terminology had followed a quite different conceptual path from the early Middle Ages.

This idea can be reinforced if we look beyond the etymologies presented above and consider the literature to which Brunner first drew attention: *Hausväterliteratur*, the explicitly neo-Aristotelian equivalent of the more strictly empirical English husbandry tracts.[55] One of the earliest examples of this genre, the *Calendarium Perpetuum, et Libri Oeconomici* of Johannes Coler, announced in its preface that

> The whole world has to admit and say / that a *gute Wirtschafft* is / *ars artium & scientia scientiarum*, an art above all arts / which all hard-working *Hauswirt(e)* have diligently studied for a lifetime / and will surely study until the end of the world / but there will never more be found / anyone who has completed their study of this art.[56]

The exclusively agricultural nature of this 'art' is emphasised by the two parts of the calendar, the first being a listing of agricultural activities month by month, the second being a more systematic market calendar. The 'libri oeconomici' that follow (the entire text bound together in Göttingen's Niedersächsische Staats- und Universitäts Bibliothek is some 2,000 pages in all, the calendars taking up just under 300 pages) consists

54. Carl Menger, *Untersuchungen über die Methode der Socialwissenschaften, und der Politischen Oekonomie insbesondere* (1883), *Gesammelte Werke* Bd. 2, ed. Friedrich Hayek, J. C. B. Mohr (Paul Siebeck), Tübingen 1969 pp. 8–9: here 'theoretische Nationalökonomie' deals with the general nature and laws of 'volkswirtschaftlichen Erscheinungen', while the 'practical sciences of *Volkswirtschaft*' deal with the principles of appropriate and purposeful (*zweckmässigen*) action in the domain of the economy—economic policy and financial science being the examples he gives for this.

55. For a general survey see Manfred P. Fleischer, 'The First German Agricultural Manuals', *Agricultural History* Vol. 55 (1981) pp. 1–15.

56. Johannis Colerus, 'Vorrede' *Calendarium Perpetuum, et Libri Oeconomici*, Paul Helwig, Wittenberg 1604, p. ii.

of six books, beginning with 'Oeconomiae', followed by an examination of the work to be carried out in the house (cooking, baking, milling, brewing, the most extensive section, from ch. 6 on the different sorts of beer to ch. 16 on drunkenness). The third book is devoted to cooking recipes, the fourth to viticulture, the fifth to gardening, the sixth to woodcutting. The seventh book, following this in a new section devoted to agriculture, is headed *Georgia oder Georgica genand*, the title of the second chapter stating that 'Agriculture is a Christian/honest/useful/praiseworthy / and necessary sustenance / not at all to be despised / or dismissed'. This explicit linkage of agriculture to Christian morality is a common feature of *Hausväterliteratur*, as is the expression of rule within the household in a more general political language:

> The *Oiconomia* is a *Monarchia*, that is / such a form of rule / within which only one rules and governs / that is / the *Wirth im Hause* / he must be sole ruler in the house /and everything in the *gantzes Haus* / has to be directed by him /as seafarers are guided by the Pole Star. And so a wife / all children / all servants and maids / they must respect the Wirt and be obedient. . . . Viel können nicht regieren zugleich / Nur einer gehört in ein Königreich.[57]

This work was revised and republished in 1645 in a generously illustrated folio format, its frontispiece busily depicting rural life and labour presided over by Adam, the first 'Hausvatter', and Noe, the first viticulturalist (figure 2.1).

Other notable works of the period were von Thumbshirn's *Oeconomia* (1617) and Hering's *Oeconomischer Wegweiser* (1689). But the most interesting example of this genre in the seventeenth century is von Hohberg's *Georgica Curiosa* (1682), to which Brunner devoted his *Adeliges Landleben*.[58]

57. Last sentence bold in original—Coler, *Oeconomia oder Hausbuch* Bk. I ch. 4 pp. 3–4. (Bound up with the Calendar but paginated separately.)

58. Otto Brunner, *Adeliges Landleben und europäisches Geist*, Otto Müller, Salzburg 1949. The book is essentially a case study of the declining world of rural nobility, seen through the prism of von Hohberg's life and activities, contrasting the moral order of the household to the very different world of 'industrial society', as Brunner sees it. While his account of householding and economic order retains its original force, the manner in which this is contrasted to 'market society' can only be sustained because of the lack of any consideration of the transition from *Haus* to *Markt* (p. 245). There is however a considerable distance from the seventeenth century to the 1930s, when the conceptual order which Brunner has in mind was first consistently articulated. Peter Miller has emphasised that *Adeliges Landleben*, far from being the elegy to a lost world of rural nobility that Brunner thought it, documents the real cosmopolitanism of a provincial culture that would in the eighteenth century form the basis for a European Enlightenment—'Nazis and Neo-Stoics: Otto Brunner and Gerhard Oestreich before and after the Second World War', *Past and Present* No. 176 (2002) pp. 181–82.

Figure 2.1:
Frontispiece to Johannes Coler, *Oeconomia Ruralis et Domestica* (1645)
Source: Niedersächsische Staats- und Universitäts Bibliothek, Göttingen

Hohberg remarks in his preface that 'economy' is an inconsequential term, echoing the marginal place that it had among the classical Greek authors—while it was of course important, it was not something that needed any lengthy examination. Nonetheless,

> So that no-one might object / that I deal with *Wirthschafft* / And do not state / what it is / I had originally thought it unnecessary / because in any case everyone knows it is that / without which human life cannot exist / but to put it most concisely / *Oeconomia* is nothing but / taking prudent care / in establishing successfully a *Hauswirthschafft* / and maintaining it.[59]

Following this preface Hohberg lists over five and a half pages all the relevant literature in Greek, Latin, German, French, Italian, and Spanish that bears on this point, including among the English texts Smith's *De Republica Anglorum*, Tusser, and North. The sheer extent of this survey makes plain that this is a work of literature, rather than a practical manual, but it still covers much of the ground already noted in Coler and others: cookery, medicine, gardening, arable cultivation, the care of cattle, the care of bees, and concluding with woodcutting—eighty-two chapters in the first volume, and eighty-three in the second. Volume II chapter VII covers 'What a *Haus-Vatter* must generally look out for in the *Wirtschaft*', beginning with the observation that

> where there is no man there is no mastery; where mastery is lacking / there is no respect; where there is no respect / everyone does what they like; where this happens / one seldom pays any attention to the advice of another; where this is lacking / seldom does any good come of it.[60]

But the next chapter turns to the way in which the *Hausvater* must watch the seasons and changes in the weather, underscoring the manner in which this conception of rule is embedded in a very practical appreciation of the rural life.

Hohberg's text is elaborate and lengthy, but the general arguments he advances, the materials he presents, and the assumptions he makes about economic and political order can also be found in many simpler and shorter books that subsequently appeared: C. Fischer's *Fleissiges Herren-Auge* (1690);

59. W. H. von Hohberg, *Georgica Curiosa. Was ist: Umständlicher Bericht und klarer Unterricht von dem Adelichen Land- und Feld-Leben*, Johann Friedrich Endter, Nuremberg 1682 Bd. 1 n.p.
60. Hohberg, *Georgica Curiosa*, Vol. 2 p. 101.

S. Fischer's *Unterrichteter Hauß-Vater und Kluger Gärtner* (1705); Meier's *Arcana et curiositates oeconomicae* (1706); an anonymous *Kleine Sorgfältige Haußhalter* (1710); another anonymous *Der arbeitsame Land und Haußvater* (1710); J. J. Becher's *Kluger Haus-Vater, Verstandige Haus-Mutter* (1714), which includes advice on how to get spots off clothes;[61] von Rohr's *Vollständiges Hauß-Haltungs-Recht* (1716); and Hoffmann's *Klugheit Haußzuhalten, Oder: Prudentia Oeconomica* (5 vols. 1744–1755). Among these was also an extremely lavish folio work, Florinus's *Oeconomus Prudens et Legalis. Oder Allgemeiner Klug- und Rechtsverständiger Haus-Vatter,*[62] published like Hohberg's book in Nuremberg, and arguably a plagiary of that work.[63] In 1769 Fischer's *Fleissiges Herren-Auge* was republished, noting that while there was no shortage of books on householding, Fischer's work had already gone through three new editions, and was now presented in a fifth 'purged of much material, in part of no use and in part superstitious' under a new title: *Der kluge Wirtschafts-Beamte*.[64] That the genre retained its popularity into the last third of the eighteenth century is confirmed by Münchhausen's six-part work *Der Hausvater*, consisting of hundreds of pages of material published between 1764 and 1773. Facing the title page in the second edition was an engraving depicting the study of a *Hausvater* (figure 2.2):

> On his table he has the works of Linnaeus and Virgil; dried herbs and fish; a magnifying glass; a telescope; a magnetic needle; and other mathematical instruments scattered around; and on a note to one side are the words *Labor ipse voluptas*, a reminder that one should never see work as an evil and avoid it, but must rather seek the greatest pleasure in constant activity.
>
> In drawers under the table is a collection of insects, fish, worms, mussels and other preparations of sea, plant, and animal; in another cupboard dried herbs are ordered.
>
> On the other side there are on different shelves a burning-glass; an electrising machine; boxes with magnifying glasses, an air-pump, and its parts; and all kinds of strange things stored while under the influence of wine. Alongside them on a bookshelf there hangs a pair of scales, a thermometer, and an artificial magnet.
>
> In front of the window there are two cupboards containing samples of minerals, earth, and stone, between which there hangs a barometer.[65]

61. 'Allerhand Flecke aus dem Kleidern zu bringen', pp. 309–12.
62. Christoph Riegel, Nuremberg 1702, reissued as a 'new edition' in 1705, and then in a genuine second edition in 1719.
63. H. Haushofer, 'Das Problem des Florinus', *Zeitschrift für Agrargeschichte und Agrarsoziologie* Jg. 30 (1982) pp. 168–75.
64. 'An der Leser' n. p., Gabriel Nicolaus Raspe, Nuremberg 1769.
65. O. von Münchhausen, *Der Hausvater*, Th. I, Hannover 1766 pp. xxviii–xxix.

Figure 2.2:
Frontispiece to Münchhausen, *Der Hausvater* (1766)
Source: Niedersächsische Staats- und Universitäts Bibliothek, Göttingen

Besides the usual arguments about the members of a household and their tasks, Münchhausen also makes use of a significant analogy:

> The entire nature of the house must interrelate like a clock; each wheel must exactly fit another and be capable of keeping all the others in motion. No wheel can stay still, for otherwise it harms the entire machine; if attention is paid only to one wheel, leaving the others to rust, so eventually they will all be brought to a halt, and the damage is obvious.[66]

This mechanical image of the internal management of the household is a new departure for this literature, and points to a looming convergence with what would become political economy: a conception of economic organisation detached from the model of the classical household, from the hierarchy and mutual obligation that created its internal order, and also from the moral order which that hierarchy and obligation presupposed.

However, the process of detachment was a very lengthy one; as will be demonstrated below, it was only completed in the course of the twentieth century. My point in beginning this essay with Hutcheson is that this process really only began in the mid-eighteenth century, and then did so by *refounding* sociability and moral order upon a general conception of human behaviour, abandoning the conception of the household structured and ordered through social rank and personal obligation. It was Adam Smith's critique of Hutcheson that provided a framework for this new order, represented in his two books, *Theory of Moral Sentiments* (1759) and *Wealth of Nations* (1776). But as is also demonstrated below and in the following essays, it took a very long time—more or less two centuries—for the significance of Smith's partially realised project to be generally appreciated. English political economy as it developed in the first half of the nineteenth century simply ignored most of the arguments that Smith had put forward, even though these British economists presented themselves as the heirs of Adam Smith. Instead, Malthus, James Mill, and Ricardo used some of his economic categories to construct a restricted model of economic relationships which entirely wrote out of the plot any sense that an economic order presupposes a moral order, and hence requires or presupposes a plausible account of human sociability. The political economy of Malthus, James Mill, and Ricardo quickly turned out to be something of an interlude, although their work was seized on by a young Karl Marx and rewritten as a critique of contemporary society that, for a variety of contingent reasons, survived into the late twentieth century as the core of

66. Ibid. p. 337.

an economic critique of modernity.[67] What has also survived is Marx's term 'classical political economy', or 'classical economics', to cover not only the English writers of the early nineteenth century, but also the work of Adam Smith. As I will show, in so doing he seriously blurred our perspective upon Adam Smith, and this is a terminology best forgotten.

However, the prime focus here is upon the shifting usage of 'economy' and its cognates. If we now turn back to where we were with Francis Hutcheson, it is evident that we need to look beyond the category 'political economy' to the set of semantic relationships that it sets in play—the conceptual framework that lends it meaning. First we can register the return of the term with Rousseau's entry 'Économie (Morale et Politique)', published in the *Encyclopédie* in November 1755:

> ECONOMIE or OECONOMIE, (Morale et Politique). This word economy comes from oikos, house, and from nomos, law, and denotes originally nothing more than the wise and legitimate government of the house for the common good of the whole family. The meaning of the term has been later extended to the government of the great family, which is the state. To distinguish these two senses, the latter case is called *économie générale*, or *politique*; and in the other case, *économie domestique*, or *particuliere*. It is only the former that is at issue in this article. For *économie domestique*, see FATHER OF THE FAMILY.[68]

This leads into an extended discussion of forms of family authority, as compared with those prevailing in the state, the analogy then being rejected as unsuitable, save for one common factor: an obligation upon heads of household and of the state to care for the well-being of their respective charges. The political domain is introduced via another analogy, this time borrowed from Hobbes, which conceives the sovereign as the head of a 'body politic', law and customs forming the brain, proceeding on to commerce, industry, and agriculture, which form

> the mouth and stomach which prepare the common subsistence; public finances are the blood which a wise *economy*, performing the functions of the

67. For some of the complex issues involved here see my '"A Lost Connection": Max Weber and the Economic Sciences', in Karl-Ludwig Ay, Knut Borchardt (eds.) *Das Faszinosum Max Weber. Die Geschichte seiner Geltung*, UVK Verlagsgesellschaft, Konstanz 2006 pp. 313–29. It might also be noted here that the revival in the later twentieth century of the term 'political economy' as the description of a 'critical economics', or of a synthesis of law, policy analysis, and economics, has no real connection with this original usage.

68. Jean-Jacques Rousseau, 'Discours sur l'économie politique', *Oeuvres complètes de Jean-Jacques Rousseau* t. 3, Gallimard, Paris 1964 p. 241.

> heart, sends out to distribute nourishment and life throughout the entire body; the citizens are the body and the members that make the machine move, live, and work, and no part of which can be hurt without the painful impression of it being straightaway conveyed to the brain, if the animal is in a state of health.[69]

The body politic is, Rousseau argues, a moral being endowed with a will; and the determination of this general will is the first task of public economy.[70] And so it turns out that the subject matter of Rousseau's entry is not, like Montchrétien, a disquisition on the various economic activities that add to the wealth of the kingdom, but an account of 'public economy' whose first rule is to establish what the General Will might be. *Économie politique* here therefore implies no particular kind of activity, but describes the internal organisation and functioning of a political structure that resembles the household model only to the extent that the heads of both have an obligation to care for their charges.

However, the following year François Quesnay published his first article in the *Encyclopédie*, 'Fermiers (Econ. Polit.)', beginning with the definition:

> Farmers are those who take out leases and lend value to the goods of the countryside, and who obtain the wealth and resources most essential for the maintenance of the state; hence the occupation of the *farmer* is a very important matter in the kingdom, and merits close attention on the part of the government.[71]

Agricultural activity remains here the foundation of the kingdom, and as such this simply extends a conception of human needs and activities that runs back to the Greeks; but as in Rousseau, the household has disappeared, and with it the order that it had created. A new kind of 'economy' was needed for the regularities of economic activity. Quesnay and his collaborators

69. Ibid. p. 244.
70. Ibid. p. 245.
71. 'Fermiers' (October 1756), in Quesnay, *Œuvres économiques complètes et autres textes* t. 1, ed. Christine Théré, Loïc Charles, Jean-Claude Perrot, L'institut Nationale d;Études Démographiques, Paris 2005 p. 128. In English, the word 'farm' derives from the medieval Latin *firma*, meaning a fixed payment relating to a lease, or a rent; hence 'farmer' is someone responsible for a lease, or the payment of a rent (OED). Quesnay employs the term here in its agricultural sense: a farmer using horses, a *métayer* using the less efficient oxen, hence demonstrating the advantages of farming to agriculture. Through another derivation from *firma*, as a signature to an agreement, the English language acquired the word 'firm' as a business organisation; while modern Italian uses the term *fattoria* for what the English call 'a farm'.

would within a few years recreate the state as a giant household whose internal structure was characterised by separate classes of activity, linked together by a circulatory system embodied in the image of the *Tableau Économique*. The name that this movement later adopted—Physiocracy—implied that the economy was a natural order, an arrangement of human affairs that ran itself and in which rulers were enjoined *pas trop gouverner*—not to govern too much. It was however also a natural order, with a natural source that set it in motion: not human activity, but nature, agricultural production.

Arguments about the 'strength of a nation' and the sources of wealth had been a commonplace back to the early seventeenth century. Manufacturers, or merchants, or farmers, these were all at one time or another identified as a class forming the basis of national wealth, the prescription for the revival of the strength of the nation being the deliberate encouragement of this or that class of producer, as could be shown by considering the better circumstances enjoyed by England, or France, or Holland, as the case might be. These were a version of populationist arguments—instead of simply associating a large population with the wealth of a state, particular sections of the population were advanced as the source of such wealth—hence the path to wealth lay in more farmers, or more craftsmen, or more merchants, or even more sailors.[72]

Some of these arguments made use of the idea of commerce and exchange, conceiving the flows between trading countries in terms of money and gold, implying that the growth of commerce itself was the path to wealth.[73] 'Commerce' in this context meant foreign trade, and in particular, the relation of foreign trade to the power of states. Melon for instance opens his *Essai* supposing that there are three islands in the world, each of the same size and number of inhabitants, producing the one good best suited to its land—corn, wool, or 'beverages' (*boissons*). Equal numbers work in each island, and the yield of their work is sufficient for the three islands combined. Since each island produces but one good, trade between them will result, each setting aside a part of its own product to exchange with that of the other islands. On these assumptions, 'Needs and

72. See Ryan Walter's discussion of 'The State's Strength and Wealth' in his *Critical History of the Economy: On the Birth of the National and International Economies*, Routledge, London 2011 pp. 35–49.

73. For a thorough examination of the idea of 'commerce' in mid-eighteenth-century France see Philippe Steiner, 'Commerce, commerce politique' in Loïc Charles, Frédéric Lefebvre, Christine Théré (eds.) *Le cercle de Vincent de Gournay: Savoirs économique et pratiques administratives en France au milieu du XVIIIe siècle*, Institut National d'Études Démographiques, Paris 2011 pp. 179–200.

exchanges will be equal, and so the balance of commerce will be equal'.[74] If, on the other hand, one island—for instance, the corn producer—should improve itself to such an extent that it can also produce what it had previously obtained from the other islands, what would then happen? Melon suggests that under these conditions the other islands will compel the corn-producing island to specialise completely in corn, so that interchange might flow once again freely between them. And this leads to his definition of commerce: 'the exchange of superfluities for necessaries'.[75] Melon had also posited an extension of the number of islands, to those producing sugar, salt, or tobacco, and so developing a series of producers whose goods ranged from necessaries to 'superfluities', or luxuries. This led naturally into a consideration of the impact such developing trade might have on these societies, whether it might corrupt societies, which in turn lead to arguments both against the export of grain and the import of 'luxuries', severely limiting prospects for the expansion of trade. Regarding this line of argument, Montesquieu proposed that

> The natural effect of commerce is to bring about peace. Two nations that trade together render themselves mutually dependent; if one is interested in buying, the other has an interest in selling; and all unions are founded upon mutual needs.
>
> But if the spirit of commerce unites nations, it does not at all unite them in their particulars. We see in those countries seized with the spirit of commerce that all human actions are trafficked, and all moral virtues; the smallest things for which humanity asks are made or given for money.
>
> The spirit of commerce produces in men a sense of exact justice, opposed on one side by banditry, and on the other by those moral virtues which allow us to refrain from a fixed and constant discussion of interests, and allows one to neglect our interests for the sake of others.[76]

As Istvan Hont has demonstrated,[77] a complex web of argument over wealth, exchange, and national wealth developed from such ideas, but not one related directly to the concept of economy discussed here. Linked to 'commerce' was an extensive literature recommending either bounties or

74. Jean François Melon, *Essai politique sur le commerce*, 2nd edition, n. p. 1736 p. 2.
75. Ibid. pp. 8–9.
76. Montesquieu, *De l'Esprit des lois*, Livre XX ch. 2, Éditions Garniers, Paris 1973 t. 2 p. 3.
77. Istvan Hont, 'Jealousy of Trade: An Introduction', in his *Jealousy of Trade: International Competition and the Nation-State in Historical Perspective*, Harvard University Press, Cambridge (MA) 2005 pp. 30ff.

duties to lend advantage to the home country in overseas trade. In all of these writings the welfare of a nation was identified with particular groups of actors, or particular forms of taxation, or particular policies—such argument was by example, and empirical: 'commerce' was identified with particular policies. The idea that exchange itself might be the source of an economic rationality, in which agents engaged in open and free commerce to their mutual benefit, and that it was the expansion of such commerce itself that was the proper object of economic reflection, was as we shall see something first properly formulated by Turgot; but this remained without resonance, and the idea was recovered around a century later, only then firmly associating 'commerce', '*trafic*', '*Verkehr*', 'exchange' with 'economy'.

The argument that Quesnay and his associates developed was novel because of its departure from this empirical problematic within which exchange was conceived, and the adoption of the idea that there were different classes of producer and consumer within the nation, linking them together in a manner which established a necessary connection and a hierarchy: 'The rich farmer employs and maintains the peasant; the peasant supplies to the poor citizen the majority of the goods required for the needs of life'.[78] Agriculture was simply assumed to be the foundation of the kingdom, and as he made clear the following year in the opening lines of another entry for the *Encyclopédie*, all other activities were secondary:

> The principal articles of commerce in France are grain, wine and spirits, salt, hemp and flax, wool and other products furnished by animals: the manufacture of cloth and other common fabrics can significantly augment the value of hemp, flax, and wool, and provide subsistence to many men who would be occupied by these very advantageous works.[79]

Appended to this article was an early version of fourteen *Maximes de gouvernement économique*, among which he asserted that

> I. 'The work of industry[80] does not multiply wealth'. Indeed, the artisan 'destroyed as much in subsistence as he produced with his labour'.[81]

78. Quesnay, 'Fermiers', op. cit. p. 147.
79. Quesnay, 'Grains (Économie polit.)', (November 1757), *Œuvres économiques* t. 1, op. cit. p. 161.
80. Here industry should be understood as 'human industry', as in Adam Smith.
81. Quesnay, 'Maximes de gouvernement économique', *Œuvres économiques* t. 1, op. cit. p. 198.

III. 'The work of industry that employs men to the detriment of cultivating landed property (*biens-fonds*) is harmful to the population and the growth of wealth'.[82]

VI. 'A nation that has great commerce in its own agricultural commodities can always maintain, at least for itself, a considerable trade in handicraft goods'.[83]

XI. 'One cannot know, from the condition of the balance of commerce between various nations, the commercial advantage and the amount of wealth of each nation'.[84]

XIV. 'In mutual commerce, the nations that sell the most necessary or most useful commodities have an advantage over those which sell luxury goods'.[85]

These early maxims articulated a principle that would become the chief point of criticism of Quesnay's ideas: that agriculture was uniquely productive, that manufacturing activity, while important, was neutral as regards the production of wealth, that the 'natural order' was an agricultural order, and that the wealth of a nation turned upon its agricultural output. It should however be remembered that these principles were intended to counter the still-prevalent argument that a large population was a prerequisite of a flourishing state. Mirabeau's *L'Ami des hommes* for example argued that the wealth of a nation lay in the size of its population, that luxury consumption diminished wealth, and that agriculture was the most profitable mode of employment.[86] In July 1757 Quesnay had made a convert of Mirabeau, persuading him that a large population was not the cause, but the effect, of wealth; and that the proper object of analysis was therefore not population, but wealth. The two articles published in the *Encyclopédie* sketched out some of these ideas, but it was only with the printing in 1758 of the *Tableau Economique* that the real novelty of Quesnay's conception of the economy became evident.

The *Tableau* is a visual representation (figure 2.3) of the flows of payments moving from agricultural producers to landed proprietors and thence to producers of manufactured goods, who then in turn recycled their incomes into purchases of manufactures and agricultural products—the flow of the net product from the 'productive' to the 'sterile' class and back again. This is an annual movement; hence the economic cycle is the

82. Ibid. p. 199.
83. Ibid. p. 200.
84. Ibid. p. 203.
85. Ibid.
86. Mirabeau, *L'Ami des hommes ou Traité de la population*, 3 parts, Avignon 1756.

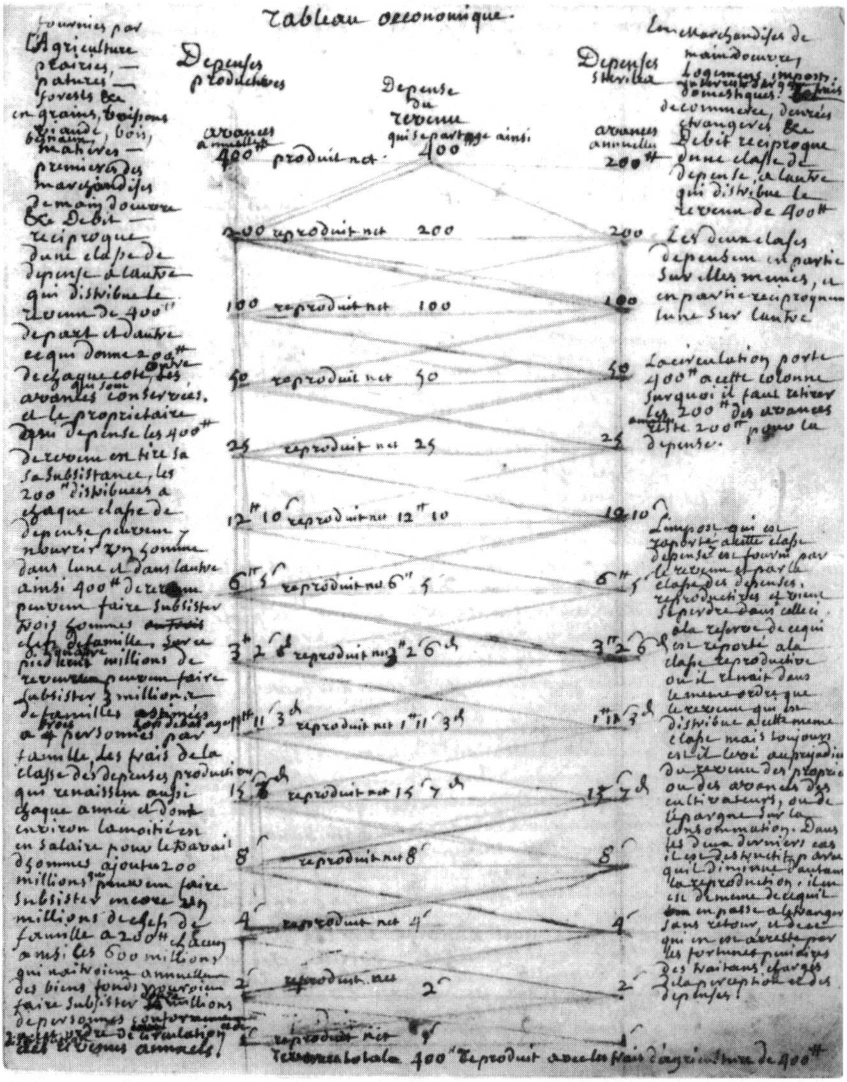

Figure 2.3:
Quesnay's first draft version of the *Tableau Economique* (1758)[87]
Source: Archives nationales, M784 no. 71-1

annual agricultural cycle. The three classes of society are linked through their incomes and expenditures, the value produced by agriculture gradually dissipating in the course of its circulation between the classes, exemplifying Rousseau's idea of money as the lifeblood of the economic system. Following each annual harvest, agricultural products would be exchanged

87. *Œuvres économiques* t. 1, op. cit. p. 571.

for manufactured goods, so that the 'sterile class' or artisans and manufacturers gained food and wine, while the 'productive class' received in turn manufactured goods. Quesnay interposed a third class, that of landed proprietors, who received the entire net product of the land in the form of rent, returning half of this revenue to the agricultural sector as purchases of food and wine, and transferring the other half as 'sterile expenditures' to the manufacturers of luxury goods, who then in turn spent half of their income on food and wine and the other half on manufactured goods—and so on through the year, until the entire system ran down to nothing and the next harvest started the sequence once more.

As Loïc Charles has demonstrated,[88] the *Tableau* was initially developed as a kind of graphic curiosity, but Mirabeau's *Philosophie Rurale, ou Économie générale et politique de l'agriculture*[89] traced at length the implications of the circulation engendered by the successive expenditures represented by lines zigzagging between the three classes. By the mid-1760s, when Adam Smith was in Paris, the *Économistes* were rapidly gaining adherents, and their writings were moving away from arguments about agriculture itself towards the broader problem of Economic Government—government according to a natural order.[90] Thus, for example, we find Le Trosne defining economic science and good government as follows:

> Economic science being nothing but the application of natural order to the government of societies, it is also constant in its principles and as susceptible of proof as the most exact of the physical sciences. . . . The Science of Government will then be simple and as easy as it is today complicated. One glance at its principles will suffice to judge and appreciate each operation; the Administrators of peoples, immune from the faults of error and surprise, will be certain of procuring the happiness of men through the implementation of the invariant laws of the natural order.[91]

By the later 1760s this 'new science' was given the name 'Physiocracy'. As *Économistes* they had identified the flows between classes that sustained

88. Loïc Charles, 'The *Tableau Économique* as Rational Recreation', *History of Political Economy* Vol. 36 (2004) pp. 457–58.

89. 3 vols. Amsterdam 1763.

90. See Philippe Steiner, 'Administration and Œconomic Government in Quesnay's Political Economy', in Roberto Baranzini, François Allisson (eds.) *Economics and other Branches – In the Shade of the Oak Tree: Essays in Honour of Pascal Bridel*, Pickering and Chatto, London 2014 pp. 123–34.

91. G. F. Le Trosne, *Recueil de plusieurs morceaux economiques*, Desaint, Paris 1768 pp.7–9.

the kingdom; as Physiocrats they developed this into a general conception of the origin and progress of societies:

> There is a natural society, previous to any convention between men, based upon their constitution, on their physical needs, on their evidently common interest.
>
> In this primitive state men have the *rights* and reciprocal *obligations* of an *absolute* justice, for they have a physical necessity, and are as a consequence *absolute* for their existence.
>
> *No rights without duties, and no duties without rights.*
>
> The *rights* of each man, previous to conventions, are the *liberty* to provide for his subsistence and his well-being, the *property* in his person and those things acquired by the labour of his person.
>
> His duties are labour to supply his needs, and respect for liberty, for personal property, and for the moveable property of others.[92]

In 1767 Quesnay published a revised set of 'Maximes' in the first volume of *Physiocratie ou constitution naturelle du gouvernment le plus avantageux au genre humain*, presenting a similar shift away from his original conception of the production and circulation of goods originating in agriculture, and placing much greater weight on sovereignty and economic government. Maxim XXV reads in its entirety:

> *That one preserve the complete freedom of commerce*; for THE MOST CERTAIN POLICE OF INTERNAL AND EXTERNAL COMMERCE, THE MOST PROFITABLE TO THE NATION AND TO THE STATE, CONSISTS IN THE FULL FREEDOM OF COMPETITION.[93]

Contemporary criticism however ignored this movement towards an idea of economic government; instead, Physiocracy was widely condemned for advancing the idea that the manufacturing class was 'sterile' with respect to the production of wealth, and that all taxes should be united in a single tax on the net product of agriculture, since this was the original source of wealth. The critique of Physiocracy thus fastened on to

92. Pierre-Samuel Du Pont de Nemours, *De l'origine et des progrès d'une science nouvelle*, Paris 1768 pp. 17–18.

93. Quesnay, 'Maximes générales du gouvernement économique d'un royaume agricole', *Œuvres économiques* t. 1, op. cit. p. 571. See for a detailed account of this usage of 'freedom of competition', and its relation to the watchwords *laissez faire, laissez passer*, Auguste Oncken, *Die Maxime laissez faire et laissez passer, ihr Ursprung, ihr Werden*, K. J. Wyß, Bern 1886 pp. 83–90 where Oncken discusses Maxime XXV, and the way that Quesnay here implies that phrasing but does not use it, instead stating that 'le monde va de lui-même' (p. 83).

principles elaborated in the early 1760s, and simply ignored the later elaboration of the 'new science'. Consequently the reputation of Physiocracy survived into the nineteenth century only as a caricature—sterility of manufacturing, agriculture the unique source of wealth, and a single tax upon the net produce of agriculture.

But this should not be allowed to obscure the manner in which, during the 1760s, the *Économistes* altered prevailing conceptions of economic order. Important to note here is the work of Turgot, who developed in his *Réflexions sur la formation et la distribution des richesses* a conception of the formation and circulation of wealth arising out of exchanges between the three classes of society. Written in 1766, published part by part in the *Ephémérides du Citoyen* from 1769 to 1770, and not published as a book until 1788, this work proposed that society was initially divided into two labouring classes, one of which laboured in the fields, and the other of which took their produce and worked it up into a form suitable for the use of men and women. The former was a *classe produtrice*, which 'produces, or rather, draws from the land ever-renewing wealth which provides all society with subsistence and materials for all needs'; the second was a *classe stipendiée*, which 'sells to the first its labour, receiving in exchange its subsistence'.[94] With the development of property in land these two classes were joined by a third, that of landed proprietors, who were able engage landless labourers to work their land, thus effecting a separation between landed property and agricultural labour. Landed proprietors, being the only members of society not needing to pursue any particular form of employment, were thus available for justice, administration, the army, and the navy, forming a *classe disponible*. Exchanges of goods between these classes gave rise to a system of values (*valeur courante*) that regulated exchange, where 'every good has the two essential properties of money, of measuring and representing all value; and, in this sense, every good is money'.[95]

> One can see that . . . how the cultivation of land, factories of all kinds, and all the branches of commerce, roll upon a mass of *capitals* or accumulated moveable wealth which, having been first advanced by entrepreneurs in each of these different classes of work, must return each year to them with a constant profit. . . . It is this advance and constant return of capitals that constitutes what *one has to call the circulation of money*; this useful and fecund circulation is what

94. A. R. J. Turgot, *Réflexions sur la formation et la distribution des richesses*, n. p. 1788 p. 14 §8.
95. Ibid. §39; 'Reciprocally, all money is essentially a commodity'. §40.

> animates all the works of society, which maintains movement and life in the body politic, and which one has good reason to compare with the circulation of blood in the animal body.[96]

Turgot had died in 1781, and delay in publication until 1788 in book form blunted the novelty of these arguments as compared with the treatises published in this period by Genovesi and Steuart. And it was the latter's text, appearing the year after Turgot had written *Réflexions*, that became the first since Montchrétien to formally announce itself as a treatise on political economy: the *Inquiry into the Principles of Political Œconomy.*[97]

While Steuart sought to reduce the 'complicated interests of domestic policy' to principles,[98] he hastened to add that

> It goes little farther than to collect and arrange some elements upon the most interesting branches of modern policy, such as population, agriculture, trade, industry, money, coin, interest, circulation, banks, exchange, public credit, and taxes.[99]

On the following page he went on to criticise the French love of 'systems', 'mere conceits' which are 'no more than a chain of contingent consequences, drawn from a few fundamental maxims'.[100] Whereas Turgot had developed a conception of the circulation of capital and money between classes, Steuart reverted to a version of the older household model to secure internal economic order.

Opening the first Book with the statement that 'Œconomy in general is the art of providing for all the wants of a family, with prudence and frugality', Steuart proceeded to argue that

> If any thing necessary or useful is found wanting, if any thing provided is lost or misapplied, if any servant, any animal, is supernumerary or useless, if any one sick or infirm is neglected, we immediately perceive a want of oeconomy. . . . The

96. Ibid. pp. 84–5 §67.

97. Sir James Steuart, *An Inquiry into the Principles of Political Œconomy: Being an Essay on the Science of Domestic Policy in Free Nations*, 2 vols., A. Millar, T. Cadell, London 1767; it was published in Dublin in 1770, in German translation in 1769–70, and in French translation in 1789; Antonio Genovesi, *Delle Lezioni di Commercio o sia d'Economia Civile*, 2 vols., Naples 1765, 1767. Note should also be made here of Pietro Verri's *Degli elementi del commercio*, first published in his periodical *Il caffè* in 1764, developed then into *Meditazioni sulla economia politica* (Livorno 1771).

98. Ibid. 'Preface' p. v.

99. Ibid. p. viii.

100. Ibid. p. ix.

> whole oeconomy must be directed by the head, who is both lord and steward of the whole family. . . . The better the oeconomist, the more uniformity is perceived in all his actions, and the less liberties are taken to depart from stated rules.[101]

This conception is then applied to the state, not arguing like Rousseau that the sole common factor between private household and the kingdom was a duty of care, but rather that 'in a state there are no servants, all are children'. The statesmen was in turn not free to establish 'what oeconomy he pleases, or in the exercise of his sublime authority to overturn at will the established laws of it'; instead the art of political oeconomy was

> to adapt the different operations of it to the spirit, manners, habits, and customs of the people, and afterwards to model these circumstances so, as to be able to introduce a set of new and more useful institutions.
>
> The principal object of this science is to secure a certain fund of subsistence for all the inhabitants. To obviate every circumstance which may render it precarious; to provide every thing necessary for supplying the wants of the society, and to employ the inhabitants (supposing them to be freemen) in such a manner as naturally to create reciprocal relations and dependencies between them, so as to make their several interests lead them to supply one another with their reciprocal wants.[102]

Men do therefore have 'reciprocal wants', and indeed Steuart opens the second chapter by declaring that 'Man we find acting uniformly in all ages, in all countries, and in all climates, from the principles of self-interest, expediency, duty, or passion'.[103] But these reciprocal wants do not lead to any sort of self-acting equilibrium in the meeting of wants, or indeed in the moral order required to determine how the distribution of goods and property resulting from this might be considered just. In the older household model there was a hierarchy of social rank that secured this; Steuart retains the household model, but without its internal moral order. Nor does this model have any alternative form of order, save that directly supplied by the intervention of the statesman. Consequently the role of the statesman or legislator is a constant work of putting people in their right place, adjusting the State machine as if it were a clock constantly in danger of going wrong:

> I only speak of governments which are conducted systematically, constitutionally, and by general laws; and when I mention princes, I mean their councils.

101. Ibid., Book I Introduction pp. 1–2.
102. Ibid. pp. 2–3.
103. Ibid. p. 6.

> The principles I am enquiring into, regard the cool administration of their government; it belongs to another branch of politics, to contrive bulwarks against their passions, vices and weaknesses, as men. . . .
>
> It is of governments as of machines, the more they are simple, the more they are solid and lasting; the more they are artfully composed, the more they become useful; but the more apt they are to be out of order.
>
> The Lacedemonian form may be compared to the wedge, the most solid and compact of all mechanical powers. Those of modern states to watches, which are continually going wrong; sometimes the spring is found too weak, at other times too strong for the machine: and when the wheels are not made according to a determined proportion, . . . they do not tally well with one another; then the machine stops, and if it be forced, some part gives way; and the workman's hand becomes necessary to set it right.[104]

It is easy to see from this why Smith, when drafting *Wealth of Nations*, could suggest that 'Without once mentioning it, I flatter myself, that every false principle in it, will meet with a clear and distinct confutation in mine'.[105] Smith had a very different kind of 'system', of 'natural liberty', related to a conception of human sociability already outlined almost twenty years previously in *Theory of Moral Sentiments*.

In *Wealth of Nations* Book IV, 'Of Systems of political Oeconomy', Smith presents his critique of the 'two systems' of political œconomy: the mercantile system (the 'system of commerce') in eight chapters, concluding with a ninth chapter developing his criticism of Physiocracy, or the 'agricultural school'. The preamble to Book IV runs as follows:

> Political œconomy, considered as a branch of the science of a statesman or legislator, proposes two distinct objects; first, to provide a plentiful revenue or subsistence for the people, or more properly to enable them to provide such a revenue or subsistence for themselves; and secondly, to supply the state or commonwealth with a revenue sufficient for the publick services. It proposes to enrich both the people and the sovereign.
>
> The different progress of opulence in different ages and nations, has given occasion to two different systems of political œconomy, with regard to enriching the people. The one may be called the system of commerce, the other that

104. Ibid. pp. 249–50. see also S. R. Sen, *The Economics of Sir James Steuart*, G. Bell & Sons, London 1957, especially ch. 4, 'Steuart's Economics of Control'.

105. Adam Smith, Letter 132: to William Pulteney, Kirkcaldy, 3 September 1772, *The Correspondence of Adam Smith*, ed. Ernest Campbell Mossner and Ian Simpson Ross, *Works and Correspondence of Adam Smith* Vol. 6, Oxford University Press, Oxford 1977 p. 164.

> of agriculture. I shall endeavour to explain both as fully and distinctly as I can, and shall begin with the system of commerce. It is the modern system, and is best understood in our own country and in our own times.

The system of commerce is explained in terms of diverse restraints on trade, and not primarily through discussion of principles expounded in the literature on commerce, trade, and money.[106] This is the currently existing 'modern system', whereas the 'agricultural system' 'probably never will do any harm in any part of the world' (WN IV.ix.2) and is entirely hypothetical. Smith rehearses in this chapter the usual criticisms made of Physiocracy: that agriculture is uniquely productive, that agricultural labour is therefore the sole form of productive labour, and that manufacturing produces no net gain. Where he differs from such criticism is in his praise for the Physiocratic insistence on perfect liberty, together with their representation of the wealth of a nation as the annual production of consumable goods. Istvan Hont suggests[107] that these remarks should be read in the light of the fragments dating from 1755 cited by Dugald Stewart, where Smith had criticised the manner in which 'statesmen and projectors' treat man 'as the materials of a sort of political mechanics':

> Projectors disturb nature in the course of her operations in human affairs; and it requires no more than to let her alone, that she may establish her own designs.[108]

As Hont points out, Smith endorsed Physiocracy in *Wealth of Nations* because he saw in their conception of a natural order the same logic that he had already exposed in his Glasgow lectures; he differed from the Physiocrats, however, in believing that their approach would 'thwart this natural course, . . . force things into another channel', that it was 'unnatural', and that any government following such prescriptions would be 'oppressive and tyrannical'.[109] Quesnay and his followers were 'projectors', seeking reform through forcibly changing the course of nature; and when in 1790 Smith realised that there was a danger that such ideas might

106. There are comments on Mun, *England's Treasure by Forraigne Trade* (1764) at IV.i.7 and 10.

107. Istvan Hont, 'Adam Smith and the Political Economy of the "Unnatural and Retrograde" Order', in his *Jealousy of Trade*, op. cit. pp. 355, 358.

108. Dugald Stewart, 'Account of the Life and Writings of Adam Smith, LL.D', in Adam Smith, *Essays on Philosophical Subjects*, Oxford University Press, Oxford 1980 p. 322.

109. Loc. cit.

actually be put into practice, he added an emphatic critique of the 'man of system' to the final edition of *Theory of Moral Sentiments* (VI.ii.2.17).

This then is the context in which Smith elaborates his conception of natural liberty. He notes that the *Tableau Economique* initially assumes 'a state of the most perfect liberty' (WN IV.ix.27) and while some relaxation of this assumption was subsequently made, he suggests that Quesnay acts like a doctor who supposes 'that the health of the human body could be preserved only by a certain precise regimen of diet and exercise, of which every, the smallest, violation necessarily occasioned some degree of disease or disorder proportioned to the degree of the violation' (WN IV.ix.28). But, Smith goes on, it would seem that the human body remained in a state of health under the most diverse array of regimens, and that the body contained within itself 'some unknown principle of preservation' which was capable of resisting the bad effects of 'even a very faulty regimen'.

> Mr. Quesnai, who was himself a physician, and a very speculative physician, seems to have entertained a notion of the same kind concerning the political body, and to have imagined that it would thrive and prosper only under a certain precise regimen, the exact regimen of perfect liberty and perfect justice.

However, 'the natural effort which every man is continually making to better his own condition' is capable of acting against and correcting 'the bad effects of a political œconomy, in some degree, both partial and oppressive'. Hence even bad policy should not be capable of halting altogether

> the natural progress of a nation towards wealth and prosperity, and still less of making it go backwards. If a nation could not prosper without the enjoyment of perfect liberty and perfect justice, there is not in the world a nation which could ever have prospered. (IV.ix.28)

A system of natural liberty could not be forcibly introduced, and was also capable of functioning under a variety of regimes. The 'art of economy' lay, for Smith, 'not in superimposing the natural order on the actual one, but rather in discovering how natural progress asserts itself'.[110] There is here no necessary connection of the progress of a nation to a particular political form. The Physiocratic conception of natural liberty, later articulated as Economic Government, was necessarily the creation of the political

110. Hont, 'Adam Smith', op. cit. p. 375.

order; natural liberty could only prevail once the barriers to its realisation had been removed by the very order which prevented it coming about. Smith's conception of natural liberty was different:

> All systems either of preference or of restraint, therefore, being thus completely taken away, the obvious and simple system of natural liberty establishes itself of its own accord. Every man, as long as he does not violate the laws of justice, is left perfectly free to pursue his own interest his own way, and to bring both his industry and capital into competition with those of any other man, or order of men. The sovereign is completely discharged from a duty, in the attempting to perform which he must always be exposed to innumerable delusions, and for the proper performance of which no human wisdom or knowledge could ever be sufficient; the duty of superintending the industry of private people, and of directing it towards the employments most suitable to the interest of the society. (WN IV.ix.51)

Hence it is in the last chapter of Book IV, 'Of Systems of political Œconomy', his evaluation of the 'Agricultural School', that he first of all criticises their idea of 'perfect liberty' as a prerequisite for the progress of wealth, then refounds this progress upon ordinary human activity; while the entirety of Book IV can be taken as a critique of the stance taken by Steuart's own *Inquiry*, in which political œconomy was the instrument of a legislator.

Wealth of Nations is not itself a 'system of political economy', for he there elaborates an idea already sketched in 1755, that 'Little else is requisite to carry a state to the highest degree of opulence from the lowest barbarism, but peace, easy taxes, and a tolerable administration of justice; all the rest being brought about by the natural course of things'.[111] In opposing the mercantile system and the Agricultural School he is opposing the very idea of economic government. The concepts which he introduces—division of labour, exchange, wealth as the product of annual labour, the distinction between productive and unproductive labour, definitions of and distinctions between prices, the identification of sources of profit—do not amount to the identification of an economic domain to be directed with particular instruments; they are instead concepts that help us understand the manner in which wealth is created through the interactions of free agents engaged in sociable conduct. *Wealth of Nations* is clearly based upon an economy of exchange: this is the link to *Theory of Moral*

111. Smith, 1755 Fragment, cited by Stewart, 'Account', op. cit. p. 322.

Sentiments. It begins with a chapter on the division of labour because the path to wealth is through the greater productivity of human labour, not through the wise conduct of commerce, nor by encouraging particular manufactures, nor increasing the size of the population, nor through the control of bullion. Early critics of *Wealth of Nations* failed to see the point of this, and complained of the work's faulty architectonics. The English political economists went further: they simply jettisoned the internal order that Smith had so painstakingly created in *Theory of Moral Sentiments*, cannibalising the terminology of wage, price, and profit, shoehorning it into a theory of distribution in which three classes interacted, and prices were determined by inputs of labour. In so doing they made Smith into a political economist of their own kind.

This would however prove to be a particularly British preoccupation. Jean-Baptiste Say adopted a more Smithian differentiation of form of rule from economic liberty, rejecting any idea that political economy concerned itself with the prosperity of a nation through the enumeration of good practice in promoting trade, improving agriculture, or expanding the working population. As he so rightly wrote, where to stop?[112]

> Political economy only deals with agriculture, commerce, and the arts in the relationships which they have to the growth or diminution of wealth, and not in the manner in which they are conducted.[113]

It was a science of the laws underlying the creation of wealth, and it was these laws to which the idea of 'economy' now related. He had opened the first edition as follows:

> For the progress of a science it is no bad idea to establish the field across which its studies might extend, and the object which such studies set themselves; otherwise one seizes here and there on a small number of truths without knowing their connection, and many errors without being able to discover their falsity.

112. Jean-Baptiste Say, *Traité d'économie politique*, variorum edition, ed. Emmanuel Blanc et al., *Oeuvres Complètes* t. 1.1, Economica, Paris 2006 p. 5. This line of argument was added to the second edition of 1814.

113. Say, *Traité*, p. 5 (addition to 1814 edition). Note the echo here of the sentiment that political economy is social science 'applied to administration and legislation on agriculture, manufacturing, trade, public works, navigation, taxation, or all the means required to make families subsist and nations prosper'. Quoted from Dupont de Nemours's journal *L'Historien*, 19 (10 December 1795) in Michael Sonenscher, 'Ideology, Social Science and General Facts in Late Eighteenth-Century French Political Thought', *History of European Ideas* Vol. 35 (2009) p. 28.

> At the time that Smith wrote one confused *Politics* or, properly speaking, the science of government, with *political economy*, which shows how wealth is formed, distributed and consumed. This confusion is perhaps solely attributable to the inappropriate name that has been given to studies of this kind. Because *economy* signifies the laws which rule the house, the interior; and because the word *politics* seems to apply this idea to the political family, to the city, one wanted to use political economy for all the laws which guided the interior of the political family.[114]

The laws of the production of wealth therefore became entangled with all these other laws. In the second edition this line of argument is generalised but condensed, moving more directly to the point that the wealth of a nation was more or less independent of its political organisation. 'A state can prosper under all forms of government, if it is well administered';[115] if political liberty is more favourable to the growth of wealth, then this is an indirect, rather than a direct, cause. There had, argued Say, been a constant tendency to confuse the principles which constituted good government with those that were the foundation of the increase of wealth, whether this be public or private wealth. This was a criticism one could make of Steuart, also one that could be made of the *Economistes* in nearly all their writings, and of Jean-Jacques Rousseau in his *Encyclopédie´* article; it is of course also exactly the argument that Smith made in *Wealth of Nations* Book IV chapter ix. But since Adam Smith, Say continued, the term 'political economy' had been reserved for the science of wealth, and 'politics' for the relations between a government and the people, and between independent governments.[116]

In effect, therefore, Say split politics from economics, although the latter retained the name 'political economy'. And he did so for reasons that can be understood against the arguments outlined above, arguments to which he referred in seeking to explain the path he had chosen. Adam Smith was exempted from the general criticism that the subject of study had hitherto been diffuse and poorly defined; but Say did criticise Smith and subsequent writers for a want of scientific method, Say introducing his own methodological distinction between general or constant facts, and particular or variable facts:

> *General facts* are the result of the action of the laws of nature in all similar cases; *particular facts* are also the result of the action of the laws of nature, for

114. Say, *Traité*, p. 2 (1803).
115. Say, *Traité*, p. 3 (1814).
116. Say, *Traité*, pp. 3–5 (all editions).

> they are never violated; but they are the result of many modified actions, the one by the other in a particular case.[117]

From this, Say is able to elaborate his definition of political economy as showing

> how wealth is born, expands, and is destroyed; the causes which favour its development, or bring about its decline; its influence on the population, the power of the state, the well-being or tribulations of peoples. [It is an exposition of *general facts*, constantly the same in similar circumstances.][118]

As such, political economy was distinct from statistics, which deals with production and consumption at a particular place, or at a particular time.[119]

This organisation of the subject matter of political economy under the heads of production, distribution, and consumption was not clearly established in the structure of the first edition, but was explicitly introduced in the second: five books were rearranged into three, and those three dealt in turn with production, distribution, and consumption:

1803 Edition	1814 Edition
Book I De la Production	Book I De la Production des Richesses
Book II Des Monnaies	Book II De la Distribution des Richesses
Book III De la Valeur des choses	Book III De la Consommation des Richesses
Book IV Des Revenus	
Book V De la Consommation	

Together with revisions and additions to the text, this gave the second edition the classic structure that would be reproduced in most general treatises until the end of the century.

However, this sharpening of focus also highlighted the manner in which, for Say, political economy was directed to the wealth created by human labour. And here there quickly developed a divergence with British writers, who during the same period developed an analysis of political economy that turned upon the distribution of *value*. Quite what they

117. Say, *Traité*, p. 6 (1803 version; later editions referred to the 'nature of things' rather than the 'laws of nature').

118. Say, *Traité*, p. 6 (1803, sentence in brackets added in second edition). In the fourth edition of 1819, Say changed his terminology of 'general' and 'particular' fact into 'things that exist' and 'things that happen' (p. 7).

119. Say, *Traité*, p. 9.

meant by this, and the difficulties to which its systematic elaboration gave rise, will be described in rather greater detail in chapter 6, since in order to understand Karl Marx's reading of Adam Smith, James Mill, and David Ricardo we need to establish what they wrote, and hence what he read. Here we can briefly summarise the background to the publication of Ricardo's *Principles of Political Economy and Taxation* in 1817, and consider the implications of what political economy had become around 1820 in Britain by considering McCulloch's entry 'Political Economy' in the 1823 supplement to the *Encyclopaedia Britannica*.

In the first few years of the nineteenth century Robert Malthus became widely considered Britain's most prominent 'political economist', on the strength of his *Essay on the Principle of Population as it affects the future Improvement of Society*, first published in 1798 and with a new revised edition in 1803. Intended as a critique of Godwin's conception of human improvement, the *Essay* took familiar arguments about population and reorganised them in terms of a balance between the natural increase of a population and the constraint on population growth presented by the means of subsistence. That population was central to any consideration of political economy had been emphasised in the lectures that Dugald Stewart had given during the early 1800s in Edinburgh, where he noted that the term 'political economy' was intimately related to wealth and population, 'or to what have sometimes been called *the resources of a State*'.[120] Malthus's reputation as a political economist led directly to his appointment in 1804 as Professor of History and Political Economy at the East India College, where he taught until his death in 1834, preparing cadets for service in India and using Smith's *Wealth of Nations* as a textbook.

Malthus's population argument was not merely speculation. The population of England had begun an exponential rise around the mid-eighteenth century, passing the 6 million mark in the late 1750s and stabilising on a linear growth path at around 10.65 million in 1816.[121] Wheat prices began a secular rise in the early 1790s, coinciding with the onset of the French wars;[122] in 1793 Britain became a net importer of wheat, a condition that

120. Dugald Stewart, *Lectures on Political Economy* Vol. 1, Thomas Constable, Edinburgh 1855 p. 9. 'Among the various objects of Political Economy, one of the most important and interesting has been always understood to be *the augmentation of the numbers of the people*; and accordingly, I propose to begin the course with an examination of the principal questions to which this subject has given rise'. Ibid. p. 31.

121. E. A. Wrigley, R. S. Schofield, *The Population History of England 1541–1871: A Reconstruction*, Cambridge University Press, Cambridge 1989, pp. 528–29 Table A3.1.

122. B. R. Mitchell, *British Historical Statistics*, Cambridge University Press, Cambridge 1988 Table XIV.17: Grain Prices 1771–1880.

persisted for the next two centuries. Poor harvests, a growing population, and the state of war in Continental Europe led to a peak in prices in 1801, and many parishes resorted to a system of 'outdoor relief', a direct subsidy to poor families whose basic foodstuff had become so expensive.

Malthus responded by developing his existing argument concerning the relation of the size of the population to subsistence into a demonstration that poor relief merely further increased the price of bread, since the supply of grain was more or less fixed in the short run. In a pamphlet of 1800 he argued that

> the attempt . . . to increase the parish allowances in proportion to the price of corn, combined with the riches of the country, . . . is, comparatively speaking, the sole cause, which has occasioned the price of provisions in this country to rise so much higher than the degree of scarcity would seem to warrant, so much higher than it would do in any other country where this cause did not operate.[123]

Rather than the speculative argument starting from the divergent rates of growth of population and means of subsistence exposed in the *Essay*, Malthus here presents an elementary analysis of the price mechanism which does however rely upon very similar conceptions. Invoking Adam Smith as an authority, he notes how Smith had decomposed the price of a commodity into a 'natural price',[124] a 'normal profit', and an element which proportioned supply to demand. Noting that when a commodity is scarce, its price in the marketplace is chiefly governed by the third element, Malthus then supposes that a shortfall in production has left sufficient corn for forty people, whereas there are fifty who wish to purchase it, ranked in descending order from 1 to 50 in order of the cash they have available.[125] Since the fortieth person has two shillings, this becomes the price of the corn, while those from 41 to 50 have insufficient funds to purchase at this price. However, he goes on, if the ten poor men are given a shilling each, the whole fifty can afford two shillings, and so the price will rise:

> The two shillings of a poor man are just as good as the two shillings of a rich one; and, if we interfere to prevent the commodity from rising out of the reach

123. T. R. Malthus, *An Investigation of the Cause of the Present High Price of Provisions*, reprinted in E. A. Wrigley, David Souden (eds.) *The Works of Thomas Robert Malthus* Vol. 7, William Pickering, London 1986 pp. 6–7.

124. Its cost of production plus additional storage and transportation costs.

125. I have made the ranking here more numerically explicit than Malthus does, since this is one of the most interesting features of his argument.

> of the poorest ten, whoever they may be, we must toss up, or draw lots, raffle, or fight, to determine who are to be excluded.[126]

And so Malthus presents the price mechanism as having an inexorable logic beyond all appeal to human charity; a line of argument that eventually became the stock in trade of the economist.

In 1804 James Mill extended this approach to support free trade in grain, criticising the argument advanced by James Anderson that the appropriate response to both pauperism and the price of grain was to protect domestic agriculture.[127] However, in 1804 new legislation endorsed the bounty system and raised the thresholds and rates for bounties and duties. Then early in 1815 debate on the matter resumed in Parliament, a new law being passed in March which removed all bounties and duties, introducing merely a threshold price above which imports were free, and below which they were banned. During February 1815 Malthus, Edward West, Robert Torrens, and David Ricardo all published pamphlets on the matter, with Ricardo's pamphlet concisely setting up a model in which three distinct classes (labourers, proprietors, and farmers) were defined by their revenues, and related through the interdependency. A fixed amount was allocated for wages, so the greater the number of labourers, the less each would get; and wages varied inversely with profits, so that if workers did achieve higher wages, this was only at the expense of profits. Since wages and profits were in a simple inverse relationship, it was rental payments which lent this model its dynamic, and these were regulated by comparison with the costs of production on the least fertile land. Assuming that the least fertile land paid no rent, that the rate of profit was uniform, and that grain had to sell at a common price, the decreasing costs of production on better lands were matched by increases in rental payments so that the rate of profit remained uniform across lands of dissimilar quality.[128] It can be argued that if we make a distinction between a short market period and a long period, Ricardo's analysis is clearly focused on the latter, where contingent fluctuations and human action no longer obscure the clear regularities resulting from economic activity. Ricardo consequently had

126. Malthus, *Investigation*, op. cit. pp. 7–8.
127. James Mill, *An Essay on the Impolicy of a Bounty on the Exportation of Grain*, London 1804.
128. David Ricardo, 'Essay on the Application of Capital to Land, with Observations shewing the Impolicy of any Great Restriction of the Importation of Corn and that the Bounty of 1688 did not Lower the Price of it', in Piero Sraffa, with Maurice Dobb, *Works and Correspondence of David Ricardo* Vol. 4, Cambridge University Press, Cambridge 1951 pp. 12–15.

no need to make reference to the human behaviour, wants, and desires that had been central to the arguments about virtue, economy, and commerce to which Adam Smith and many others had previously addressed themselves. More importantly, as we shall see, the absence of any such reference would also separate Ricardo, Malthus, and Mill from the mainstream of economic argument that was already developing in France and Germany, and which by the end of the nineteenth century would reorganise economic analysis around human action and its contexts.

Following publication of the *Essay on Profits* in 1815 Ricardo was vigorously encouraged by Mill to extend arguments that had been expressed in terms of a rate of profit and quarters of wheat into a theory of distribution which, by early the following year, had been recast in terms of exchange value and its relation to labour. Ricardo's *Principles of Political Economy and Taxation* was duly published in April 1817, its first chapter being 'On Value', and as Piero Sraffa makes clear in his editorial introduction, the first six chapters of *Principles* were structured as a critique of Smith's early chapters on value, rent, price, wages, and profits.[129] Quoting directly from Adam Smith regarding the rate of exchange between a beaver and deer in a society of hunters, Ricardo supports the idea that their relative values reflected the amount of labour time it took to kill each of them—so that one beaver would be worth two deer.

> If the quantity of commodities realized in commodities, regulate their exchangeable value, every increase of the quantity of labour must augment the value of that commodity on which it is exercised, as every diminution must lower it.[130]

Problems would arise with relative values once different amounts of capital were introduced, but henceforth political economists would for the most part treat value as a quantity of labour, linking the process of production directly to inputs of labour, relative prices as a reflection of labour embodied in a commodity, and distribution between wages and profits supposed to be in a fixed, inverse relationship.

There were a number of inconsistencies in the first edition of the *Principles*, not all of which were attributable to the haste with which it had been written and set: a second edition introduced corrections and revisions in 1819, and a third in 1821 added a new chapter, considering the impact of machinery on the different classes of society. Contemporary reception of

129. David Ricardo, *Principles of Political Economy and Taxation*, in Sraffa Dobb, *Works and Correspondence* Vol. 1, p. xxiv.
130. Ricardo, *Principles*, op. cit. p. 13.

this work in the reviews was almost universally hostile, save for those written by James Mill and J. R. McCulloch, the latter assuming the role of principal propagator of Ricardian political economy. It was therefore something of a coup for the Ricardian camp when McCulloch authored the entry for 'Political Economy' in the Supplement to the Fourth Edition of the *Encyclopaedia Britannica* in 1823. But if one examines McCulloch's exposition, it soon becomes clear that he mangles some key aspects of Ricardo's arguments, and appears to owe more than a little to Say.[131]

McCulloch initially defines political economy as

> the science of the laws which regulate the production, distribution and consumption of those material products which have exchangeable value, and which are either necessary, useful, or agreeable to man.[132]

The first part of this definition comes straight from Say, but the fact that James Mill's own *Elements of Political Economy* (1821) was organised in a similar manner[133] is suggestive of how quickly Say's schema had caught on. McCulloch then emphasises, however, that this is a '*science of values*', relating to those goods 'obtainable only by labour; and as no one will voluntarily sacrifice the fruits of his industry, without receiving an equivalent in return, they are truly said to possess exchangeable value'.[134] McCulloch repeats this basic point several times in the first two pages, clearly implying that the distinction between goods that have use value and those that have exchange value is a property of the goods themselves as the products of labour (as Smith argued)—and not of any particular relationship of a consuming/using agent to such goods (as Say argued).

He then returns to an expanded definition:

> The science of Political Economy is exclusively conversant with that class of phenomena, which the exertion of human industry exhibits. Its object is to

131. As Terry Peach notes, while McCulloch was an enthusiastic and prolific disciple of Ricardo, he was capable of veering seriously off-message: 'Indeed, it was McCulloch himself who gave the lie to the alleged victory of Ricardo's ideas when, in his entry on Political Economy for the Supplement to the fourth edition of the *Encyclopaedia Britannica,* (1823), he declared that the "exchangeable value of commodities . . . is held *almost universally* [emphasis added] to depend on their *relative abundance or scarcity in the market, compared with the demand*"'. Peach, 'Introduction' to *David Ricardo: Critical Responses* Vol. I, Routledge, London 2003 p. 14.

132. J. R. McCulloch, 'Political Economy', Supplement to *Encyclopaedia Britannica* 4th edition (1823), cited from separate 1825 reprint p. 2.

133. Mill has four books: Production, Distribution, Interchange, and Consumption.

134. McCulloch, 'Political Economy', op. cit. p. 2. Malthus and Say are said by McCulloch to have lost sight of this point.

> ascertain the means by which this industry may be rendered most productive of necessaries, comforts, luxuries, and enjoyments, or of wealth in the proper sense of the word; by which this wealth may be most advantageously distributed among the different classes of the society; and by which it may be most profitably consumed.[135]

Political economy, he went on, was not a speculative science, but one of fact and experiment. However, there was a distinction to be made between the physical sciences on the one hand, and the moral and political sciences on the other. The conclusions of the former applied in every case; those of the latter 'in the *majority* of cases',[136] for its principles did not exercise precisely the same influence on the conduct of every individual. It was a principle of both the science of morals and of political economy that

> By far the largest proportion of the human race have a much clearer view of what is conducive to their own interests, than it is possible for any other man, or select number of men to have, and consequently that it is sound policy to allow every individual to follow the bent of his inclination, and to engage in any branch of industry he thinks proper.[137]

This was not like the laws that regulated the planetary system: 'it will hold good in nineteen out of twenty instances, but the twentieth may be an exception', for the conclusions of the economist 'are drawn from contemplating the principles which are found to determine the condition of mankind, as presented on the large scale of nations and empires'.[138]

I have quoted McCulloch at length here to demonstrate how far a political economy which was supposedly Smithian deviated from Smith, and an economist who was supposedly Ricardian deviated from Ricardo. It would be fairer to view McCulloch as peddling a garbled version of Say; for example, he reproduces unacknowledged Says's distinction of political economy from statistics, then returning to the definition of political economy once again, states that we should understand by production not 'the production of matter . . . but the production of *utility*', which is straight out of the second edition of Say's *Traité*.[139] And when McCulloch approaches the question of the gains from trade, his presentation, derailed by the properties of wine and wool for England and Portugal respectively, at first

135. Ibid. p. 4.
136. Ibid. p. 5.
137. Loc. cit.
138. Ibid. p. 6.
139. 'il y a création, non pas de matière, mais d'utilité'—Say, *Traité*, op. cit. p. 81.

implies that the gains from international trade depend upon absolute, and not comparative, advantage.[140] McCulloch's writings would continue to dominate the field of political economy in Britain into the 1830s; John Stuart Mill's *Essays on some Unsettled Questions of Political Economy* would not appear until 1844, the first essay being his lucid exposition of Ricardo as the originator of the theory of comparative advantage,[141] at the same time initiating the idea that all previous accounts of the benefits of trade consisted 'in affording a vent for surplus produce'.[142]

John Stuart Mill had learned his economics from his father, James Mill, who lectured him on the principles of political economy on their daily walks, the thirteen-year-old then writing up the monologue each day.[143] James then used these notes to draft his *Elements of Political Economy*, which became in this way more or less a Ricardian catechism. However, while James was completing this book John was in France, where he stayed for some time with Jean-Baptiste Say, a friend of his father. When John published his own *Principles of Political Economy* in 1848 he was quite explicit that this work was intended to update and displace Smith's *Wealth of Nations*,[144] and in this he was entirely successful: Mill's *Principles* became the central English reference work for the remainder of the century—providing the foundation for Marshall's own reworking of political economy during the 1870s, Edgeworth continuing to recommend it as a textbook in the Oxford of the 1900s, and in 1909 William Ashley bringing out a new edition.[145] The enduring readability of this text rather casts in doubt the usual assumption that Mill's *Principles* was essentially a continuation of Ricardo's *Principles*.

If, as Ashley argued, Mill's 'abstract science' were basically Ricardian, then we should relate this to the Ricardo of *Principles*: a model of distribution between labour, capital, and land in which it is assumed that the share of labour is fixed (underpinned by Malthus's arguments about

140. McCulloch, 'Political Economy', op. cit. p. 29. See ch. 4 fn. 38.

141. Not a term, however, that Mill employs—he talks of 'the advantage which nations derive from a mutual interchange of their productions'. 'Of the Laws of Interchange Between Nations; and the Distribution of the Gains of Commerce among the Countries of the Commercial World', in J. M. Robson (ed.) *Collected Works of John Stuart Mill* Vol. 4, University of Toronto Press, Toronto 1967 p. 232.

142. Loc. cit.

143. Donald Winch, 'James Mill and David Ricardo' in James Mill, *Selected Economic Writings*, ed. Winch, Oliver & Boyd, Edinburgh 1966 pp. 188ff.

144. John Stuart Mill, *Principles of Political Economy with Some of Their Applications to Social Philosophy, Collected Works* Vol. 2, [Toronto 1965] p. xcii.

145. John Stuart Mill, *Principles of Political Economy with Some of Their Applications to Social Philosophy*, ed. W. J. Ashley, Longman, Green, London 1909.

population and poverty), that the general rate of profit is determined by the profits of agriculture, that the rate of profit in agriculture is inversely related to rent, and that the level of rent is governed by a differential principle according to which the most distant/least fertile land bears no rent, and that rental payments incrementally increase to ensure that the profits of agriculture are uniform across different fertilities/locations. Ricardo's model was designed to deal with a specific problem, the price of agricultural produce, and to support the argument that only free trade can defer the tendency of the general rate of profit to fall, leading to a stationary state. This was where Ricardo's arguments on foreign trade fitted into his system, although the chapter on trade in his *Principles* comes and goes without any such explanation.

Mill by contrast clearly stated that he distinguished between the

> laws of the Production of Wealth, which are real laws of nature, dependent upon the properties of objects, and the modes of its Distribution, which, subject to certain conditions, depend on human will. The common run of political economists confuse these together, under the designation of economic laws, which they deem incapable of being defeated or modified by human effort.[146]

In making this distinction Mill moves a considerable distance from Ricardo, whose work had been focused exactly upon such 'laws' of distribution. Furthermore, he also abandoned the core of Ricardo's value theory and explicitly adopted that of Say: that 'labour produces utilities, not objects'.[147] Consistent also with the idea that distribution was conditioned by human will, Mill's account of low wages and their relation to poverty also deviates from the positions of Malthus and Ricardo:

> By what means, then, is poverty to be contended against? How is the evil of low wages to be remedied? If the expedients usually recommended for the purpose are not adapted to it, can no others be thought of? Is the problem incapable of solution? Can political economy do nothing, but only object to everything, and demonstrate that nothing can be done?

146. Mill, *Autobiography*, in *Collected Works* Vol. 1 [Toronto 1981] p. 255.

147. Mill, *Principles of Political Economy*, *Collected Works* Vol. 2 [Toronto 1965] p. 46. 'What we produce, or desire to produce, is always, as M. Say rightly terms it, an utility. Labour is not creative of objects, but of utilities. Neither, again, do we consume and destroy the objects themselves; the matter of which they were composed remains, more or less altered in form: what has really been consumed is only the qualities by which they were fitted for the purpose they have been applied to'.

> If this were so, political economy might have a needful, but would have a melancholy, and a thankless task.[148]

Ricardo had adopted from Malthus the principle that the problem of poverty was essentially one of an oversupply of labour, and that any attempt to alleviate this condition through charity would be ineffective. Mill instead proposes that the 'habits of the labouring people'[149] be altered, through the education of their children, and by action aimed at removing extreme poverty for one generation: emigration to the colonies, and the development of a new class of small landed proprietors.

Limited though such meliorative measures might be, underlying Mill's argument was a conception of human agency absent from 'the political economists of the old school'. Mill had sought to define the scope of political economy in an essay first published in 1836, and in so doing suggested that

> Political Economy presuppose[s] an arbitrary definition of man, as a being who invariably does that by which he may obtain the greatest amount of necessaries, conveniences, and luxuries, with the smallest quantity of labour and physical self-denial with which they can be obtained in the existing state of knowledge.[150]

This formulation prefigures the argument that Jevons developed in his own *Theory of Political Economy*, and is suggestive of how it could be that Marshall developed his own early version of marginalist analysis from a study of Mill's *Political Economy*.[151]

Notwithstanding Marshall's own disingenuous disavowal of the influence upon his work of Stanley Jevons,[152] it can be said that Jevons himself contributed to the assimilation of Mill to Ricardo when, in the second edition of his *Theory of Political Economy,* he added a lengthy preface reviewing

148. *Principles* op. cit. Book II ch. 13 §1 p. 367.

149. *Principles* op. cit. Book II ch. 13 §3 p. 374.

150. Mill, 'On the Definition of Political Economy; and on the Methods of Investigation Proper to It', *Collected Works* Vol. 4 p. 326. He goes on: 'It is true that this definition of man is not prefixed to any work on Political Economy'.

151. See the discussion of Marshall's reworking of Mill in Simon J. Cook, *The Intellectual Foundations of Alfred Marshall's Economic Science: A Rounded Globe of Knowledge*, Cambridge University Press, Cambridge 2009 ch. 5 pp. 150 ff.

152. Letter 133, Marshall to Léon Walras, 1 November 1883, John Whitaker (ed.) *The Correspondence of Alfred Marshall, Economist* Vol. 1: *Climbing 1868–1890*, Cambridge University Press, Cambridge 1996 p. 169; where Marshall claims not 'to have accepted' Jevon's doctrine of final utility, having taught it in the course of Cambridge lectures before *Theory of Political Economy* was published in 1871.

the development of mathematical economics, closing with the following judgement:

> When at length a true system of Economics comes to be established, it will be seen that that able but wrong-headed man, David Ricardo, shunted the car of Economic science on to a wrong line, a line, however, on which it was further urged towards confusion by his equally able and wrong-headed admirer John Stuart Mill. There were economists, such as Malthus and Senior, who had a far better comprehension of the true doctrines (though not free from Ricardian errors), but they were driven out of the field by the unity and influence of the Ricardo-Mill school. It will be a work of labour to pick up the fragments of a shattered science and to start anew, but it is a work from which they must not shrink who wish to see any advance of Economic Science.[153]

Jevons was however seemingly unaware that a quite different way of developing a science of political economy had emerged during the first two decades of the nineteenth century, one which owed something to Smith, but also a great deal to Critical Philosophy. When in 1871 Carl Menger published his *Grundsätze der Volkswirthschaftslehre*, he defined as 'goods' 'utilities . . . related to the satisfaction of human needs'.[154] A long footnote was appended to this statement, beginning with Aristotle's conception of goods, proceeding on through Forbonnais, Le Trosne, and Say; and listing as the first relevant German authors Soden, Jakob, and Hufeland. These three writers were the principal architects of the new *Nationalökonomie* created in the early 1800s. Among them, Jakob's definition of a good is the most pithy: 'Everything that serves the satisfaction of human needs'.[155] Jakob was also Say's German translator,[156] his own textbook of 1805 following the organisation and argument of Say's *Traité* so clearly that it amounts to a précis of that text. And like Schlözer,[157] and following Say, Jakob made a clear distinction between state and economy, or politics and economics.

153. William Stanley Jevons, *The Theory of Political Economy*, 2nd ed., Macmillan, London 1879 p. lvii.

154. Carl Menger, *Grundsätze der Volkswirthschaftslehre*, Wilhelm Braumüller, Vienna 1871, p. 2.

155. Ludwig Heinrich Jakob, *Grundsätze der National-Oekonomie oder National-Wirthschaftslehre*, Halle 1805 §23.

156. Jean-Baptiste Say, *Abhandlung über die Nationalökonomie*, 2 vols., trans. L. H. Jakob, Halle 1807.

157. Christian von Schlözer, *Anfangsgründe der Staatswirthschaft oder die Lehre von dem Nationalreichthume*, Vol. 1, Riga 1805 §12.

The expurgation of exchange, interest, and human need from the British political economy of the early nineteenth century was not emulated by German writers interested in developing a science of political economy following on from Adam Smith. Prompted by what he saw as the lack of system in Adam Smith's *Wealth of Nations*, a new translation of which had just appeared,[158] Soden set out to provide a more systematic basis for the new science, defining it as

> the *Natural Law* of *sociable* mankind with respect to the maintenance and promotion of its physical welfare, and in the same way that the Law of Nations outlines the laws according to which *nations*, in the reciprocal condition of co-existence, must adhere in every respect; so *Nazional-Oekonomie* provides the principles which . . . must be adhered to, such that every member of every nation achieves the highest possible degree of physical welfare, and maintains this position.[159] (1805, pp. v, vi)

The leading principle of *Nationalökonomie* was then described as 'the highest perfection of the physical condition of sociable mankind' (1805, p. 14), underscoring the impact that the contemporary intellectual fashion for Critical Philosophy had beyond the confines of philosophy and ethics.

Gottlieb Hufeland, the third writer named by Menger, was like Jakob a professor of law who had become a 'Kantian'—and both, like Soden, found their way to Adam Smith via Kant's new philosophy. Hufeland's *Neue Grundlegung der Staatswirtschaftskunst* began with a review of the relative merits of James Steuart and Adam Smith as systematic theorists of economic life. Smith's *Wealth of Nations* had quickly been translated into German, but found at first little resonance among university professors, although like the Physiocrats, Smith was more widely read by lay members of local literary and economic societies than university scholars. The German 'Smith reception' proper began with the publication of the second translation in the mid-1790s, coinciding with the developing wave of enthusiasm for Critical Philosophy. And as Hufeland noted in his introductory remarks, it was only towards the end of the 1790s that there were clear signs that Smith had been read *and* understood.[160]

Soden and Jakob, observed Hufeland, had dubbed their new field of study *Nationalökonomie*, and while he did not find this very objectionable,

158. Adam Smith, *Untersuchung über die Natur und Ursachen des Nationalreichthums*, 4 vols., trans. Garve and Dörrien, Breslau 1794–96.

159. J. H. von Soden, *Die Nazional-Oekonomie*, Vol. 1, Leipzig 1805 pp. v, vi.

160. Gottlieb Hufeland, *Neue Grundlegung der Staatswirthschaftskunst* Vol. 1 Gießen 1807 n. p.

he suggested that it would be 'better and clearer' to use a German expression, *Volkswirthschaft*—which is indeed the root term that became generally accepted about a century later. This latter expression was more suitable, he thought, because it expressed a clear distinction with respect to *Staatswirthschaft*, the generic term that Cameralists had used to describe the domain of economic life in an intellectual system where no distinction was made between 'state' and 'society'. The problem with the German word *Wirtschaft*, he noted, was that it implied a governing person—it recalled the Aristotelian head of household on the one hand, and the more down-to-earth figure of the farmer or innkeeper on the other (*Landwirt*, or simply *Wirt*). Such a figure was absent from the *Volkswirtschaft*, 'where many thousands pursue their economic life' (*wirthschaften*).[161] This he later clarified as a 'sphere of goods', goods being defined as any medium for the realisation of human purposes; hence the 'sphere of goods' was a domain of autonomous human economic activity independent of state action.[162]

Jakob noted in the preface to his *Grundsätze* that he had used Sartorius's *Handbuch* for some years,[163] but that he had come to the view that some of Smith's ideas were obscured by the form of presentation adopted.[164] He proceeds to redefine the state and its affairs in a manner that denies it a decisive role in the formation and distribution of wealth, analogously to the manner in which Say had clearly separated politics from political economy. The expression 'state', Jakob argues, can only be used to refer to *public* affairs; state property is therefore merely a part of national property (*Volksvermögen*), separate from it and for use in pursuit of public and common ends.

> *Staatswirthschaftslehre* can be in fact nothing other than *financial science* or *Policey*, insofar as care for public order is part of good public economy.[165]

As suggested above, German writers were able to manipulate derivations from *Wirtschaft* and from *Ökonomie* to make a distinction which existed in English and French, but for which there was no ready vocabulary available.

161. Loc. cit. p. 14.
162. Loc. cit. pp. 17–18, 116.
163. Georg Sartorius, *Handbuch der Staatswirthschaft zu Gebrauche bey akademischen Vorlesungen, nach Adam Smith's Grundsätzen ausgearbeitet*, Berlin 1796.
164. See my *Governing Economy: The Reformation of German Economic Discourse 1750–1830*, Cambridge University Press, Cambridge 1988 pp. 164–68 for a discussion of Sartorius's treatment of Smith.
165. Jakob, *Grundsätze*. op. cit. p. vi.

Today *Volkswirtschaftslehre* is the generic term of 'economics', and *Nationalökonomie* has fallen into disuse, but of course it is plain to everyone that 'economics' is a university discourse embodied in textbooks, and popular discourse related to economic growth, welfare, or the banking crisis is not 'economics' in this sense. But during the nineteenth century the propensity for German professors to approach their subject by making definitions and distinctions drew upon a broad terminology which facilitated clear distinctions, even if none of them became permanently established, or like Menger, a writer changed his mind about which domain belonged to which term.

If we consider Jakob's textbook, the most striking feature is its plan of organisation. At the end of the introduction, he states that *Nationalökonomie* deals with three principal issues:

1. The formation and increase of national wealth.
2. The principles of the most advantageous distribution of national wealth among the members of society.
3. The consumption of national property and the various effects of the same.[166]

Or, in other words, the trinity of production, distribution, and consumption introduced by Say in the second (1814) edition of his *Traité*. Jakob not only stated that *Nationalökonomie* dealt with the production, distribution, and consumption of wealth; his book is divided up in this way too. And this structure became established itself in Germany: Wilhelm Roscher's *System der Volkswirthschaft*, a major mid-century work, likewise followed the same structure, albeit with an additional chapter on the circulation of goods interpolated between Books I and II.[167]

Jakob, Soden, Hufeland, and Schlözer created a new conception of economic life separate from the work of state administration, hitherto thought to provide the essential framework for orderly conduct of production and consumption.[168] This did however remain very general in outline, and in many cases it was simply taught alongside the traditional practical areas of economic administration, such as agriculture and forestry, finance, and botany. In 1826 Karl Heinrich Rau, since

166. Ibid. p. 12 §20.

167. Wilhelm Roscher, *System der Volkswirthschaft* Bd. 1: *Die Grundlagen der Nationalökonomie*, J. G. Cotta, Stuttgart 1854.

168. For a summary of the principles of Cameralism see my 'Cameralism and the Sciences of the State', in Mark Goldie, Robert Wokler (eds.) *The Cambridge History of Eighteenth-Century Political Thought*, Cambridge University Press, Cambridge 2006 pp. 525–46.

1822 professor in Heidelberg, published the first volume of a textbook that was to end this equivocal state of affairs. Three volumes of his new *Lehrbuch der politischen Oekonomie*—Rau chose to revert to a name for the subject generally accepted outside Germany and more recognisable for French or English readers—were published between 1822 and 1837. The work ran into many editions, the last revised edition appearing in 1876.

The first volume of the *Lehrbuch* deals with 'Die Volkswirthschaftslehre' —'those characteristic laws which can be perceived in the economic activities of peoples regardless of the intervention of government'.[169] It begins by making a clear distinction between private and public economics. 'Private economics' was composed of the rules governing the optimum satisfaction of needs through the acquisition, maintenance, and use of material goods. 'Public economics' by contrast dealt with the satisfaction of needs by the allocation of material goods on the part of the state—it had a strictly redistributive character, recirculating goods produced in the 'private economy' using revenues derived from taxation. Whereas the *Volkswirthschaft* is conceptualised by the individual pursuit of self-interest, there are general aims of the state that the individual cannot attain unaided, and so the role of government in the economy is to intervene to ensure that these general aims are secured. Rau's conception of the economy does not have the kind of internal theoretical structure that had been established by Malthus and Ricardo. Although he announces the intention of developing a theory of economic forces based upon natural laws, the volume merely enumerates economic objects without regard to their mutual relationship in production, distribution, and consumption; 'natural laws' simply secure the existence of certain regularities; they do not link human conduct to a particular structure of production or distribution. It is for this reason that Rau's *Lehrbuch* is able to encompass Say and Ricardo without any conflict: their conceptual structures are ignored and their arguments treated as so many observations on the workings of the economy. This eclecticism is reinforced by the subsequent editions. The second volume, first published in 1828 and devoted to economic welfare, consistently distinguishes between the wealth of an individual and the wealth of a people, only the latter being the proper object of economic analysis. The function of the state is strictly limited to the facilitation of individuals' desire to better their conditions, through educational provision and the promotion of commercial enterprise. But once past the initial principles, the work becomes a review of

169. Karl Heinrich Rau, *Lehrbuch der politischen Oekonomie* Bd. 1, Heidelberg 1826 p. x.

specific measures fostering enterprise or removing hindrances to individual enterprise. Thus we read, under the heading 'Promotion of Exchange or Encouragement of Trade', about newspapers, fairs, weights and measures, money, roads, railways, canals, and bridges. Later we can read that savings and insurance are to be promoted, and gambling restricted. The third volume, published in 1832 and devoted to 'financial science', examines the proper employment of state expenditure and the relation of taxation to such employments, and inevitably reinforces the broadly descriptive impression.

However, we should pause and ask ourselves: who read these texts, and why? In Britain discussion of political economy would, until the last third of the nineteenth century, be a component of liberal public discourse, a way of thinking about the world that fed, in a very general way, into arguments about social and political reform embraced by both workers' organisations and new liberal institutions such as the British Association for the Advancement of Science or the London Statistical Society. Its principles were argued out in periodicals such as the *Edinburgh Review*, or the *Quarterly Review*, later the *Fortnightly Review*, *The Academy*, or *The Nineteenth Century*.[170] John Stuart Mill's *Principles of Political Economy* established an orthodoxy that survived almost to the end of the century. But it was a work directed to an educated general reader, not to any kind of specialised reader. An 'economist' was in Britain simply anyone who took an interest in the contemporary literature of political economy.

In Germany, however, Rau's text was written by a university professor for a different purpose: for use by law students alongside the course of lectures on economics which they attended as part of their training. A degree in law was required for entry into public administration, and was generally regarded as the appropriate preparation for all kinds of employment in business and administration. This imperative provided professors of political economy with their chief employment, and to do this work they needed textbooks like those of Rau, whose *Lehrbuch* survived in one form or another into the last third of the century. Roscher's *System der Volkswirthschaft* carried the subtitle 'A Textbook and Work of Reference for Businessmen and Students',[171] and a dedication to Dr. J. P. Falkenstein,

170. See my 'Economic Societies in Great Britain and Ireland', in M. Augello, M. Guidi (eds.) *The Spread of Political Economy and the Professionalisation of Economists*, Routledge, London 2001 pp. 32–52.

171. 'Ein Hand- und Lesebuch für Geschäftsmänner und Studierende'.

Royal Saxon Minister of State. As befitted a textbook, it began with 'Basic Concepts', the first of which was

> §1. We call goods everything recognised as being of use for the satisfaction of human needs.

And then Roscher cites Hufeland to the effect that it is the human mind, the idea of means and ends, which posits such objects as goods.[172] With changing human needs the boundaries and hierarchy of goods altered, argued Roscher, and so the constitution of value was from the beginning linked to changing human needs. The use value of an object is the greater, the more general and urgent these needs are, and the degree of completeness, certainty, the longer and more pleasantly it fulfils these needs. In support of this statement he cites Genovesi's *Economia civile*.[173] The distinction of use and exchange value is traced back to Aristotle, Locke, and the Physiocrats, and he suggests that the sum of all economic goods in the possession of a physical or legal personality is 'property'. Consequently, 'All continuing activity involving the acquisition and use of a property is called *Wirthschaft*'.[174] Such activity was characterised by self-interest, seeking to accumulate as great an amount of goods as possible, and lose as few as possible. But a balance was struck by 'communal feeling' (*Gemeinsinn*), which created a higher, well-ordered organism called *Volkswirthschaft*.[175]

However attenuated this linkage of economic activity to self-interest, moderated by communal feeling, might be, the emphasis upon human needs and their role in creating 'utility' was clearly different from the way in which British political economy talked of wages and profits and the laws of distribution. In fact, Carl Menger began with Rau and Roscher, his annotated copy of Rau's *Lehrbuch* providing an initial orientation for the analysis of his 1867–68 notebooks.[176] Whereas Jevons believed that he had to abandon the British legacy from Malthus to Mill if he were to

172. Hufeland, *Neue Grundlegung*, Bd. 1 op. cit. p. 41.

173. Antonio Genovesi, *Delle Lezioni di Commercio o sia d'Economia Civile* Parte Seconda, Naples 1767 ch. 1, §7 p. 12: 'Turning now to our proposition, I say that it is plain that no thing has a price except in respect of our needs. And it follows first of all from this, that the value of a thing is proportioned to the power it has to satisfy our needs. A thing that can satisfy the most needs, or one need many times, has a higher price, or is held in higher regard, than one that does not have that, or which can only meet a few needs, or at the same time'.

174. Roscher, *Grundlagen*, op. cit. p. 14 §11.

175. Ibid. p. 15 §12.

176. See Carl Menger, *Carl Menger's Zusätze zu den 'Grundsätze der Volkswirtschaftslehre'*, Hitotsubashi University Library, Tokyo 1961; Kiichiro Yagi, *Austrian and German Economic Thought*, Routledge, London 2011 ch. 3, espec. pp. 32–33.

develop a new form of economic reasoning, Menger built upon an established tradition, and drew attention to this in detailing his sources.

Menger's *Grundsätze* began by identifying four conditions necessary for a thing to be a good:

1. A human need
2. A property of the thing which made it suitable for the satisfaction of this need
3. Recognition of this causal relation on the part of the person
4. Disposition of the thing so that it can actually be employed to satisfy a need[177]

All four conditions turn on the economic agent, so that for example discussion of the price of a good would be related not only to the number of persons seeking a particular good, but to the intensity of their need for this good compared with that for all the other goods they might wish to acquire. Exchange is motivated by the same logic, the striving for the most complete satisfaction of need. Within the framework presented by Menger, the domain in which individuals engage in economic activity is radically subjectivised; but this is mainly because in his *Grundsätze* he is seeking to establish the relationship between individual need and its satisfaction, not present a complete analysis of the way in which individual activity is transformed into an economic dynamic through exchange.

It could be argued that Menger introduced a small, but critical, revision to Roscher's presentation of human needs and economic goods, for his definition of the latter is very close to, but not quite identical with, that given by Roscher.[178] He breaks away from long-established tradition by rejecting the pertinence of a distinction between use value and exchange value. While some economists had argued that non-economic goods do have use value (water, air), he notes that some French and English economists had sought to dispose of 'use value' and replace it with 'utility'. But this he says is mistaken:

> Utility (*Nützlichkeit*) is the suitability of a thing for the satisfaction of human needs, and so (as the *acknowledged* utility) a general precondition for the

177. Menger, *Grundsätze*, op. cit. p. 3.

178. 'The activity of men directed to the aims we have mentioned we call in their totality their *Wirthschaft*, and we call the goods in the quantities given above and the exclusive object of the same: *economic* goods (*wirthschaftlichen Güter*), in contrast to those for which men find no practical impulse to economic activity'. Menger, *Grundsätze*, op. cit. p. 52.

> quality of being a good. Non-economic goods are also useful, since they are themselves just as well suited to the satisfaction of our needs as economic goods, and this suitability has also to be *acknowledged* by a person; otherwise they could not assume the quality of being goods.[179]

Value, he argued, was a function of human needs, not of the goods themselves, and this value varied in relation to the magnitude of a person's needs, acknowledgement of such need, and the capacity to act upon such acknowledgement. It was not until 1884 that his student von Wieser coined the term *Grenznutzen* to express the final portion of satisfaction supplied by a good;[180] and in the 1880s another student, Böhm-Bawerk, coined the term *Nutzleistung* to identify the 'provision of utility' of a good,[181] underscoring the perceived quality of a good rather than the good per se. 'Provision of utility' was always in respect of a subjective evaluation, which evaluation was expressed by human action—'economising' action. And Böhm-Bawerk's own 1882 lecture course began with a definition of *Wirtschaftlichkeit* expressed in terms that echo conceptions encountered centuries before:

> Whoever conforms in their action to the principle of *Wirtschaftlichkeit* acts economically—is a *guter Wirt*; whoever acts contrary to such principles acts uneconomically—is a *schlechter Wirt*. In every economic action a balance has to be struck between utility and sacrifice. This calculation is characteristic for the economy. Some economists have therefore defined economy in terms of calculation, evaluation. But this is too narrow: economy is calculated action.[182]

There are some parallels here with Jevons, although Jevons simply assumed that value entirely depended upon utility, and then by introducing a calculus of pleasure and pain made the point that it was an economic subject who registered shifts between pleasure and pain:

> A unit of pleasure or pain is difficult to conceive; but it is the amount of these feelings which is continually prompting us to buying and selling, borrowing and lending, labouring and resting, producing and consuming; and it is from

179. Ibid. p. 84.

180. Ibid. p. 107; Friedrich von Wieser, *Über den Ursprung und die Hauptgesetze des wirthschaftlichen Werthes*, Alfred Hölder, Vienna 1884 p. 126.

181. Eugen von Böhm-Bawerk, *Kapital und Kapitalzins. Erste Abtheilung: Geschichte und Kritik der Kapitalzins-Theorieen*, Verlag der Wagner'schen Universitäts-Buchhandlung, Innsbruck 1884 p. 266.

182. Eugen von Böhm-Bawerk, *Innsbrucker Vorlesungen über Nationalökonomie*, ed. Shigeki Tomo, Metropolis Verlag, Marburg 1998 p. 44.

> the quantitative effects of the feelings that we must estimate their comparative amounts.[183]

These 'amounts' vary according to duration and intensity, and from this Jevons is able to construct a histogram of declining intensities over time, presenting this then as a downward-sloping curve.[184] But what distinguishes Jevons from Menger is that the terminology of pleasure and pain allowed Jevons to balance declining intensities of pleasure, either over time or with greater amounts consumed, against increasing amounts of pain incurred in creating the means of acquiring goods—a balance of consumption against work:

> Pleasure and Pain are undoubtedly the ultimate objects of the Calculus of Economy. To satisfy our wants to the utmost with the least effort—to procure the greatest amount of what is desirable at the expense of the least that is undesirable—in other words, to maximise comfort and pleasure, is the problem of Economy.[185]

The 'final degree of utility' declines with the increased consumption of a commodity, while the larger the wages earned the less is the pleasure derived from any further increment.[186] As Michael White has demonstrated, Jevons in drawing upon Jennings's 'natural laws' of psycho-physiological political economy ended up positing a universalist model of human action, such that the circumstances in which an action was performed had no bearing upon the marginalist calculus governing that action.

While Jevons introduced a subjectivist theory of economic action, this was purely formal, presupposing a universal decision-making subject. As such it was simply the inverse of early nineteenth-century British political

183. William Stanley Jevons, *The Theory of Political Economy*, Macmillan, London 1871 pp. 13–14.

184. Ibid. pp. 36, 37.

185. Ibid. p. 44. In the second edition 'Economy' was replaced by 'Economics'—1879 p. 40. The histogram of diminishing marginal utility which Jevons had used 'in my lectures during seven or eight years past' is on p. 55 of the first edition. White demonstrates the sources upon which Jevons's conceptions of 'balance' drew as contemporary mechanics and energetics, 'In the Lobby of the Energy Hotel: Jevons's Formulation of the Postclassical "Economic Problem"', *History of Political Economy* Vol. 36 (2004) pp. 228–71.

186. Jevons, *Theory*, op. cit. pp. 62, 169. This whole calculus is more complex than it seems, and has been thoroughly exposed by Michael White, 'The Moment of Richard Jennings: The Production of Jevons's Marginalist Economic Agent', in Philip Mirowski (ed.) *Natural Images in Economic Thought: 'Markets Read in Tooth and Claw'*, Cambridge University Press, Cambridge 1994 pp. 197–230.

economy, where individual agency had no place and instead the focus of attention was on the 'law of distribution' and the 'law of value'. We seem therefore to have arrived at the modern 'abstract' conception of economic action: subjective and universalist. But we are in fact some way from the end of our story—about one hundred years, in fact. As White has emphasised, Jevons presented a theory of wealth, not a logic of choice.[187] Suffused with contemporary developments within physics, mechanical and electrical engineering, and physiological psychology, Jevons's conception of economics had sources quite different from the work of his German and French contemporaries. While there was a superficial resemblance to the arguments of Menger and Walras, neither of these dealt in the universalist terms to which Jevons's sources in the natural and life sciences propelled him.

Jevons drowned in a swimming accident in 1882, just at the point when the new 'marginalist' economics was about to move beyond the work of a few specialists: within ten years it would be increasingly accepted as the basis of 'modern economics' throughout Europe and North America. But Jevons was not without influence in Britain. As Alon Kadish has demonstrated, during the 1880s Oxford was the centre of English political economy, stimulated originally by the teaching of Arnold Toynbee, and after his death in 1883, his legacy was nurtured by the student members of the Oxford Political Economy Club, including William Ashley and Edwin Cannan.[188] Both remained 'Jevonian' economists throughout their lifetimes, disavowing the Marshallian path for the new university subject marked out in the inauguration of the Cambridge Economics Tripos in 1903. Ashley's response was a turn to economic history; Cannan wound up as the founding professor of political economy at the London School of Economics, where he taught a robust non-Marshallian economics to a new generation of students, including Lionel Robbins.

Jevons also introduced Edgeworth, his Hampstead neighbour, to economics,[189] while in 1882 Philip Wicksteed purchased a copy of the second edition of Jevons's *Theory of Political Economy* and in 1885 used its principles in his critique of Marx's *Capital* volume I.[190] Wicksteed's own interest in political economy had however been fired by a rather different source:

187. White, 'In the Lobby of the Energy Hotel' op. cit. p. 262.

188. Alon Kadish, *Apostle Arnold: The Life and Death of Arnold Toynbee 1852–1883*, Duke University Press, Durham (NC) 1986; and *The Oxford Economists in the Late Nineteenth Century*, Oxford University Press, Oxford 1982.

189. Peter Newman, 'Francis Ysidro Edgeworth (1845–1926)', in *F. Y. Edgeworth: Mathematical Psychics and Further Papers on Political Economy*, ed. Peter Newman, Oxford University Press, Oxford 2003 p. xxv.

190. Lionel Robbins, 'The Economic Works', in C. H. Herford, *Philip Henry Wicksteed: His Life and Work*, J. M. Dent, London 1931 p. 229.

Henry George's *Progress and Poverty* (1879), which directed his attention to the welfare of the individual and also led to an interest, which he shared with Arnold Toynbee, in the problem of poverty as the central problem of economics.[191] Unlike Toynbee, however, he approached this problem in a quite systematic manner. In 1888 Wicksteed published a small popular primer which devoted its first fifty pages to a discussion of the acceleration of falling bodies, the velocities of balls thrown in the air, the expansion and contraction of iron bars when heated or cooled, and the enjoyment gained by sitting in a Turkish bath as the temperature is increased, all of which was devoted to the single purpose of identifying the importance of what he called 'marginal usefulness', 'marginal effectiveness', but also 'marginal utility'.[192] In what could almost count as a parody of Jevonian physics, Wicksteed expounds the choices made by Böhm-Bawerk's 'schlechter Wirt' as follows:

> The clumsy housekeeper spends a great deal too much on one commodity and a great deal too little on another. She does not realise or follow the constant changes of condition fast enough to overtake them, and buys according to custom and tradition. Her system of expenditure is viscous, and cannot change its levels so fast as the channels change their bore. She can never get her marginal utilities balanced, and therefore, though she drives as hard bargains as any one, and always seems to "get her money's worth" in the abstract, yet in comfort and pleasure she does not make it go as far as her neighbour does, and never has "a penny in her pocket to give to a boy," a fact that she can never clearly understand because she has not learned the meaning of the formula, "my coefficient of viscosity is abnormally high."[193]

Wicksteed explicitly acknowledged his debt to Jevons in his *Common Sense of Political Economy* (1910), where he also noted that Jevons's principles were not limited to the economic domain, for the

> general principles which regulate our conduct of business are identical with those which regulate our deliberations, our selections between alternatives, and our decisions, in all other branches of life. . . . We must regard industrial and commercial life, not as a separate and detached region of activity, but as an organic part of our whole personal and social life.[194]

191. Herford, *Philip Henry Wicksteed*, op. cit. pp. 197, 199, 211.
192. Philip H. Wicksteed, *The Alphabet of Economic Science*, Macmillan, London 1888 pp. 45–46.
193. Wicksteed, *Alphabet*, op. cit. pp. 126–27.
194. Philip H. Wicksteed, *The Common Sense of Political Economy* Vol. 1, ed. Lionel Robbins, George Routledge, London 1933 p. 3.

For Wicksteed, political economy was ruled by a calculus applicable to all other domains, an extension made possible by his logico-mathematical version of human conduct unconstrained by social context: 'In current language "economy" means the administration of any kind of resources (time, thought, or money, for instance) in such a way as to secure their maximum efficiency for the purpose contemplated. It is administration with a minimum of waste'.[195]

Laying out the Jevonian vision in this way suggests what it might have been in Jevons that Marshall found so unacceptable. Marshall had begun in the 1870s with Mill, the awkward nature of the transition he had to make being evident in the textbook *Economics of Industry* (1879), which he wrote with his wife Mary for university extension classes.[196] When Marshall eventually published his *Principles of Economics* volume I in 1890 this was a very different kind of book from Jevons's *Theory of Political Economy*. For one thing, it was very discursive, the first one hundred pages being a long historical account of the development of economic society and of economic analysis; but it was also more comprehensive, dealing with industrial organisation, labour supply, and also introducing the term 'national dividend' to describe the annual aggregate output of an economy.[197] He also introduced a new definition:

> §1. POLITICAL ECONOMY, or ECONOMICS, is a study of man's actions in the ordinary business of life; it inquires how he gets his income and how he uses it. Thus it is on the one side a study of wealth and on the other, a more important side, a part of the study of man.[198]

The shift of terminology to 'economics' was widely accepted; in any case, the 'political' sense of 'political economy' had by now been emptied of much of its meaning, the new science of production and distribution rendering the body politic a shell within which inexorable economic laws worked their way out. 'Wealth' was now initially defined by Marshall as 'desirable things' called commodities, or goods, although not all goods would be considered wealth. There are material and immaterial goods, transferable and non-transferable, first and second order, or, as Marshall

195. Wicksteed, *Common Sense*, op. cit. pp. 13–14.
196. See my discussion of this work in 'Economic Manuals and Textbooks in Great Britain and the British Empire 1797–1938' in Massimo M. Augello, Marco E. L. Guidi, (eds.) *The Economic Reader*, Routledge, London 2012 pp. 54–57.
197. Alfred Marshall, *Principles of Economics* Vol. 1, Macmillan, London 1890 p. 560.
198. Ibid. p. 1.

noted, consumers' and producers' goods. Echoing Say, he notes that man cannot create material things, only utilities; and that this is effected by labour, defined along the Jevonian lines as exertion undertaken with a view to something other than the pleasure or pain arising directly from work.[199]

Nowhere does Marshall commit himself to a final and definitive statement of the nature and purpose of economics. Instead, we have very broad and preliminary statements which are then elaborated and rendered more precise in the course of the development of the text. This does contribute to the apparent looseness of the text, and we look in vain for the kind of definition that we can find in Jevons. We can however establish Marshall's position on the definition of economics and the nature of economic action by considering his response to claims from William Cunningham that Marshall had a universalist conception of 'economic man', imputing late-Victorian ideas to economies of all times and in all places. Marshall was here quite clear: far from subscribing to the view that the same motives have been at work through the ages, producing similar results and hence demonstrating the constancy of economic laws, Marshall described his *Principles* as follows:

> The whole volume is indeed occupied mainly in showing how similar causes acting on people under dissimilar conditions produce more or less divergent effects. The leading motive of its argument is the opposite of that which Dr. Cunningham ascribes to it.[200]

As Marshall had noted,

> The economist must be greedy of facts; but facts by themselves teach nothing. History tells of sequences and coincidences; to interpret these and draw lessons from them requires the aid of reason. . . . Economic science is but the working of common sense, organized and equipped with a machinery of general analysis and reasoning adapted for collecting, arranging, and drawing inferences from some particular class of fact.[201]

If, then, Marshall retreats from Jevons's reductivist conception of economic action and the economic domain to a more contextual and differentiated, not to say diffuse, idea of action and its context, where then does

199. Ibid. pp. 106–17.
200. Alfred Marshall, 'A Reply', *Economic Journal* Vol. 2 (1892) p. 508.
201. Marshall, *Principles*, op. cit. p. 94.

the modern conception that economics is a behavioural science of human action, formalised and mathematised, an 'algebra of action',[202] come from? Marshall's *Principles* was until the 1920s the unchallenged international reference for modern economic thinking; in Britain it remained influential until at least the 1940s. Given the apparent persistence of Marshallian economics in Britain, at what point was its pragmatic stance abandoned?

The proximate cause was the publication in 1932 of Lionel Robbins' *Nature and Significance of Economic Science*, in which Robbins settled upon the definition:

> Economics is the Science which studies human behaviour as a relationship between ends and scarce means which have alternative uses.[203]

He arrives at this conclusion having started with an attempt to 'delimit the subject-matter of Economics',[204] citing definitions by Marshall, Davenport, Cannan, Beveridge, and Pigou as evidence of a lack of clear agreement.[205] Robbins recognised that economics had developed from diverse and practical origins, and suggests that it was only recently that 'it had become sufficiently unified for the identity of the problems underlying these different enquiries to be detected'.[206] He suggests that the prevailing consensus in English-speaking countries would be to relate economics to the study of the causes of material welfare.[207] But he develops his argument, leading from this point to his famous definition, solely with respect to the writings of Cannan, his teacher. He avoids any confrontation with Marshall's approach to economics; he instead takes to pieces the second chapter of Cannan's *Wealth*, a text based on Cannan's first-year teaching at LSE from 1898 onwards, and first published in 1914. The difficulty that Cannan has in distinguishing 'economic' from 'non-economic' activity is

202. I take this phrase from Apostolos Doxiadis, Alecos Papadatos, and Annie Di Donna, 'Claude Lévi-Strauss (1908–2009)', *FT Magazine* 27 February 2010.

203. Lionel Robbins, *The Nature and Significance of Economic Science*, Macmillan, London 1932 p. 15.

204. Ibid. p. 1.

205. Robbins, *Nature*, op. cit. fn. 1 pp. 1–2: 'Economics is the science of men earning a living' (Marshall); 'Economics is the science which treats phenomena from the standpoint of price' (Davenport); 'The aim of Political Economy is the explanation of the general causes on which the material welfare of human beings depends' (Cannan); economics is 'the study of the general methods by which men co-operate to meet their material needs' (Beveridge); economics is the study of economic welfare, the latter being 'that part of welfare which can be brought directly or indirectly into relation with the measuring rod of money' (Pigou).

206. Ibid. pp. 2–3.

207. Ibid. p. 4.

highlighted,[208] and he proposes that the solution to this difficulty is to focus upon the choices made by economic subjects—their economising activity.[209] There are consequently no intrinsic 'economic goods' whose accumulation as 'wealth' forms the proper object of economics; there are no intrinsic 'economic ends', and Robbins illustrates this by referring to the services of prostitutes and the sale of indulgences in making the point that 'all conduct coming under the influence of scarcity has its economic aspect'.[210] There is simply a form of behaviour, the act of choice between various means to achieve particular ends. And so while he presented explicit arguments for the delimitation of economic analysis, there is an implication that economic analysis, conceived as the study of economising choices, can be extended far beyond what was then considered the proper domain of economic analysis.

The footnotes to the first edition of *Nature and Significance* suggest that Robbins had arrived at this position through his reading of Austrian economists, especially von Mises and Schumpeter, an impression fostered by reference and allusion. But as Susan Howson has shown from a study of Robbins's own drafts and lecture notes, it is evident that his argument was formed by the end of 1928, owing 'most to Wicksteed', there being 'nothing particularly "Austrian" about it'.[211] The Oxford lecture notes from the Spring Term of 1929 to which Howson here refers make more than one reference to Wicksteed, but in the 1932 book Wicksteed is thanked alongside von Mises in the preface, only then to disappear from the main exposition, which is dominated by references to Austrian literature.[212] Robbins did study this literature intensively from 1925 to 1927, but Howson shows that this was not the primary source from which he developed his new definition of economics. And in drawing upon Wicksteed, he made a link back to Jevonian universalism, and short-circuited the Marshallian emphasis upon contingency.

At the time little attention was paid to where Robbins's arguments might lead; economists continued to study what they considered to be uncontroversially 'economic phenomena', notwithstanding Robbins's argument that there were no inherently economic phenomena, only the activity

208. Ibid. p. 11.
209. Ibid. p. 12.
210. Ibid. p. 27.
211. Susan Howson, 'The Origins of Lionel Robbins's *Essay on the Nature and Significance of Economic Science*', *History of Political Economy* Vol. 36 (2004) p. 426. Fn. 1 to the definition on p. 15 refers to Menger, von Mises, Fetter, and Strigl—three Austrians and an American.
212. There are only five direct references to *Common Sense* in the entire book: pp. 31, 55, 76, 88, 92.

of decision-making under constraint. His stance was contested in the 1930s, partially accepted in the 1940s, and only unambiguously entered 'common knowledge' in the 1960s. Indeed, it was as late as 1976 when Samuelson's *Economics* for the first time clearly adopted Robbins's definition.[213] Only in the later 1950s did Gary Becker begin to apply economic theory, conceived as a calculus of choice, to areas hitherto not thought to be 'economic'—crime, education, and marriage—following on from the argument advanced by Robbins in 1932.[214] The extension of economic theory into issues of public choice date from around the same time, beginning with Downs's *Economic Theory of Democracy* (1957), continuing on to Buchanan and Tullock's *Calculus of Consent* (1962) and Mancur Olson's *Logic of Collective Action* (1965). These works picked up the radical implications of Robbins's arguments in *Nature and Significance*, although in the interim Robbins had become a quite different kind of economist.[215]

Since then, of course, the 'economisation' of political language—the use of economic rhetoric in the expression of public policy—has become endemic, drawing legitimation from the academic literature of public choice. The broader political appeal of economic arguments has nonetheless had a longer history. We can first detect it in arguments concerning 'national efficiency' in the 1890s, the idea that Britain was 'falling behind' the economic success of Germany and America; it developed during the 1920s in the Soviet Union, the drive to increase both agricultural and industrial production becoming a murderous imperative; it became generalised in post-war Western democracies, where political parties campaigned on promises of more houses, more schools, more hospitals, all of this built upon constant and unending economic growth. As we will see in the following chapter, this idea of 'economic growth', and international competition measured in terms of rates of growth, was only possible once there was a positive number as a measure of economic activity. However, the creation of a systematic framework for the measurement of national income and its variation created a new instrument of economic management, itself contributing to the economisation of politics and political language in Western party states.

It should however be clear from the foregoing that conceptions of 'economy' have been changing for the last couple of millennia, and there is little

213. Roger E. Backhouse, Steve G. Medema, 'Defining Economics: The Long Road to Acceptance of the Robbins Definition', *Economica* Vol. 76 (2009) p. 812.

214. Ibid. p. 814.

215. Following sharp criticism from von Mises, Robbins wrote in 1950 to Ludwig Lachmann that Mises 'commits the major error of identifying the logic of choice with the whole field of economic action'. Susan Howson, *Lionel Robbins*, Cambridge University Press, Cambridge 2011 p. 680.

reason to think that this process of change and redefinition has come to an end. Some might insist that our modern understanding of routine economic activity is in some way superior to earlier understandings; but if this view is underpinned by an appeal to the rigour of modern economics, then we should bear in mind that all genuine scientific knowledge is flux, committed to the discarding of present certainty and its replacement by new certainties. A better understanding of this process can teach us to be wary of 'new ideas' that might not, after all, be so new. The foregoing suggests no sense of progress in the changing sense of 'economy', rather a real heterogeneity, from its origin with the Greeks to the present. There has been no uniform 'narrowing': the 'dismal science' came and went in the first half of the nineteenth century, and then underwent a temporary revival in the 1950s. Rather than search back for present meanings, or seek to identify anticipations and dawning realisations, I have reversed the flow and tracked words and meanings through the centuries, showing just how long it took for our current understanding of 'economy' and 'economics' to emerge. If, ultimately, this chapter has taken the form of a scholarly shaggy-dog story, its sense lies as much in the length of the telling, as in the point it reaches.

CHAPTER 3

The Measurement of Economic Activity and the Growth Metric: Constructing National Income in Britain, 1907–1941

Our present object is to discover what determines at any time the national income of a given economic system and (which is almost the same thing) the amount of its employment.

—John Maynard Keynes, *The General Theory of Employment, Interest and Money* (1973)[1]

This chapter is about how a concept, national dividend, first exposed by Alfred Marshall in *Principles of Economics*, elaborated by Pigou in his *Wealth and Welfare*, was then transformed into a number, and how that process took more than forty years.

In chapter 18 of his *General Theory* Maynard Keynes restates his 'theory of employment', and opens by distinguishing the independent variables of the system from the dependent. He takes as 'given' the existing skills and quantity of labour, technique, the degree of competition, consumer tastes, and the organisation of the labour process. The independent variables are listed as the propensity to consume, the schedule of the marginal efficiency of capital, and the rate of interest. The dependent variables are the volume of employment and the national income measured in wage units.[2]

1. John Maynard Keynes, *The General Theory of Employment, Interest and Money*, *Collected Writings of John Maynard Keynes* Vol. 7, Macmillan, London 1973 p. 247.
2. Ibid. p. 245.

Insofar as these variables relate to empirically ascertainable entities, they were in 1936 only very roughly sketched out. Keynes acknowledged this in chapter 4, where he commented on some of the more recalcitrant aspects of 'national dividend', but without, of course, introducing any numbers—because no reliable or generally accepted magnitudes existed at the time for the UK. The *General Theory* proposed the existence of systematic relationships between variables whose precise dimensions remained indefinite, or disputed. The habit, still prevalent today, of treating Keynes's *General Theory* as the origin of a modern macroeconomics takes for granted a statistical foundation that was still in the 1930s at a very rudimentary stage. This elision obscures a very significant gap between the theoretical prospect offered by Keynes's book, and the capacity to represent the empirical reality to which it appealed.

The success of the 'Keynesian Revolution' in Britain would require that this gap be bridged, that the empirical content of theoretical variables could be filled in. Only with the outbreak of war three and a half years after publication of the *General Theory* would it become a tool for the management of national economies, rather than a compelling theoretical system. Academic economists were quickly recruited into government service, and the creation of a reliable statistical framework for economic management was quickly identified as their principal initial objective. The budget of April 1941 was supplemented with an official *Analysis of the Sources of War Finance and Estimate of the National Income and Expenditure in 1938 and 1940* (Cmd. 6261) that deployed for the first time a national accounting framework together with relevant statistical data. This was, therefore, the inaugural moment of that 'Keynesian economic management' which clearly separates post-war from pre-war government policy. Discussion of this usually turns on the theoretical foundations of modern macroeconomics. But without a consistent statistical basis, economic management would not have been possible.

Although academic economists were recruited to the British wartime administration at a very early stage,[3] most returned to academic employment once hostilities ceased. Not until the mid-1960s did British economists begin to make a significant contribution to peacetime government administration.[4]

3. See Alec Cairncross and Nita Watts, *The Economic Section 1939–1961: A Study in Economic Advising*, Routledge, London 1989; and also for the important area of aircraft production that accounted for almost a quarter of UK domestic output, Alec Cairncross, *Planning in Wartime: Aircraft Production in Britain, Germany and the USA*, Macmillan, Houndmills 1991, and Ely Devons, *Planning in Practice: Essays in Aircraft Planning in War-time*, Cambridge University Press, London 1950.

4. Indeed, in the early 1960s most 'economic policy' had no input at all from trained economists; see P. D. Henderson, 'The Use of Economists in British Administration', *Oxford Economic Papers* Vol. 13 New Series (1961) pp. 5–26.

'Keynesian economic management'[5] was in postwar Britain largely the creation of civil servants untrained in economics, the relationship to and employment of academic economists episodic and casual. However, those who departed in 1945 did leave behind a permanent legacy in a framework for government finance based upon National Income estimates, the landmark 1941 budget being the first to make explicit use of national accounting concepts.

But it is not enough just to have a national accounting framework. The Germans had something similar by 1944, but no numbers.[6] And numbers are hard to come by. The first British national census was in 1801; prior to this date all English population statistics have had to be laboriously reconstituted from parish records.[7] Trade data has a rather longer history—Great Britain and Ireland have always traded most intensively with their European neighbours and this is documented back to 1701 in Elizabeth Boody Schumpeter's important compendium of trade statistics.[8] These raw data were generated by the operations of the customs service at British and Irish ports, a sea border being the most reliable guarantee that official trade returns reflect the intensity of economic activity.

But as was revealed in the tariff reform campaign at the start of the new century, there remained considerable uncertainty about the actual and prospective structure of British trade. Strategic planners found shortly before the First World War that it was necessary to set up a special committee to determine, among other things, the degree to which the British economy depended upon its trade with the prospective enemy state, Germany. The Runciman Committee discovered that

> in 1911 Britain had imported 16 million tons of goods from Germany and countries bordering the Baltic, and had exported to them just over 29 million tons of goods. This trade represented just over a quarter of all Britain's imports by value and just over a fifth of its exports. When these crude figures were broken down they showed that, for example, over half of all butter and

5. Insofar as policy can be thought of as 'Keynesian'—see Neil Rollings, 'British Budgetary Policy 1945–1954: A "Keynesian Revolution"?', *Economic History Review* Vol. 41 (1988) pp. 283–98, which summarises discussion among English economic historians of the extent to which postwar management could be considered 'Keynesian'.

6. See Adam Tooze, *Statistics and the German State, 1900–1945: The Making of Modern Economic Knowledge*, Cambridge University Press, Cambridge 2001 espec. ch. 7, 'World War II and the Return of Macroeconomics'.

7. See E. A. Wrigley, R. S. Schofield, *The Population History of England 1541–1871: A Reconstruction*, Cambridge University Press, Cambridge 1989.

8. Elizabeth Boody Schumpeter, *English Overseas Trade Statistics 1697–1808*, Oxford University Press, London 1960, Tables 5 and 6.

> margarine eaten in Britain came from here, as did no less than 70 per cent of all sugar. If trade across the North Sea were suspended, the timber industry would lose half its raw materials and the flax spinning industry would lose all of them. Germany supplied Britain with over 30 per cent of all its steel, 60 per cent of its zinc, half of its electric motors and no less than four-fifths of its coal tar dyes.[9]

This kind of detail on the interdependence of national economies was unreadable in the published statistics. And if this were true of Britain's overseas trade, the implications for data on the domestic economy itself were not good.

During the interwar years a great deal of effort was devoted to remedying this deficiency. The initial task was the formulation of a conceptual apparatus that would permit the existing statistical base to be employed in the construction of national income statistics. However, academics and government officials worked independently of the machinery of administration, so there was no systematic effort to reorganise or augment the existing machinery for the collection and publication of official statistics. And so, viewed from the new perspective of government wartime requirements in early 1940, things seemed to have advanced little since 1914:

> It may be difficult to imagine it now but up to 1940 the government felt no particular need for such macroeconomic data [on industrial production, food consumption, or employment]. There were no official estimates of GNP or consumer spending, only the sketchiest of estimates of the balance of payments, nothing at all on stocks, profits, and capital formation. Economic statistics were relegated to unreadable monthly journals and annual abstracts. If they were used at all, it was usually in the most unsophisticated way with no attempt to produce a time series or adjust for seasonal and other specific factors. Fragments of statistical information went on the file like other fragments of information.[10]

However, the idea of estimating and comparing numerically national economies was not in the 1930s a novel one. Estimates of the 'strength of

9. David French, *British Economic and Strategic Planning 1905–1915*, George Allen and Unwin, London 1982 pp. 61–26.

10. Cairncross and Watts, *The Economic Section*, p. 57. This is Cairncross's personal comment on the situation in early 1940 when the Economic Section was formed. He also cites Harry Campion's remark that, when asked by the Cabinet Office on his first day at work for some employment figures in the engineering industry, he told them that what they wanted was in the *Ministry of Labour Gazette*. But the Cabinet Office had no copy; so Campion went out at lunchtime and bought them one (p. 51).

a nation' run back to the seventeenth century—Petty's *Political Arithmetick* of 1691 states its aim to be the demonstration that a small country with a small population may be equivalent in wealth and strength to a large country and a large population, with Holland and France the respective candidates. Many seventeenth-century writers perceived simple populousness to offer a road to wealth; others argued about the nature of the employments concerned. As Richard Stone shows, Petty's *Political Arithmetick* was itself a response to an earlier work that purported to demonstrate that the power and trade of the country were in decline.[11] 'Strength of a nation' arguments were throughout the seventeenth and eighteenth centuries ultimately addressed to the question of a nation's military potential, and warfare among the Continental European powers was a regular occurrence throughout the eighteenth and for most of the nineteenth century, only terminating in 1871 with the unification of Germany. There then followed a period of rapid industrialisation in which competition between the great powers became economic rather than military, although with the 'industrialisation' of warfare foreshadowed by the American Civil War this in turn became the harbinger of further military conflict.

Hence economic power, together with its prospective rise and decline, were very much a matter of public debate in the later nineteenth century, especially in a Britain whose industrial pre-eminence was challenged by newly industrialising economies. The work of Alfred Marshall provided a new analytical framework. The central concept was the 'national dividend', introduced by Marshall in the first edition of his *Principles* with words echoing the opening of Smith's *Wealth of Nations*:

> The labour and capital of the country, acting on its natural resources, produce annually a certain Net aggregate of commodities, material and immaterial, including services of all kinds. This is the true net annual revenue of the country, or as we may say the NATIONAL DIVIDEND. . . . it is a continuous stream always flowing, and not a reservoir or store, or in the narrower sense of the word a "Fund" of capital.[12]

This captures the essential character of national income, that it is an annual aggregate of economic activity of all types and, importantly, a flow and not a stock. But it is more than that. As Pigou stated in his review of the fifth edition of Marshall's *Principles*, it is a 'practical instrument of great power designed for service in the concrete solution of social

11. Richard Stone, *Some British Empiricists in the Social Sciences 1650–1900*, Cambridge University Press, Cambridge 1997 pp. 36–47.
12. Alfred Marshall, *Principles of Economics* Vol. 1, Macmillan, London 1890 p. 560.

problems'.[13] Pigou firmly linked this conception to the development of welfare economics, his *Wealth and Welfare* being organised with respect to the concept of national dividend—its relation to welfare, its magnitude, distribution, and variability.[14]

The welfare economics that Pigou founded was a conceptual schemata lacking a necessary empirical foundation in much the same way as sketched above for Keynes's *General Theory*. At this time, the available official statistics can be summarised as follows:

1. Decennial Population Census data starting in 1801.
2. Taxation data, distributed under the following heads:
   Consumer taxes and duties (Customs and Excise)
   Land and property taxes
   Post Office revenue
   Income tax (Inland Revenue)
   County and police rates
   Water and gas rates
   Poor rates receipts
3. Board of Trade data on exports and imports
4. Factory Inspectors' returns[15]

The inadequate and piecemeal nature of official statistics was acknowledged, and work already directed to redressing this gulf between a conceptual structure and the data needed for it to realise its potential for social and economic policy. In September 1908 Henry Macrosty (1865–1941) read a paper to the Economic Section of the British Association noting that

> The politics of to-day are economists' politics—Socialism, Tariff Reform, Old Age Pensions, Wage Boards, Railway Nationalisation, the Eight Hours' Day—and not only have we nothing decisive to say, but nobody asks us to say anything.[16]

13. Arthur C. Pigou, review of Marshall, *Principles of Economics* (5th edition), *Economic Journal* Vol. 17 (1907) p. 534.
14. Arthur C. Pigou, *Wealth and Welfare*, Macmillan, London 1912—the titles of the four main parts of the book.
15. In 1907 the Census of Production was added; then in 1909 the creation of a National Insurance scheme provided some data on employment; in 1911 Surtax was introduced; and then much later in 1921 there followed motor vehicle duties.
16. H. W. Macrosty, 'Proposals for an Economic Survey of the United Kingdom', *Economic Journal* Vol. 19 (1909) p. 2. Macrosty would run the Office of the Census of Production until formally appointed Assistant Director alongside Flux in 1911. After the war the Board of Trade formally established a reorganised Statistical Department directed by Flux as Assistant Secretary, with Macrosty as Senior Principal. Flux and Macrosty should therefore be regarded as the joint heirs of Sir Robert Giffen as official statisticians. See the obituary notice for Macrosty by M. G., *Journal of the Royal Statistical Society* Vol. 104 (1941) pp. 85–90.

Economists, he argued, had established a secure position for themselves as pure theorists, and the purchase of pure theory on such questions was strictly limited. Instead, emphasis needed to be placed upon fact-gathering, and he called upon the British Association or the Royal Economic Society to inaugurate an 'economic survey' of the United Kingdom, combining existing data on the organisation of the economy trade by trade and supplementing it with independent enquiry.

He was in fact to be involved in a partial version of this, for during 1907 the first Census of Production had been carried out by the Board of Trade.[17] Alfred Flux was appointed Statistical Adviser to the Census in 1908, being given the title of Director in 1911 when the first report was fully published. Flux's subsequent career was as a government statistician in the Board of Trade, although in 1908 he could be counted among the leading British economists of the day.[18] Despite the limitations of the census design and execution—it presents employment and net output of branches of production by size of establishment for the year 1907—he sought to draw out of it material that might assist estimation of the national income, for he reasoned this was simply the obverse of all goods and services produced minus exports plus imports.[19] He continued:

> The goods consumed, however, when regarded as the exchange equivalent of income, are valued after passing through the hands of merchants, wholesale and retail, processes of adaptation for use after acquisition by the consumer

17. Britain was something of a latecomer in this regard, regular surveys of industrial production having been initiated in the United States in 1850; Canada adopted a similar measure on Confederation; Australia adopting an annual survey in 1903; and New Zealand moved to a quinquennial system in 1887. The second British Census followed in 1912, but the war and then postwar government economies postponed the organisation of the third census until 1924—A. W. Flux, 'The Census of Production', *Journal of the Royal Statistical Society* Vol. 87 (1924) pp. 351–53.

18. Joint Senior Wrangler in 1887, 1889 fellow of St. John's College, Cambridge, where he was attracted to the study of economics by Marshall. In 1893 he went to Manchester, where he developed teaching on economics and commerce in advance of the formation of the Faculty of Commerce, being the first to be given the title of Stanley Jevons Professor of Political Economy in 1898. He left Manchester in 1901 for a chair in political economy at McGill University, from where he returned to the Board of Trade in 1911. In 1904 he published the first 'post-Marshallian' textbook, *Economic Principles*. See his *Oxford Dictionary of National Biography* entry by Henry Clay, revised by John Whittaker.

19. A. W. Flux, 'Gleanings from the Census of Production', *Journal of the Royal Statistical Society* Vol. 76 (1913) p. 576. For a contemporary summary of the results of the Census applicable to the concept of national dividend see A. L. Bowley, 'The Census of Production and the National Dividend', *Economic Journal* Vol. 23 (1913) pp. 53–61. For a summary of the official remit of the first census, and a comparison with the surveys of other countries, see Flux, 'The Census of Production' pp. 354ff.

> not being valued, as one does not set a value on the work done by oneself in preparing, for example, food for eating. A line has to be drawn somewhere, and the most easily-defined line is drawn when the last process of exchange before consumption takes place is reached.

For this one need to know the value of goods as they left the producers; value added in transport and trade; and the value of services. The first could be established with some degree of certainty from the Census of Production; the second was more complicated to ascertain; while the third raises the issue that in the course of the new century services would steadily become the most important sector of the national product, so that the quinquennial Census of Production would in fact record an ever-shrinking component of total economic activity.[20] In any case, as Henry Macrosty made plain in discussion of Flux's 1913 presentation to the Royal Statistical Society, the powers of the Census of Production Office were strictly limited by act of Parliament, and any extension of its inquiries, into for example the details of working capital, capital stock, and reserves in the form of investments and securities (including hidden reserves) would require a further act of Parliament.[21]

Not only did the outbreak of war redirect attention to more urgent questions than census design, the problem of war finance highlighted another problem related to the estimation of national income. The budget for the financial year 1913–14 covered planned expenditure of £197.5 million, with revenue flowing from the following sources:

Income tax (£47.3 m.)
Estate duties (£27.2 m.)
Spirits, wine, and beer (£43.4 m.)
Tobacco (£18.3 m.)
Tea and sugar duties (£9.8 m.)
Stamp duties (c. £10 m.)
Post Office (£30 m.)
Sinking Fund (residual)

Indirect taxation of alcohol, tobacco, tea, and sugar accounted for over one-third of total revenue; income tax started at £160 per annum. The

20. Flux concluded with an estimate of national income of £2 bn. For 1907, plus or minus 10%. A particular problem that he identified concerned the valuation of capital stock—p. 580.
21. Macrosty, 'Discussion on Mr. Flux's Paper' ('Gleanings') p. 591.

subsequent problems of war finance can be read straight out of these figures: a fiscal base so heavily skewed to the indirect taxation of basic items of mass consumption was unsuited for the rapid increase of government revenue or, alternatively, the rapid reduction of domestic consumption. The highly regressive structure of the fiscal base rendered it extremely inflexible and entirely unsuited to a rapidly changing financial framework. The yawning budgetary gaps that developed as a result were covered by domestic and foreign loans, management of which remained a major preoccupation for governments into the later 1920s.[22]

The sheer scale of this financial problem highlighted two things: first, the exclusion of most of the working population from direct taxation meant that the Inland Revenue possessed a very inexact picture of aggregate incomes; and second, the sheer incapacity of indirect taxation to yield significant increases in government revenue indicated something about consumer preferences and elasticities of demand for the goods in question. But in Britain these two issues were the provinces of respectively the Inland Revenue and the Customs and Excise, so there was no compelling administrative motivation to address the issues in a systematic manner. However, one of the most insightful commentators on Flux's 1913 paper, Josiah Stamp, was throughout the war an official of the Inland Revenue, promoted in 1916 to Assistant Secretary, the moving spirit behind the wartime excess profits duty, and joining in 1919 the Royal Commission on Income Tax. In 1920–21 he gave the Newmarch lectures, whose theme was 'Current Statistical Problems in Wealth and Industry'. This provided an early postwar benchmark for the resumption of those issues raised before the war by Flux and Macrosty.

In reviewing the existing sources, Stamp first drew attention to the lack of utility of income tax data when the threshold was set, as in Britain, above the average income.[23] Second, he pointed out that it was possible to estimate earnings for those below this threshold by using data from the occupational census for those in employment, then apply these estimates to the whole of the occupational group. Third, value added in production could be derived from the Census of Production, the resultant figure forming the fund that provides income and hence approaching aggregate income from the output side in the same way that Flux had earlier

22. E. V. Morgan, *Studies in British Financial Policy, 1914–25*, Macmillan, London 1952, pp. 89ff.
23. J. C. Stamp, *Wealth and Taxable Capacity*, P.S. King & Son, London 1922 pp. 58–59.

suggested. However, he summarised the prevailing state of knowledge as follows:

> At this date (February 1921) we have no very clear idea as to the actual number of people engaged in industry, though, of course, we know how many come within insured classed under the extended schemes. Still less do we know the numbers in the separate industries, and any information we have as to the increase in piecework rates or time rates is difficult to apply, because these fundamental facts are missing at present. The Census result will help to resolve many doubts, as it will give us a new and more secure basis on which to work. The lowering of the exemption limit to £130 at a time when there has been a general increase of wages has brought a very large number into this class of official statistics. Formerly, the income tax statistics were almost clear of weekly wage-earners, but now some four million at least come within the figures.[24]

Stamp had by this time left government service and so had no direct involvement in the development of official statistics. However, he collaborated with Bowley in an estimation of the national income for 1924 based around income tax returns and data on wages paid by employers for that year, combined with the 1921 Population Census, concluding that the income per head in Britain in 1924 was around the same level as in 1911.[25] When in 1928 Flux was made president of the Royal Statistical Society his address took up this issue, but as Yule pointed out in moving the vote of thanks, his conclusion, that national income had doubled from 1907 to 1924, was vitiated by price changes: 'The greater part of the remainder of his Address unfortunately has to be devoted to showing how very difficult it is to attach any precise significance to that ratio'.[26] The problem lay not only in the construction of an adequate price index, which was at this time under discussion,[27] but that the nature of goods and services was rapidly changing—examples noted are street lighting, motorbuses, and electrical goods. Stamp in his remarks drew a clear distinction between the physical apprehension of activity in the Census of Production, and the accounting method when dealing with the same activity from the point of view of

24. Stamp, *Wealth and Taxable Capacity*, pp. 70–71.
25. A. L. Bowley, J. C. Stamp, *The National Income, 1924*, Oxford University Press, Oxford 1927.
26. Udney Yule moving the Vote of Thanks to A. W. Flux's Presidential Address of 20 November 1928, *Journal of the Royal Statistical Society* Vol. 92 (1929) p. 27.
27. See A. L. Bowley, 'Notes on Index Numbers', *Economic Journal* Vol. 38 (1928) pp. 216–37, summarising the Newmarch Lectures of 1928 that he had delivered.

taxation data.[28] This point was re-emphasised in a meeting of the Society in January 1929, where Bowley, Stamp, and Macrosty contributed to discussion of Flux's own 1924 estimates.[29]

Substantial preparatory work on the determination of national income had therefore been done by 1930, but the focus would soon shift to the work of Colin Clark in Cambridge, appointed on Keynes's suggestion as lecturer in statistics in 1931. Born in 1905, and therefore a generation removed from Bowley (born 1869) or Stamp (born 1880), Clark had in 1928 gained a second-class degree in chemistry from Oxford, his interest in economics stimulated however by G. D. H. Cole through the University Labour Club, of which he was an active member.[30] In May 1929 he joined the Merseyside Social Survey, but left in February 1930 for the Economic Advisory Council, where he came to the attention of Keynes.

Coinciding exactly with his Cambridge appointment was Clark's preliminary review of British economic statistics bearing on an assessment of economic activity, published in September 1931.[31] He runs through in turn export and import statistics, estimates of the employed population, of output and of consumption, and productivity per head in manufacturing industry. This is, as Flux later noted, a virtuoso performance,[32] but the urgency with which Clark was at this time working is graphically highlighted by the inclusion in his article of a spidery hand-drawn graph of exports by value over the period 1913 to 1930 (figure 3.1).[33] Presumably lacking both time and resources to turn this important diagram into a more professionally composed graph, the editors simply copied Clark's own sketch into the pages of the *Journal*, helping us once more appreciate

28. Stamp in *Journal of the Royal Statistical Society* Vol. 92 (1929) p. 29.

29. 'Discussion of the National Income', *Journal of the Royal Statistical Society* Vol. 92 (1929) pp. 163–82, especially the contribution by W. H. Coates, pp. 173ff.

30. An Oxford contemporary recalled of Clark at the time: 'at Oxford we had a very superior Economics Club, which people like Robbins would come to, Colin was a member of it. There would for example be an argument about the Miners' Strike, and the Professors would all be saying how wicked it was, and how could the country survive; and then Colin would produce some statistics about the levels of profit, and argue that the owners could afford to pay the miners twice as much given the profits they were making. But this idea of bringing actual figures into an academic discussion was, at that time, a bit surprising'. KT Interview with Christopher Saunders, Hove 4 July 1995.

31. Colin Clark, 'Statistical Studies relating to the Current Economic Position of Great Britain', *Economic Journal* Vol. 41 (1931) pp. 343–69.

32. A. W. Flux, review of Clark, *The National Income, 1924–31* in *Economic Journal* Vol. 43 (1933) p. 279. Flux notes in the course of his review that Clark presents in conclusion calculations 'needed to give reality to some of Mr. J. M. Keynes' monetary formulae' (p. 279).

33. Clark, 'Statistical Studies', p. 345.

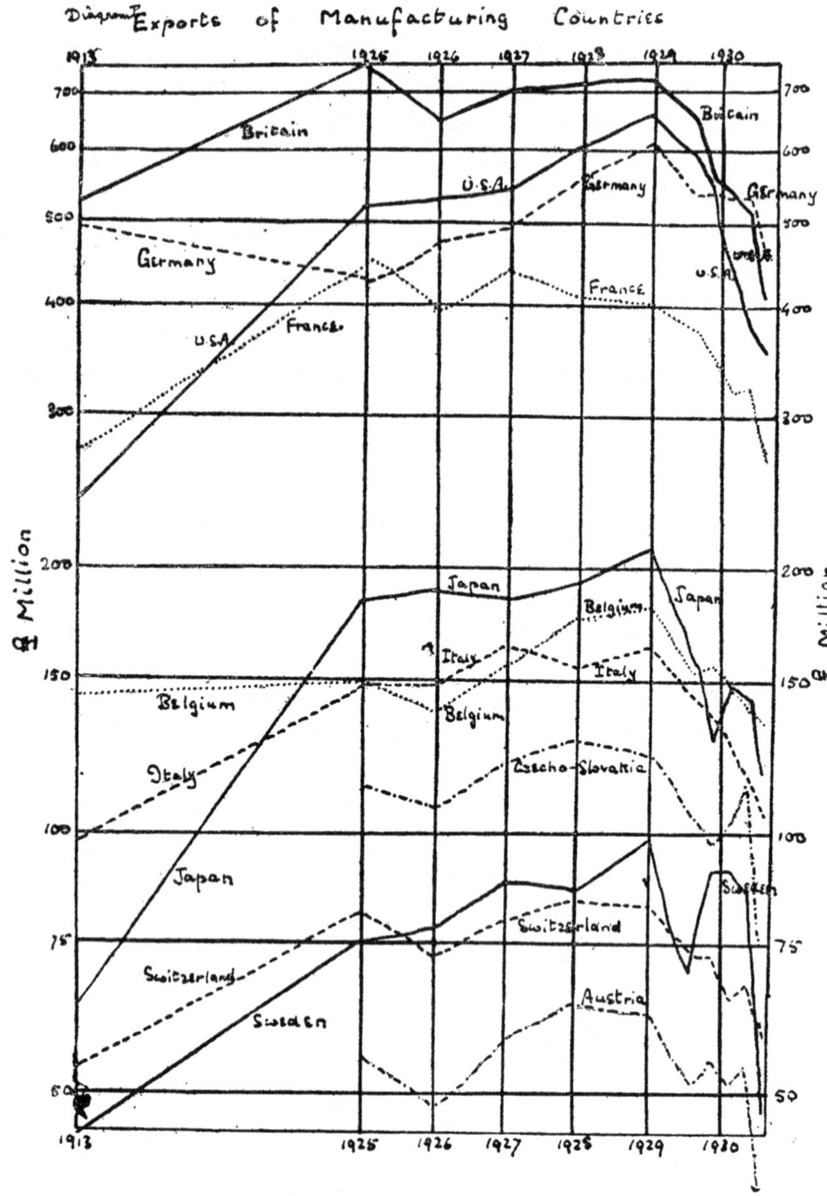

Figure 3.1:
Colin Clark, Exports by Value over the Period 1913 to 1930, Various Countries (1931).

the rudimentary technical conditions under which the first estimates of national accounts were made.

The following year Clark succeeded in publishing a succinct overview of the issue, his introductory remarks voicing a familiar lament:

> In many ways it has been a weary business making bricks without straw, and I think it is about time a little plain speaking was done about the disgraceful condition of British official statistics.[34]

He drew attention to the way that the Census of Production made use of an antiquated form of industrial classification rendering it impossible to compare its results with those of the Census of Population, or with those of the Unemployment Insurance statistics. Five different classifications of employer were used by five different government departments: the Board of Trade, the Census Office, the Ministry of Labour, the Inland Revenue, and the Home Office.[35] In addition to this, he noted that both the Balfour and the Macmillan committees had urged the publication of industrial profits, and that the Inland Revenue was ready to undertake it; but the Federation of British Industries opposed the idea on the grounds that it would give employees useful bargaining information.

Clark was however able to open his account with a definition of the National Income more comprehensive than hitherto articulated:

> The national income for any period consists of the money value of the goods and services becoming available for consumption during that period, reckoned at their current selling value, plus additions to capital reckoned at the prices actually paid for the new capital goods, minus depreciation and obsolescence of existing capital goods, and adding the net accretion of, or deducting the net drawings upon, stocks, also reckoned at current prices. Services provided on a non-profit-making basis by the State and local authorities (e.g. defence, elementary education) are included in the total at cost price; but where these services are 'sold' in the market (e.g. postal services, municipal tramway services) they are included on the basis of the charge made. Where taxation is

34. Colin Clark, The *National Income 1924–1931,* Macmillan, London 1932 p. vi.
35. Appendix 6 contains examples of this, contrasting employment in branches of industry during 1924 as recorded by the Census of Production, the Unemployment Insurance Statistics, and the Wage Inquiry. Even where the three sources agreed on a common term—for instance 'tinplate'—we find that employment is given by one as 23,000, and by the other two as 28,000; likewise 'shipbuilding' is a common category, but employment in this branch of industry is either 136,000, 175,000, or 129,000, depending upon which source you use. *National Income*, appendix 6 pp. 160–1.

> levied upon particular commodities and services, such as the customs and excise duties on commodities or the entertainment tax, such taxes are not included in the selling value.[36]

The remainder of the book wrestles with the diverse and diffuse sources through which this clear definition might be empirically realised. Writing in 1932 Clark did not of course have access to an up-to-date Census of Population, the most recent version being for 1921, since when of course there had been considerable change both in the size and in the occupational structure of the population. Nor did he have access to the results of the third Census of Production in 1930, having to rely on the published results of the 1924 census. He therefore turned to Health Insurance statistics, which showed the number entitled to benefits, including the sick and the unemployed as well as the insurable population in work. Unemployment statistics were used in the same way; the difference between the two sets then indicating the number of workers in domestic service and in agriculture, where for the latter separate annual figures were available. On this basis, once the number in different categories of employment were established, he could estimate rates of pay and then derive the incomes received by different groups. A 1929 inquiry into the catering trade, for instance, suggested that average weekly incomes were 52s. 6d. for males, and 28s. 6d. for females. Likewise it was possible to estimate average weekly earnings of policemen as 60s., and postal workers at 57s. 6d. If the numbers employed in the catering trade, as policemen, or in the postal services could then be determined, multiplying the one by the other would give an estimate of total incomes for these occupational groups. Clark's method was to proceed systematically through the employed population in this way, so that eventually he could arrive at figures for weekly, monthly, and annual earnings that could then be aggregated.

But the output side was more problematic, for the Census of Production did not cover transport, distribution, and services, which together amounted to more than half the national income.[37] No other source was available for reliable estimates, and imposing fixed percentages for various stages (as had been done for the 1907 census) was, so far as Clark was concerned, pure guesswork. Capital stock and depreciation was another problem. But, ever-resourceful, Clark turned to sources such as the

36. Clark, *National Income 1924–1931*, pp. 1–2.
37. Clark discussed his estimates in comparison with those of Stamp and Bowley in his 'The National Income and the Net Output of Industry', *Journal of the Royal Statistical Society* Vol. 96 (1933) pp. 651–59.

'Inhabited House Duty'[38] to estimate the annual value of dwellings, and the Society of Motor Manufacturers for guidance on the depreciation of commercial vehicles.[39]

These acrobatics did not go unchallenged. Clark's book was subjected to a scathing review in the *Journal of the Royal Statistical Society*,[40] and the reviewer dismissed Clark's presentation of the JRSS paper: 'his methods are so faulty that his results must be omitted in any serious discussions on the question of national income'.[41] Such criticism was however disregarded, for Clark's work continued, supported by the research of Feavearyear on consumption.[42] Clark also devised a new method for the continuous estimation of national income based first on statistics of consumption and investment, and second on wages and profits.[43] Implicitly, therefore, he had arrived at the now-familiar tripartite approaches to national income accounting, based upon income, expenditure, or output; but also leaving the last of these to one side, presumably on the grounds that the difficulties presented by the Census of Production for the determination of the output of industry, agriculture, and services were simply too great. In 1934 he was then able to update all of his estimates with the results of the 1931 Population Census, final reports from the 1930 Census of Production, and the Seventy-Sixth Report of the Commissioners of the Inland Revenue.[44]

Nonetheless, such progress as was made did not entirely resolve difficulties with the estimation of key national accounting variables. In his 1941 (posthumous) inaugural address as president of the Royal Statistical Society Henry Macrosty raised the problem of a continuing absence of important statistical data, an issue to which he had first drawn attention in 1908; and he went on to warn of the danger in forming judgements on the basis of imputed population sizes and incomes. He too is critical of Clark:

> I turn to the *Economic Journal* for 1938, and there I find in an article by Mr. Clark on page 444 a table in which he shows *quarter by quarter* from 1929

38. Clark, *National Income 1924–1931*, p. 109.
39. Ibid. p. 113.
40. 'E. C. S.' [E. C. Snow], review of Clark, *The National Income, 1924–31*, *Journal of the Royal Statistical Society* Vol. 96 (1933) pp. 110–14.
41. Snow responding to Clark, 'The National Income and the Net Output of Industry', p. 658.
42. A. E. Feavearyear, 'Spending the National Income', *Economic Journal* Vol. 41 (1931) pp. 51–60; and 'The National Expenditure, 1932', *Economic Journal* Vol. 44 (1934) pp. 33–47.
43. Colin Clark, 'The National Income and the Theory of Production', *Economic Journal* Vol. 43 (1933) p. 205.
44. Colin Clark, 'Further Data on the National Income', *Economic Journal* Vol. 44 (1934) pp. 380–97.

> to 1937 figures, precise to the last million pounds, for such categories as, *inter alia*, 'Balance of Payments', 'Total Investment', 'Total Private Consumption', 'Gross National Income'. I simply don't believe it.[45]

Despite such scepticism, and Clark's departure for Australia in 1937, work on these problems did not falter. Stamp and Bowley continued their work. In 1938 the newly founded National Institute of Economic and Social Research (NIESR) commissioned the London School of Economics with the conduct of a systematic investigation of national income, and during the year before the outbreak of war Bowley directed research, collaborating from the autumn of 1939 with Harry Campion.[46] When in June 1940, as president of the Royal Statistical Society, Bowley came to give his valedictory address, he chose the topic 'national income', just as had Flux in November 1928.[47] Stamp for his part published a comprehensive international survey of national accounting methodologies,[48] remarkable for its scope given his preoccupations as chief executive of the London, Midland, and Scottish Railway, and as a director of the Bank of England. In September 1939 Stamp became chief adviser to the government on economic co-ordination. In November 1939 the Central Economic Information Service was formed, headed by Stamp and Sir Horace Wilson, head of the Treasury; its first appointments in December were John Jewkes, Austin Robinson, and Harry Campion. From these appointments there grew the eventual formation in January 1941 of the Economic Section, and the parallel creation of the Central Statistical Office (CSO) under the directorship of Harry Campion. In this way the empirical labours of Bowley, Stamp, and Clark during the interwar years were eventually joined to a central administrative institution linked to government policy.

The conceptual framework originally laid down in Keynes's *General Theory* had also undergone modification in the new wartime setting. During November 1939 Keynes had published a series of newspaper articles, reappearing in February 1940 as the pamphlet *How to Pay for the*

45. Henry Macrosty, 'Economic Statistics: Retrospect and Prospect', *Journal of the Royal Statistical Society* Vol. 104 (1941) p. 5.
46. See A. L. Bowley, *Studies in the National Income 1924–1938*, National Institute of Economic and Social Research, Economic and Social Studies I, Cambridge University Press, Cambridge 1942. Campion was reader in economic statistics at Manchester University and secretary of its Economics Research Section.
47. A. L. Bowley, 'Some Constituents of the National Income', *Journal of the Royal Statistical Society* Vol. 103 (1940) pp. 491–518.
48. J. C. Stamp, 'Methods Used in Different Countries for Estimating National Income', *Journal of the Royal Statistical Society* Vol. 97 (1934) pp. 423–55.

War.[49] Here Keynes famously reversed the premise of the *General Theory*—instead of examining the manner in which an economy might be prevented from reaching a full-employment equilibrium, Keynes now asked how an economy could be maintained at full capacity and civilian consumption cut without inflationary pressures developing. The elimination of unemployment under wartime conditions would he suggested do two things: it would tend to cause wages to increase as labour shortages emerged, while at the same time consumer prices would increase independently because of a shortfall of food and other goods. The solution was as follows:

> The right plan is to restrict spending power to the suitable figure and then allow as much consumer's choice as possible how it should be spent.[50]

The alternative to this was inflation: prices would adjust demand to supply, but with harmful long-term consequences. If, however, demand were adjusted to supply through fiscal means, consumers would defer present purchasing power, rather than lose it.

> The net result of these proposals is to increase the consumption of young families with less than 75s. a week, to leave the *aggregate* consumption of the lower income group having £5 a week or less nearly as high as before the war (whilst at the same time giving them rights, in return for extra work, to deferred consumption after the war), and to reduce the aggregate consumption of the higher income group with more than £5 a week by about a third on the average.[51]

This apparently simple assertion rests of course on the years of research into official statistics outlined above, for to make sense of the sums chosen by Keynes one also needs to know how many persons there are in the categories to which he refers. And as Clark had pointed out in the early 1930s, even these data were then unknown.

49. Keynes's formulation of the problem of war finance prompted a number of pamphlets and articles—see Barbara Wootton, 'Who Shall Pay for the War?', *Political Quarterly* Vol. 11 (1940) pp. 143–54, published in the April–June issue; and H. O. Meredith, 'The Finance of War', *Political Quarterly* Vol. 11 (1940) pp. 59–73, in the January–March issue.

50. Maynard Keynes, *How to Pay for the War, Collected Writings of John Maynard Keynes* Vol. 9, Macmillan, London 1972 p. 372.

51. Keynes, *How to Pay for the War*, p. 380. The following year Nathan and Kuznets were involved in analogous arguments about capacity and the feasibility of President Roosevelt's production targets—see Fogel, *Political Arithmetic*, pp. 56–57.

The pressures of wartime economic administration quickly made it possible to address lacunae of this nature. The creation of the Central Statistical Office in early 1941 was partly a response to the great amount of statistical work already done in the course of 1940, and partly to the new importance assigned to the introduction of a common statistical framework for the organisation and direction of the war economy. It was decided by the government that inflation should not be used as a means to suppress private consumption in favour of war production. Excess purchasing power was instead to be absorbed through additional taxation, and for this to be effective it was first necessary to estimate the actual level of excess. Hence allowance had to be made for the subsidies necessary to stabilise the cost of living, and assuming that this stabilised gross incomes, total volume of money demand needed to be established. By subtracting the amount of goods and services coming on the market an 'inflationary gap' could be identified, representing the amount of excess demand that had to be siphoned off. By late 1940 government conceived of pressures in the economy in terms of an 'output gap' separating the level of demand from the capacity of factors of production to meet these demands.[52]

The 1941 budget articulated these conceptions:

> Upon this theoretical foundation the actual budget arithmetic was based: on the assumption of a given national income, the amounts of voluntary saving and of revenue on the previous basis of taxation were estimated, and the remaining gap between total money demand and the value of goods and services become available was taken as the amount of new taxation to be imposed.[53]

As Kaldor pointed out, any review of the financial condition of the nation required the use of a national accounting framework, and could not be built around existing government accounts, as all budgets had done in the past.[54] Moreover, this approach carried the implication that the economic aim of governments should be stability and growth of the national income, rather than the more narrowly financial considerations traditionally associated with reviews of government income and expenditure. It is, remarked Kaldor, 'on the assumption of this wider responsibility that our best hopes lies for the post-war world'.[55]

52. R. S. Sayers, '1941—The First Keynesian Budget', in C. Feinstein (ed.) *The Managed Economy: Essays in British Economic Policy since 1929*, Oxford University Press, Oxford 1983 p. 106.
53. Ibid. pp. 108–9.
54. Nicholas Kaldor, 'The White Paper on National Income and Expenditure', *Economic Journal* Vol. 51 (1941) p. 181.
55. Ibid.

Henceforth, governments would be held increasingly responsible for national welfare; low unemployment and economic growth became the dominating concerns of all successive governments until the early 1980s, when it came to be argued that low unemployment and growth were not necessarily complementary, but more than likely incompatible objectives. This ideological shift did not however alter the relationship of government and economy that had developed in the early postwar years. As Kaldor points out above, the creation of a national accounting framework altered the given objective for economic management independently of the academic backgrounds or personal inclinations of politicians and civil servants directing the formation and execution of policy.

However, it was not merely the framework which lent 'Keynesianism' meaning as a new way of governing of a national economy. The word 'statistics' originally denoted information (not necessarily numerical in form) about the state. Effective management of enterprises has always relied on a variety of sources of information. Over time, as enterprises grew beyond the capacity of individuals to direct and control all stages of their operations numerical information came to predominate, and in turn procedures were developed to systematise this data through increasingly sophisticated forms of cost accounting. The same can be observed in economic administration; but as this chapter has shown, assembling and co-ordinating national statistics adequate to a national accounting framework was a long and difficult process. The new imperatives in managing a wartime economy gave these diverse efforts the necessary final impetus, integrating a new theoretical framework with the national income data appropriate for co-ordinated macroeconomic management.

PART II

Reading—Reception

While any reading of a text has a particular context, it is also implicitly guided by a set of assumptions, some of which might help understanding, others being a definite impediment. Economists have always acknowledged the canonical status of *Wealth of Nations*, but have generally approached the text with the questions and instruments with which they are familiar, converting Smith's eighteenth-century analysis of commercial society into modern terms. Since the 1980s historians of political thought have done a great deal to remedy the problems with this approach,[1] but little attention has been paid to the structure of the text itself. *Wealth of Nations* had its origins in Adam Smith's Glasgow lecture courses of the 1750s; after his return from France in 1766 he spent six years in Kirkcaldy drafting the work, moving in 1773 to London, where he completed it. The least we could do would be to assume that the work is put together in a particular way for a reason; and we should bear this in mind when seeking the arguments that Smith constructed.

In the nineteenth century the name of Adam Smith was synonymous with free trade, but twentieth-century commentators noted the apparent absence from his arguments of the principle of comparative advantage, the core of a 'modern' theory of international trade. Chapter 4 approaches this familiar issue from a different angle, setting to one side this modern

1. My article 'Adam Smith: Critical Theorist?', *Journal of Economic Literature* Vol. 37 (1999) pp. 609–32 is a survey of the recent critical reception of Smith's work, in conclusion drawing attention to the paradox that the 'historical Smith' of our modern understanding is necessarily a *reconstruction* of meaning available to Smith's contemporary readers, the authenticity and validity of this understanding being secured by historical argument.

theory and instead examining the way in which Smith in *Wealth of Nations* discusses international trade, its costs and benefits. It would of course be paradoxical if Smith had no understanding of the principle of opportunity cost that underlies the theory of comparative advantage. He begins his book with a chapter on the advantages of specialisation, elaborating the relationship between the division of labour and exchange through the first three chapters. This is followed by a chapter on money and value, the metric through which exchanges can be equalised in a world of specialisation created by the division of labour. Unless it can be shown that Smith suddenly switched arguments when moving from the discussion of trade between men and women to that between nations, we should start from the assumption that his book does in fact contain some recognition of the principle of opportunity cost upon which all argument about economic exchange turns. Smith's 'misconceptions' are clearly more the creation of modern commentary than of Adam Smith. Chapter 5 examines the debate surrounding another of these: whether the motivations of human action that Smith sets forth in *Theory of Moral Sentiments* are compatible with those underlying *Wealth of Nations*. Here we are interested not primarily in the structure of these books, but in that of the arguments made about them. This explicit shift between the reading of a text in chapter 4, and the reception of a text represented by the history of its readings, serves to highlight the way in which we can refresh our approach to canonical texts, and in so doing learn new things about them.

CHAPTER 4

Reading 'Trade' in *The Wealth of Nations*

Textbooks generally attribute the foundation of our modern understanding of the gains from trade to chapter 7 of David Ricardo's *On the Principles of Political Economy and Taxation* (1817). Ricardo there advanced an account of trade between England and Portugal that drew attention to the welfare gains for both if each specialised in the production of goods where a comparative advantage existed. Hitherto, the textbook story goes, writers had thought of trade and specialisation in terms of absolute advantage, such that the pattern of international trade reflected the relative costs of producing the same good in different locations. A shift of emphasis to the opportunity costs of producing a range of goods opened up a new argument concerning the gains from trade through the exploitation of comparative advantages: a country might benefit from specialising in the production of a good in which it enjoyed no absolute cost advantage. Hence trade between rich and poor countries could be to the advantage of both. This new argument provided a theoretical rationale for the constant expansion of commerce, and irrevocably linked the growth of capitalism to free trade.

But if we examine Ricardo's treatment of this issue in chapter 7 we find that it is sketchy to say the least. It has been suggested, in mitigation of the evident deficiencies in Ricardo's exposition, that the key passages on the advantages of trade were simply inserted into Ricardo's book at the prompting of James Mill.[1] More recent work discounts this

1. Mill's 'Commerce Defended' of 1808 presents a vigorous defence of the gains from trade based on specialisation—James Mill, *Selected Economic Writings*, ed. D. Winch, Oliver and Boyd, Edinburgh 1966 pp. 108 ff. For the argument about Mill's intervention see William O. Thweatt, 'James Mill and the Early Development of Comparative Advantage', *History of Political Economy* Vol. 8 (1976) pp. 207–34.

hypothesis.[2] Nevertheless, it was certainly John Stuart Mill who is responsible for Ricardo's reputation as the originator of our economic theory of the gains from trade.[3] In an essay written in 1829 or 1830, he stated that

> Of the truths with which political economy has been enriched by Mr. Ricardo, none has contributed more to give that branch of knowledge the comparatively precise and scientific character which it at present bears, than the more accurate analysis which he performed of the nature of the advantage which nations derive from a mutual interchange of their productions. Previously to his time, the benefits of foreign trade were deemed, even by the most philosophical enquirers, to consist in affording a vent for surplus produce, or in enabling a portion of the national capital to replace itself with a profit.[4]

Mill went on to formulate the nature of comparative advantage in a manner still recognisable today:

> To render the importation of an article more advantageous than its production, it is not necessary that the foreign country should be able to produce it with less labour and capital than ourselves. We may even have a positive advantage in its production: but, if we are so far favoured by circumstances as to have a still greater positive advantage in the production of some other article which is in demand in the foreign country, we may be able to obtain a greater return to our labour and capital by employing none of it in producing the article in which our advantage is least, but devoting it all to the production of that in which our advantage is greatest, and giving this to the foreign country in exchange for the other. It is not a difference in the *absolute* cost of production which determines the interchange, but a difference in the *comparative* cost.[5]

The remainder of Mill's essay was addressed primarily to the distribution of the gains from trade between nations, but in the passage cited here he

2. Roy J. Ruffin rebuts the hypothesis in his 'David Ricardo's Discovery of Comparative Advantage', *History of Political Economy* Vol. 34 (2002) pp. 736–38.

3. Ch. 3 §4 of James Mill's *Elements of Political Economy* (1st edition 1821; 3rd edition 1826) contains a tidied-up version of Ricardo's argument regarding the gains from trade, noting that 'it is not greater absolute, but greater relative, facility, that induces one of them to confine itself to the production of one of the commodities, and import the other'. Mill, *Selected Economic Writings* op. cit. p. 273.

4. J. S. Mill, 'Of the Laws of Interchange Between Nations; and the Distribution of the Gains of Commerce among the Countries of the Commercial World', in his *Essays on Some Unsettled Questions of Political Economy, Collected Works of John Stuart Mill* Vol. 4, Routledge and Kegan Paul, London 1967 pp. 232–33. The *Essays* were first published in 1844.

5. Mill, 'Of the Laws of Interchange Between Nations', p. 233.

formulates the 'Ricardian' position in a manner both more clear, and concise, than Ricardo ever managed.

However, Mill's later *Principles of Political Economy* (1848), a work which explicitly set out to 'modernise' Adam Smith's *Wealth of Nations*, buries Ricardo's argument in the few pages of Book III chapter 17. The function of comparative advantage in promoting the wealth of all nations is no longer given any special prominence. Henceforth arguments concerning the benefits of free trade were generically associated with Adam Smith's conception of natural liberty, rather than with any special form of economic reasoning. Indeed, it could be argued that the argument from comparative advantage only became conventional in the twentieth century, with the work of Eli Heckscher and Bertil Ohlin. In practice, of course, 'free trade' more or less disappeared off the radar for international economic development from 1914 to the early 1950s, and so we are faced with the paradox that, at the zenith of nineteenth-century free trade, this economic ideology was linked firmly to the name of Adam Smith, who, according to twentieth-century economists, was supposed to have had the wrong sort of theory.[6]

Smith had opened *Wealth of Nations* with a chapter on the division of labour, emphasising the importance of unimpeded specialisation for economic development. This was however elaborated only with respect to the process of production, the linkage to exchange being connected not prospectively to the benefits of trade, but retrospectively, to a 'propensity to truck and barter'. Nonetheless, the title of Book I chapter 3—'That the Division of Labour is Limited by the Extent of the Market'—appears to point the way from domestic specialisation to the benefits of foreign trade. The general principles that Smith outlines in Books I and II of *Wealth of Nations*, together with his emphasis on natural liberty, were mobilised in the course of the nineteenth century as the intellectual source and justification for the doctrine of free trade. And Smith appeared to have provided the license for this approach later in Book IV, where he develops a

6. See Arthur I. Bloomfield's initial survey in his 'Adam Smith and the Theory of International Trade', in A. S. Skinner, T. Wilson (eds.), *Essays on Adam Smith*, Oxford University Press, London 1975 p. 455. There is of course an extensive literature on this. Myint has drawn attention to the close relationship between Smith's theory of international trade and his treatment of domestic economic development (H. Myint, 'Adam Smith's Theory of International Trade in the Perspective of Economic Development', *Economica* Vol. 44 New Series [1977] pp. 231–48); while more recently Smith's emphasis on economies of scale has led to a partial rehabilitation—see Bruce Elmslie, Antoinette M. James, 'The Renaissance of Adam Smith in Modern Theories of Trade', in R. F. Hébert (ed.) *Perspectives on the History of Economic Thought* Vol. 9: *Themes on Economic Discourse, Method, Money and Trade*, Edward Elgar, Aldershot 1993 pp. 63–76 who emphasise (p. 67) the importance of Smith's conception of exchange and the division of labour.

critique of the 'mercantile system' which, it is assumed, starts from principles expounded in Books I and II.[7]

Today general opinion endorses John Stuart Mill's judgement that Ricardo is the originator of the modern theory of international trade. The year 1776[8] is certainly acknowledged as a turning point for economic analysis in general, but the crucial step with respect to international trade was taken by Ricardo in 1817 with his sketch of a theory of comparative advantage.[9] This however remained largely a monument until Heckscher and Ohlin introduced, in 1919 and 1924[10] respectively, an elaboration of Ricardo's very simple model, and this has survived as the core for international trade. We might also note here that Heckscher himself made a significant contribution to the idea that 'mercantilism' was the counterconcept of free trade,[11] and this notion has survived up to the present.

It is not part of my purpose here to review commentary upon Smith's analysis of international trade in *Wealth of Nations*. Instead, I contend that Smith's own arguments have for so long been pulled apart and reassembled for other purposes, passages being cited without regard for their place in the work as a whole, that direct contact with Smith's own line of reasoning has been lost. Instead, I wish to redirect attention to what Smith actually wrote, and the precise sequence in which he developed his analysis. I will demonstrate that Smith's analytical structure is consistent, but idiosyncratic. The point here lies in this demonstration, not in the evaluation of Smith's arguments. It will I hope become apparent that Book IV is after all not simply an elaboration of Book I, and that Smith's account of the genesis of and gains from trade begins at the end of Book II, flowing out of his 'capital theory', and not directly from the arguments

7. Robert A. Blecker provides an intelligent 'rational reconstruction' that seeks to reconcile the arguments of Book III with those of Book I—see his 'The "Unnatural and Retrograde Order": Adam Smith's Theories of Trade and Development Reconsidered', *Economica* Vol. 64 (1997) pp. 527–37.

8. Smith's principal subsequent addition to *Wealth of Nations*, the new Book IV ch. 8 'Conclusion of the Mercantile System' in the third edition of 1786, does not modify his original position and serves chiefly to clarify the underlying argument before turning to his treatment of the Physiocrats—see below.

9. Douglas Irwin attributes the first outline of a theory of comparative advantage to Mill (1814) and Torrens (1815), although the passages he adduces do little more than rephrase what Smith had already written in *Wealth of Nations* Book IV, as argued below—see *Against the Tide: An Intellectual History of Free Trade*, Princeton University Press, Princeton NJ 1997 pp. 89–90.

10. See H. Flam, M. J. Flanders (eds.) *Heckscher-Ohlin Trade Theory*, MIT Press, Cambridge (MA) 1991.

11. E. F. Heckscher, *Mercantilism*, new edition in two volumes, Routledge, London 1994; first published in Swedish in 1931, translated into German in 1934, into English in 1935, with a revised edition in 1955.

concerning specialisation and the division of labour in Book I. Indeed, seen in this light Smith's 'theory of international trade' looks more like Böhm-Bawerk's capital theory than any conception of vent for surplus or absolute or comparative advantage.[12]

Ever since *Wealth of Nations* was published in March 1776, readers have paid most attention to the early parts of the work; among the numerous summaries and extracts of Smith's work there is only one that deals in detail with the later books.[13] From the first, readers noted the curious ordering of topics adopted by Smith, and the intrusion of digressions that appeared to obstruct the smooth elaboration of his argument. Garnier in 1802 went so far as to provide a reading guide which rearranged the work; this survived in all French editions to mid-century; and, translated into English, in more than thirty editions of the text from 1805 to 1869. It was also reprinted in the third edition of Jeremiah Joyce's *Complete Analysis; or, Abridgment of Dr. Adam Smith's Inquiry into the Nature and Causes of the Wealth of Nations*;[14] and Joyce's treatment of Books I and II, together with Garnier, was the basis of Wolseley P. Emerton's *An Analysis of Adam Smith's Inquiry into the Nature and Causes of the Wealth of Nations Pt. I.*[15] From this, we might reasonably infer that Garnier's views on Smith's narrative strategy would have been, for at least two-thirds of the nineteenth century, those most commonly encountered by the average reader, not only in Britain and America, but also in most of Continental Europe.

So what approach to Smith did Garnier recommend? His preface was divided into three: a summary exposé of Smith's 'doctrines' as compared to those of the Physiocrats; a 'method' to ease the study of Smith's work; and a comparison of the wealth of France and Britain conducted in Smith's terms. The original English translation of Garnier's preface excluded this third section, subsequent editions reprinting this version. Garnier characterised Smith's doctrine as 'simple and true'.[16] But, he continued, this

12. Böhm-Bawerk opens his theoretical account of capital with the statement that all human production involves the 'spatial displacement of material' (*Raumversetzung des Stoffes*) (p. 11) and proceeds to define capital as an intermediate good involved in 'roundabout production' which takes varying amounts of time: Eugen von Böhm-Bawerk, *Positive Theorie des Kapitals (Kapital und Kapitalzins Zweite Abtheilung)*, Verlag der Wagner'schen Universitäts-Buchhandlung, Innsbruck 1889.

13. S. H. Hodwala, *An Analysis of Adam Smith's Inquiry into the Nature and Causes of the Wealth of Nations. Books III–V*, Commercial Press, Bombay 1901.

14. G & W. B. Whittaker, London 1821.

15. James Thornton, Oxford 1877; in 1880 Emerton brought out Part II, and in 1881 reissued the whole in one volume, primarily aimed at students in Oxford.

16. Germain Garnier, 'Préface du traducteur'. II. Une méthode pour faciliter l'étude de l'ouvrage de Smith", in his edition of *Recherches sur la nature et les causes de la richesse des nations*, H. Agasse, Paris An X 1802 p. xxiij.

does not strike the reader at once, for Smith has in common with other English writers a 'want of method' and a lack of appropriate 'didactic forms'—Smith, Garnier suggests, appears to have taken up his pen and just started writing in the first flush of enthusiasm for the marvels of the division of labour. Only subsequently does he define value, the laws that govern it, its composition, and the relationships among its various elements—preliminary notions all of which should, Garnier suggests, precede presentation of the mechanism of wealth. Smith also broke the flow of his narrative with long digressions—Garnier notes five, three of them in Book IV[17]—and while they were in themselves excellent, the reader lost sight of the principal object. Instead, Garnier suggests an order more in conformity with the natural chain of ideas, 'and for this reason best suited to teaching'. He begins

> by observing that Smith's entire doctrine on the formation, increase, and distribution of wealth is contained in his first two books, and the other three can be read separately, as separate treatises which in truth confirm and develop his doctrine, but do not complete it.[18]

Book III is a historical and political account of the natural progress of societies, and of the reasons why Europe has followed a contrary path; Book IV is a 'polemical treatise' criticising all hitherto existing systems of political economy, and above all that which he calls the 'mercantile system', of great influence on the financial legislation of European governments, and principally that of Britain. Book V deals with state expenditure and the most equitable and advantageous manner of taxation. These three Books can be read separately, being easily understood by every reader with a grasp of the body of doctrine outlined in the first two books.

> I therefore deal here with these first two books as a complete work, which I divide into three parts.[19]

Garnier does later provide a brief outline of Books IV and V, but his approach to the work as a whole and his account of the relative importance of the various parts was quickly accepted, and has generally prevailed up to the present.

17. Garnier, 'Préface', p. xxv.
18. Garnier, 'Préface', p. xxvj.
19. Garnier, 'Préface', pp. xxvij–xxviij. The parts run as follows: the first deals with value; the second with the general nature of wealth; and the third with the increase and distribution of wealth.

But *Wealth of Nations* has always been much more than this, and an alternative reading strategy is adopted here, taking its inspiration from 'Practical Criticism'.[20] To begin with, I assume that Smith composed his book in a particular way for a reason. He returned from his European tour and a spell in London to live with his mother at Kirkcaldy in 1767 and, reputedly, scarcely left the place until 1773, when he went back to London. During the six years in Kirkcaldy he worked on his book, and then dictated it to an amanuensis. For all my reluctance to read texts in terms of intentionality and 'authorship', we should at least give Smith credit for having put a great deal of time and thought into the composition of his book. Consequently, if we today find anomalies in the structure and argument of the work, our default position should be that this is more likely to be the outcome of the way we read it, rather than the way he wrote it. Furthermore, he made no revisions to the text after the third edition of 1786, whereas he continued to revise and rewrite *Theory of Moral Sentiments*, the final edition appearing in 1790, the year he died.

We need therefore to embark upon the kind of 'naive' reading that the principles of Practical Criticism dictate, looking at the text stripped of markers and interpretation, so that we might begin to discern arguments that were already buried by the practices of early nineteenth-century editors—Garnier, Buchanan, McCulloch—who supposed that editorial work amounted to the identification and correction of Smith's errors. *Wealth of Nations* is therefore read at face value: the structure of his argument is given priority, as it takes shape paragraph after paragraph, page after page, noting the reiterations and the connections made with earlier related points. For the moment I place on one side all wider context, borrowings and oversights, and Smith's influence on later writers; nor do I seek a thematic thread running through the book that can be linked to his other writings. The focus is here entirely upon the *sequence* of the argument formed in *Wealth of Nations*. This is not to deny the importance of intellectual context, nor of subsequent interpretation. But we should first register clearly what Smith actually wrote, and what he did not write. We therefore simply skip Book I entirely; while this does contain principles

20. The purpose of 'Prac Crit' was to direct attention to what is actually on the page, rather than associations with a received canon in the mind of the reader. Presenting students with samples of text stripped of reference to author or period, students struggled to evaluate them, and tended to favour exactly those texts that had been excluded from the canon for lack of literary merit—in their teachers' eyes, most students could not really tell 'good' from 'bad' literature and verse. The merits of Practical Criticism are considerable when dealing with texts embedded within generations of received opinion. See I. A. Richards, *Practical Criticism: A Study in Literary Judgement*, Kegan Paul, Trench, Trubner, London 1929.

central to his later arguments, they do not provide the explicit basis from which he begins, and I am here focusing on this explicit line of argument. A rather different work will begin to emerge: one that is better structured than has usually been assumed, where important general arguments are introduced and developed in the later books, which do more than provide the historical and critical context for principles previously elaborated.

Smith begins his account of the nature of international trade in the last chapter of Book II, where he discusses the different employments of capital, identifying four types corresponding to the different phases of the production process. Capital can be employed in the procurement of raw produce; in the use of this raw produce in the manufacture of goods; in the distribution of these goods to various markets; and in their sale to consumers. All persons whose capitals are employed in one of these trades are 'productive labourers'. But there are both more and less productive employments for capital:

> No equal capital puts into motion a greater quantity of productive labour that that of the farmer. Not only his labouring servants, but his labouring cattle, are productive labourers. In agriculture too nature labours along with man; and though her labour costs no expence, its produce has its value, as well as that of the most expensive workmen. (II.v.12)

There is a hint here of a feature of Smith's 'capital theory' that becomes an important theme of the following books: the 'efficiency' of capital, its capacity to increase wealth, is measured by the amount of labour that it employs. Underlying this is another criterion that Smith exposes later in Book IV: the importance of an investor being able to oversee directly the work of investment—straightforward in agriculture and certain forms of manufacturing, difficult in distant trading ventures. This principle trumps a fundamental point made in Book I. There it is argued that scope for the extension of the division of labour in agriculture is restricted, limiting the contribution agricultural production can make to the increase of wealth. By contrast, from the later sections of Book II agricultural investment is treated as the prime contributor to wealth, an idea which then informs the entire argument of Book III.

This new principle rests on the idea that agricultural labour directs the work of nature, which is the primary source of profit:

> It is the work of nature which remains after deducting or compensating every thing which can be regarded as the work of man. It is seldom less than a fourth, and frequently more than a third of the whole produce. No equal quantity of

> the productive labour employed in manufactures can ever occasion so great a reproduction. In them nature does nothing; man does all; and the reproduction must always be in proportion to the strength of the agents that occasion it. The capital employed in agriculture, therefore, not only puts into motion a greater quantity of productive labour than any equal capital employed in manufactures, but in proportion too to the quantity of productive labour which it employs, it adds a much greater value to the annual produce of the land and labour of the country, to the real wealth and revenue of its inhabitants. Of all the ways in which a capital can be employed, it is by far the most advantageous to society. (II.v.12)

Manufactures are next in importance to agriculture in adding value to the national product, while that employed in exports comes third. Here we begin to see why we need to begin Smith's analysis of international trade at the end of Book II.

> The country, indeed, which has not capital sufficient for all those purposes, has not arrived at that degree of opulence for which it seems naturally destined. To attempt, however, prematurely and with an insufficient capital, to do all the three, is certainly not the shortest way for a society, no more than it would be for an individual, to acquire a sufficient one. (II.v.20)

The final chapter of Book II therefore points strongly towards the argument of Book III, arguing that there is an optimal sequence for the investment of capital: beginning with agriculture, on to manufacture, and then lastly to overseas trade. The foundation for the argument concerning European economic development outlined in Book III is therefore built directly on this analysis of the relative advantages of different employment of capitals.

It is also in this final chapter of Book II that Smith introduces some comments upon American economic development. The rapid increase in the wealth of the American colonies is attributed to capital being invested principally in agriculture, the export and coastal trade being largely in the hands of merchants resident in Britain. Manufactured goods beyond those of the most rudimentary kind were chiefly imported from Europe; and this state of affairs would only be altered by protective measures for American producers, diverting capital from more productive to less productive ends and hence slowing the annual increase of wealth. This already foreshadows the key later argument on the gains from trade; Smith here suggests that Americans have a comparative advantage in agricultural production, and so they should specialise in this line of activity.

He then turns to three broad divisions of trade: domestic, foreign, and the 'carrying trade', the use of British shipping to trade between foreign ports. There are two features of importance here. First, the 'return on capital employed' is conceived in a physical sense—commodities flowing from one place to another over varying periods of time, reproducing in this way capitals employed in the trade itself and in the goods which are traded.

> When it sends out from the residence of the merchant a certain value of commodities, it generally brings back in return at least an equal value of other commodities. When both are the product of domestick industry, it necessarily replaces by every such operation two distinct capitals, which had both been employed in supporting productive labour, and thereby enables them to continue that support. The capital which sends Scotch manufactures to London and brings back English corn and manufactures to Edinburgh, necessarily replaces, by every such operation, two British capitals which had both been employed in the agriculture or manufactures of Great Britain. (II.v.25)

When applied to foreign trade, this argument is then used to show that one of the capitals 'replaced' is foreign. It is important to keep in mind here that the efficiency of capital is measured by the amount of (domestic) productive labour that it sets to work. Even if the returns were as rapid as in domestic trade, the capital employed in foreign trade will give only half 'the encouragement to the industry or productive labour of the country'. Since however returns are slow in foreign trading, the rate of circulation of capital in domestic trade is much higher than in foreign trade. This argument is further extended to distant trading where foreign goods are purchased through the sale of other foreign goods, although the initial trade would necessarily have been effected with domestic goods. The delay in receipt of any return, and the lack of stimulus to capital and labour in the home country when only the profit from such activity is repatriated, renders this form of economic activity even less attractive.[21]

> The capital, therefore, employed in the home-trade of any country will generally give encouragement and support to a greater quantity of productive labour in that country, and increase the value of its annual produce more than an

21. Arthur Bloomfield picks up on this line of argument, but translates it into modern terms as 'transport costs'—'Adam Smith and the Theory of International Trade', pp. 465–66.

> equal capital employed in the foreign trade of consumption: and the capital employed in this latter trade has in both these respects a still greater advantage over an equal capital employed in the carrying trade. The riches, and so far as power depends upon riches, the power of every country, must always be in proportion to the value of its annual produce, the fund from which all taxes must ultimately be paid. But the great object of the political œconomy of every country, is to encrease the riches and power of that country. It ought, therefore, to give no preference nor superior encouragement to the foreign trade of consumption above the home-trade, nor to the carrying trade above either of the other two. It ought neither to force nor to allure into either of those two channels, a greater share of the capital of the country than what would naturally flow into them of its own accord. (II.v.31)

We have therefore a natural ranking of employments for capital, first by domestic activity, then by the constraints posed by space and time on the periods of circulation of capitals employed in trade. This latter point is underwritten by the argument that the efficient use of capital is also related to the capacity of the owner to oversee its employment—the further from home that capital is employed, the greater the difficulty in ensuring that it is put to good use.

Books III and IV are constructed on these foundations—and Smith is remarkably consistent in reiterating these basic principles and reintroducing them at different stages of his argument. Private profit directs the flow of capital to its most efficient use, to where the returns are greatest; and where agriculture is the most profitable employment, 'the capitals of individuals will naturally be employed in the manner most advantageous to the whole society' (II.v.37). But in Europe the profits of agriculture appear to be low; fortunes are made in manufacturing and trade, not in agriculture, despite the fact that there remains considerable scope for agricultural investment. Why then, asks Smith, are urban traders at such an advantage? The following two books seek to answer this conundrum.

As with other eighteenth-century writers, Smith's contrast of agriculture and manufacture is doubled by that between country and town, notwithstanding the rural location of much early manufacturing enterprise:

> The great commerce of every civilized society, is that carried on between the inhabitants of the town and those of the country. (III.i.1)

Agricultural production is held to be necessarily prior to that of the town, for it is the rural surplus that subsists the town; and so urban economic activity can only increase if agriculture is flourishing, whether this be at home or abroad.

> That order of things which necessity imposes in general, though not in every particular country, is, in every particular country, promoted by the natural inclinations of man. If human institutions had never thwarted those natural inclinations, the towns could no-where have increased beyond what the improvement and cultivation of the territory in which they were situated could support; till such time, at least, as the whole of that territory was completely cultivated and improved. (III.i.3)

Likewise manufactured goods are required in the countryside, so that country people are drawn into the towns to exchange their produce—the inhabitants of the town and those of the country 'are mutually the servants of one another' (III.i.4). In North America, Smith continues, surplus capital was not employed in distant trading, but rather in the purchase and improvement of uncultivated land. And he concludes this opening chapter with a reiteration of the natural hierarchy in the employment of capital established in Book II chapter 5 and the observation that, in modern Europe, this had been inverted: manners and customs introduced by their original government 'necessarily forced them into the unnatural and retrograde order' (III.i.9).

This first chapter of Book III therefore elaborates an account of the natural progress of society out of the natural sequence for the employment of capital, concluding on exactly the same point made at the end of Book II chapter 5—that the development of European societies had followed an unnatural course. Since this unnatural course has been dictated by manners fostered by an earlier form of government, the next step is to outline quite how a form of human government might engender 'inverted manners and customs'. This is therefore a historical question, and the second chapter examines the neglect of agriculture in Europe after the fall of the Roman Empire. Whereas the Romans had divided and redivided land, the decline of the towns led to new centres of power based in the countryside, such that land was not only a means of subsistence, but also of power. Landholding became concentrated, and the tenants of a landowner his subjects. But, observes Smith, great proprietors were seldom great improvers:

> If the expence of his house and person either equalled or exceeded his revenue, as it did very frequently, he had no stock to employ in this manner [in improvement of land]. If he was an œconomist, he generally found it more profitable to

> employ his annual saving in new purchases, than in the improvement of his old estate. To improve land with profit, like all other commercial projects, requires an exact attention to small savings and small gains, of which a man born to a great fortune, even though naturally frugal, is very seldom capable. The situation of such a person naturally disposes him to attend rather to ornament which pleases his fancy, than to profit for which he has so little occasion. (III.ii.7)

And so here we can see emerging another important thread in Books III and IV, a kind of proto-Weberian *habitus* in which action is conditioned by legal and political circumstances. Whereas the political economy that followed on from Smith—of the Mills, Malthus, and Ricardo—imputed economic action according to the agent's formal position in an abstract system of production and distribution, Smith demonstrates here a far more nuanced approach, of greater explanatory power in the understanding of economic development. Not only do great proprietors show little practical interest in agricultural improvement; their retinues of tenants and slaves have in turn no incentive to improve land. What made a difference, for better or for worse, to the course of agricultural improvement was not the presence or absence of capital as such, but the motivations of landowners and tenants respectively, arising from the structure of incentives in which they found themselves. Institutional forms therefore engendered behaviour either favourable or unfavourable to economic development. As we shall see, Smith considered agricultural development to have the best chances of development where merchants retired to the countryside and brought with them a commercial spirit.

Book III chapter 3 considers the same post-Roman period from the point of view of the towns, originally occupied by poor tradesmen, who travelled with their wares, paying taxes and duties as they passed through manors or crossed bridges. In time, these and other revenues were farmed, as a rent for which citizens of emergent towns became jointly liable, leading in turn to the formation of corporations. New trading centres tended to side with the king against rural lords, forming islands of order in a sea of 'every sort of violence'. The Italian city-states were the first to achieve in this way some measure of opulence and security:

> The inhabitants of trading cities, by importing the improved manufactures and expensive luxuries of richer countries, afforded some food to the vanity of the great proprietors, who eagerly purchased them with great quantities of the rude produce of their own lands. The commerce of a great part of Europe in those times accordingly, consisted chiefly in the exchange of their own rude, for the manufactured produce of more civilized nations. (III.iii.15)

Having engendered a taste for refined goods, merchants sought to capitalise on the demand by local manufacture, saving the expense of carriage and the uncertainties of distant trading. Once established, any surplus from such manufacture was in turn made available for 'distant sale', whether the raw material be of domestic or foreign origin. An alternative model is then mooted by Smith, where an inland location inhibits the development of distant trading, and the resulting local abundance in agricultural produce reduces the price of foodstuffs, encouraging workmen to settle there; they

> find that their industry can there procure them more of the necessaries and conveniencies of life than in other places. They work up the materials of manufacture which the land produces, and exchange their finished work, or what is the same thing the price of it, for more materials and provisions. They give a new value to the surplus part of the rude produce, by saving the expence of carrying it to the water side, or to some distant market; and they furnish the cultivators with something in exchange for it that is either useful or agreeable to them, upon easier terms than they could have obtained it before. The cultivators get a better price for their surplus produce, and can purchase cheaper other conveniencies which they have occasion for. They are thus both encouraged and enabled to increase this surplus produce by a further improvement and better cultivation of the land; and as the fertility of the land had given birth to the manufacture, so the progress of the manufacture re-acts upon the land, and increases further still is fertility. The manufacturers first supply the neighbourhood, and afterwards, as their work improves and refines, more distant markets. For though neither the rude produce, nor even the coarse manufacture, could, without the greatest difficulty, support the expence of a considerable land carriage, the refined and improved manufacture easily may. (III.iii.20)

Hence, Smith continues, a piece of fine cloth weighing eighty pounds contains in it not only the price of eighty pounds of wool, but of several thousand weights of corn, which is the maintenance of the working people and their immediate employers. Corn, which could not have been carried abroad, is

> in this manner virtually exported in that of the complete manufacture, and may easily be sent to the remotest corner of the world. In this manner have grown up naturally, and as it were of their own accord, the manufactures of Leeds, Halifax, Sheffield, Birmingham, and Wolverhampton. Such manufactures are the offspring of agriculture. (III.iii.20)

Smith links the extension of trade to the reproduction of capital, and the manner in which he thinks of the employment of capital with respect to the labour which it sets to work—the greater the amount of 'industry' any one unit of capital employs, the greater its effectiveness in the promotion of national wealth—is extended here into an argument concerning the best distribution of that 'industry' within a country. There are important implications in this line of thought for Smith's later arguments concerning the relationships established between trading countries, and the manner in which countries differing in natural circumstances and endowments of capital and labour can engage in mutually beneficial trade.

He next passes to the 'retrograde' nature of European development—the fourth chapter of Book III is entitled 'How the Commerce of the Towns contributed to the Improvement of the Country'. There are three ways in which this occurs:

1. By affording a 'great and ready market' for the raw produce of the country further production of agricultural commodities is stimulated. As before, this is not confined to the home country, but is extended to all agricultural producers. However, the home country gains the greatest benefit from this trade, for lower carriage costs mean that growers get a better price, while from the standpoint of consumers the cost of home produce might be the same as for the produce of more distant markets.
2. The wealth of town dwellers is applied to the purchase of land, frequently uncultivated land. Merchants often aspire to the status of country gentlemen, and as such become the best improvers, given their commercial sense.
3. Commerce and manufactures gradually introduce 'order and good government' to all inhabitants of a country.

We might note here once more how, in the second point, Smith argues that what begins as a modish inclination ends as a positive outcome for the increase of national wealth.

> A merchant is accustomed to employ his money chiefly in profitable projects; whereas a mere country gentleman is accustomed to employ it chiefly in expence. (III.iv.3)

But this is not simply a prejudice; Smith immediately notes that in a country without foreign commerce there is no prospect of exchanging surplus produce, and so a great proprietor simply consumes the produce of his lands in 'rustick hospitality' (III.iv.5). He then resumes the argument of Book IV chapter 2, linking the power of government to the system of landed property. However, this system was undermined by foreign commerce and manufactures—economic activities attributed to the towns, but whose outcome was unforeseen by any party:

> A revolution of the greatest importance to the publick happiness, was in this manner gradually brought out by two different orders of people, who had not the least intention to serve the publick. To gratify the most childish vanity was the sole motive of the great proprietors. The merchants and artificers, much less ridiculous, acted merely from a view to their own interest, and in pursuit of their own pedlar principle of turning a penny wherever a penny was to be got. Neither of them had either knowledge or foresight of that great revolution which the folly of the one, and the industry of the other, was gradually bringing about. (III.iv.17)

And so, Smith concludes, throughout Europe the improvement of agriculture had been caused by the commerce of the cities, contrary to the natural course of development. This contrary form of development was, being unnatural, consequently hesitant and uncertain—unlike the progress that was evident in the North American colonies, whose wealth was securely founded in agriculture.

This reading of Book III in the context of the final chapter of Book II opens a new perspective. Accustomed as we are to think of Book III as a 'historical' account of the progress of nations, we instead find an argument related closely to Smith's account of the productivity of capital, measured by the amount of labour it sets to work; a conception of the conditions of economic action and economic 'personality'; and a contrast of European and North American development along the axis of economic development led by manufacturing and agriculture respectively. No wonder Smith was, in the eighteenth century, sometimes thought to be a Physiocrat.

Book IV opens with an introduction which divides all systems of political oeconomy into two: the mercantile and the agricultural systems. The former is, he considers, 'the modern system'. What is then 'modern' about the 'mercantile system'?

The first chapter outlines the principles of the 'commercial, or mercantile System', linking it initially with the idea that wealth consists in gold and silver, an idea rooted in the dual function of money as means of payment and measure of value (IV.i.2). A rich country, he goes on, is supposed to have much money; and there is some truth in this, since money is indeed required to prosecute foreign wars. Smith's subsequent argument is not directed against the folly of confusing money with wealth, but rather to policies that pursue the accumulation of money, rather than wealth. Efforts to hinder the export of bullion directly harmed trade, since merchants regarded gold and silver as the most convenient means for the purchase of foreign goods. And in a second line of argument, he points out that bullion could easily be smuggled, given its lack of bulk. Faced with such policies, merchants developed doctrines that rationalised their interests:

> That foreign trade enriched the country, experience demonstrated to the nobles and country gentlemen, as well as to the merchants; but how, or in what manner, none of them well knew. The merchants know perfectly in what manner it enriched themselves. It was their business to know it. But to know in what manner it enriched the country, was no part of their business. This subject never came into their consideration, but when they had occasion to apply to the country for some change in the laws relating to foreign trade. It then became necessary to say something about the beneficial effects of foreign trade, and the manner in which those effects were obstructed by the laws as they then stood. (IV.i.10)

Their arguments proved effective and the British government directed its attention to the balance of trade.

> From one fruitless case it was turned away to another case much more intricate, much more embarrassing, and just equally fruitless. The title of Mun's book, *England's Treasure in Foreign Trade*, became a fundamental maxim in political œconomy, not of England only, but of all other commercial countries. The inland or home trade, the most important of all, the trade in which an equal capital affords the greatest revenue, and creates the greatest employment to the people of the country, was considered as subsidiary only to foreign trade. It neither brought money into the country, it was said, nor carried any out if it. The country therefore could never become either richer or poorer by means of it, except so far as its prosperity or decay might indirectly influence the state of foreign trade. (IV.i.10)

Here again Smith reiterates his argument that capital employed in domestic trade provides a greater return than capital invested in foreign trade, for it brought about the highest level of employment, which in turn stimulated 'effectual demand', and since bullion was the most convenient store of value, easily transferred from one place to another, the quantity in any one place was likewise regulated by the effectual demand, stabilising its price. Therefore, if money was scarce, this meant that effectual demand was low—the means to acquire money were lacking. This is the important thrust of Smith's argument, and he dismisses the need to demonstrate that wealth is not money:

> It would be too ridiculous to go about seriously to prove, that wealth does not consist in money, or in gold and silver; but in what money purchases, and is valuable only for purchasing. (IV.i.17)

The point of his argument is different.

Money is desired, he reasons, for what can be purchased with it. Bullion is durable, transportable, and steady in value; it is therefore much sought after by those who wish to acquire goods. However, having reviewed the use of bullion in foreign wars, Smith concludes that only the king of Prussia had sought to accumulate money, and that in all eighteenth-century wars circulating money appears to have played a minor role. The costs of the previous war had in fact been defrayed by the export of commodities.

> The importation of gold and silver is not the principal, much less the sole benefit which a nation derives from its foreign trade. Between whatever places foreign trade is carried on, they all of them derive two distinct benefits from it. It carries out that surplus part of the produce of their land and labour for which there is no demand among them, and brings back in return for it something else for which there is a demand. It gives a value to their superfluities, by exchanging them for something else, which may satisfy a part of their wants, and increase their enjoyments. By means of it, the narrowness of the home market does not hinder the division of labour in any particular branch of art or manufacture from being carried to the highest perfection. By opening a more extensive market for whatever part of the produce of their labour may exceed the home consumption, it encourages them to improve its productive powers, and to augment its annual produce to the uttermost, and thereby to increase the real revenue and wealth of the society. (IV.i.31)

Here, much later in the book, Smith refers back for the first time to the title of Book I chapter 3—'That the Division of Labour is limited by the Extent of the Market'. Trade between two countries is of mutual benefit; trade permits specialisation. It does not matter that Smith thinks of the commodities traded as a domestic surplus;[22] what is important is that he conceives the benefits of trade as flowing from a mutual adjustment in the

22. I.e., as a 'vent for surplus'; Smith does adhere to the idea that exported goods are a surplus over and above domestic demand, but this is not important in his explanation of the gains from trade.

distribution of domestic resources—of capital and labour, since it is the increase of the former which permits the division of labour to advance, limited only by the 'extent of the market'. This particular brand of political oeconomy, he concludes, in supposing that wealth lay in gold and silver, sought to restrict imports and augment exports (IV.i.35). These twin principles provide the organising framework for the next six chapters.

Of interest here is the way that Smith makes his argument, rather than its details. First he looks at 'import substitution'.[23] From individual issues he quickly moves to a general point concerning the relation between the prevailing level of 'industry' and the amount of capital than can employ it:

> No regulation of commerce can increase the quantity of industry in any society beyond what its capital can maintain. It can only divert a part of it into a direction into which it might not otherwise have gone; and it is by no means certain that this artificial direction is likely to be more advantageous to the society than that into which it would have gone of its own accord. (IV.ii.3)

Individuals seek the best employments for their capital; for reasons earlier outlined—the time taken for the realisation of returns on capital, and the problems of control and supervision—each individual will invest as near home as possible. 'Home' is the centre 'round which the capitals of the inhabitants of every country are continually circulating, and towards which they are always tending' (IV.ii.6). Capital employed in the home trade puts a greater proportion of domestic industry into motion than that employed in foreign trade or consumption; and the investor is able to see that the capital is put to the best possible use, hence the most profitable use. And it is in exactly this context that we encounter Smith's famous metaphor:

> As every individual, therefore, endeavours as much as he can both to employ his capital in the support of domestick industry, and so to direct that industry that its produce may be of the greatest value; every individual necessarily labours to render the annual revenue of the society as great as he can. He generally, indeed, neither intends to promote the publick interest, nor knows how much he is promoting it. By preferring the support of domestic to that of foreign industry, he intends only his own security; and by directing that industry in such a manner as its produce may be of the greatest value, he intends only his own gain, and he is in this, as in many other cases, led by an invisible hand

23. Ch. 2 'Of Restraints upon the Importation from foreign Countries of such Goods as can be produced at Home'.

> to promote an end which was no part of his intention. . . . By pursuing his own interest he frequently promotes that of the society more effectually than when he really intends to promote it. I have never known much good done by those who affected to trade for the publick good. It is an affectation, indeed, not very common among merchants, and very few words need be employed in dissuading them from it. (IV.ii.9)

The individual, argues Smith, can judge the best employment of capital better than a statesman or a lawgiver. The very best state policy would only achieve what individuals, pursuing their own ends, generally bring about. Regulation is, therefore, either redundant, or harmful. And this returns us to the argument concerning the advantages of trade:

> What is prudent in the conduct of every private family, can scarce be folly in that of a great kingdom. If a foreign country can supply us with a commodity cheaper than we ourselves can make it, better buy it of them with some part of the produce of our own industry, employed in a way in which we have some advantage. The general industry of the country, being always in proportion to the capital which employs it, will not thereby be diminished, no more than that of the above-mentioned artificers; but only left to find out the way in which it can be employed with the greatest advantage. It is certainly not employed to the greatest advantage, when it is thus directed towards an object which it can buy cheaper than it can make. (IV.ii.12)

And so to use modern terminology: in an open economy trade inflows prompt internal readjustments in the employment of capital and labour, the produce of which will be exported in exchange for the imported goods, increasing the wealth of the country accordingly. There is not the slightest suggestion in this that trade arises out of natural advantages such as location, topography, or natural resources: there are no grounds in any of the foregoing to conclude that Smith's account of the gains from trade rests on the idea of absolute advantage. The underlying idea is quite plainly that the gains from trade, where international trade is thought expedient, rest on comparative advantage, on the rearrangement of capital and labour through the mechanism of the division of labour.

Having made this point, he does then introduce the absolute advantage argument: that to make wine in Scotland would cost thirty times more than anywhere else and so would be a poor use of resources.

> But if there would be a manifest absurdity in turning towards any employment, thirty times more of the capital and industry of the country, than would

> be necessary to purchase from foreign countries an equal quantity of the commodities wanted, there must be an absurdity . . . of exactly the same kind, in turning towards any such employment a thirtieth, or even a three hundredth part of either. (IV.ii.15)

An absolute disadvantage, such as this, would therefore, if pursued, simply tie up capital and labour more profitably employed elsewhere. Nonetheless, having reviewed various restrictive practices he concludes the chapter on a qualified note:

> To expect, indeed, that the freedom of trade should ever be entirely restored in Great Britain, is as absurd as to expect that an Oceana or Utopia should ever be established in it. Not only the prejudices of the publick, but what is much more unconquerable, the private interests of many individuals, inevitably oppose it. (IV.ii.43)

Chapter 3 turns to restraints on the import of goods from countries with whom an unfavourable balance of trade is thought to exist. This extends the bilateral argument made so far into a multilateral one, arguing that although a 'balance' might not exist between two countries, taking into account substitutions and adjustment to the mix of exports and imports with respect to third countries would show that an overall balance existed. Whereas under free trade between France and England the balance would probably be in favour of France, this would not be a general disadvantage if cheaper and better French wines were substituted for previous imports of Portuguese wine. It was not however possible to make this argument with any degree of accuracy since there was no firm evidence that could be used in estimating the balance, and this leads Smith into a digression on bills of exchange and the banking system. Returning from this, Smith once more makes his general point, built upon the analysis of employments of capital and labour to be found in Books I and II:

> Nothing, however, can be more absurd than this whole doctrine of the balance of trade, upon which, not only these restraints, but almost all the other regulations of commerce are founded. When two places trade with one another, this doctrine supposes that, if the balance be even, neither of them either loses or gains; but if it leans in any degree to one side, that one of them loses, and the other gains in proportion to its declension from the exact equilibrium. Both suppositions are false. A trade which is forced by means of bounties and monopolies, may be, and commonly is disadvantageous to the country in whose

> favour it is meant to be established, as I shall endeavour to shew hereafter. But that trade which, without force or constraint, is naturally and regularly carried on between any two places, is always advantageous, though not always equally so, to both.
>
> By advantage or gain, I understand, not the increase of the quantity of gold and silver, but that of the exchangeable value of the annual produce of the land and labour of the country, or the increase of the annual revenue of its inhabitants. (IV.iii.c.2)

By engaging in foreign trade, each country provides a market for a part of the surplus product of the other; this 'replaces' the respective capitals employed, and so in this way some inhabitants of a country will indirectly receive their income and maintenance from the activities of others. And concluding the chapter, Smith ties this up by suggesting that the balance of trade doctrine should be replaced by that of 'the balance of produce and consumption'.

The main lines of Smith's arguments have now been exposed, and we can briefly note their further development. The fourth chapter deals in a few pages with the effect of 'drawbacks' or tax relief on exported goods. Smith considers this to be a relatively harmless favour to merchants that does not disturb the existing allocation of capital, nor the balance between employments. But here again, it serves to point up Smith's leading principle: that consideration of foreign trade is necessarily linked to consideration of the disposition of capital and labour in the domestic economy. This is further underlined in the following chapter, dealing with bounties or export premia. These are payments made to foreigners so that they might buy goods that a country should not be producing; a bounty is thus a remedy for a want of demand that works by reducing the price to overseas purchasers. Hence domestic labour and capital is tied to one sector when it could be more profitably redeployed to another, offending against the best deployment of capital and labour.[24]

The sixth chapter is entitled 'Treaties of Commerce', and takes the 1703 Methuen Treaty as its principal example, reproducing the text in its entirety. Article I binds the Portuguese sovereign to admit British

24. Ricardo deals at length with the issue of bounties in ch. 22 of his *Principles*, but directs his attention entirely to their impact upon prices and the level of profit, not to the larger issue of the disposition of labour and capital—D. Ricardo, *On the Principles of Political Economy and Taxation*, ed. P. Sraffa, M. H. Dobb, *Works and Correspondence of David Ricardo* Vol. 1, Cambridge University Press, London 1951.

woollen cloth at the level of duties prevailing before it was prohibited. This involves no preferential treatment of British woollens. In return, Article II provides that the British sovereign will admit Portuguese wines subject to a tariff no higher than the prevailing duty on French wines minus one third (IV.vi.5). Portuguese wine is therefore afforded a permanent retail price advantage in respect of rival French wines. Smith notes that the terms of the treaty are advantageous to Portugal and disadvantageous to Britain. His subsequent discussion turns on the access to Portuguese gold, which was the rationale for the Methuen Treaty, but we should note that its terms relate back to the argument made in chapter 3 regarding the limitations of arguments regarding the 'balance of trade' between two countries. Smith introduced instead a model of multilateral trade; the Methuen Treaty is dealt with here only because it is a clear example of an existing commercial treaty. This was however the model that Ricardo took up, ignoring Smith's dismissal of conceptions of the 'balance of trade' implicit in bilateral models; and this was to prove a fatal move, since the two-good, two-country model became the core of the theory of international trade. Before concluding our discussion of Smith, we now need to consider how Ricardo constructed his own argument on trade, so that we might properly appreciate why the coherence of Smith's arguments on the gains from international trade was so quickly lost to view.

Ricardo's exposition of the gains from trade is based squarely on the Methuen Treaty: there are two countries, and the goods are wine and wool. As with the initial chapters of his *Principles*, Ricardo develops his argument as a critique and elaboration on Smith; but he ignores the bulk of what can be found in *Wealth of Nations*, forcing upon it a perspective in which the governing issue is the rate of profit, not the 'wealth of the nation'. Chapter 7 of *Principles* is not part of any general argument developed by Ricardo; the preceding chapter completes the argument that began with the discussion of value in chapter 1, and what then follows is at best a corollary, considering whether foreign trade might increase the amount of value in a country.

The rather tortured nature of Ricardo's chapter 'On Foreign Trade' is made clear by the way it begins by distinguishing 'value' from 'enjoyment', or welfare, then arguing that an extension of foreign trade cannot augment the amount of value in a country, for no matter how great the mass of imported commodities, their value is constant in domestic terms. He further contends that expenditure on imported commodities will diminish, in equal measure, the effective demand for domestically produced goods. What then might the 'gains from trade' be? Ricardo denies that the principles governing exchange within one economy are applicable to exchanges made between economies:

> The same rule which regulates the relative value of commodities in one country, does not regulate the relative value of the commodities exchanged between two or more countries.[25]

This distinction is alien to Smith, who when differentiating domestic and foreign trade introduces arguments relating to time and space that do modify the conditions of exchange, but not the principle regulating such exchange. And it gets even worse. Under a system of 'perfectly free commerce', states Ricardo,

> each country naturally devotes its capital and labour to such employments as are most beneficial to each. . . . It is this principle which determines that wine shall be made in France and Portugal, than corn shall be grown in America and Poland, and that hardware and other goods shall be manufactured in England.[26]

While the first sentence is compatible with the idea of opportunity cost, the examples he gives strongly suggest absolute advantages. In the next paragraph Ricardo considers the level of profits, arguing that while profits might equalise between London and Yorkshire, this will not occur between countries under open and free commerce, for in his argument capital and labour are immobile between countries.

These early passages in Ricardo's chapter on foreign trade entirely lack the systematic approach of Smith. Each paragraph seems to start an entirely new line of argument unconnected with that preceding, lending some plausibility to the suggestion that Ricardo had inserted these passages on trade at the behest of James Mill, but failed to integrate them with his own argument. And it is only six pages into the chapter that Ricardo suddenly changes tack and begins a discussion of production in a closed economy, contrasted with the employment of resources in an open economy. Portugal is the closed economy, and England the partner in an open economy. By comparing the number of men in each required to make respectively wine and cloth, Ricardo can show that trade between them results in a greater production of wool and cloth than would prevail if no

25. Ricardo, *Principles*, p. 133.
26. Ricardo, *Principles*, pp. 133–34.

trade took place. But since he insists on dealing in labour time, his conclusion runs as follows:

> Thus England would give the produce of the labour of 100 men, for the produce of the labour of 80. Such an exchange could not take place between individuals of the same country. The labour of 100 Englishmen cannot be given for that of 80 Englishmen, but the produce of the labour of 100 Englishmen can be given for the produce of the labour of 80 Portuguese, 60 Russians, or 120 East Indians.[27]

We have seen that Smith had developed out of Book II an elaborate argument on the gains from trade before introducing the 'wool and wine' model. Ricardo simply begins from this model; it is neither apparent that he takes it from Smith, nor that Smith was writing about the Methuen Treaty. It could be said that Ricardo, arguing through 'wool and wine' in this way, introduced a major confusion into discussion of the gains from trade of which Smith is entirely innocent. Even where Ricardo introduces the idea of technical innovation, capital investment, and consequent readjustment to the pattern of trade, he argues from wine and wool rather than, as in Smith, capital and labour.[28] English wool and Portuguese wine do initially represent absolute production advantages enjoyed by England and Portugal respectively, a point which is easily grasped; but which blurs the distinction between comparative and absolute advantages. Furthermore, in *Wealth of Nations* France served as an alternative supplier of wines, suggesting that while French wine might end up more expensive than that of Portugal, the consumption of better French wine in reduced quantities might still raise the general level of welfare. From his starting point it is clear that this sort of argument would not interest Ricardo, and highlights the difference between Smith's concern with wealth and welfare, and Ricardo's with the rate of profit.

James Mill sought to clarify aspects of Ricardo's account in his *Elements of Political Economy*, in section IV of the chapter on 'interchange': 'Occasions on which it is the interest of Nations to exchange Commodities with one another'. He sets up the problem much more clearly by choosing corn and cloth as the goods, assuming that two countries have no natural advantage, but that one might enjoy an advantage in labour productivity over the other for both goods. He chooses numbers for Poland and England, cloth and corn, showing that in some cases there would be an

27. Ricardo, *Principles*, p. 135.
28. Ricardo, *Principles*, pp. 137–38.

advantage in Poland importing cloth in exchange for corn, in other cases not, concluding:

> When a country can either import a commodity or produce it at home, it compares the cost of producing at home with the cost of procuring from abroad; if the latter cost is less than the first, it imports.
>
> The cost at which a country can import from abroad depends, not upon the cost at which the foreign country produces the commodity, but upon what the commodity costs which it sends in exchange, compared with the cost which it must be at to produce the commodity in question, if it did not import it.[29]

The entire exposition takes less than four pages, and is considerably more lucid than Ricardo. The importance of clear definition and exposition, not to mention choosing suitable numbers in an example, was underscored by McCulloch's own brief treatment of this issue in his *Encyclopaedia Britannica* entry 'Political Economy' of 1823. No explicit mention is made here of productivity differences; his numerical example (Poland and England, wool and wheat) simply assumes this, and having selected numbers that inadvertently present complementary absolute advantages, derives from this an argument about exchanges based upon comparative advantages.[30] The more often this passage is read, the murkier it becomes, and one can only conclude that McCulloch's own grasp of the underlying logic was tenuous. This suspicion is reinforced by the way that he next cites a passage from Mill's *Commerce Defended* of 1808, which talks in general terms of the advantages of trade, but not specifically in terms of comparative advantage where there is no absolute advantage.[31]

This brief excursion into the early history of 'Ricardian' trade theory serves to point up one major fact: by the 1820s Adam Smith's own account

29. Mill, *Elements*, op. cit. p. 273.

30. J. R. McCulloch, *Political Economy*, reprinted from Supplement to the *Encyclopaedia Britannica* Vol. 6 Part 1 (1823), London 1825, p. 29 col. 2. The choice of numbers and the unarticulated introduction of the differential productivity of labour—he works not in different numbers of hours or men, but in the same number of men producing different quantities—obscures the point he seeks to make.

31. Marx did not understand the principle of comparative advantage either. Making notes on Mill's *Unsettled Questions* in the summer of 1845, he wrote down (in German) the following passage from pp. 2–3 of Mill's text: 'The bargain is still advantageous to the foreigner, because the commodity which he receives in exchange, though it has cost us less, would have cost him more'. Marx added the comment: 'Schöner Unsinn!'—*Karl Marx, Friedrich Engels Gesamtausgabe* Bd. IV/4 p. 329, Dietz Verlag, Berlin 1988.

of the advantages and disadvantages of international trade had been entirely effaced, and henceforth the principles advanced by Ricardo and the two Mills would form the basis of any discussion. However incoherent McCulloch's attempt to expound these principles might be, he was clear that these were the relevant principles. And, in time, commentators would look for these principles in Smith's *Wealth of Nations* and fail to find them, concluding that Smith lacked a consistent account of the growth of international trade.

From the above we can draw two conclusions. First, Smith's narrative structure is much tighter than usually credited, for I have shown how closely his arguments are built progressively upon previously elaborated concepts and propositions. Apart from one reference back to the account of division of labour in Book I, all of the citations above follow in sequence. It is possible to understand Smith's line of argument by reading one paragraph after another. True, the care with which he went to work tended to load his prose with qualifications and deviations, a matter for complaint by readers from the later eighteenth century to the present. But underlying this diffuseness there is a remarkably consistent argument.

Second, I have shown that Smith does indeed conceive the gains from trade in a framework that highlights the comparative, and not absolute, advantages from which the gains from trade flow. Furthermore, this account of the gains from trade underlies a model of international economic development far broader in scope than that of Ricardo. Indeed, once this underlying structure in Smith's work is clarified, one is unavoidably struck by the lack of purpose and system in the account of trade to be found in Ricardo's *Principles*. The clarity of the Ricardian model of comparative advantage is spurious; read in context, it prompts more questions that it resolves. His principal discussion of the gains from trade turns out on closer inspection to be poorly structured, dominated not by larger conceptions of the efficiency with which resources are employed for the generation of welfare, but with the much more limited issue of the impact upon prices and profitability.

But we also know that the reputation of Smith as a proponent of the welfare gains from free trade does not rest upon these arguments; this reputation is derived instead from the general principles he advanced, not from a clear understanding of the analysis he developed in Books III and IV of *Wealth of Nations*. Throughout the nineteenth century, Smith's name was associated with free trade because of the principle of natural liberty, and because the 'division of labour is limited by the extent of the market'. Having here demonstrated that there is a far more sophisticated, yet unacknowledged, analysis of the gains from trade buried in the *Wealth of Nations*, we are left with the paradox that it has made little impression during the two centuries of debate over the gains and losses in international trade. Nobody seems to have noticed; or, perhaps, it has been assumed that the substance of Smith's analysis of foreign trade is inconsequential. Nonetheless, there has been a larger purpose here: to direct attention to the importance of a close reading of Smith's words.

CHAPTER 5

Das Adam Smith Problem and the Origins of Smith Scholarship

In 1892 L. L. Price read a paper on Adam Smith to the annual meeting of Section F of the British Association. He opened as follows:

> It is with a feeling of some hesitancy that I submit to the Economic Section of the British Association these fragmentary and inadequate remarks. To say anything new on Adam Smith is not easy; but to say anything of importance or profit, which has not been said before, is well-nigh impossible.[1]

The idea that serious discussion of Adam Smith had run its course was a commonplace in later nineteenth-century Britain. But that Price shared this view is itself significant, for he was part of that Oxford generation of political economists which included W. J. Ashley, L. T. Hobhouse, Llewellyn Smith, W. A. S. Hewins, and also of course Edwin Cannan, all of whom graduated between 1881 and 1887 and were members of the Oxford Economic Society.[2] Arnold Toynbee's early death had brought Alfred Marshall to Balliol as his successor and heir apparent to the Oxford chair; only the premature death of Henry Fawcett in late 1884[3] took him away again to

1. L. L. Price, 'Adam Smith and his Relation to Recent Economics', *Economic Journal* Vol. 3 (1893) p. 239. Price (1862–1950) had graduated in Lit Hum in 1885, became the first Toynbee Trust lecturer in 1886, and was a fellow of Oriel College, Oxford from 1888 to 1923.
2. During the 1880s Oxford was at the centre of British political economy—see Alon Kadish, *The Oxford Economists in the Late Nineteenth Century*, Oxford University Press, Oxford 1982.
3. Fawcett was fifty-one and died from pneumonia.

Cambridge. Moreover, in 1891 Price had published an account of political economy 'from Adam Smith to Arnold Toynbee', the first chapter summarising some aspects of *Wealth of Nations* and mentioning *Theory of Moral Sentiments* just once, as a treatise published in 1759.[4] There was no mention of the work at all in his address to Section F. The name of Smith was firmly linked to one book, the *Wealth of Nations*, and Dugald Stewart's outline of Smith's larger project was as good as forgotten.

Since the 1860s English-language editions of *Wealth of Nations* had been published more or less annually,[5] and *Theory of Moral Sentiments* at regular intervals (1861, 1871, 1880, 1887, and 1892). There was however little serious discussion of these individual works;[6] and none at all of their putative relationship. The fact that McCulloch's 1828 edition of *Wealth of Nations*, with its extensive critical notes, was last published more or less unaltered in 1872 suggests that Smith's work had by the 1880s long passed into the limbo of famous works that were bought, perhaps read through, but not studied. As Haldane remarked, while Smith would be remembered as the founder of modern political economy, the *Wealth of Nations* was decidedly not, as Buckle had once argued, 'the most important book ever written'. Indeed,

> As we become removed by an ever-increasing distance from the prejudices and opinions which Adam Smith once for all shattered, their magnitude and importance appears to grow smaller. It is safe to affirm that even the battle between Free Trade and Protection will never again be fought upon the ground from which Adam Smith drove his opponents. Here, as in almost every other particular, the controversies of political economy turn upon new issues, however they may resemble the old disputes in name.[7]

And so Haldane regarded *Wealth of Nations* in much the same way as Bagehot did—as 'a very amusing book about old times'.[8] They also concurred on the importance, or rather lack of it, of *Theory of Moral Sentiments*—for

4. *A Short History of Political Economy in England from Adam Smith to Arnold Toynbee*, Methuen, London 1891 ch. 1: 'Adam Smith. (1723–1790.) The Division of Labour' p. 4. The book was part of the University Extension Series.

5. See Keith Tribe, with Hiroshi Muzuta (eds.) *A Critical Bibliography of Adam Smith*, Pickering and Chatto, London 2002 pp. 366–67.

6. An exception that should be noted is J. A. Farrer, *Adam Smith (1723–1790)*, Sampson, Lowe, Marston, Searle, & Rivington, London 1881, which contained an extensive discussion of *Theory of Moral Sentiments*.

7. R. B. Haldane, *Life of Adam Smith*, Walter Scott, London 1887 pp. 12–13.

8. Walter Bagehot, 'Adam Smith as a Person', *Fortnightly Review* Vol. 20 New Series (1876) p. 37.

Bagehot it was a once well-regarded book but was no longer of much philosophical value.[9] Haldane thought it 'delightful reading . . . in every reference, excepting that of the systematic study of the subject which it professes to expound. . . . As a work on Moral Philosophy it is dull and unedifying'.[10]

If we also bear in mind that biographical detail for Smith has always been very slight, and that at this time the same few biographical points originally culled from Dugald Stewart's 'Account of the Life and Writings of Adam Smith, LL.D.' were the only context given to his writings, then we can begin to appreciate how anodyne and routine accounts of Smith had become in the Britain of the early 1890s. The name of Adam Smith was one firmly associated with *Wealth of Nations*; the early political economists had developed their theories of value and distribution in criticism of this work; but by the time that John Stuart Mill published his *Principles* in 1848 Smith was firmly part of the past of political economy. His name lived on generally associated with free trade and economic liberty, but without serious examination of the arguments that Smith had advanced in support of these principles. During the century following his death there was very little scholarly engagement with the writings of Smith[11] in the English language that went beyond that of the political economists in the first two decades. His early editors—Playfair, Buchanan, McCulloch, Wakefield—understood their work as the identification, explanation, and correction of Smith's errors, so that the bulk of their commentary and notes is devoted to their own (allegedly superior) explanations. They were entirely uninterested in the intellectual and political contexts within which Smith had composed his works.

There is one notable exception to this sorry story: the publication in 1861 of the second volume of Buckle's *History of Civilization in England*, which contained a detailed commentary on Smith's two books and which presented the first coherent account of Smith's intellectual project after Stewart's 'Account'. But this went unremarked in discussions of political economy in Britain; and Haldane's casual dismissal of Buckle cited above refers only in passing to a passage in the first volume,[12] otherwise studiously ignoring the more extensive arguments that Buckle advanced in the second. This was entirely typical of what passed for comment on Smith in Britain from 1860 to 1890.

9. Ibid. pp. 26–28.
10. Haldane, *Life* p. 57.
11. Besides Stewart, Buckle, and Farrer.
12. Henry Thomas Buckle, *History of Civilization in England* Vol. 1, John Parker and Son, London 1857 p. 194.

This was of course about to change. When Price published his *Short History* Edwin Cannan was already working on his *History of Theories of Production and Distribution*, a book that would establish new standards for the appraisal of historical works in political economy. Following its submission to Macmillan, it was read for them by Foxwell, who evidently understood very little of it, and Macmillan rejected it in May 1892.[13] Cannan found a new publisher and settled to revise the manuscript, publication following in May 1893. Sales were disappointing: 169 copies in 1893, 81 in 1894, and 21 copies up to May 1895.[14] Macmillan declined the opportunity to distribute the book in the United States; as his publisher explained, 'It is not apparently a question of price but of want of demand for such a book'.[15]

Edwin Cannan was a man of independent means and so these setbacks did not deflect him from pursuit of his interest in political economy. In the spring of 1895 the manuscript of Smith's lectures came into his hands and in the autumn of 1896 Smith's *Lectures on Justice, Police, Revenue and Arms* was published by Oxford University Press.[16] Quite apart from the very important substance of these lectures, Cannan set entirely new standards for the editing of Smith's texts, redirecting attention to the question of Smith's sources in the composition of his two works, and the nature of the project upon which he had engaged. Nonetheless, when he turned to the substantive import of the lectures in the 'Editor's Introduction' it is clear that his thoughts turned primarily on the evidence that could be found in the *Lectures* for the originality, or lack of it, of *Wealth of Nations*, and not on the place of this book within Smith's larger body of work. At this time Cannan, along with most other English writers, seems to have been unaware that this latter issue had been subjected to debate in Germany.[17]

13. Macmillan and Co. to Cannan, 5 May 1892, London Correspondence with Publishers I 1890–1916. BLPES Archive, Cannan Collection 1018 f.2; H. S. Foxwell, Reader's Report on Cannan, 'English Political Economy' 6 May 1892, Macmillan Archives, BL Add. Ms. 55946 f.63–70 (Foxwell's letter is transcribed in the letterbook and therefore postdates the letter of rejection).

14. Percival & Co., to Cannan, 28 May 1895 34 King Street, Covent Garden BLPES Cannan Collection 1018 f.16. The book was published by Rivington, Percival & Co, the title page bearing the date 1894.

15. Percival & Co., to Cannan, 20 February 1893, 34 King Street, Covent Garden BLPES Cannan Collection 1018 f.12.

16. See my discussion of this in 'Adam Smith in English: From Playfair to Cannan' in *Critical Bibliography of Adam Smith* pp. 43–45.

17. Some of this German literature is listed in the 'Bibliography' to Haldane's *Life* (Inama-Sternegg (1876), Leser (1874), Wilhelm Neurath (1884), Oncken (1874, 1877), Oesler (1871), Skarżyński (1878), Stöpel (1879)); but Haldane refers to none of this in his book, and in any case the bibliography was compiled by John Anderson of the British Museum, not by Haldane.

The following year August Oncken published a survey of German writing on Smith, remarking that

> It does not seem to be understood in Great Britain that, on the Continent, there is a difference of opinion about one fundamental point in Adam Smith's system—a difference which, at one time, gave rise to some sharp polemics, and which is not yet settled. The question may be stated thus: —Are the two principal works of Adam Smith, the *Theory of Moral Sentiments* (1759) on the one hand, and the *Inquiry into the Nature and Causes of the Wealth of Nations* (1776) on the other, two entirely independent works, contradicting each other in their fundamental principles, or are we to regard the latter simply as a continuation of the former, though published at a later date, and both as presenting, when taken together, a comprehensive exposition of his moral philosophy?[18]

As Oncken noted, the publication of the *Lectures* dissolved this 'Adam Smith Problem' once and for all. Argument that the first book was owed chiefly to the influence of Hutcheson and Hume, while the inspiration for the second came from French sources encountered during his time in France—the line taken by the most extreme exponent of the 'Problem', Witold Skarżyński—was fatally undermined by the clear presentation of many of the arguments later elaborated in *Wealth of Nations* in a text originating in 1763, before Smith had left for France, and in a framework which strongly suggested the presence of a general project of which the two books were merely part.

Some thirty years later much of this argument had been revised and integrated into a new appraisal of Smith's work, notably by writers in North America such as Morrow, Viner, and Hollander, who all presented lectures at the University of Chicago during the winter of 1926 to 1927 to mark the 150th anniversary of the publication of *Wealth of Nations*.[19] But the first indication that these hitherto 'German' discussions had any resonance in the English language can be found at the very end of the 1890s. First of all, Leslie Stephen's essay on Adam Smith for the *Dictionary of National Biography* noted the importance of Hasbach's 1891 *Untersuchungen*, and concluded his account of *Wealth of Nations* by listing other monographs on Smith's relation to other writers: these are Oncken's 'A. Smith und Immanuel Kant' (1877), Feilbogen's 'Smith und Turgot'

18. August Oncken, 'The Consistency of Adam Smith', *Economic Journal* Vol. 7 (1897) p. 444.

19. Published in the *Journal of Political Economy* Vol. 35 (June 1927) and then separately as J. M. Clark et al., *Adam Smith, 1776–1926*, University of Chicago Press, Chicago 1928.

(1893), and Skarzynski's 'Adam Smith als Moralphilosoph und Schöpfer der Nationalökonomie'.[20]

The following year Bastable published an extensive review essay on the *Lectures* which was also distinguished by its attention to German commentary. He opens by noting the recent extension of materials available for an understanding of the origins of political economy, noting the work of James Bonar (on Smith's library), Hollander's work on Ricardo, the new edition of Turgot's *Réflexions*, the Harvard edition of Cantillon, the edition of Quesnay's *Tableau* edited by Henry Higgs under the auspices of the British Economic Association—and the work of Schelle, Hasbach, Oncken, Bauer, and Knies.[21] Drawing upon these sources, Bastable invents a new 'Adam Smith Problem', suggesting that comparison of the *Lectures* with the *Wealth of Nations* would reveal what Smith really had taken from the Physiocrats, identifiable by arguments present in the latter but absent from the former. Bastable then argues that the linking of a distributive structure to the components of price does come from the *Tableau*:

> The physiocratic idea that the sum of produce is divided by economic laws amongst definite classes, themselves called into existence by economic conditions, was a fascinating one, which the writer of a great constructive work would naturally appreciate and employ in his own way. This is precisely what Adam Smith has done. He has worked the conception of shares of produce into his theory of the factors of prices. Rent, profit, and wages appear as the determining elements or, in his language, 'component parts' of the price of commodities.[22]

This contrasts with the fact that wages are the only component considered in *Lectures*. Cannan in his introduction to the *Lectures* had simply listed the principal discrepancies between *Wealth of Nations* and the *Lectures*; Bastable next considered their relative importance for Smith's arguments.

> The most important omission, however, is that of the two opening sections of the lectures on 'Cheapness or Plenty', entitled 'The Natural Wants of Mankind', and 'The Arts are subservient to the Natural Wants of Mankind'. These sections, brief as they are, indicate by their position that, in Adam Smith's opinion, the first problem for the economic student is the character of man's needs.[23]

20. Leslie Stephen, 'Adam Smith', *Dictionary of National Biography* Vol. 53, Smith, Elder, London 1898 pp. 9, 10.
21. C. F. Bastable, 'Adam Smith Lectures on "Jurisprudence"', *Hermathena* Vol. 10 (1899) p. 200.
22. Ibid. p. 203.
23. Ibid. p. 207.

We should first of all note that Bastable considers that the organisation of Smith's argument gives us guidance on what he is seeking to argue—a perspective as rare then as now. This enables him to highlight the importance for Smith of that very un-English economic concept of 'man's needs'. Bastable then directly commented upon Hermann's *Staatswirthschaftliche Untersuchungen*, stating that Hermann, in placing 'needs' before 'productive effort', did not correct, but revive, Smith's arguments from the period before he became acquainted with Physiocratic argument:

> The study of Society as an economic machine presupposes the existence of objects for which that machine is to work. Had there been no disturbing influence, it is at least possible that the opening chapters of the *Wealth of Nations* would have described the growth of wants in civilized societies, and shown how their increasing subdivision and differentiation insensibly produced a corresponding division of employments, and permitted more effective, because more specialized, kinds of labour. But the aspect of society as working to produce, overshadowed, in the minds of the French economists, the parallel view of society as using its products. 'Accumulation' became more important than 'satisfaction'; and Adam Smith was persuaded to abandon this section of his system, contenting himself with laying down, at an advanced part of his treatise, that 'consumption is the end and purpose of all production' (Book IV chap. 8), and introducing scattered notices of the effect of changes in the modes of expenditure. If his connexion with France enabled him to gain a more scientific position in respect to the partition of produce, may it not have induced him to abandon quite as valuable a conception, viz. the dependence of the economic system on the nature and variation of human wants?[24]

While the foregoing only sketches the English appraisal of Smith in the late nineteenth century, it would be hard to find anything of English provenance that might have motivated the sophistication of these remarks. The casual mention of Hermann in this context was also highly unusual—it is true at this time that many British economists followed developments in recent Continental theory much more closely than often credited, but when writers fell to thinking about Adam Smith this disposition was entirely absent. The idea that one might profit from attention to foreign commentary on an English, Scottish, or Irish writer was quite alien. By contrast, Bastable shows (quite unselfconsciously) what happened if one did. But this line of argument cannot be extended here, for it is time that

24. Ibid. pp. 207–8.

we examine more directly the course taken by German commentary on Smith in the second half of the nineteenth century.

First of all, I am not intending here to deal with the phenomenon of *Smithianismus*.[25] I disregard here the casual linkage of Smith's name with 'abstract', 'formal' economic principles that became a reflex for German historical economists, and reached its nadir with Schmoller's 1897 inaugural address as rector of the University of Berlin.[26] I have dealt elsewhere with the publishing history of Smith's works in German, and so will not directly address this issue either.[27] I will restrict myself here to demonstrating that the German elaboration of *Das Adam Smith Problem*, whose German attribution is reflected in precisely this phrasing, was indeed a mistaken idea, but one which stimulated argument about the significance of Smith's work and the nature of any project that he might have been pursuing. As we have seen, such argument was absent from English commentary on Smith; and more generally, while the origination of English 'Smith scholarship' is largely attributable to the efforts of Edwin Cannan, the placing of Smith in a wider intellectual context was first essayed by German scholars long before Cannan's work.

Central to the German story is the translation, and immediate popularity, of Buckle's *History of Civilization* volume 2. This work remained the touchstone for later discussion since few German scholars had direct access to *Theory of Moral Sentiments* in German translation, and it was not as usual for Germans in the 1860s and 1870s to read English as later became the case. Two German translations of *Theory of Moral Sentiments* had been published in the eighteenth century (1770 and 1791/95); the second, edited and commented on by Kosegarten, was an important work in its own right. But German university libraries did not routinely purchase translations of English works at this time,[28] and no new German edition was available to readers until Eckstein's edition of 1926. Discussion among German scholars during the second half of the nineteenth century of the importance of *Theory of Moral Sentiments* developed in the

25. In its positive sense this was best represented by John Prince-Smith—see Harald Hagemann, Matthias Rösch, 'German Economists in Parliament (1848–1919)' in M. M. Augello, M. Guidi (eds.), *Economists in Parliament in the iberal Age (1848–1920)*, Ashgate, Aldershot 2005 pp. 176–78.

26. Outlined very perceptively by August Oncken as a 'Correspondent' of the British Economic Association in his 'New Tendencies in German Economics', *Economic Journal* Vol. 9 (1899) pp. 462–69.

27. See my 'The German Reception of Adam Smith' in *Critical Bibliography* pp. 120–52; the following draws in part on this account.

28. For example, the Heidelberg Universitätsbibliothek does possess the first translation, but not that of Kosegarten.

absence of readily available copies of the work; debate over the importance of *Theory of Moral Sentiments* for an understanding of Smith's work failed to prompt even one reissue of an existing translation. Put more bluntly: many of those who argued in German about *Theory of Moral Sentiments* had quite probably not read the book.

The origin of the 'Problem' lies in Hildebrand's *Nationalökonomie der Gegenwart und Zukunft*, which opened with a critique of Smith and his 'School'. Towards the end of this first chapter, having repeated List's allegation of 'cosmopolitanism' against Smith, Hildebrand turned to deal with Smith's atomistic conception of civil society, and the 'egoism' of his analysis.[29] The main line of criticism that Hildebrand made was ethical, rather than historical, the 'philosophical context' that he sketched out for Smith not being one which took account of *Theory of Moral Sentiments*. A few years later, composing his own critique of political economy, Knies noted Hildebrand's charge that Smith assumed self-interest always to coincide with the common good; he pointed out that Hildebrand was merely repeating here a misconception which by then was into its third generation. Knies was emphatic that, although Smith had treated self-interest as the basic human motivation in the economic domain,[30] the idea that unhindered individual action necessarily leads to the common good was a later accretion, and had no origin with Smith himself. This is demonstrated by a series of citations from *Wealth of Nations* where for one reason or another Smith contrasts the individual interest to the common good.[31] He also demonstrates that this habitual identification of the common good with the pursuit of self-interest can be seen at work in Stirner's translation, where a passage that in Smith reads: 'By pursuing his own interest he frequently promotes that of the society more effectually than when he really intends to promote it' becomes in Stirner: 'If every individual pursues his

29. B. Hildebrand, *Die Nationalökonomie der Gegenwart und Zukunft*, Literarische Anstalt (J. Rütten), Frankfurt am Main 1848 pp. 29–33. This was conceived as the first of two volumes, dealing with the economic systems of 'the present'; but no treatment of 'the future' ever appeared.

30. Proper appreciation of Smith's argument on self-interest and self-love is of course very recent; Pierre Force's *Self-Interest before Adam Smith: A Genealogy of Economic Science*, Cambridge University Press, Cambridge 2003 clarifies the nature of these terms and their linkage to Rousseau. The routine attribution to Mandeville of the relation of self-interest to public good in Smith has likewise been dealt with by E. J. Hundert's *The Enlightenment's 'Fable': Bernard Mandeville and the Discovery of Society*, Cambridge University Press, Cambridge 1994. In my reconstruction of nineteenth-century arguments about these matters there seems little point in 'correcting' errors that would be commonplace for well over another century.

31. K. Knies, *Die politische Oekonomie vom Standpunkte der geschichtlichen Methode*, C. A. Schwetschke und Sohn, Brunswick 1853 pp. 149–50.

own interest, he promotes the interest of the society more effectively than if this had been his intention'.[32] Knies points to two other passages where the same elision is made by Stirner, and emphasises that such error only goes to reinforce a general misapprehension of Smith's position on the pursuit of self-interest and the realisation of the common good:

> the two principles—that private selfishness (*Privategoismus*) is the sole source of individual economic activity, or the sole such source to be considered; and that through free exercise of self-interest on the part of the individual the common good will be most effectively promoted—must be emphatically distinguished.[33]

Knies then passes to other systems of political economy, but returns to Smith following his account of Physiocratic doctrine, concluding:

> Not even the most decided admirer of the great Scot can doubt, once he has become more closely acquainted with their writings, that Smith henceforth stands on the broad shoulders of his Physiocratic friends. Smith adopted the greater part of their important results, together with their argument, which involved the interest of consumers; and besides this one will find hardly any discussion in his book as unsatisfactory as that where he seeks to oppose the doctrine of the Physiocrats, at the close of a work which, reputedly, he wished to dedicate to his teacher Quesnay. . . . it certainly cannot be regarded as a matter of coincidence that his stay in France falls between the publication of his *Theory of Moral Sentiment* [*sic*] and the political economy of his *Inquiry*.[34]

This appears to be the first explicit statement of the idea that there was a shift in approach between *Theory* and *Inquiry*, and that the explanation for the shift lies in Smith's encounter with French economists and philosophers. Although here stating the idea, Knies's book was not responsible for its diffusion, for as he later complained, it sold very slowly, and the second edition only appeared thirty years later.[35]

It might be helpful to summarise the chronology that will dominate the following discussion. Knies's comments (as with Bastable above) regarding the impact of Physiocratic argument was a common contextual move, for of course the Physiocrats were the only set of writers explicitly

32. Ibid. p. 150.
33. Ibid.
34. Ibid. pp. 179–80.
35. Knies, 'Vorwort' to *Die politische Oekonomie vom geschichtlichen Standpuncte*, C. A. Schwetschke und Sohn, Brunswick 1883 pp. iii, v.

named in Book IV of *Wealth of Nations*. The other 'system of Political Œconomy' was the 'Mercantile System', in which policy rather than systematic argument was the object of analysis. Given that the *Tableau* was first published in 1758, and then reprinted in condensed form in Mirabeau's *Philosophie rurale* of 1763, the timing here is very close. *Theory of Moral Sentiments* was written up from Smith's lectures and published in 1759. This was in the middle of the Seven Years' War, during which it can be surmised that literary communication between France and Britain would have been curtailed. The lectures published by Cannan date from the period immediately preceding Smith's resignation,[36] presenting therefore the state of argument and understanding with which he embarked for France in early February 1764. This was just one year after the Treaty of Paris had ended the war with France; he returned in October 1766, and spent the bulk of the following ten years preparing *Wealth of Nations* in Kirkcaldy. As we shall see, during the later nineteenth century this chronology could be easily resolved into the idea that *Theory of Moral Sentiments* was a predominantly 'English' work, and that any analytical differences with *Wealth of Nations* could be attributed to his lengthy and direct contact with French intellectuals.

The main lines of this disjunction were first clearly outlined in the second volume of Buckle's *History of Civilization*,[37] a work which was not only immediately translated into German by Arnold Ruge,[38] but which (unlike Knies's book) was an immediate literary success in Germany.[39] Buckle considered *Theory* and *Inquiry* to be 'two divisions of a single subject':

> In the *Moral Sentiments*, he investigates the sympathetic part of human nature; in the *Wealth of Nations*, he investigates its selfish part. And as all of us are sympathetic as well as selfish; in other words, as all of us look without as well as within, and as this classification is a primary and exhaustive division of our motives to action, it is evident, that if Adam Smith had completely accomplished his vast design, he would at once have raised the study of human nature to a science, leaving nothing for subsequent inquirers to ascertain the

36. See Cannan's 'Editor's Introduction', A. Smith, *Lectures on Justice, Police, Revenue and Arms*, Oxford University Press, Oxford 1896 p. xx.

37. H. T. Buckle, *History of Civilization in England* Vol. 2, Parker, Son, and Bourn, London 1861 pp. 432ff.

38. H. T. Buckle, *Geschichte der Civilisation in England* Bd. 2, C. F. Winter'sche Verlagshandlung, Leipzig 1861.

39. The second edition of the entire work appeared in 1864 and 1865; it was reprinted in 1868 and 1874 by Carl Winter, while another edition appeared from Heimann of Berlin in 1870.

> minor springs of affairs, all of which would find their place in this general scheme, and be deemed subordinate to it.[40]

In principle, Smith's projected total science of human nature would result from the systematic application of inductive method, establishing in this manner principles that were applicable to all areas of social life. But this objective required vast intellectual and physical resources; and so, suggested Buckle, Smith had instead settled upon a solution to be achieved in stages: he would initially make use of a deductive approach and divide the indivisible, human nature, in two. Thus *Moral Sentiments* presupposed that humans were sympathetic in their interaction with others, while *Wealth of Nations* presupposed that the fundamental human motivation was selfish. A first approximation of the laws of political economy could be realised in this way:

> He, therefore, selects one of those aspects, and generalizes the laws as they are exhibited in the selfish parts of human nature. And he is right in doing so, simply because men, in the pursuit of wealth, consider their own gratification oftener than the gratification of others. Hence, he, like the geometrician, blots out one part of his premises, in order that he may manipulate the remaining part with greater ease. But we must always remember, that political economy, though a profound and beautiful science, is only a science of one department of life, and is founded upon a suppression of the facts in which all large societies abound.[41]

Smith, Buckle suggested, supplied in one line of argument the premises absent in the other, providing in this way a basis for a future unified science of human nature.

There was no direct response to this line of argument in Britain. But in Germany, where those advocating an 'inductive' methodology identified themselves as historical economists, this ambivalence was rejected. Historicists argued with increasing vehemence that Smith followed a deductive procedure, that is, adhered to a conception of human action independent of time and place, and so both his principles and his conclusions should be rejected. But since Buckle had suggested a form of historical explanation for Smith's arguments, this did permit an argument to develop that was to transform all future discussion of the work of Adam Smith. In the early 1860s Hildebrand founded a new journal dedicated to

40. Buckle, *History of Civilization*, pp. 432, 433.
41. Ibid. p. 436.

economics and statistics—the first in the German language, strictly speaking. As editor, he opened the first issue with a statement of 'the present tasks of the science of political economy', a historical review of the recent development of economics in which the work of Smith played a prominent role. Noting the similarities between the Physiocrats and Adam Smith, Hildebrand suggested that they shared the contemporary moral philosophical view that self-interest is the sole necessary motivation for human action, hence basing upon this conception their economic laws. An appended footnote noted the contrast between *Moral Sentiments* and *Wealth of Nations*, referring to Buckle's attempt at a resolution of this contradiction by treating them as complementary springs of human action.[42] Hildebrand went on to criticise Smith's association of economic motivation with natural laws, suggesting that natural liberty could just as well lead to a mutually destructive system of exploitation as to national welfare. But while the idea of natural laws based upon self-interest was according to Hildebrand untenable, this did not mean that economic actions were arbitrary. The task of economics was instead to provide a historically grounded understanding of the prevailing economic culture.[43] From this perspective much of *Wealth of Nations* might be salvaged, Hildebrand thought.

A dissenting voice here was that of Hermann Roesler, a professor of the Staaswissenschaften at Rostock, who sought to lay bare the moral turpitude and logical confusion in Smith's writing, rooted as it was in the illusions of the Enlightenment.[44] But a more positive note was struck by August Oncken in 1874, publishing a lecture in which he first outlined his ideas on the importance of Smith's writings. He does maintain that the visit to France had a major and lasting effect—Smith returned from France, according to Oncken, determined to compose a great work[45]—which demonstrates that French influences on Smith were not necessarily mobilised to deprecate the achievement of *Wealth of Nations*. Oncken then determined to mark the centenary of *Wealth of Nations* with a reassessment of Smith, his original working title being *The Wealth of Nations from an Ethical Standpoint*—but the work came out a year late under the title *Adam Smith*

42. B. Hildebrand, 'Die gegenwärtige Aufgabe der Wissenschaft der Nationalökonomie', *Jahrbücher für Nationalökonomie und Statistik* Bd. 1 (1863) p. 7.

43. Ibid. pp. 139–43.

44. H. Roesler, *Ueber die Grundlehren der von Adam Smith begründeten Volkswirthschaftstheorie*, Verlag von Andreas Deichert, Erlangen 1868 pp. iii, iv. The work was republished in 1871 with revisions emphasising that Smith's ideas were largely borrowed from the Physiocrats, and especially from Turgot.

45. A. Oncken, *Adam Smith in der Culturgeschichte*, Verlag von Faesy & Frick, Vienna 1874 p. 4.

und Immanuel Kant.[46] In the first section of the book he took up the problem raised by Buckle—given that Smith's economic theory was but one part of a wider system, how might one go about reconstituting that system on the basis of *Wealth of Nations* and *Moral Sentiments*? Oncken's solution, echoing readings of Smith more common earlier in the century, suggested that a *Staatslehre* was contained in the fifth book of *Wealth of Nations*, complete with an exposition of the objectives of a state and the means commanded to achieve those objectives. *Wealth of Nations*, argued Oncken, was not just an economic treatise, as the great majority of previous writers had supposed: it contained both 'eine Oekonomik *und* eine Politik'.[47] And since an ethics was to be found in *Moral Sentiments*, together the two books presented the classic triad—ethics, politics, and oeconomy, component parts of a practical philosophy that went back to Socrates.

A more critical account of Smith's system and its genesis was published the same year, by Lujo Brentano, identified with the Younger Historical School and hence generally critical of Smithian economics. Emphasis was placed upon the fact that Smith's visit to France fell between the publication of *Moral Sentiments* and *Wealth of Nations*, and that during his twelve months in Paris he associated with Helvetius and others. The influence this had on Smith, argues Brentano, can be seen in the change that came about in his basic ideas. In *Moral Sentiments*, he suggests, Smith explicitly rejects self-love as a motivating factor, Brentano citing in support a passage from Smith.[48] By the time he comes to write *Wealth of Nations*, however, Smith has changed his mind; he fully shares the ideas of Helvetius, who had depicted selfishness as the motivating force behind human conduct. Elsewhere in *Wealth of Nations*, Brentano continues, we encounter the conception that all men are naturally equal, an idea he shares with the Encyclopaedists, for whom human differences are solely the consequence of variations in education, legislation, or government. State power should according to Smith be restricted to the protection of natural liberty, property, and public order, and any

46. A. Oncken, *Adam Smith und Immanuel Kant: Der Einklang und das Wechselverhältniss ihrer Lehren über Sitte, Staat und Wirthschaft*, Duncker und Humblot, Leipzig 1877 p. ix.

47. Oncken, *Adam Smith*, p. 14.

48. L. Brentano, *Das Arbeitsverhältniss gemäss dem heutigen Recht*, Duncker und Humblot, Leipzig 1877 p. 61, citing Part VII, §3 ch. 1: 'That whole account of human nature, however, which deduces all sentiments and affections from self-love, which has made so much noise in the world, but which, so far as I know, has never yet been fully and distinctly explained, seems to me to have arisen from some confused misapprehension of the system of sympathy'. A. Smith, *The Theory of Moral Sentiments*, ed. D. D. Raphael, A. L. Macfie, Oxford University Press, Oxford 1976 p. 317.

care of the legislator for the individual is held to be an imposition. Consequently, Brentano continued, Smith favoured the abolition of all economic legislation and its replacement with rule by natural economic laws.[49] Which was in turn the central tenet of the Physiocrats, hence the basic ideas of Smith are Physiocratic:

> A. SMITH has refuted their theory only with respect to relatively minor doctrines, and in doing so fell into new errors. Apart from these differences, A. SMITH is himself a Physiocrat.[50]

This might be thought a somewhat bald judgement, but an even more blunt statement of the same position soon followed. Witold von Skarżyński had completed a doctorate at the University of Berlin on Boisguillebert,[51] providing him with a background in early eighteenth-century French economic thought. He then sought to complete his habilitation at Breslau, where Brentano was professor, possibly thinking that this would lend his own criticism of Smith a readier reception. However, while in Berlin he had also taken private lessons with Eugen Dühring, who seems to have exerted a very powerful influence on Skarżyński's style of argument. In 1874 Dühring, then a privatdozent at the University of Berlin, had engaged in a personal and vitriolic exchange with Adolph Wagner in the pages of the *Berliner Börsenzeitung*.[52] Dühring therefore made his name, and style of argument, notorious beyond Berlin, and since Dühring is generously cited in his Habilitation dissertation and the style of argument owes much to him, it is little surprise that it was duly rejected by the Faculty. Skarżyński abandoned his academic ambitions, returned to Poland to run the family estate, and later becoming a member of the national assembly. But he did publish his second thesis, and this work has long been identified as the most zealous exposition of the 'Problem'; what it lacks in substance it more than makes up in forcefulness.

It is not entirely unfair to say that Skarżyński's book on Smith simply amplified and extended the position outlined by Brentano above, although by stretching the argument over four hundred pages and more it

49. Brentano, *Das Arbeitsverhältniss*, pp. 62–63.
50. Ibid.
51. W. von Skarżyński, 'Pierre de Boisguillebert und seine Beziehungen zur neueren Volkswirthschaftslehre', dissertation, Faculty of Philosophy, University of Berlin 1873.
52. See Wolfgang Drechsler, 'Herrn Eugen Dühring's Remotion', *Journal of Economic Studies*, Vol. 29 Nos. 4–5 (2002) p. 269.

becomes more than a little thin and repetitive. He opens with a rhetorical question:

> *Should* Adam Smith *be considered an original moral philosopher, and subsequently as the creator of political economy and hence as an independent, path-breaking thinker?*[53]

The short answer, according to Skarżyński, is no; and his book amounts to relentless repetition of the point that there is absolutely nothing positive to be said about Smith. It is nonetheless worth considering how he constructs this position.

A reference to Buckle opens the argument, noting how Buckle had contrasted the way Smith in his first book placed human sentiment in the relationship prevailing between persons, while in *Wealth of Nations* this was relocated in man himself and linked to the pursuit of self-interest. He does not mention here the manner in which Buckle sought to resolve the polarity he had introduced. Skarżyński then proceeds to expand upon Dugald Stewart's biographical memoir of Smith, blocking in the nature of science in the Enlightenment, the importance of the deductive method and Hutcheson's allegiance to it, and, importantly, Scotland's economic and cultural situation in the mid-eighteenth century. This all comes from Buckle, as does the succeeding account of Smith as a professor of philosophy, where Skarżyński suggests that the principal reason that it took Smith twenty-four years from his 1752 lectures to their final development and publication was the time it took to borrow piece by piece from others the principles he employed.[54] The fact that Hume's *Enquiry Concerning the Principles of Morals* was published in 1751 explains the seven years it took him to publish *Moral Sentiments*, while the meeting with Turgot accounts for the twenty-four years it took to write *Wealth of Nations*. This argument, together with illustrative parallels between Smith and Hume, is taken directly from Dühring, for Skarżyński's book itself is largely assembled out of passages from Buckle, Dühring, and Roscher. Basically, argued Skarżyński, Smith borrowed most of *Moral Sentiments* from Hume, without however understanding what he borrowed.[55] So much for the period before the trip to France: up to this point his economic thinking had not developed in any respect beyond that of Hume.

53. W. von Skarżyński, *Adam Smith als Moralphilosoph und Schoepfer der Nationaloekonomie: Ein Beitrag zur Geschichte der Nationaloekonomie*, Verlag von Theobold Grieben, Berlin 1878 p. iv.
54. Ibid. p. 54.
55. Ibid. p. 77.

> Under the influence of Hutcheson and Hume Smith was an Idealist, so long as he remained in England. After three years of contact with the materialism that prevailed in France, he returned to England a materialist. The contrast between *Theory* (1759), written before his visit to France, and the *Wealth of Nations* (1776), written after his return, can be quite simply explained in this way. There is no need for Buckle's critical sophistries to explain such a straightforward situation. Certainly then Smith is not the great and original thinker he is made out to be—but should political economy introduce a doctrine of infallibility that is so discredited in religion?[56]

As for the substance of Smith's political economy—that all came from the Physiocrats, and Smith merely systematised what he found in France. Skarżyński summarises his position as follows:

1. As far as the history of economics goes, not Smith, but the Physiocrats, are the creators of the science of political economy, with Hume as their principal forerunner, Smith building on them.
2. As far as economic theory goes, although Smith made much of 'labour as the source of wealth', he did not make this a consistent axiom in his work, nor make it a guide for his practice.[57]

One might sympathise with the Breslau examiners; Skarżyński's argument is derivative and poorly constructed even by contemporary standards. But it is worth outlining here, for while Skarżyński's name is frequently cited in connection with 'Das Adam Smith Problem', the substance of his argument is never reported. And we might simply dismiss this uncompromising, but ill-argued, repudiation of Smith's originality on any score if it were not that it reproduced relatively accurately the reflex of the 'more extreme'[58] members of the Younger Historical School when confronted with Smith.

Even careful historical reconstruction could go astray, however. Emil Leser sought to elaborate the relationship between Smith and Hume by using John Hill Burton's *Life and Correspondence of David Hume*, but his arguments get off to a bad start when evaluating Burton's [mis]identification of the 'Smith' that Hume met in March 1740 and concludes that this was

56. Ibid. p. 183. By this allusion Skarżyński stands revealed as a *Kulturkämpfer* too, suggestive of his degree of identification with German cultural politics.

57. Ibid. p. 258.

58. John Neville Keynes's characterisation, not mine: see *The Scope and Method of Political Economy*, Macmillan, London 1891 pp. 26–27.

Adam Smith himself.[59] He consequently assumes that the acquaintance of Smith and Hume began before Smith went to Oxford.[60] This misinterpretation considerably extends the period during which Hume and Smith were personally acquainted and leads him to rewrite much of Smith's early development in the light of Hume's influence; providing a context, and not seeking to reducing Smith to Hume as Skarżyński had done, but nonetheless contributing to some misunderstanding of Smith's intellectual sources.

A different approach to Smith's work was taken by Zeyss, who focused directly upon the theme of 'self-interest'. He points out that the critique of Rochefoucauld and of Mandeville that can be found in *Theory of Moral Sentiments*[61] contradicts the idea that all Smith's work was characterised by a focus upon self-interest, a perspective from which, instead of pointing to a disjunction between the two books, there is the distinct possibility of assimilating the philosophical foundation of *Wealth of Nations* to that of *Theory of Moral Sentiments*, a strategy that took much longer to become accepted. He also makes the simple but nonetheless worthwhile point that no one (including Hume) thought to point to a disjunction between *Theory of Moral Sentiments* and *Wealth of Nations* in Smith's lifetime, rather suggesting that such a disjunction was a later fabrication. Unlike many writers, then and now, who work back from the later to the earlier book, he also deals first with *Theory of Moral Sentiments* before turning to *Wealth of Nations*, enabling him to conclude that in every respect its principles were in conformity with *Theory of Moral Sentiments*.[62]

Zeyss placed discussion on fresh ground, but his study was quickly followed by criticism that he had in his treatment of *Theory of Moral Sentiments* failed to mention Farrer's earlier book,[63] demonstrating that German

59. But as Thorold Rogers had already demonstrated with the use of Balliol College's Buttery records (*An Inquiry into the Nature and Causes of the Wealth of Nations* Vol. 1 Clarendon Press, Oxford 1869 p. vi), Adam Smith arrived in Oxford early in July 1740 and left in August 1746.

60. E. Leser, *Untersuchungen zur Geschichte der Nationalökonomie*, Gustav Fischer, Jena 1881 pp. 5–8.

61. R. Zeyss, *Adam Smith under der Eigennutz: Eine Untersuchung über die philosophischen Grundlagen der älteren Nationalökonomie*, Verlag der H. Laupp'schen Buchhandlung, Tübingen 1889; Zeyss opts to cite from Smith in English; and in pp. 39–76 cites extensively from *Theory of Moral Sentiments*. He also reviews recent French and English writings, citing Delatour's book (*Adam Smith, Sa vie, ses travaux, ses doctrines*, Guillaumin, Paris 1886) and Bagehot's 1876 *Fortnightly Review* article.

62. R. Zeyss, *Adam Smith under der Eigennutz*, p. 92.

63. W. Hasbach, *Untersuchungen über Adam Smith und die Entwicklung der politischen Ökonomie*, Duncker und Humblot, Leipzig 1891; on p. 20 fn. 1 Hasbach notes that he came across Farrer's book on Smith too late to take account of it in the text. Farrer had written the best monograph on Adam Smith as a philosopher, according to Hasbach. Delatour, Zeyss, and Paskowski do not by contrast mention him.

scholars paid more attention to publications in other languages than did their English counterparts. Hasbach had also completed a study specifically directed to the Physiocrats and Adam Smith, and so his commentary on Smith began from considerable acquaintance with the economic arguments of the time. In this second study he develops his account of Smith as a moral philosopher in the context of teaching in Scotland during the first half of the eighteenth century, devoting a chapter to Smith's place in English-language ethics and another to 'Adam Smith's Natural Theology'. There are flaws in his treatment—for example, instead of seeking in Grotius and Pufendorf sources for the overall arguments of *Wealth of Nations*, he instead seeks concepts such as value and price in their writings, but he does then go on to suggest that Smith did not take the idea of economic liberty from earlier economic writings, but developed it from Shaftesbury's ethics.[64]

Hence, despite the routine disparagement of Smith by German historical economists, there was an increasing body of German-language writing which represented in the early 1890s an understanding of Smith considerably more sophisticated than anything to be found in English at this time. Oncken, who as we saw had begun writing about Smith some twenty years previously, responded to this by publishing a detailed account of the genesis and course of the 'Adam Smith Problem', raising the question: was Smith now misunderstood in much the same way that Smith had misunderstood his predecessors? He referred directly to Schmoller's 1897 address in suggesting that there was now in Germany a systematic downgrading of Smith among academic economists, that no one would admit allegiance to his work. But what, he asked, if the contemporary image of Smith were false? That Smith in fact occupied a position more progressive than the current received opinion? This would indeed be an 'Adam Smith Problem'.[65] And out of this reappraisal Oncken was able to take stock of the Smith reception in Germany during the second half of the nineteenth century and recover a clearer view of the problem. He could also draw upon Rae's *Life*, Bonar's catalogue of Smith's library, and also of course Cannan's edition of the *Lectures* to dismiss the entire topic of a 'transition' in Smith's work centred upon the period in France. If the transformation theory were correct, Oncken asks how one would explain the following:

1. That Smith continued to revise and republish *Theory of Moral Sentiments* until shortly before his death

64. Ibid. pp. 175–76.
65. A. Oncken, 'Das Adam Smith-Problem', *Zeitschrift für Socialwissenschaft* Jg. 1 (1898) p. 26.

2. That there is no mention of this conversion in the later works of the Physiocrats, nor is there any sign of this having been communicated to Hume
3. That directly after his return from France Smith prepared a third edition of *Theory of Moral Sentiments* which appeared the following year, 1767, and that in this edition he strengthened his criticism of Mandeville and Rochefoucauld

Furthermore, if Smith were so influenced by French materialist philosophy, how come there are virtually no relevant works in the library as catalogued by Bonar? Brentano had laid great emphasis upon Helvetius's *De l'esprit*, but this was not in Bonar's catalogue; neither was any other work by Helvetius; Holbach's *Système de la Nature* was not there either. The *Lectures* finished the transformation theory off completely: quoting Millar's comments upon the organisation of Smith's lectures, Oncken could show that the framework of *Wealth of Nations* was complete before Smith went to France. And finally, Smith had emphasised the systematic character of his work in 1790, recalling in the advertisement to *Moral Sentiments* that he had promised a continuation of his account of the principles of law and government, and that he had not entirely given up on this project.[66] So there was no contradiction in the procedure followed by Smith in his two books; and it was also now clear that these two books were part of a larger project. The criticism of 'Smithian economics' on the part of historical economists had resulted, not in the eclipse of his work, as Schmoller thought, but in its renewal.

As we have seen, the absence of a current edition of *Moral Sentiments* had not obstructed discussion of its relationship to the argument of *Wealth of Nations* during the final decades of the nineteenth century.[67] German interest in Smith's 'philosophy' continued developing, culminating in 1926 with the publication of Eckstein's translation of *Theory of Moral Sentiments* together with an editorial apparatus upon which the Glasgow edition later leaned very heavily.[68] Eckstein went further than providing a new translation: he established a standard text out of the

66. Ibid. pp. 31–33.
67. Although Oncken had claimed in 1877 that no German translation of *Moral Sentiments* existed—*Adam Smith und Immanuel Kant*, p. 108, n. 1.
68. In an interesting extension of his comments upon Smith, Eckstein remarked that very few German scholars seemed to have read Smith in the original, underlining the suspicion that much of Smith's 'philosophical' reputation was drawn directly from the translation of Buckle—see W. Eckstein, 'Adam Smith als Rechtsphilosoph', *Archiv für Rechts- und Wirtschaftsphilosophie* Bd. 20 (1927) p. 378.

different editions, provided a detailed editorial apparatus including an index of technical terms, and prefaced the whole with a comprehensive survey of the place of *Moral Sentiments* in the work of Adam Smith.

The principal text of Eckstein's edition is the sixth edition, based however upon a systematic comparison with the five previous versions of the book. In this he followed the procedure introduced by Cannan for his edition of *Wealth of Nations*, which is based on the last edition published in Smith's lifetime (the fifth edition) but where a thorough comparison had been made with the text of the first edition. By default, therefore, Eckstein's German edition became the standard edition of *Moral Sentiments*, and was later acknowledged as such by the editors of the Glasgow Edition.[69] The sixty-page introduction to the edition provides a thorough survey of the work and its reception. It opens with the remark, 'Adam Smiths Leben ist arm an äußeren Ereignissen', a sober recognition of the limitations of biography as an explanatory source for Smith's project that was, by this time, well overdue.[70] Smith himself, suggests Eckstein, always regarded *Moral Sentiments* more highly than *Wealth of Nations*, an assessment which had in the course of the nineteenth century been reversed—while *Wealth of Nations* stood at the beginning of the development of political economy, *Moral Sentiments* stood rather at the close of a line of ethical theory and had consequently been passed over by more recent ethical philosophy. This neglect was however unwarranted, and Eckstein suggests somewhat obliquely that the work had a relevance to the moral sciences that had been largely overlooked. Moreover, not only had the work been an immediate success in Britain, it was very well received in both France and Germany; indeed, in Continental Europe *Wealth of Nations* was when it appeared generally thought of as a new work 'by the author of the *Theory of Moral Sentiments*'. Its decline into relative obscurity in the course of the nineteenth century was moreover assisted by a series of misconceptions concerning the composition and revision of the work. The fact for example that, on his return from France, Smith issued a third

69. D. D. Raphael, A. L. Macfie, 'Preface' to *The Theory of Moral Sentiments*, Oxford University Press, London 1976. The original two-volume edition of Eckstein was reissued by Felix Meiner in 1977 as a one-volume work with a new bibliography in their standard series Philosophische Bibliothek; since then it has twice been reissued with an updated bibliography, in 1985 and in 1994. Since the publishers did not reset the second edition, the important note that Eckstein included on the deviations between the various editions of *Moral Sentiments* is now located in the middle of the book (pp. 275–81), and not where one would normally expect it, at the end of the main text.

70. A. Smith, *Theorie der ethischen Gefühle* (1926), trans. and ed. W. Eckstein, Felix Meiner Verlag, Hamburg p. xi. The opening sentence can be translated as: 'Adam Smith's life was notably uneventful'.

edition of *Theory of Moral Sentiments* which varied from the second in very minor respects could have been employed at any time to rebut the idea that Smith underwent some kind of conversion to materialist philosophy while in France; but this did not happen, since even Rae's biography in 1895 provides an erroneous account of Smith's successive revisions to the first edition.[71] Likewise, speculation regarding Smith's waning religious belief can be shown to be unwarranted; successive revisions to the text might indicate a growing Deist conviction, but there is no convergence with the beliefs of his long-dead friend, David Hume.[72] Eckstein also includes a judicious settling of accounts with the debates of the later nineteenth century, emphasising that the moral world comprehends the economic world and not the other way around, while it was equally false to read into Smith's account of sympathy a conception of benevolence which he clearly rejected.[73]

As if to underline this new basis for an appreciation of the work of Smith a German translation of the *Lectures* appeared in 1928.[74] In his introduction Jastrow recalled Hasbach's emphasis upon Dutch, German, and Scottish natural law traditions in seeking a lineage for Smith's own conception of 'natural liberty'; he also pointed out that if there were similarities here with the Physiocrats, this was because they substantially drew on the same traditions as Smith, not because Smith had borrowed from them. The *Lectures*, dating as they do from a period before Smith's encounter with Physiocracy, provide evidence for this and consolidate the advance in Smith scholarship that Oncken had anticipated in 1898.[75] Hasbach's sometimes rather laboured arguments had in turn been published before the discovery of the student notes in 1895, the existence of which now made it easier to place Smith in his intellectual context without resort to argument concerning the inconsistency of his conceptions of human motivation, or speculation over his experiences in France. The implications of this, and the importance of the *Lectures*, were outlined in

71. Ibid. pp. xxxvi, xl.

72. Ibid. p. xlix.

73. Ibid. p. lviii. Eckstein also published an overview of *Moral Sentiments* the following year which provides a resumé of many of the arguments advanced in his Introduction: 'Adam Smith als Rechtsphilosoph', *Archiv für Rechts- und Wirtschaftsphilosophie* Bd. 20 (1927) pp. 378–95.

74. A summary of the lectures based on the Cannan edition of 1896 had already been published by Artur Sommer as 'Das Naturrechtskolleg von Adam Smith', *Archiv für Rechts- und Wirtschaftsphilosophie* Bd. 20 (1927) pp. 378–95, i.e., immediately following on from Eckstein's article noted in fn. 72.

75. A. Smith, *Vorlesungen über Rechts-, Polizei-, Steuer- u. Heereswesen*, Nach der Ausgabe von Edwin Cannan, intr. J. Jastrow, H. Meyer's Buchdruckerei, Halberstadt 1928 p. vi.

greater detail in an article published while the new translation was in the press.[76]

It is striking that these writings from the 1920s both settled accounts with the Adam Smith Problem and laid a sound foundation for the elaboration of a more nuanced and sophisticated understanding of Adam Smith's significance. On neither count, however, was this achievement adequately realised. Adam Smith was by now increasingly written about in English by writers who treated him as a canonical economist. Bastable's excursion into German literature remained an isolated deviation. Edwin Cannan had made reconsideration of Smith as a historical figure once more possible for English-language scholarship, but Cannan was an economist interested in the history of economics, not a historian of political thought. That German scholars had debated the wider significance of Smith's work since the later 1860s went largely unremarked, save for the recognition that there had been some discussion of an Adam Smith Problem. Cliffe Leslie had reviewed Roscher's *Geschichte der National-Oekonomik in Deutschland* in the mid-1870s but directed his attention to historiographical and methodological issues, not to the substance of Roscher's work.[77] The English 'historical economists' looked to Henry Maine, not to Knies, Hildebrand, or even Schmoller, for their inspiration.[78] When a summary of August Oncken's survey of the 'Adam Smith Problem' was published in the *Economic Journal* in 1897 this appears to have introduced to English readers for the first time arguments that went back forty years. Germany of the 1920s was succeeded by Germany of the 1930s; the liberal values with which the name of Smith was associated were preserved most notably among those German who emigrated, and the impetus given to scholarship by Sommer, Jastrow, and above all Eckstein dissipated. Friedrich List became the foremost

76. J. Jastrow, 'Naturrecht und Volkswirtschaft. Erörterungen aus Anlaß der deutschen Ausgabe von Adam Smith Vorlesungen', *Jahrbücher für Nationalökonomie und Statistik* Bd. 126 (1927) pp. 689–730. The last piece that Jastrow published before his death also drew attention to a new Smithian discovery, Scott's account in *Economic Journal* Vol. 45 (1935) of an early draft of the *Wealth of Nations*, concluding with the remark 'das missing link ist gefunden'—see 'Ein neuer Adam-Smith-Fund und der Aufbau des nationalökonomischen Lehrbgebäudes', *Zeitschrift für Nationalökonomie* Bd. 8 (1937) pp. 338–80.

77. T. E. Cliffe Leslie, 'The History of German Political Economy', first published in the *Fortnightly Review* 1 July 1875, reprinted in *Essays in Political and Moral Philosophy*, Hodges, Foster and Figgis, Dublin 1879 pp. 167–78. The preceding essay on Adam Smith notes the work of Buckle, but in identifying the 'two paths of descent' leading from Smith states that the first relates to Ricardo, and the second to Malthus and Mill (p. 151); hence Leslie treats Smith in terms of deductive and inductive methods, despite his comments on natural law.

78. See my essay 'The Historicisation of Political Economy?', in B. Stuchtey, P. Wende (eds.) *British and German Historiography 1750–1950*, Oxford University Press, Oxford 2000 pp. 211–28.

popular economist in the Germany of the 1930s.[79] Shortly after the war two condensed editions of *Wealth of Nations* were published,[80] but nothing in the 1950s and 1960s. Eckstein's edition of *Theory of Moral Sentiments* was not republished until 1977, since when it has constantly been available. It was Hans Medick's book on the Scottish Enlightenment[81] that re-established the link with the level of discussion that had existed in the 1920s, although the coincidental increase of Anglophone discussion of Smith served to deflect attention away from this.

Medick's book thus stands at the point of renewal of an interest in Smith, the Scottish Enlightenment, and eighteenth-century political thought that is still today gathering pace. Our understanding of Smith's sources and borrowings is now far in advance of the state of scholarship in the 1970s when, finally, a modern reference edition of Smith's writings began publication. One purpose here has been to illuminate the sometimes unhistorical nature of the 'history of thought'. It is a fact too little remarked that most of the commentary upon Smith with which we are familiar is of very recent provenance. Partly this is a product of the work that has been done in the history of political thought, reconnecting Adam Smith to the rapidly expanding field of Enlightenment studies. But the history of economics has also mostly been practised by economists, rather than historians; hence the literature of the history of economics has tended to mirror the foreshortened perspective of the literature of economics in general. For all the familiarity of *Das Adam Smith Problem*, the modern commentary on the matter treats it as a problem with one of two possible solutions: Smith either changed his mind between writing his two books, or he did not, for all the world like one of the entries in Flaubert's 'Dictionnaire des idées reçues'. How this came to be considered a problem, and the manner in which it found resolution—what might be considered the truly historical object of a history of economics—was last considered in any detail by Oncken in 1897. While we now know immeasurably more about Adam Smith in his time, we still know relatively little about what he subsequently, and successively, became.

79. A drastically condensed version of *Wealth of Nations* was published in 1933, with the text taking up 258 pages; the editor remarks that a modern reader could not be expected to plough through all five books—Adam Smith, *Natur und Ursachen des Volkswohlstandes*, trans. and ed. Friedrich Bülow, Alfred Kröner Verlag, Leipzig 1933 p. v.

80. Adam Smith, *Die Theorie des Aussenhandels: Inquiry into the Nature and Causes of the Wealth of Nations B. IV. Ch. 1–3 1776*, ed. A. Skalweit, Vittorio Klostermann, Frankfurt am Main 1946; Adam Smith, *Untersuchungen über Natur und Ursprung des Volkswohlstandes*, Georg Westermann Verlag, Braunschweig 1949; the latter included Book I chs. 1–3 and Book IV chs. 1–8 and was approved for use in schools.

81. Hans Medick, *Naturzustand und Naturgeschichte der bürgerlichen Gesellschaft*, Vandenhoeck und Ruprecht, Göttingen 1973.

PART III

Economics as the Theory of Industrial Society

The golden age, which blind tradition hitherto has placed in the past, lies before us.
—Strap-line of *Le Producteur. Journal de l'industrie, des sciences et des beaux arts*, 1825–26

To each according to his capacity, to each capacity according to its works.
—Strap-line of *L'Organisateur. Journal de la doctrine Saint-Simonienne*, 1829–30

In the conventional narrative of the history of economics, the political economy of Karl Marx and the general equilibrium analysis of Léon Walras belong to different eras and mindsets: Marx developing in *Das Kapital* Bd. 1 (1867) an account of the capitalist mode of production from his critique of Ricardo and Smith, hence looking back to the early nineteenth century; Walras publishing at about the same time his *Éléments d'économie politique pure* (1874–77), a general equilibrium account of an economic system that looks forward to the twentieth century. The impact that each had on the development of economic thinking in the twentieth century is also very different: Marxian analysis forming the core of a critique of capitalism, while Walrasian general equilibrium became during the 1930s the basis for a neoclassical microeconomics which was vigorously contested by critics of capitalism during the 1960s and 1970s. Nonetheless, the works of Marx and Walras share something very important: they are different answers to the same Saint-Simonian question regarding the nature of exchange and distribution in modern society: how the contributions made to production by industrious men and women were reflected in the distribution of the fruits of their labour. 'From each according to his abilities, to each according to his contribution' was Marx's vision for a transitional socialist society in 1875,[1] entirely unaware that the year before Walras had embodied this principle in a system of simultaneous equations. The very different economic frameworks that Marx and Walras developed are in fact variant responses to Saint-Simonian ideas of the 1820s and the 1830s, in particular conceptions of equality and exchange in an 'industrial society'. However, the development of a predominantly anglophone economics in the latter half of the twentieth century was linked to a narrative of its origins in which the international history of economics was rewritten as one of the diffusion, first from Britain, then from the United States, of 'modern economics'. Gide and Rist, authors of the first modern history of economic thought, devoted a whole chapter to 'Saint-Simon, the Saint-Simonians and the Origins of Collectivism',[2] placing it between a chapter on Sismondi and one which dealt with Owenism, Fourier, and Louis Blanc. And while there is a chapter on utopian socialists in Heilbroner's seminal *Worldly Philosophers* that includes some remarks on Saint-Simon and Fourier,[3] Robert Owen is placed centre stage because by the 1950s it was assumed that the story of nineteenth-century political economy was primarily an Anglo-Scottish story. Gide and Rist, Frenchmen writing about the history of political economy at the very beginning of the twentieth century, therefore provide a helpful corrective to this strictly fictional story.

According to Gide and Rist, the new industrial society envisaged by the Saint-Simonians would involve the transformation of politics into a positive science of production, the task of government being the optimisation of individual capacities with the aim of improving the physical and moral condition of all. Economic government would replace political government; the administration of things would replace authority over men. Industrialism, as seen by the Saint-Simonians, was distinguished from the vision of economic liberals by this new role for government.[4] An end to the exploitation of man by man; the organisation of labour; the distinction of the industrious from the idle; the problem of the distribution of wealth resolved into the distribution of property; and the question of why

1. Karl Marx, 'Kritik des Gothaer Programms', *Werke* Bd. 19 p. 20.
2. Charles Gide, Charles Rist, *Histoire des doctrines économiques depuis les physiocrates jusqu'à nos jours*, J. B. Sirey, Paris 1909 pp. 230–65.
3. And also rather cheekily tags on a discussion of John Stuart Mill—Robert L. Heilbroner, *The Worldly Philosophers*, Simon and Schuster, New York 1953 pp. 96–127.
4. Gide, Rist, *Histoire*, op. cit. pp. 240, 242.

incomes resulting from the unequal division of wealth were themselves unequal—these were the watchwords and issues of the 1820s, some of which clearly found their way into Marx's rhetoric and eventually became attributed to him. However, the purpose of the following two chapters is not primarily to redraft the history of political economy in the nineteenth century, but to demonstrate how we might approach economic writing with new questions, and in so doing discover new answers. The consistent failure of commentators to measure Marx's reading of political economy against what he actually read presents an easy target. By considering the circumstances in which Marx first came to read Say, Smith, Ricardo, Mill, and McCulloch, and the evidence of how he read them, it is possible to shed fresh light on the unfinished project for which *Das Kapital* Bd. 1 was, eventually, the only published part.

With Léon Walras the problem is rather different. The broad outlines of his life and work—the fact that his father Auguste published two treatises on political economy, that there is a somewhat unorthodox backstory to his appointment to an assistant professorship in Lausanne in 1870, the publication in two parts of his *Éléments*, his extensive correspondence with contemporary economists, the fact that his work only became better known through the appointment of his successor, Vilfredo Pareto—this is all reasonably familiar. However, the construction of modern neoclassical microeconomics in a general equilibrium framework has led to an emphasis upon the technical and formal aspects of 'Walrasian economics' which has as little to do with the work of Léon Walras as 'Marxist economics' has to do with the work of Karl Marx. Modern economists generally subscribe to the view that there is a distinction to be made between positive and normative statements, and that questions of equity belong among the latter. Further, the formal and mathematical structure of 'Walrasian economics' is thought to exemplify positivist rigour; while it might be acknowledged that Léon Walras had some ideas that today seem distinctly odd, recent commentary presumes these can be simply detached from his 'achievement' and quietly ignored. Chapter 7 demonstrates that such cherry-picking is untenable; that Walras devised his general equilibrium model precisely to exemplify his 'odd ideas', in particular, to demonstrate the conditions of possibility of a Saint-Simonian 'from each according to their abilities, to each according to their contribution'. Justice and equality lie at the heart of Walras's economics; and the point of so demonstrating is to suggest that these ideas are also implicit in modern 'Walrasian economics', that arguments about justice and equality are not merely normative, ethical, issues external and extraneous to economic analysis.

And so the next two chapters examine texts and arguments with a view to identifying different kinds of success and failure. It has often simply been assumed that Marx succeeded in identifying the underlying dynamics of modern economies, and their crisis-ridden form of development. By comparing his arguments with the sources which he used, I suggest that the outcome is more mixed; that his 'critique of political economy' eventually produced more of a variation upon the French radical arguments of the 1840s that he and Engels had so vehemently rejected. While *Das Kapital* Bd. 1 is an impressive analytical synthesis that, importantly, adds contemporary English material on the factory system to an existing French critique of British economic development, and discounting its radical incompleteness, it does not actually make the arguments that Marx wished it to make. Nonetheless, soon enough it was assumed that it did. The case with Léon Walras is rather the reverse: he did succeed in creating an argument about the conditions under which an economic system could achieve justice and equality, but this very success has been completely obscured by the way that some of his ideas were appropriated by neoclassical economists. As with the approach in Part II, this distinction between the construction of a text and its subsequent reception helps us see more clearly through the fog of commentary and elaboration, seeking to expose arguments in the terms in which they were originally constructed.

Marx and Walras not only shared a common heritage in utopian communism and programmes for social and economic reform. The different ways in which they responded to this heritage were also subsequently joined together in an unanticipated manner: while the course of the Russian Revolution was marked by struggles between political groupings claiming to be the true exponents of Marxism, the organisation of the Soviet and East European economies was by the 1960s increasingly shaped by planners working within a general equilibrium framework, and this work continued right up to the collapse of the Soviet Union. By contrast, wherever the principles of 'Marxian political economy' were systematically applied to the organisation of real enterprises, the outcome was fudge and muddle.[5]

5. In her book *Karl Marx Collective: Economy, Society and Religion in a Siberian Collective Farm* (Cambridge University Press, Cambridge 1983) Caroline Humphrey lucidly demonstrates the limitations of trying to run a collective farm on the basis of Marx's economic categories, as prescribed in the statutes governing its administration and the textbooks written for the use of administrators—see ch. 2.2 'Theoretical Basis for the Internal Economy of the Collective Farm', and ch. 2.3 'The Collective Farm and the State in Soviet Theory'. See also Nigel Swain, *Collective Farms Which Work?* Cambridge University Press, Cambridge 1985.

The idea that a collectivised socialist economy could be elaborated in terms of a general equilibrium model was first fully stated in the early 1900s.[6] It was however the seizure of power by the Bolsheviks in the course of the Russian Revolution that transformed this academic question into a real prospect for economic organisation. The extensive and lasting dislocation brought about by the Civil War and War Communism shattered many of the institutional linkages through which markets could function, so that for the early 1920s it could be said that the Russian economy was centralised, but unplanned.[7] The foundation of a central planning office (GOSPLAN) in 1921 made possible the articulation of a conception of equilibrium in the economy as a whole[8] as a system of material balances, which then formed the basis for the formation of five-year plans used for economic administration in the 1930s. Jasny suggests that the conception of equilibrium which he and other economists employed could be traced back to Quesnay's *Tableau*,[9] which in the 1860s had been the inspiration for the circulation and reproduction schemes published by Engels in *Capital* volume II. By the early 1900s there was a substantial literature discussing Marxian issues of circulation and production cycles. In the 1950s and 1960s, however, the development of mathematical modelling and linear programming necessarily transformed these elementary conceptions into something more akin to the formal representation that Walras had envisaged.[10] Indeed, when the function of market prices in planned economies had been raised in the early 1930s, H. D. Dickinson had used Cassel and Pareto to argue that a collectivised economy would function in the optimal manner that text-books described a capitalist economy as functioning, the condition of the contemporary world economy rather underlining his point about

6. Enrico Barone, 'Il Ministro della Produzione nello Stato Collettivista', *Giornale degli Economisti* 8 (1908) pp. 267–93, 392–414; translated in Friedrich von Hayek, *Collectivist Economic Planning*, George Routledge and Sons, London 1935 pp. 245–90.

7. A comment made by Kritsman in 1929—see Athar Hussain, Keith Tribe, *Marxism and the Agrarian Question*, 2nd edition, Macmillan, London 1983 pp. 259–61.

8. 'Equilibrium, be it a dynamic one, of the economic body of a country is the highest requirement, each violation of which at once leads to a crisis, and compels conjections of the permitted departures from its requirement'. Vladimir Gustavovich Groman, 'On Certain Regularities Empirically Discovered in our National Economy', *Planovoe khozyaistvo* No. 1 (1925) p. 91, quoted in Naum Jasny, *Soviet Economists of the Twenties: Names to Be Remembered*, Cambridge University Press, London 1972 p. 110.

9. Jasny, *Soviet Economists of the Twenties*, op. cit. p. 104.

10. See Ivan Boldyrev, Olessia Kirtchik, 'General Equilibrium Theory behind the Iron Curtain: The Case of Victor Polterovich', *History of Political Economy* Vol. 46 (2014) pp. 435–61.

optimality.[11] The more recent tendency to pitch the differences between plan and market along the axes of individual liberty and the free flow of information, an approach that dates from Mises and was developed by Hayek, has obscured the fact that, by the 1960s, there was a distinct convergence in the advanced modelling of capitalist and socialist economies. And from the perspective of Saint-Simon this would have all made a great deal of sense.

While Saint-Simonians looked forward to a bright future in which bankers and engineers collaborated on major infrastructure projects, such as the construction of the French railway network and the Suez Canal,[12] Étienne Cabet was more concerned with the perfection of social and political organisation, in his eyes the final realisation of the revolutionary vision of Robespierre and St. Just. Exiled to London in the later 1830s, he composed a utopian novel modelled on Mercier's *L'an deux milles quatre cents quarante* (1795) and incorporating much of Robert Owen's New World Order. When he returned to Paris in early 1839 he arranged for its anonymous publication as a book by Francis Adams about the voyage of a fictional Lord William Carisdall to Icaria, translated from the English by 'Th. Dufruit, master of languages'; but in 1842 this was published under his own name, and with a striking title-page that presents a concise inventory of contemporary socialist vocabulary (figure 6.1).

The central diamond lists love, justice, mutual security, universal insurance, organisation of work, machines used for the profit of all, expansion of production, equal distribution of products, suppression of poverty, the advance of improvement, marriage and family, continual progress, abundance, and arts. Paired above it are 'All for one, one for all'; and below it 'to each according to his needs, from each according to his capacity'.

Likewise exiled to London in the wake of the 1848 Revolution, Louis Blanc later fleshed out this idea in describing a Runnymede picnic:

> The next day there was a trip out into the country. . . . There was going to be a picnic on the island where the great charter of English liberties, Magna Carta,

11. 'Thus there is, in theory, no ground for the assertion that a socialist community, lacking a free market for intermediate goods, would be unable to regulate production in accordance with the principles of scarcity and utility. In fact we may go so far as to say that only in a socialist community, where production can be carried on in the full light of statistical measurement and publicity, is it possible to realise the true principles of economic valuation'. H. D. Dickinson, 'Price Formation in a Socialist Community', *Economic Journal* Vol. 43 (1933) p. 246.

12. For a recent overview see Pamela Pilbeam, *Saint Simonians in Nineteenth-Century France: From Free Love to Algeria*, Palgrave, Basingstoke 2014: for the Suez Canal project pp. 125–29, and railway development pp. 76–77.

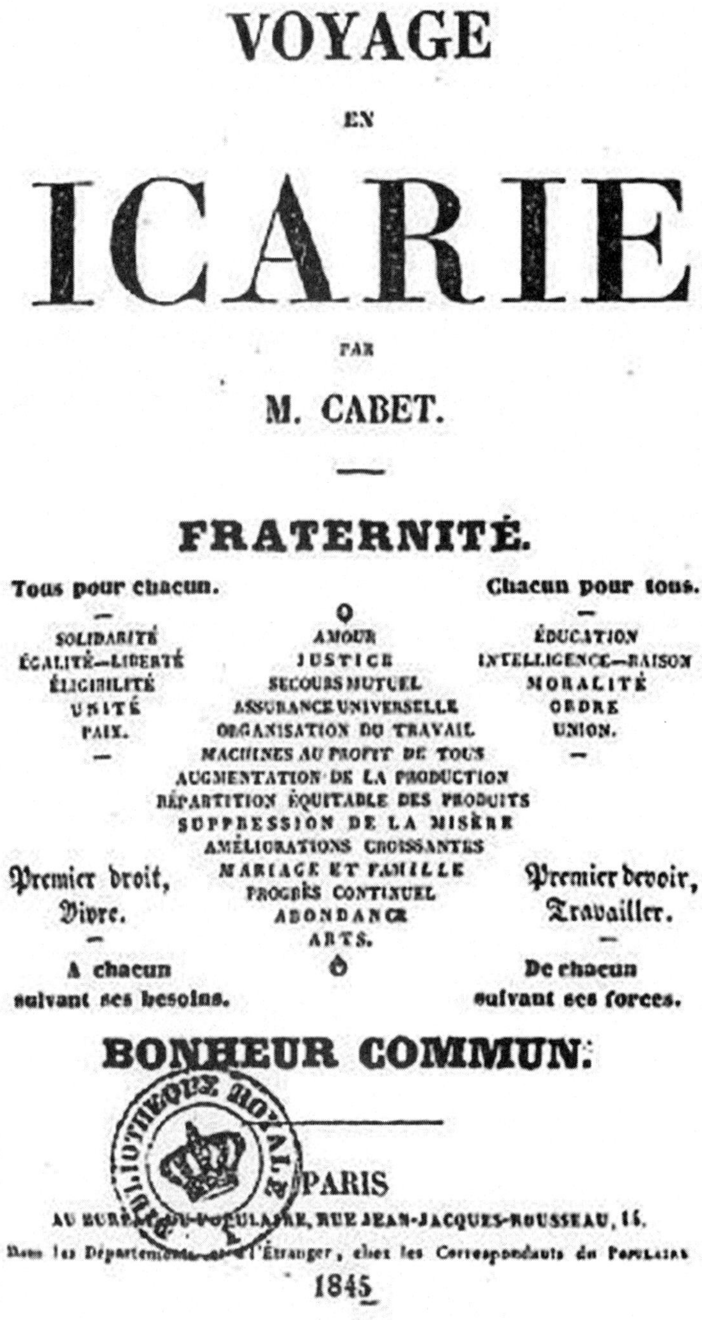
VOYAGE

EN

ICARIE

PAR

M. CABET.

FRATERNITÉ.

Tous pour chacun. — SOLIDARITÉ, ÉGALITÉ—LIBERTÉ, ÉLIGIBILITÉ, UNITÉ, PAIX. —

Chacun pour tous. — ÉDUCATION, INTELLIGENCE—RAISON, MORALITÉ, ORDRE, UNION. —

O
AMOUR
JUSTICE
SECOURS MUTUEL
ASSURANCE UNIVERSELLE
ORGANISATION DU TRAVAIL
MACHINES AU PROFIT DE TOUS
AUGMENTATION DE LA PRODUCTION
RÉPARTITION ÉQUITABLE DES PRODUITS
SUPPRESSION DE LA MISÈRE
AMÉLIORATIONS CROISSANTES
MARIAGE ET FAMILLE
PROGRÈS CONTINUEL
ABONDANCE
ARTS.
Ô

Premier droit, Vivre. — A chacun suivant ses besoins.

Premier devoir, Travailler. — De chacun suivant ses forces.

BONHEUR COMMUN.

PARIS

AU BUREAU DU POPULAIRE, RUE JEAN-JACQUES-ROUSSEAU, 14.

Dans les Départements et à l'Étranger, chez les Correspondants du POPULAIRE

1845

Figure 6.1:
Title-page to Cabet, *Voyage en Icarie* (1845)[13]

13. Source: gallica.bnf.fr / Bibliothèque nationale de France.

had been signed. Our party was made up of persons of both genders, of very different social positions, fortune, and intelligence, but who shared a sentiment of mutual and enlightened benevolence. There were some disbursements to be made, provisions to be collected: this was the business of those with wine in their cellars and money in their purses. At the appointed hour we were all at the agreed rendezvous. The boats were waiting; we boarded, and set off. Those who knew how to row took up the oars without being asked, and while they happily tired themselves propelling the boat, the others watched the passing Thames riverbank, played with the children, or talked with the ladies. When we set foot on land the matter of conveying our provisions to the designated spot arose . . . the strongest claimed the privilege of picking up the precious burden, each being happy to take his turn in being useful. We arrived. It fell to the ladies to look after the arrangement of our countryside feast, and the children joyfully helped them. It goes without saying that during our repast no pretence disturbed the harmony, whether concerning the greater or lesser merit of a particular guest, or any small difference in the small services provided or required. The rowers, who had made so much effort, did not think of asking for anything that would detract from those who had not rowed. The prettiest perhaps attracted more attention, but it would have seemed very strange that they demand the best wines and the most delicate dishes on account of their beauty. Each ate according to his appetite, drank according to his thirst. And so the evening passed very pleasantly, and everyone gave of their best. One sang, another played guitar, a third recited charming verses in his own way. No one was asked to do anything they could not, nobody refused to do what he could, and everyone was cordially thanked, even if not all had contributed to the pleasures of the day in the same degree or manner. In short, we were thankful to have passed such pleasant hours together, and we promised to do it again as soon as possible.[14]

14. Louis Blanc, *Histoire de la revolution de 1848* t. 1, C. Marpan and E. Flammarion, Paris 1880 pp. 155–56.

CHAPTER 6

Karl Marx's 'Critique of Political Economy': A Critique

If there is anything clearly exposed in political economy, it is the fate attending the working classes under the reign of Free Trade. All those laws developed in the classical works on political economy, are strictly true under the supposition only, that trade be delivered from all fetters, that competition be perfectly free, not only within a single country, but upon the whole face of the earth. These laws, which A. Smith, Say, and Ricardo, have developed, the laws under which wealth is produced and distributed – these laws grow more true, more exact, then cease to be mere abstractions, in the same measure in which Free Trade is carried out. . . . Thus it can justly be said, that the economists – Ricardo and others – know more about society as it will be, than about society as it is. If you wish to read in the book of the future, open Smith, Say, Ricardo.

—Karl Marx, 'Speech on Free Trade', *Northern Star*, 9 October 1847[1]

In late 1844 Marx began work on a book that he would continue to write for the next thirty years, but never complete. Many books remain unfinished in one way or another, but with Marx this would have major ramifications; for his posthumous reputation came to rest upon arguments that he had himself left incomplete. *Das Kapital* Bd. 1 was eventually published in 1867, then reorganised for the second edition of 1872, then revised for the French edition of 1872–75. Since then others have sought to bring into

1. Karl Marx, 'Speech on Free Trade', Northern Star 9 October 1847, in Karl Marx, Friedrich Engels, Historisch-Kritische Gesamtausgabe, Marx-Engels-Verlag, Berlin 1927–35 (henceforth MEGA) Bd. I/6 pp. 429–30.

some kind of order the mass of published and unpublished writings, fragments, drafts, and notes that he left on his death in 1883—for someone who only found a settled existence during the 1860s, Karl Marx managed to preserve an extraordinary volume of paper during more than twenty years of a semi-peripatetic existence. Friedrich Engels began the process of creating a coherent legacy, bringing out the third and fourth editions of *Das Kapital* Bd. 1, putting together second and third volumes for this work, seeing to the publication in German of *Misère de la philosophie*, and creating a corpus of popular 'Marxist' texts: *Anti-Dühring* (1878), *Socialism: Utopian and Scientific* (1880), and *The Origin of the Family, Private Property and the State* (1884). Karl Kautsky continued this work, publishing a reading guide to *Capital* in 1886, and editing Marx's notes from the 1860s into *Theorien über den Mehrwert* (1905–10). This process has continued to the present day,[2] the new *Gesamtausgabe* publishing manuscripts and notes which have given a new lease of life to argument about the structure and status of *Das Kapital* that had begun in the 1920s.[3]

In the following I will rely primarily on the original *Gesamtausgabe* edition,[4] initiated in the later 1920s under the direction of David Ryazanov, but who was in 1931 ousted from the position of chief editor and then eventually shot in 1938, mainly for being an old Menshevik.[5] The edition achieved an excellent balance between textual reliability and unobtrusive editorial contextualisation; it remained radically incomplete, but included all of Marx's writings up to 1850. When in the 1970s a new *Gesamtausgabe* began publication, the editors opted for a different editorial strategy. It had long been evident that Marx sought to develop his ideas through

2. For readers unfamiliar with this history, a potted history of 'Marxism' is appended.

3. Henryk Grossmann, 'Die Änderung des ursprünglichen Aufbauplans des Marxschen *Kapital* und ihre Ursachen', *Archiv für die Geschichte des Sozialismus und der Arbeiterbewegung* Bd. 14 (1929) pp. 305–38. Grossman opens as follows: 'Remarkable as it may seem, the complex of questions concerning the construction of Marx's principal text, as well as it relationship to both the *Theories of Surplus Value* on the one hand and the earlier *Contribution to a Critique of Political Economy* on the other, has never been the object of any investigation'.

4. Referenced here as 'MEGA'; material from the new *Gesamtausgabe* is referenced in full, as with the Dietz *Werke* edition. The new *Gesamtausgabe* has four series: I being published and unpublished writings; II *Das Kapital* and its preparatory work; III Correspondence; IV notebooks. Series II begins in 1850, the editors assuming that Marx did not begin his work on the project that became *Das Kapital* until he came to London.

5. For details of the editorial principles governing the first MEGA see Rolf Hecker, 'Rjazanovs Editionsprinzipien der ersten MEGA', in Carl-Erich Vollgraf, Richard Sperl, Rolf Hecker (eds.) *David Borisovič Ryazanov und die erste MEGA*, Argument-Verlag, Berlin 1997 pp. 7–27.

endlessly commenting, drafting, revising, and rewriting. Rather than use the mass of the resulting manuscript material to inform editorial work on a usable new edition, the new editors simply converted this manuscript material into print.[6] Whereas Ryazanov initiated the first collected edition of Ricardo's writings in any language,[7] the new editors betray no interest in, or knowledge of, the material upon which Marx drew. They have failed to produce a reference edition of *Das Kapital* Bd. 1, instead reprinting the first four German editions of Bd. I, plus the first French and English translations. It is for this reason that I use in the following my own facsimile copy of the 1867 edition of *Das Kapital* Bd. 1, since I am at least sure that this is what the book looked like in 1867, and the new *Gesamtausgabe* edition offers no real advance on this position.[8]

My premise here is that the vision of his project that Marx formed in the mid-1840s turned out to be a chimera.[9] His 'critique of political economy' aimed to disclose the 'laws of motion of the capitalist mode of production', its origins, functioning, and prospective demise. With his turn to political economy in 1844 he began the construction of a 'Marxian' political economy that would culminate in 1867 with the publication of *Das Kapital* Bd. 1. No further volumes were published in his lifetime, but from the mass of notes, drafts and plans that he left at his death some sixteen years later Friedrich Engels eventually assembled second and third

6. In 1975 I asked my supervisor Maurice Dobb about the planned twenty volumes for *Capital*, and he simply dismissed the new material as 'undated postcards and the like'. Jonathan Sperber on the other hand seems to think that sheer volume is a good thing—see his *Karl Marx: A Nineteenth-Century Life*, W. W. Norton, New York 2013 p. xiv.

7. Edward Gonner published the first modern edition of Ricardo's *Principles* in 1891 and a selection of the articles and essays in 1923. A draft letter (August 1936) from Ryazanov reveals that he had completed a translation of Ricardo's writings, letters, and speeches, forming the basis for a Collected Works that at that time was unique in any language and which was eventually published in five volumes in 1955–61, without however Ryazanov being named as translator—Vollgraf, Sperl, Hecker, *David Borisovič Ryazanov*, op. cit. p. 261; also Denis Melnik, 'The Diffusion of Ricardo's Theories in Russia', in Gilbert Faccarello, Masahi Izumo (eds.) *The Reception of David Ricardo in Continental Europe and Japan*, Routledge, Abingdon 2014 pp. 203–4, 208 fn. 7.

8. The *Werke* edition of *Das Kapital* Bd. 1 is based on the 4th 1890 edition, by which time it is impossible to discern what the original edition had looked like. The most reliable and accessible edition of *Das Kapital* Bd. 1 currently in print is the facsimile of a 1932 Berlin edition with an introduction by Karl Korsch, published by Anaconda, Cologne 2009. This is a reset version of the 2nd 1872 edition.

9. The general lines of my argument here follow that of Gareth Stedman Jones in a number of recent essays, in particular the closing sections of 'The Young Hegelians, Marx and Engels', in Gareth Stedman Jones, Gregory Claeys (eds.) *Cambridge History of Nineteenth-Century Political Thought*, Cambridge University Press, Cambridge 2011 pp. 556–600.

volumes, fostering the illusion that a coherent Marxian political economy existed. Marx himself appears to have given up the struggle long before his death; the materials that he left indicate that he was losing the power of synthesis that was so marked in earlier writings, and that in any case he was changing his mind about the global scope and history of the capitalist mode of production which was here the object of his analysis.[10] Nor can it be said that *Das Kapital* Bd. 1 forms an adequate foundation for a distinctively Marxian political economy; as will be shown below, that text retains its linkage to the French socialist critique of political economy from which he had already sought to mark himself off in *Die heilige Familie* of 1845. Marx read English political economy in a French context, assimilating an existing French critique of English political economy, making it his own, then disavowing the sources upon which he had drawn. The fact that Marx's own version of all this was recounted so obstinately and forcefully, first by Marx, then by Engels, and then by generations of 'Marxists', not least among them the editors of the new *Gesamtausgabe*, has deflected attention from Marx's sources, as it also has from the rather significant issue that all the core literature of political economy with which Marx was familiar was published before the 1840s, when he first started to read it.[11]

As the epigraph to this essay suggests, Marx sought an understanding of the structure of civil society in political economy, specifically in a 'critique' of political economy—this was the subtitle of all of his principal writings.[12] What however did he conceive 'political economy' to be, and how was the work of 'critique' supposed to reveal a truth which had been otherwise hidden within the discourse of political economy? I will seek

10. Whereas the preface to the first edition of Bd. 1 implies that the capitalist mode of production is a global force, the way in which it has always been read, the French edition shifts ground. In his 1881 response to Vera Zasulich he maintains that he '*expressly* restricted the "historical fatality" of this movement to the *countries of Western Europe*' (First Draft of Letter to Vera Zasulich in *Karl Marx, Friedrich Engels, Gesamtausgabe* Bd. I/25 Dietz Verlag, Berlin 1985 p. 219). This 'express restriction' is unique to the French edition, not appearing in the first or second German editions—he refers Zasulich to *Le Capital* t. 1, Maurice Lachatre, Paris 1872 p. 315. col. 2.

11. Much is sometimes made of Marx's 'Notes on Wagner' of 1879/80 ('Randglossen zu Adolph Wagners "Lehrbuch der politischen Ökonomie"', *Werke* Bd. 19 pp. 355–83), although the work in question, Adolph Wagner's *Lehrbuch der politischen Oekonomie Bd. 1 Allgemeine oder theoretische Volkswirthschaftslehre mit Benutzung von Rau's Grundsätzen der Volkswirthschaftslehre Theil 1 Grundlegung* is, as the full title indicates, not an original work by Adolph Wagner, but rather his re-edition of Rau's 1826 textbook; and so the full force of Marx's critique is, yet again, turned upon old arguments, not new ones.

12. From 'Kritik der Hegelschen Rechstphilosophie' (1843) through *Zur Kritik der politischen Oekonomie* (1859) to *Das Kapital: Kritik der politischen Oekonomie* Bd. 1 (1867). Then there is of course *Die heilige Familie, oder Kritik der kritischen Kritik* (1845).

here an answer to these questions on the basis of what Marx actually read and wrote.[13] In particular, I ignore the accounts that Marx later gave of his early development, since they clearly involve a teleology that I wish here to avoid.[14] I will first of all provide an account of how Marx initially came to identify political economy as a body of writing that repaid attention; second, an outline of Marx's first reading of political economy, considering what he did actually read in it, and how he responded to what he read; and third, what he made with what he read—where his 'critique of political economy' eventually led him.

MARX'S EARLY FORMATION: FROM BONN TO PARIS VIA BERLIN, COLOGNE, AND BAD KREUZNACH

On 15 April 1841, then aged twenty-two, Karl Marx was awarded a doctorate by the Philosophy Faculty of the University of Jena for a dissertation on the 'Differenz der demokratischen and epikurischen Naturphilosophie'. He had begun the study of law at Bonn in 1835,[15] then after two semesters moved to Berlin, where he continued his legal studies until the Winter Semester of 1838–39, during which the only course he attended was on the law of inheritance. During his first Winter Semester of 1836–37 he studied Roman private law with Savigny and Criminal Law with Gans, back to back as Kelley points out in his seminal article on Marx's early studies.[16] Although he later shifted his interest to philosophy, beginning his thesis in

13. Thomas Kemple's imagining of 'Marx's Desk' is an interesting approach to this problem, but treats Marx's own statements about his writing as unmediated evidence of his actual reading and writing practice: Kemple, *Reading Marx Writing: Melodrama, the Market, and the 'Grundrisse'*, Stanford University Press, Stanford 1995 pp. 49ff.

14. The same scepticism informs Michael Evans's important essay on the 1844 Manuscripts—see 'Karl Marx's First Confrontation with Political Economy: The 1844 Manuscripts', *Economy and Society* Vol. 13 (1984) p. 118. The importance of Margaret Fay's essay 'The Influence of Adam Smith on Marx's Theory of Alienation', *Science and Society* Vol. 47 No. 2 (1983) pp. 129–51 should be noted here, as also the well-informed discussion of Jürgen Rojahn, 'The Emergence of a Theory: The Importance of Marx's Notebooks exemplified by Those from 1844', *Rethinking Marxism* Vol. 14 No. 4 (2002) pp. 29–46.

15. Marx took six courses in his first semester, three on law (Encyclopaedia, Institutions and History of Roman Law), two in Classical Studies (Greek and Roman Mythology, Homer) and one on Modern Art History. In the 1836 Summer Semester he took three courses in law (History of German Law, European Law of Peoples, Natural Law) and one on Propertius's elegies. 'Abgangszeugnis der Universität Bonn für Marx; Bonn 1836 August 22', MEGA Bd. I/1.2 p. 194.

16. Savigny lectured from nine to eleven every morning, and Gans from twelve to one every day except Wednesdays: Donald R. Kelley, 'The Metaphysics of Law: An Essay on the Very Young Marx', *American Historical Review* Vol. 83 (1978) p. 352 fn. 9.

1839, this involved a change of emphasis rather than of disciplines, since as Kelley points out, law and philosophy were in Justinian's Digest of Roman Law (Pandects) a single identity. This was for two reasons: first, law was a 'true science', 'since it was universal and viewed the world in terms of cause and effect, and, second, . . . unlike natural science it proposed as its principal object the common good of society'.[17] If 'political economy' is here substituted for 'law' we can already discern the logic of Marx's later turn to the study of political economy, although there is no evidence that he showed any interest in the subject before Engels's outline of political economy introduced him to it in late 1843.

What is certain is that during 1837–38 Marx made an attempt to systematise his studies in a substantial treatise, and in so doing discovered the basic fallacy of the 'metaphysics of law' in Savigny's *Das Recht des Besitzes*.[18] The fallacy was Savigny's derivation of private property from the historical chance of wilful seizure, so that in Savigny property was simply possession, retrospectively legitimated through law. This was precisely the point that Gans made in his 1839 critique of Savigny and, in subsequently aligning himself with Gans's critique and against Savigny, Marx moved towards the work of Hegel, away from the study of law and to the study of philosophy. But it would take a few years before it became clear quite where this led.[19]

Having gained his doctorate, Marx travelled in early June 1841 to Bonn in the hopes of beginning an academic career, but by the autumn it was clear that a career of this kind was closed to him.[20] The principal reason was commonplace enough: the number of students studying law had sharply declined, reducing in turn the opportunities for young academics to get started on the path to a university chair. In the early 1830s there had been a surge in the number of law students, producing a glut of candidates for the conventional careers in state administration to which a degree in law, philosophy, or theology naturally led, employment as a university professor being one of these state employments. Toews notes that by 1840 there were some 2,500 unsalaried jurists in the Prussian bureaucracy awaiting appointment to positions for which they were

17. Ibid. p. 353.

18. Marx described his intellectual development in a long letter of 10 November 1837 to his father; most of the surviving letters from this period are replies from his father (who died in 1838)—see MEGA Bd. I/1.2 pp. 213–21.

19. Kelly, 'Metaphysics', op. cit. pp. 357–58. For a summary of the Young Hegelians and the divisions of the later 1830s see Gareth Stedman Jones, 'Introduction' to Karl Marx, Friedrich Engels, *The Communist Manifesto*, Penguin Books, London 2002 pp. 74–95.

20. David Rjazanov, 'Einleitung zum ersten Bande', MEGA Bd. I/1.1 pp. xxxviii–xxxix.

qualified.[21] There emerged a kind of intellectual proletariat, young men without secure incomes or prospect of employment, fired by philosophical controversy. This is also suggestive of the emergent division between 'Left' and 'Right' Hegelians; many of the latter occupied permanent university positions to which the former aspired. This was then the radicalised milieu in which young educated men without fixed employment engaged in controversy and bitter polemics, establishing transient periodicals that lent their opinions wider circulation.

Without the prospect of an academic career, Marx shifted his attention to political journalism. In the autumn of 1841 he joined in discussions concerning the foundation of a newspaper that could be a political counterweight to the established *Kölnische Zeitung*, but was not immediately involved when the *Rheinische Zeitung* was inaugurated during the winter of 1841–42. Other issues had distracted him—the death of his future wife's father in early March 1842, and writing various pieces for other publications. Not until the spring of 1842 did he write something for the new newspaper, a long article on the freedom of the press, which appeared in six parts between 5 and 19 May.[22] In June 1842 he became editor, his profile at this time being that of a moderate liberal with a polemical style.[23] When in October Friedrich Engels passed through Cologne on his way to England the contrast between the two was plain. Marx had just rejected an article by Engels on the King of Prussia, where Engels argued that Prussia was on the brink of a liberal revolution which would lead to the abolition of the monarchy and the creation of a republic.[24] Such radicalism had no place in Marx's thinking at this time.

In late October and November 1842 Marx published five articles about debate in the Provincial Assembly over the theft of wood from privately owned forests. Marx made a distinction between growing wood and fallen wood, appropriation of the former requiring that it be 'forcibly separated from its organic context', rendering such removal an act of theft. However, fallen timber had not been so forcibly separated, 'the wood collector only making a judgement that the nature of property has made itself, for it only possesses the tree, and the tree no longer possesses the fallen branch'.[25]

21. John Edward Toews, *Hegelianism: The Path Toward Dialectical Humanism, 1805–1841*, Cambridge University Press, Cambridge 1980 pp. 213–15.

22. Rjazanov, 'Einleitung', MEGA Bd. I/1.1 pp. xliv–xlv.

23. See the judicious summary of Marx's development at this time in Evans, 'Karl Marx's First Confrontation', op. cit. pp. 116–19.

24. David Gregory, 'Karl Marx's and Friedrich Engels' Knowledge of French Socialism in 1842–1843', *Historical Reflections* Vol. 10 No. 1 (1983) p. 146.

25. Marx, 'Debatten über das Holzdiebstahlsgesetz', MEGA Bd. I/1.1 pp. 268–69.

And he went on: 'if every infringement of property is theft, without distinction and without more precise definition, would not all private property be theft? Do I not by my private property exclude any third party from this property?' (MEGA Bd. I/1.1 pp. 269–70). While this appears to echo Proudhon's *Qu'est-ce que la propriété*, the way in which Marx constructs his argument runs back to Gans's critique of Savigny, and not to Proudhon, who distinguished between property and possession in a different manner—we do not know when Marx first read Proudhon, although he would have heard about his book from Moses Hess. However, this linkage of possession as a physical monopoly to private property was to be important when he first came to read political economy.

However, the turn to political economy was still more than a year away. In the new year the threat of censorship increased, Marx resigning as editor on 17 March 1843, citing this as his reason (MEGA Bd. I/1.1 p. 393). He moved to Bad Kreuznach in the Pfalz, married Jenny von Westphalen there in June, and between March and August drafted his critique of the Hegelian philosophy of law, a systematic commentary on §§261–313 of Hegel's *Grundlinien der Philosophie des Rechts*. These are in Section 3 of Part Three, 'Die Sittlichkeit', Section 1 dealing with the family, Section 2 with civil society, and Section 3 with the state. Marx is here initially concerned with the way in which state, civil society, and family are distinguished from each other, moving then to consider the purpose of the state, and thence to the question of sovereignty and legislative authority. He then reviews the relation of the state to civil society, and the relationship of the *Stände* to the state, concluding with a lengthy discussion of the problem of representation. Marx thus here considers the nature of civil society solely from the standpoint of political society. Hegel's linkage of civil society to a system of needs, and his identification of political economy as a discourse upon these needs—what in retrospect one might expect Marx's critique to turn on—is however in Part Three Section 2 of the *Philosophie des Rechts*, and Marx does not address this part of Hegel's argument at all.[26]

As Gregory notes, Marx's arguments here rely heavily upon his reading of Rousseau's *Social Contract*,[27] and are of relevance here only to

26. Marx, 'Aus der Kritik der Hegelschen Rechtsphilosophie: Kritik des Hegelschen Staatsrechts (§§261–313)', MEGA Bd. I/1.1 pp. 401–553. Michael Evans provides a very lucid account of what Marx might have made of Section 2, but concedes that the surviving part of his critique of Hegel's *Rechtsphilosophie* provides no support for Marx's later contention that he had, at this time, come to the conclusion that 'the anatomy of civil society . . . has to be sought in political economy'. Evans, 'Karl Marx's First Confrontation', op. cit. pp. 120–21.

27. Gregory, 'Karl Marx and Friedrich Engels', op. cit. p. 165.

establish one point: Marx has not shown, by October 1843 when he moves to Paris to work with Arnold Ruge on the *Deutsch-Französische Jahrbücher*, any acquaintance with, or interest in, the literature of contemporary political economy. He remains politically a liberal, has now begun to discard the allegiance to Hegelian philosophy he had assumed in 1839, but lacks any particular identifiable political or philosophical position. Gregory suggests that 'he had now espoused the ideal of a democratic, secular, and republican political community in which the power of government bureaucrats, vested interests, and wealthy property-owners would (somehow) be curbed by popular sovereignty'. But it is a stretch to describe this position as belonging to 'the camp of "Jacobins" or radical democrats outside the pale of respectable political life'.[28] In September he wrote to Ruge regarding editorial policy, and he made clear his opposition to the idea that the new journal should adopt any one particular position. Communism, he wrote, was a 'dogmatic abstraction', making clear that he did not have in mind here some imaginary communism, but rather the communism expounded by 'Cabet, Dezamy, Weitling':

> This communism is itself only a striking manifestation of the humanistic principle that is infected by its opposite, the private. Abolition of private property and communism are therefore in no respect identical, and other socialist doctrines, those of Fourier, Proudhon, etc., have necessarily developed in opposition to it because it is itself only a particular, one-sided realisation of the socialist principle.
>
> And the entire socialist principle is moreover only one aspect of the *reality* of the genuine human essence.[29]

And in the conclusion to the letter he wrote:

> Our slogan must therefore be: reform of consciousness not through dogma, but through the analysis of mystical consciousness which is not clear to itself, whether this be in a political or a religious form. . . . It will become apparent that it is not a matter of drawing a line in thought between past and future, but of the *fulfilment* (*Vollziehung*) of the thoughts of the past. It will at last become plain that mankind is not beginning a *new* task, but is consciously realising its old task.[30]

28. Loc. cit.
29. Marx to Arnold Ruge, Kreuznach, September 1843, MEGA Bd. I/1.1 p. 573.
30. Marx to Ruge, September 1843, MEGA Bd. I/1.1 p. 575.

This is of course not the kind of Marx we are used to reading about. Nor is there any trace in the surviving notebooks from his stay in Kreuznach that he had actually read any Cabet and Proudhon, as opposed to having heard Moses Hess talk about them.[31] All of this would change very soon.

THE POLITICAL ECONOMY OF BLANC, ENGELS, PROUDHON, AND BURET

Once in Paris Marx went the rounds trying to drum up copy; Proudhon and Cabet were out of the city, so he would not have met them. He did however meet Louis Blanc, who promised him an article, and the use of his postal address. Marx mentions this in a letter also referring to the arrival of 'Engels's article', the package having been intercepted and the contents jumbled and damaged.[32] This article was presumably sent again later; but before considering what Engels wrote, it is worth considering what Blanc might offer Marx for the *Jahrbücher*.

In 1839 Blanc had published a series of articles in the *Revue du Progrès*, reprinted in 1841 as a pamphlet under the title *Organisation du travail*. This opened with the argument that society was divided into two sorts of people, rich and poor, tyrants and victims, and that the system of competition within which everybody was trapped was in nobody's interest. He set out to demonstrate two things: first, that competition was an exterminating system; and second, it also represented for the bourgeoisie an unceasing source of impoverishment and ruination. The salvation of all was to be found in social reform.[33] The wage system, he argued, was dominated by unlimited competition, leading to the impoverishment of all workers:

> Systematic reduction in wages, bordering on the suppression of a certain number of workers, this is the inevitable effect of unlimited competition. It is therefore only an industrial process by means of which the proletarians (*les prolétaires*) are forced to exterminate each other. (p. 13)

This process also engendered monopoly: the increase of population, the fragmentation of property, and the confusion engendered by competition

31. Marx, 'Kreuznacher Exzerpte 1843', MEGA Bd. I/1.2 pp. 118–36.

32. Karl Marx to Julius Fröbel in Zürich, Paris 21 November 1843, Karl Marx, Friedrich Engels, *Gesamtausgabe* Bd. III/1 p. 61, Dietz Verlag, Berlin 1975. The article would be 'Umrisse zu einer Kritik der Nationalökonomie', printed in the *Jahrbücher* the following year.

33. Louis Blanc, *Organisation du travail*, Administration de librairie, Paris 1841 p. 8.

fostered exploitation by 'capitalistes' (p. 45) who furthered the process of concentration: large factories absorbed small, medium-size warehouses were absorbed by larger, the artisan was displaced by the journeyman. This competitive system had reached its apogee in England, Ricardo epitomising the heartlessness of political economy:

> To know where such improvidence can lead, the madness of production, one has only to examine the industrial and commercial history of England. (p. 153)

England, he wrote, presented to the world both extreme poverty and extreme opulence (p. 56). France was on the same path:

> In 1789 France adopted all the traditions of English political economy; it became an industrial people like the English people. . . . France and . . . England, ruled by the same economic laws, and as a consequence animated by the same spirit. (pp. 62, 63)

Blanc had clearly been reading Sismondi. In particular, the concept of proletarianisation had been introduced by Sismondi in his analysis of the relation of population growth to poverty:

> Hence, the more the poor person is deprived of all property, the more he is in danger of misconceiving his revenue, contributing to the growth of a population which, lacking all correspondence to the demand for labour, can find no subsistence. This observation is old enough to have passed into the language, and to have been transmitted from the Latin language to modern languages. Romans called proletarians those who had no property; just as more than all others they were called to have children: *Ad prolem generandum*.[34]

This process of impoverishment was related to the dependence of the population upon capitalists, the reciprocity of production and consumption, the manner in which the competitive process created a surplus of goods that could not be consumed domestically and hence, Sismondi argued, the support for free trade among English political economists. In particular, this process of proletarianisation was related to the 'bounded rationality' of industrial and agricultural workers:

> The artisan who has a shop knows the demand in his market; the worker in the factory cannot know this. The cultivator, in turn, knows the demand in his

34. Jean-Charles-Léonard Simonde de Sismondi, *Principes de l'économie politique, ou de la richesse dans ses rapports avec la population*, Tome II, Livre VII ch. 2, Delauney, Paris 1819 pp. 262–63.

> market; the rural worker is not able to know the demand for his labour. The more the poor man is stripped of everything, the more disposed he is to form a family.[35]

Blanc's account of pauperism and competition to the death is of course more dramatic, and less well argued, than Sismondi's, but it is plain that Sismondi is the prime source for his economic analysis of the process of immiseration, and also of his critique of Malthus and Ricardo, the two English economists that Sismondi had named in his work. The principles of Adam Smith had served Sismondi as a constant guide; but in making the additions to Smith's arguments that he thought necessary, he had come to very different conclusions.[36] The work was as a whole structured accordingly: as a Smithian text which does, however, preserve far more of Smith's own analysis than ever found its way into the writings of Malthus and Ricardo.

It would be the mangled article by Engels that would directly prompt Marx into reading political economy, but this little pamphlet by Blanc, and the influence upon it of Sismondi, is suggestive of the change of perspective that Marx encountered in Paris. This kind of writing, about exploitation, competition, wage levels, and impoverishment, has no precedent in anything he had written in the previous seven or eight years or, so far as we can judge, had read. Not only did the move to Paris confront Marx with political rather than philosophical arguments, these political arguments were grounded in arguments about the exploitation of workers; in Blanc's case, leading to the advocacy of a system of social workshops maintained at public expense to provide the workless with work and incomes.[37] Although the influence of Blanc is here only indirect, it is certainly clear that within a few weeks of moving to Paris Marx shifted away from the position adopted in his comments on Hegel's *Rechtsphilosophie* and the letter to Ruge in October. The evidence for this is in the articles he wrote for the *Jahrbücher* and published in February 1844, by which time he had begun reading and summarising the principal works of French and British political economy.

The first of these articles reviewed Bruno Bauer's book *Die Judenfrage*, and an article from Herwegh's *Einundzwanzig Bogen aus der Schweiz* on the emancipation of Jews and Christians. Notebook evidence indicates that

35. Ibid. p. 433. This is in the extensive 'Table analytique des matières', which provides a more succint account than the text itself.

36. Sismondi, 'Avertissement' *Principes* t. 1 p. vj.

37. Ibid. pp. 76ff. See Gregory, 'Karl Marx and Friedrich Engels', op. cit. pp. 171–73 for a broader summary of Blanc's arguments.

these two parts were written in Paris and completed in December.[38] Marx first picks up Bauer's point that, while Jews may seek emancipation in Germany, so do all Germans, and that the Jews should seek emancipation as Germans, not as Jews. This is extended into a discussion of the state, following on from the critique of Hegel written in Bad Kreuznach. It then elaborates the rights of man in terms of versions of French revolutionary constitutions, where political emancipation flows from the dissolution of an older, feudal society (MEGA Bd. I/1.1 p. 596). This is all new, and comes from Blanc's own studies of the French Revolution that would be published later in twelve volumes as *Histoire de la Révolution française*, the first volume appearing in 1847. In the shorter, second part of this first article, Marx introduces money as the earthly God of the Jew as a huckster, and argues that the abolition of a society in which the god money ruled would necessarily also involve the emancipation of the Jew.

> Money is the assiduous God of Israel, before which no other God may exist. Money abases all human gods—and transforms them into a commodity. Money is the general, self-constituting value of all things. It has therefore robbed the whole world, the human world as much as that of nature, of its particular value. Money is the estranged essence of man's labour and his being, and this alienated essence dominates him, and he worships it. (MEGA Bd. I/1.1 p. 603)

Externalisation, alienation, estrangement, the domination of an alien essence which is worshipped—we can here see the idea of the fetishism of commodities taking shape, reinforced in his new critique of Hegel's *Rechtsphilosophie*, likewise written in December 1843 and which, beginning from religion as the '*phantasmic realisation* of the human essence', concludes with the positing of a class which is the 'complete loss of man', a class which can only regain itself through the complete reclamation of man: the proletariat.[39] This is however still December 1843, and Marx has yet to read any writers on political economy. But he has plainly read Blanc, and talked with him, much as he had talked with Moses Hess about Proudhon in Cologne. Marx's own reading of political economy began in early 1844, but it is already clear what will happen: he will read these prosaic writers in terms of

38. Karl Marx, Friedrich Engels *Gesamtausgabe* Bd. I/2 Apparat pp. 650–51, Dietz Verlag, Berlin 1982.

39. Marx, 'Zur Kritik der Hegelschen Rechtsphilosophie', MEGA Bd. I/1.1 pp. 607, 620. Hence Marx plugs 'the proletariat' that he had first heard about from Blanc into the model of externalisation and realisation exposed initially with respect to Jewish emancipation, and then elaborated in respect to religion. One should not allow the high-flown philosophical rhetoric to obscure the basic mechanics of what Marx does here.

the anthropology of human development that he had first articulated in late 1843, and then seek to transform what he has read into the law of movement of human history, reinvented as the law of motion of capital.

In the same double issue of the *Jahrbücher*—as it would turn out, the only issue—Ruge and Marx published the article that had first arrived in fragments, Engels's 'Outline of a Critique of Political Economy'. While Marx had assimilated some economic elements from the writings of Blanc and others, it was Engels's text that directly brought about his turn to political economy and its critique. He was of course aware of Engels's earlier contributions from England: four articles had been published in the *Rheinische Zeitung* during December 1842, and four 'letters from London' during May and June 1843 in the *Schweizerischer Republikaner*. The last of the *Rheinische Zeitung* series was from Lancashire, briefly outlining urban poverty and unemployment. Those written in May and June 1843 deal for the most part with the Chartist movement, and when read alongside Marx's writings of the time stand out for their clarity of prose and engagement with current social and political issues. The third opens as follows:

> English socialists are far more principled and practical than the French, and this is owed especially to the fact that they are in open conflict with the various churches, and are completely uninterested in religion. In large towns they usually have a hall (a meeting house) where every Sunday they listen to speeches. These are often polemics against Christianity and are atheistic, but they also often deal with aspects that touch on the life of the worker. Among their lecturers (preachers) Watts in Manchester seems to me an important man; he has written some pamphlets on the existence of God, and on political economy, showing a great deal of talent.[40]

I will come back to Watts in due course, but first we need to consider Engels's contribution to the *Jahrbücher*, written in the autumn of 1843. Marx would have first been able to read this in late December 1843, and it would leave a strong impression upon him.

Engels opens as follows:

> Political economy originated as a natural consequence of the extension of trade, replacing simple, unscientific haggling with a developed system of licensed swindling, a complete science of enrichment (*komplette Bereicherungswissenschaft*).[41]

40. Engels, 'Briefe aus England', *Schweizerischer Republikaner* 9 June 1843, MEGA Bd. I/2 pp. 370–71.
41. Engels, 'Umrisse zu einer Kritik der Nationalökonomie', MEGA Bd. I/2 p. 379.

The mercantile system developed from this, turning on the doctrine of the balance of trade. This was displaced by a revolution in economic thinking during the eighteenth century, which however remained one-sided since it did not consider the justification for private property. At the core of this system stood Smith's *Wealth of Nations* with its doctrine of free trade which, while inconsistent and immoral, represented some progress since it overthrew the mercantile system (p. 381). However, with the work of Malthus, Ricardo, and McCulloch matters steadily deteriorated, there being however one positive step that was made: the development of the law of private property. Having sketched out a history for political economy which, given its derivation of political economy from commerce, closely follows the one sketched by McCulloch in his *Discourse*,[42] Engels turns to its basic categories.

Smith, the 'economic Luther' (p. 383), showed that trade, far from being a matter of conflict and mistrust, should become a bond of union and friendship between nations and individuals. But really the doctrine of free trade was no more than a veil beneath which exploitation could be extended across the globe, and having generalised hostility between nations, liberal economy moved on to dissolve the family through the extension of the factory system.

> But the economist himself is not aware of the cause which he serves. He does not know that, for all his self-interested reasoning, he is merely a link in the chain of the general progress of mankind. He does not know that in dissolving all particular interests he only prepares the way for the great transformation towards which the century is headed, the reconciliation of mankind with nature and with itself. (p. 385)

Following trade there comes the category of value. There is, states Engels, a distinction between the real or abstract value of a thing, and its exchange value. There had been dispute about the former: English political economists argued that the real value of a thing was equivalent to its production costs, while Say maintained that it should be measured by its utility. Why should production costs be the measure of value? Because no one would sell it for less than its cost of production. This is all very confusing for Engels:

> First an abstract value, now also an abstract exchange, a trade without competition, i.e., a person without a body, a thought without a brain to produce

42. J. R. McCulloch, *A Discourse on the Rise, Progress, Peculiar Objects, and Importance, of Political Economy*, Archibald Constable, Edinburgh 1824 pp. 32ff.

> thoughts. And doesn't the economist consider that, with competition left out of things, there is no guarantee that the producer will sell his product for exactly the cost of production? What a confusion! (p. 386)

Things become even more muddled if we turn to Say, he goes on, for if the utility of something is purely subjective, then necessaries should be more costly than luxuries. Engels brings clarity into all these confusions by proposing that value is the relationship between the cost of production and utility. Price is then introduced as a further variable, and here at last Engels finds some trace of sense: that price is determined by the reciprocal relationship of cost of production and competition.

The cost of production is however divided into three elements: rent of land, profit of capital, and wages of labour. However, even the economists admit that capital and labour are the same, since capital is treated as 'stored-up labour' (p. 388). And so we have two elements of production, nature and man, the latter as both physical labour and intellectual activity. Engels then argues that the existence of price rests upon private property; for anything that is freely available, that cannot be monopolised, has no price. But land has been monopolised through a process of 'original appropriation' of communal land, excluding all besides a small minority (p. 390). This monopoly is itself the opposite of competition, so that private property is itself opposed to competition, and both are internally contradictory.

Furthermore, Engels goes on, competition is ruled by supply and demand, and these are never steady, but constantly changing:

> The economist presents his lovely theory of supply and demand, proves to you that 'too much can never be produced', while practice answers with trade crises that recur as regularly as the comets, of which we have one on average every five or seven years. Trade crises have been occurring regularly for the past eight years as consistently as the great plagues formerly did, and have brought with them more poverty, more immorality than did the plague. (p. 394).

These fluctuations destroy all values, any chance of creating a moral basis for exchange. The speculator hopes for catastrophes, especially harvest failures, and the culmination of immorality is speculation in funds.

Nonetheless, there is land enough to feed everyone, and the available productive powers are immeasurable. Malthus had created a doctrine of overpopulation in which it was always the poor who were superfluous, for whom nothing could be done. But from this doctrine one could conclude the need for a social reformation:

> From this we have learned of the deepest degradation of mankind, its dependence upon competition; it has shown us how in the last instance private property has made man into a commodity whose creation and destruction depends only upon demand; how the system of competition has consequently slaughtered millions of people, and continues to do so; we have seen all this, and it drives us on to the abolition (*Aufhebung*) of this degradation of mankind through the abolition of private property, competition, and opposed interests. (p. 400).

Upon what sources might have Engels drawn for this? He presents a robust and systematic critique of political economy in which, while making great play with dialectical contrasts—between competition and monopoly, between private property and value—he makes a more systematic critique of contemporary political economy than we find in Louis Blanc, while however sharing his combative rhetorical posture. One source for Engels is certainly the Sunday lectures of John Watts, whose *Facts and Fictions of Political Economists* appeared in 1842.[43] Watts's discussion of landed property, rent, competition, wages, immiseration, labour, and capital covers similar ground to the 'Umrisse', and Watts's discussion of Malthus and population seems a clear source for Engels;[44] although Engels directs his attention to specific concepts—value, price, competition, and property—without the references to James Mill and McCulloch we can find in Watts. We can nonetheless conclude that Engels is reworking arguments he encountered in Manchester, since none of his writings before June 1843 involved anything similar.[45] Another source for Engels was Proudhon, whose approach to political economy in terms of systems of property supplied a connection absent from the English literature. The importance of Proudhon at this time to both Marx and Engels

43. John Watts, *The Facts and Fictions of Political Economists: Being a Review of the Principles of the Science, Separating the True from the False*, Abel Heywood, Manchester 1842. Marx made some brief extracts from this work in 1845—see Karl Marx, Friedrich Engels, *Gesamtausgabe* Bd. IV/3 pp. 430–33, Akademie Verlag, Berlin 1998.

44. Watts, *Facts and Fictions*, op. cit. pp. 18ff.

45. See the discussion of the reliance of Engels on the Owenite version of political economy in Gregory Claeys, *Machinery, Money and the Millennium: From Moral Economy to Socialism, 1815–60*, Polity Press, Cambridge 1987 pp. 169–77, and of his use of Proudhon pp. 171–72.

is shown in a passage from *Die heilige Familie*, on which they collaborated towards the end of 1844:

> All developments of political economy have *private property* as their presupposition. It regards this basic presupposition as an irrefutable fact, paying little further regard to it, about which, as *Say* naively says, it only comes to talk about 'accidentally'. Now Proudhon subjects the foundation of political economy, *private property*, to critical examination, indeed the first decisive, ruthless but also scientific examination. This is the great scientific advance that he has made, an advance which revolutionises political economy and which first makes possible a genuine science of political economy. Proudhon's text 'Qu'est-ce que la propriété?' has the same significance for modern political economy as Sièyes text 'Qu'est-ce que le tiers état?' has for modern politics.[46]

While Proudhon did not treat, they went on, forms of private property—wages, trade, value, price, money, and so on—as Engels had done in his 'Umrisse', this only reflected Proudhon's 'historically justified standpoint'. Nonetheless, 'he had achieved everything that a critique of political economy on the basis of political economy was capable of doing' (loc. cit.). As we shall see, this condescension would be lent a sharper edge when in 1846 Proudhon published his new account of political economy as a *Système des contradictions économiques*.

Whatever the independent merits of Engels 'Umrisse', its principal significance is that it triggered Marx's turn to political economy in the first few weeks of 1844, and linked political economy to private property. We might also note that Engels's opening paragraph implied that the 'science of enrichment' was not based upon free exchange, wealth instead being accumulated through dupery and swindling. In his treatment of the creation and extraction of surplus value Marx would later reject this idea, insisting on the need to demonstrate how a free worker came to surrender the surplus value that that worker had created. The notebooks provide critical evidence of how in his reading Marx first adopted such ideas, and then developed them.

More awkward is how we deal with texts which he manifestly did read, but for which he either made or left no notes. The first of these is in fact Proudhon's *Qu'est-ce que la propriété*, known to him from the autumn of 1842 at the latest, but then most likely at second hand from Moses Hess. There is no record in his notebooks of his reading the work during 1843, in

46. Friedrich Engels, Karl Marx, *Die heilige Familie, oder Kritik der kritischen Kritik*, MEGA Bd. I/3 p. 203.

Paris in 1844, nor in Brussels in 1845; but the passage in *Die heilige Familie*, mostly written by Marx from September to November 1844, demonstrates his familiarity with it. In fact, by 1840 Proudhon already had a more extensive knowledge of political economy than Marx would have in late 1844—he had read Say's *Principes* and *Cours* in 1839, taking extensive notes; he actually made some notes on Cournot's *Recherches sur les principes mathématiques de la théorie des richesses* in December 1839; and he had attended Adolphe Blanqui's lectures on political economy at the Conservatoire during the winter of 1840–41. He went on to read Smith and Ricardo in 1841, re-read Book I of *Wealth of Nations* in June and July 1844 in the Blanqui edition, and in July 1844 he read Sismondi's *Études sur l'Économie politique*, along with Godwin, Chevalier, and Buret the same month.[47] In his reading of political economy during 1844 Marx was catching up with a body of literature already familiar to Proudhon, Blanc, Cabet, and several other French socialist writers, many of whom drew an explicit contrast with England and were critical of English political economy. Once he had begun to read political economy, his problem became how he might sustain a claim to have discovered something that these French writers had missed.[48]

Proudhon's definition of property was idiosyncratic: it involved the right of escheat, the feudal law under which the state had could appropriate property for which there was no owner.[49] Proudhon had in 1839 developed the argument that the biblical injunction 'Thou shalt not steal' could be extended to all cases where someone gained at the expense of another.[50] This idea of property is therefore quite distinct from possession: those who use something have a right to the possession of that thing, whether it

47. Proudhon took more than 10,000 words of notes on Say's *Principes*, for example—Bibliotheque Nationale, Nouvelles Acquisitions Françaises (NAF) 18257; VIIe Cahier in-8, 1839: pp. 29–48; he also made very extensive notes on Rossi's *Cours d'Economie politique*, and over 14,000 words on Droz's *Économie politique*—NAF 18256; Ie Cahier in-4 : pp. 78–92. My thanks to Edward Castleton for his transcriptions of these notebooks.

48. The editorial introduction to Marx's 'Economic and Philosophical Manuscripts' in Karl Marx, Friedrich Engels, *Gesamtausgabe* Bd. I/2 Apparat, Dietz Verlag, Berlin 1982 pp. 685–88 presents an entirely fictional summary of Marx's intellectual development at this point.

49. 'AXIOM: Property is the right of escheat (*le droit d'aubaine*) which the proprietor attributes to a thing which bears his mark'. Proudhon, *Qu'est-ce que la propriété? Ou Recherches sur le principe du droit et du gouvernement*, J.-F. Brocard, Paris 1840 p. 125. I quote here from the original edition to underline the point that these are formulations put forward in 1840, prior to any engagement of Marx with political economy.

50. Edward Castleton, 'Introduction. Comment la propriété est devenu le vol, ou l'éducation de Pierre-Joseph Proudhon', in Proudhon, *Qu'est-ce que la propriété?*, Livre de poche, Paris 2009 p. 63.

be means of production or a dwelling. Accordingly, Proudhon attacks individual property, the better to defend individual possession; he is not opposed to ownership in general, as usually supposed, nor is he advocating a form of communism. Likewise, he defended the right of inheritance, provided that a legacy be used appropriately, for this protected the family against the state:

> Individual *possession* is the condition of social life; five thousand years of property have demonstrated that: *property* is the suicide of society. Possession is within the law; property is contrary to law. Suppress property while conserving possession; and, by this single modification of principle, you will change everything in laws, government, economy, institutions: you chase evil off the land.[51]

In Proudhon's *Qu'est-ce que la propriété?* Marx encountered a linkage between property and political economy that was rather like his own.

Take Proudhon's treatment of the relation between the worker and what that worker produces. He proposes that

> The worker retains, even after having been paid his wage, a natural right in the thing which he has produced. (p. 90)

He then cites Charles Comte's discussion of workers who, having been employed to drain a marsh and improve land, have increased its value; and the value which they have added is returned to them in the subsistence given to them, and by the price of their daily wages, and so the improved land becomes the property of the capitalist—according to Comte. Proudhon disagrees: the right of the capitalist cannot annul that of the workers, for their wage is only a very small part of that which the capitalist has acquired. Another example follows, and a few pages later Proudhon summarises:

> The capitalist, one says, has paid the *days worked* by the labourers; to be exact, one should say that the capitalist has paid for as many *days* as the number of workers he has employed each day, which is not at all the same thing. For this immense force which results from the union and harmony of the workers, the convergence and simultaneity of their efforts, he has not paid for this at all. Two hundred grenadiers in a few hours raised the obelisk of Luxor; does anyone think that one man in two hundred days could achieve the same thing?

51. Proudhon, *Qu'est-ce que la propriété?* (Paris 1840) op. cit p. 242.

> However, as far as the capitalist is concerned, the sum of wages paid would be the same. (p. 93)

Proudhon also deals with the objection that skill and intelligence are not evenly distributed, and that some work requires a greater skill than others. Consequently, it is argued that inequality of wealth is a natural outcome of the unequal distribution of human skills and capacities. He turns this around: arguing that there is an equation in any job between the function performed and the person performing the function, he suggests that in truth the person is fitted to the function rather than the other way around, the 'economy of nature' fitting the division of labour to the specialisation of vocations (p. 105). He then summarises his own position:

> Every transaction having as its aim an exchange of products or services can be called an *operation of commerce*.
>
> He who says commerce says exchange of equal values; for if the values are not equal, and if the contractor perceives this, he will not consent to exchange, and there will be no commerce.
>
> Commerce exists only between free men; everywhere else transactions may be accomplished through violence and fraud; there is no commerce.
>
> The free man has command of reason and his faculties; is neither blinded by passion, nor constrained or prevented by fear, nor deceived by a false opinion.
>
> Hence in every exchange there is a moral obligation that one of the contractors gains nothing to the detriment of the other; that is to say, to be legitimate and true, commerce must be exempt from all inequality; that is the first condition of commerce. The second condition is that it be voluntary, that is to say, that the transacting parties are free and have complete knowledge (*pleine connaisance*). (p. 107)

Proudhon here clearly states the central problem of equal exchange that Marx sought to reconcile with the accumulation of capital: given a free exchange between worker and capitalist, and given that all value originates with the worker, how can what he later called 'surplus value' be appropriated by the capitalist? It is a clear statement of the problem at which Marx only really arrives at the end of the 1840s, in his *Lohnarbeit und Kapital*, and which would provide the overarching theme of *Das Kapital* Bd. 1.

Proudhon continues on, referring to Say and discussing the manner in which goods exchange and prices form, continually questioning the way in which economists have treated the issue of equality and distribution. Later he discusses the rent of land as defined by Ricardo, McCulloch, Malthus, and Mill (pp. 130–31); then observes that Buchanan in his commentary on Smith had treated rent as arising from a monopoly, and that Say had countered this with the argument that the true monopolist was someone who added no degree of utility to a commodity (p. 132). Quesnay's view that the land is uniquely productive is noted, whereas Smith, Ricardo, and de Tracy locate production in labour.

Political economy deals with the production, distribution, and consumption of wealth or of values; but of what values? Values are produced by human industry, that is to say, are transformations that man makes in appropriating matter for his use, and are not the spontaneous productions of nature (p. 34). Proudhon therefore located value in human industry, the producers of value being robbed of their rightful possession through the wage relation. This was not as such in contemporary France a radical or extreme idea. French liberals also employed the language of political economy in their social critiques. Pellegrino Rossi had succeeded Say at the Collège de France in 1833, and during 1836–37 his lectures denouncing the institution of slavery led him to consider the wage relation, and the remuneration of workers.[52] He then elaborated this into a critique of the manner in which the political economy of McCulloch explicitly developed the idea of the worker as a factor of production like any other. But, argued Rossi, while a surplus of commodities was a purely economic problem, an excess of labour was a social and political problem, alluding here to Louis Blanc's pamphlet on the organisation of labour.[53]

Eugène Buret developed these ideas in the prize essay he wrote for the Académie des sciences morales et politiques, the topic having been announced in 1837: 'To determine the nature and signs of poverty in several countries. Investigate the causes that produce it'.[54] Buret was awarded his prize in June 1840 in a ceremony chaired by Rossi, and Buret used the award to finance a visit to England, including his observations in *De la misère des classes laborieuses en France et Angleterre*, a text which presented both a critique of political economy's treatment of labour as a commodity, and an extended description of living conditions in contemporary France and England. Marx read the first volume of this work in the summer of 1844, making extensive notes; but he seems to have passed

52. François Vatin, 'Le travail, la servitude et la vie: La critique de l'économie politique d'Eugène Buret', in his *Trois essais sur la genèse de la pensée sociologique*, Éditions La Découverte, Paris 2005 pp. 34–35.

53. Ibid., p. 41.

54. Eugène Buret, *De la misère des classes laborieuses en France et Angleterre*, t. 1, Paulin, Paris 1840 p. ii.

quickly over the critique of laissez-faire in the hundred-page 'Introduction',[55] devoting his attention to Buret's account of living conditions in England and France. So, for example, on the face of it he skimmed over this passage entirely:

> Labour, in the case where the worker possesses no kind of capital, like day workers or factory workers (*les ouvriers des fabriques*), does not have the economic character of a commodity; the wage does not have the characteristic of a market; for the worker is not in the position of a free seller vis-à-vis the person who employs him. One could say that the capitalist is always free to use labour, and the worker is always forced to sell it. The value of labour is completely destroyed if it is not sold at each instant. Labour can neither be accumulated nor saved, which distinguishes it from genuine commodities. Labour is life, and if life is not exchanged every day for food, it soon enough perishes. For the life of man to be a commodity one would have to restore slavery.
>
> Capital, the purchaser of labour, is placed in an entirely different position; if it is not employed it ceases only to make a profit, it is not destroyed. . . . In a word, labour is not always demanded, but it is forced to constantly offer itself.[56]

Further, Buret summarises his discussion of labour as a commodity as follows:

> There are two things in the price of labour that one must be careful not to confuse, since they are subject to opposing laws. There is a quantity of labour necessary to create a product, and the remuneration of the human agents who combine in this production. This first part, included in the costs or the price of labour, tends to continuously diminish, that is to say, with the expenditure of a given amount of effort, man obtains progressively a product superior in quantity and in quality. The price of labour, in this sense, must always fall. But, in a good economic regime, to the degree that labour lowers price, the worker can be improved in welfare, morality, and independence.[57]

55. Marx's notes on the 'Introduction' to the first volume cover little more than a page—Karl Marx, Friedrich Engels, *Gesamtausgabe* Bd. IV/2 Dietz Verlag, Berlin 1981 pp. 551–52 (for the set of notes see pp. 551–79).

56. Buret, *De la misère,* op. cit. pp. 49–50. Proudhon read Buret in July 1844, but found little more than what he already knew: '*Introduction* de 100 pages, parfaitement inutile'. NAF 18261; 'Cahier B. Juillet 1844. Varia variorum': pp. 74–85.

57. Buret, *De la misère,* op. cit. Vol. 1 pp. 51–52. This argument is attributed in fn. 1 p. 52 to Henry Carey, *Principles of Political Economy,* Pt. II, Philadelphia 1838 p. 286.

Marx made no notes on this and the previous passage. Nonetheless, the affinity to positions he would subsequently adopt is plain. Vatin suggests that Marx copied several unattributed passages from Buret, in French, directly into the '1844 Manuscripts'.[58] As we shall see, these notebooks are a jumble of comments and excerpts, but have nearly always been read as if they were Marx's own writing. The final paragraphs of 'Wage Labour' (MEGA Bd. I/3 pp. 50–51) certainly quote Buret in French, then in German.[59] Unwary readers might conclude that Marx is here sketching out an early version of the idea, developed later in *Das Kapital,* of the reserve army of labour; when in fact he is quoting verbatim from a French work published in 1840.

When Marx turned to English political economy in 1844 he was a latecomer, working within a framework already established by French liberals and socialists. Unfortunately, the way in which he made notes was also very chaotic; Proudhon's notes are by contrast a model of good order; his own comments are clearly separated and prefixed with a 'P'. Marx did more or less distinguish in his notes between direct quotation, summary, and comment; in fact the new MEGA editors dutifully refer to the notebooks as 'Exzerptenhefte'. But with his habit of directly translating quotations into German, combined with the constant rewriting of notebooks and redrafting on the basis of old notes, it would be almost inevitable that he would eventually lose track of what he had thought for himself, copied or translated, paraphrased, or summarised, so that sections of a later text would contain elements of all four.[60] As Hans-Peter Müller has

58. Vatin's exclusive reliance upon French translations of Marx makes it very difficult to follow his argument, or confirm it with reference to the MEGA version. See for example the long passage quoted from Marx by Vatin, 'Le travail', op. cit. p. 65; the passages originally in French have been italicised, and two French translations consulted, but no direct notebook transcription is cited.

59. MEGA Bd. I/3 p. 51, paragraph beginning 'Der industrielle Krieg . . .' is a direct translation of one complete paragraph from Buret, *De la misère*, op. cit. Vol. I pp. 68–69: 'For its successful prosecution the industrial war requires numerous armies which it can concentrate at one point and decimate. And it is neither from dedication nor need that the soldiers of this army bear the trials laid upon them; it is solely to escape the hard necessity of hunger'. While 'l.c.p. [68,] 69' appears at the end, this is Marx's direct translation of Buret, not a summary in his own words.

60. A parallel can be drawn here with the circumstances surrounding the cases of dissertation plagiarism which led to the resignation of several prominent German politicians in 2011. Karl-Theodor zu Guttenberg, the former defence minister, plausibly argued in a subsequent interview that he had compiled material from the Web on several different computers, and in subsequently shunting it all into one text was no longer fully aware of the sources he had used, or which parts were his own and which copied from other sources. See http://www.zeit.de/2011/48/DOS-Guttenberg (accessed 5 April 2013).

observed in connection with the 1851 notebooks on technology, when creating a synopsis of his notes it was by this time usual for Marx to refer not to the page numbers of the original sources, but to the page number of his notebook from which the extract was copied.[61] One implication of this is that many later notebooks are for the most part synopses of earlier reading, so that the corpus of notebooks as a whole gradually became self-replicating, drifting in time away from any direct reference to the texts they ostensibly represent. So when Marx reviewed his notes, he would no longer have seen in them the structure of the text from which they were taken, the context to which they belonged, but merely sets of quotations and summaries that related in some way to a particular concern of his own. This would for example be one explanation for the way in which, in the early 1860s in London, Marx is still citing Smith's *Wealth of Nations* in the Garnier edition which he had read and taken notes on during the early months of 1844 in Paris.[62] It can also be demonstrated that Marx's linkage of technology to the factory, and the loss of control on the part of the worker that this represents, is an argument originally taken from Proudhon, and refigured in *Misère de la philosophie*; by the time we arrive at the much more elaborated argument in *Kapital* Bd. 1 evidence of this origin is limited to some cryptic remarks in a handful of footnotes.[63]

As with the example of the industrial reserve army of labour noted above, or the appearance of the term 'proletariat' at the close of his 1843 critique of Hegel, subsequent readers have attributed ideas to Marx that were in no respect his own, but were even commonplace for the time—the examples drawn above from Sismondi, Proudhon, Blanc, and Buret will not be isolated cases. However, let us now turn to Marx's notebooks to see what he did write down from his reading, and so judge on this more certain basis what he made of what he read.

61. Hans-Peter Müller, 'Materialismus und Technologie bei Karl Marx', in Karl Marx, *Die technologisch-historischen Exzerpte* (ed. H.-P. Müller), Ullstein, Frankfurt am Main 1981 p. lxxxv.

62. See his discussion of Smith's theory of cost price and the natural rates of wages, profit, and rent in the old version of the notebooks edited by Karl Kautsky and published as *Theorien über den Mehrwert, Werke* Bd. 26.2 pp. 214–34, Dietz Verlag, Berlin 1972. In these notebooks Smith's *Wealth of Nations* has become a text which has been dismembered so that it can be lined up against Ricardo's arguments about value and price, discussion of which *precedes* it—pp. 170–214. Hence Marx analyses Smith in terms of Ricardo, reinforcing the fact that the 'Smith' to whom he refers is to all intents and purposes the creation of Ricardo.

63. See fn. 190 below.

MARX'S READING OF POLITICAL ECONOMY IN 1844

MEGA Bd. I/3, published in 1932, contains the transcription of Marx's first notes on political economy.[64] There are nine notebooks dating from the first half of 1844, and the editors used physical and internal evidence to put them in order, providing a concise overview of their form and content (MEGA Bd. I/3 pp. 411–12). The texts which Marx read were either originally in French, or in French translation, as follows:

Jean-Baptiste Say, *Traité de l'économie politique* pp. 436–55
Jean-Baptiste Say, *Cours d'économie politique pratique* p. 455
Frédéric Skarbek, *Théorie de la richesse sociales* pp. 455–56
Adam Smith, *Recherches sur la nature et les causes de la richesse des nations* pp. 457–93
David Ricardo, *Des principes de l'économie politique et de l'impôt* pp. 493–519
James Mill, *Éléments d'économie politique* pp. 520–50
J. R. McCulloch, *Discours sur l'origine, les progrès, les objets particuliers et l'importance de l'économie politique* pp. 550–60
Destutt de Tracy, *Éléments d'idéologie* pp. 560–63
Boisguillebert, *Le détail de la France* pp. 563–68
Boisguillebert, *Dissertation sur la nature des richesses, de l'argent et des tributs* pp. 568–79
Boisguillebert, *Traité de la nature, culture, commerce et intérêt des grains* pp. 579–83

He therefore began with the leading French political economist—Say had died in 1832 but he remained the central authority in France on political economy—and followed up with Smith, Ricardo, Mill, and McCulloch in chronological order. This was the first time he read their books; he would never read right through any of them again. Later he would reuse his original notes, or dip into a copy in his own library; but he never re-engaged with these texts as connected arguments. Instead, he worked up commentary upon the notes he had already made, beginning this process in the summer of 1844, drafting the text that has come down to as the 'Economic and Philosophical Manuscripts'.

Marx read the third edition of Say's *Traité*, published in 1817. There were some revisions in this text compared with the second, chiefly reflecting

64. Also printed in Karl Marx, Friedrich Engels, *Gesamtausgabe* Bd. IV/2, Akademie Verlag, Berlin 1981.

Say's visit to England and his encounter with Ricardo in December 1814, with whom he had since corresponded over the nature of value.[65] Marx made no notes on the 'Discours préliminaire', so we lack direct evidence that he read it; he started his notes with Livre I and the discussion of value, noting the definitions of economic categories such as utility, price (as *prix courant*), wealth, productive capital, natural agents, wages and interest, trade, the accumulation of capital. He wrote down long extracts in French, with occasional summary, mostly in French too. There is a minor interjection on the sixth page (*Allerdings*), he then proceeds to around halfway through the second volume, writing down many extracts and with some linking commentary, and then skips to the 'Épitome' at the end,[66] an alphabetically ordered series of definitions of individual terms which makes up around one-third of all Marx's notes on Say's text.[67] Say here provides an alternative methodical order for reading, beginning with 'property' in the third edition: Marx follows Say's suggestion, moving straight to the entry on 'Propriété', adding in the right-hand column some 'Adnotationes ad Epitomen' in German:

I. *Principles in relation to circulation.*

1. *Private property* is a fact whose explanation does not concern political economy, but which forms its foundation.

> There is no *wealth* without private property, and in essence political economy is the *science of enrichment*.[68] There is therefore no political economy without private property. The whole of political economy rests on a fact without necessity. (MEGA Bd. I/3 p. 449)

65. See my 'Jean-Baptiste Say's Footnotes to Ricardo', in press.
66. See the discussion of this addition to the second edition of the *Traité* and the prominence here of the idea of industrious classes in Richard Whatmore, *Republicanism and the French Revolution: An Intellectual History of Jean-Baptiste Say's Political Economy*, Oxford University Press, Oxford 2000 p. 192.
67. Printed pp. 1073–165 in Jean-Baptiste Say, *Traité d'Économie politique*, ed. E. Blanc et al., Economica, Paris 2006. The Epitome was added to the second edition and retained through to the sixth. Marx's notes on this cover six of the seventeen pages dedicated to Say's *Traité*, MEGA Bd. I/3 pp. 437–55. This notebook is made out of eight 12" by 16" sheets folded in two, laid out in two columns with the notes on the *Traité* on the left. When Marx comes to comment on the Epitome, he places his remarks in the right-hand column; one might suppose he wrote the summary on the left so that he might add comments in the right. There were however so few of these that he went on to fill up the right-hand column from the front with the notes on Skarbek and the *Cours*. See Karl Marx, Friedrich Engels, *Gesamtausgabe* Bd. IV/2 Apparat pp. 739–41.
68. 'die Nationökonomie ist ihrem Wesen nach die *Bereicherungswissenchaft*'. This repeats the opening formulation of Engels's 'Umrisse', MEGA Bd. I/2 p. 379, cited above fn. 41.

This is followed by some remarks on wealth, and Marx suggests that exchange is inherent to wealth since it is composed both of necessaries and things that one is prepared to exchange. Wealth, he writes, consists of things which are 'not necessary' to someone. Following this observation he goes back to working through the 'Épitome', writing down individual definitions in French, with no further comments in the right-hand column. There then follow, from the beginning of the notebook, some excerpts without comment from Skarbek's *Théorie des richesses sociales* and Say's *Cours complet*.

From this we can conclude that Marx began his economic studies with a thorough read through of Say's *Traité*, making notes and excerpts in French, focusing in particular on the definitions that Say had appended to the work, with one major interjection in which he reveals that, while he is himself thinking all the while of property, he notices that the book he is reading does not treat it as a central category.

Next Marx turned to Smith's *Wealth of Nations*, in the 1802 Garnier edition (MEGA Bd. I/2 pp. 457–92). His excerpts and summaries were once again written in homemade notebooks, the first made from six 8″ by 10.5″ sheets, and the second (which already contained some other notes) made from seven 12″ by 16″ sheets, both folded in two.[69] It has already been noted in chapter 4 that the Garnier edition came with an extensive reading guide, but Marx makes no notes on this, beginning immediately by writing down, in French, the first sentence from the 'Introduction and Plan of the Work'. Immediately following this, however, Marx summarises in German the example of pin-making from the first chapter of *Wealth of Nations*. This suggests that he is reading this text in a way different from the way he had read Say; whereas with Say he had mostly written down extracts in French, making occasional summaries in German, Marx here moves almost immediately into German summary. And then he writes down a citation from Garnier directly translated into German, and continues on, summarising and citing in German. Soon we come to the famous passage which ends in the remark about the benevolence of the butcher, the brewer, and the baker, moving in a few lines of mixed French and German from the statement about human wisdom and the propensity to truck and barter, through the analogy with the dog-world, and a free German rendering of what is in any case a flawed French translation, where Smith's 'self-love' is first rendered by Marx as 'persönliches Interesse'; then, repeating the line he had summarised in German, he quotes

69. Karl Marx, Friedrich Engels, *Gesamtausgabe* Bd. IV/2 Apparat pp. 747, 727.

directly Garnier's rendering of 'self-love' as 'égoisme'.[70] He writes down two more passages from the Garnier translation in French, and then comments in German:

> How delightful is the circularity in Smith's demonstration. To explain the division of labour he imputes exchange. But for exchange to be possible he has already to presume the existence of the division of labour, the difference of human activity. Transferring the problem back to a primitive state does not get rid of the problem. (MEGA Bd. I/3 p. 458)

This is the only substantial observation in Marx's notes on Smith, the remaining comments being interjections or clarifications. Proceeding onwards through the text, he begins reading Book I chapter VIII on wages, writes down the first two brief paragraphs, and then immediately skips to the beginning of Book II, making notes about circulating capital, income and savings, then goes back to the beginning of Book I chapter VIII, but this time writing the opening line—'The produce of labour constitutes the natural recompense or wages of labour' (I.viii.1)—in German (MEGA Bd. I/3 p. 465), before eventually returning to Book II.

The one comment Marx makes here reveals that, while noting down the basic categories in Say and Smith, he is still thinking like a German philosopher, remarking on circularities in the argument. His summary and excerpting of Smith is dense, but the fact that he makes no comment on the structure of the work (or lack of it), or on Smith's digressions, suggests a degree of superficiality in his engagement: this is a novice reader who really does not know what to make of Smith, and so writes it all down anyway. Just over twenty pages out of a total of thirty-six are devoted to Books I and II of *Wealth of Nations*; almost seven to Book III; and ten to Book IV, overwhelmingly on the chapters dealing with the mercantile system, mostly in German, with very perfunctory notes on Smith's analysis of the Physiocrats in chapter 9. There are no notes on Book V at all.[71]

70. MEGA Bd. I/3 p. 458; WN I.ii.2–3. Pierre Force has noted Garnier's translation of Smith's 'self-love' as 'intérêt personnel' and 'egoïsme'. Garnier elides self-love, self-interest, and 'selfishness' in the same way that Max Stirner did later in his 1846/1847 German translation of *Wealth of Nations*, as discussed above—see Pierre Force, 'First Principles in Translation: The Axiom of Self-Interest from Adam Smith to Jean-Baptiste Say', *History of Political Economy* Vol. 38 (2006) pp. 321–22.

71. Proudhon had read the same edition of *Wealth of Nations* in October 1841; he made notes only on Book I, reviewed Garnier's introductory comments, and also noted that Book III would be a rich source of material for his work on property—NAF 18259; XXIIIe Cahier in-8° (octobre 1841): pp. 6–12; in 1844 he returned to Book I and made more extensive notes and comments from the Blanqui edition—NAF 18261; Cahier in-8° (juin–juillet 1844): pp. 18–45.

The new *Gesamtaugabe* editors assert that at this point Marx began composing the first of the three notebooks for the 'Economic and Philosophical Manuscripts',[72] on the grounds that there is so much Smith in the 'Manuscripts', and so little Ricardo. They assume that since Ricardo would become more important for Marx than Smith, the apparent absence of references here to Ricardo must mean that Marx had not yet read Ricardo. What, however, of the possibility that he read Ricardo, but did not at first recognise his significance? As we shall see, there are good grounds for believing that it was only after he had read Mill and McCulloch that Ricardo came clearly into focus for Marx, Smith then moving into the background. This would also explain the rapid development of a perspective upon Smith owed in part to Garnier, but chiefly to Ricardo, together with Say's notes on Ricardo in the version he read. Besides, if Marx immediately recognised the significance of Ricardo as soon as he had read *Principles*, why then read James Mill's *Elements* so thoroughly, since this was only a systematisation and simplification of Ricardo? Lacking any unambiguous evidence that Marx did break off at this point and start work on the 'Manuscripts', I will continue straight on to Marx's notes on Ricardo, Mill, and McCulloch, before turning to the work Marx did in the summer of 1844.

Marx read the second edition of the French translation of the first edition of Ricardo's *Principles*. To understand what Marx made of Ricardo it is very important that the implications of this statement are properly understood. The first edition of the translation had been published in two volumes in 1819 with notes by Say.[73] This was republished in 1835 in a 'corrected' edition together with a 'notice on the life and writings of Ricardo, published by his family'.[74] The 'Notice sur la vie' is a translation of

72. Karl Marx, Friedrich Engels, *Gesamtausgabe* Bd. I/2 Apparat p. 689.

73. David Ricardo, *Des principes de l'économie politique, et de l'impot*, 2 vols., trans. Francisco Solano Constancio, notes by Jean-Baptiste Say, Paris 1819. Constancio also translated Malthus's *Principles of Political Economy* into French—see José Luìs Cardoso, 'The Road to Heterodoxy: F. S. Constancio and the Critical Acceptance of Political Economy', *History of Political Economy* Vol. 31 (1999) pp. 479–81.

74. Title-page to David Ricardo, *Des Principes de l'Économie Politique et de l'impot*, trans. F.-S. Constancio, with notes by J.-B. Say, 2nd edition, J. P. Aillaud, Paris 1835. At the end of 'Avis au lecteur' here the translator notes that he follows the 'natural order' of the thirty-one and not twenty-nine chapters, and that chs. 5 and 8 were numerically duplicated, and accordingly marked with an asterisk in the English edition—p. lx. Allen Oakley (*Marx's Critique of Political Economy: Intellectual Sources and Evolution* Vol. 1: *1844 to 1860*, Routledge and Kegan Paul, London 1984 p. 28) states that the French translation is of Ricardo's second edition, but he confuses the second edition of the French translation with the second edition of the original.

McCulloch's *Memoir of the Life and Writings of David Ricardo, Esq. M.P.*,[75] although Marx made no notes on this at the time.[76] Nonetheless, it has already been shown in chapters 2 and 4 that McCulloch's grasp of the finer details of Ricardo's political economy was at times uncertain;[77] now we will see how McCulloch's version of Ricardo is reflected in the way that Marx reads Ricardo.

Ricardo's *Principles* went through three editions in his lifetime, the third adding a chapter on machinery which opened with Ricardo's admission that he had revised his original opinion on the effect of machinery upon employment, that both capitalists and labourers benefited from its introduction.

> My mistake arose from the supposition, that whenever the net income of a society increased, its gross income would also increase; I now, however, see reason to be satisfied that the one fund, from which landlords and capitalists derive their revenue, may increase, while the other, that upon which the labouring class mainly depend, may diminish, and therefore it follows, if I am right, that the same cause which may increase the net revenue of the country, may at the same time render the population redundant, and deteriorate the condition of the labourer.[78]

I mention this here only to emphasise that Marx would *not* have found this argument in the edition of Ricardo that he read in 1844. Much as Ricardo's new position on machinery and labour might seem to fit into the French critique of labour and competition in the 1830s and early 1840s, this revision was in the third edition published in 1821, and McCulloch would have been the last person to draw attention to it in his *Memoir*.[79] We

75. Anon. [J. R. McCulloch], *Memoir of the Life and Writings of David Ricardo, Esq. M.P.*, Richard Taylor, London 1825. This is in part based on the memoir attributed to one of Ricardo's brothers printed in *Works and Correspondence* Vol. 10 pp. 3–15.

76. But Marx came back to McCulloch in a later notebook, and the notes he made there confirm the argument being advanced here—see below.

77. Terence Hutchison concisely summed McCulloch up in describing his influence on Ricardo as 'pulling in the same direction as Mill's, that is, in politics woodenly radical, in methodology vastly oversimplified, in everything narrowly dogmatic'. 'Ricardo's Correspondence', *Economica* Vol. 20 New Series (1953) p. 269.

78. David Ricardo, *On the Principles of Political Economy and Taxation*, *Works and Correspondence of David Ricardo* Vol. 1, ed. Piero Sraffa with Maurice Dobb, Cambridge University Press, Cambridge 1951 p. 388.

79. McCulloch's discussion of *Principles* in the 1825 *Memoir* is limited to the first edition—Memoir, op. cit. p. 16. In the same year that Ricardo's third edition appeared McCulloch published an article in which he categorically stated that 'It appears, therefore, that no improvement of machinery can possibly diminish the demand for labour, or reduce the rate of wages. The introduction of machinery into

can assume that Marx was at the time unaware of this later revision to the version of Ricardo's *Principles* that he read.

It is also important here to consider some problems, both compositional and theoretical, with the first edition of *Principles*, some of which were corrected in the second. As briefly outlined in chapter 2 above, James Mill pressured Ricardo to extend the argument concerning distribution and the rate of profit outlined in his 1815 'Essay on Profits' into a book-length treatment.[80] Mill mostly offered general advice and encouragement, and did not engage in a detailed review of the drafts that Ricardo eventually produced. One task that Mill did assume was the preparation of the index, which as Sraffa points out demonstrates misunderstandings of the text; although many of the reviewers preferred the clarity of the index to the text, Samuel Bailey among them.[81] Nevertheless, one result of Mill's chivvying on one side, and Ricardo's prevarications on the other, was that the text was divided into chapters only after the whole had been written, and the resulting arrangement imposed on the book in part while it was being set, leading to two misnumbered chapters and other printing errors. These were corrected in the second edition, and the first chapter on value subdivided by headings, to which were added revisions to the end and beginning of each of the resulting five sections.

Terry Peach has provided a detailed analysis of the broader theoretical problems of Ricardo's theory of value as exposed in the first chapter of the first edition of *Principles*, which he describes as 'replete with unanswered questions, misplaced material, and internal contradictions'.[82] Ricardo opened this chapter with Smith's distinction of 'value in use' and 'value in exchange', utility being essential to exchange value, but limiting the latter further to commodities that could be increased in number by human effort under conditions of unconstrained competition. The implication of this is that commodities sell at their natural prices, which prevail when rates of profit and wages are uniform; and the exchange value of

one employment, *necessarily occasions an equal or greater demand for the disengaged labourers in some other employment*. The only hardship which it ever imposes upon the labourer, is, that in some cases it forces him to change his business' (McCulloch's emphasis)—'The Opinions of Messrs Say, Sismondi, and Malthus, on the Effects of Machinery and Accumulation, Stated and Examined', *Edinburgh* Review Vol. 35 No. 69 (1821) p. 115.

80. The composition of the book is dealt with at some length in the editorial introduction to Ricardo's *Works and Correspondence* Vol. 1 pp. xix–xxxvii.

81. Ibid. p. xxi + xxii.

82. Terry Peach, *Interpreting Ricardo*, Cambridge University Press, Cambridge 1993 p. 154.

commodities is made dependent on the quantities of labour expended upon them.[83] Next comes a somewhat convoluted discussion of the possibility of there being an invariant standard of value, which is eventually developed into a consideration of the impact upon values when commodities are produced with unequal amounts of fixed and circulating capital. This leads to what Ricardo had called a 'curious effect', where the relative prices of those commodities on which such capital is employed will vary 'in proportion to the quantity and durability of the fixed capital employed'—indeed, prices will fall as wages rise.[84] The upshot of Peach's analysis is that, in the first edition especially, Ricardo's exposition of his 'labour theory of value' was by no means unambiguous, involving both a strict 'labour expended' theory and one in which alterations to the combinations of capital and labour used in the production of a commodity introduced a 'curious effect', that prices would fall as wages rose. Important for our purposes here is that, reviewing the first edition, McCulloch stated that it was the cost of production which is the regulator of exchangeable value, this being the commodity's 'real price'. However, this was only true for Ricardo if a pure labour theory of value, unencumbered by inputs of capital, holds.[85]

In the memoir that prefaced the 1835 French edition McCulloch drew the lines even more clearly than he had in his 1818 review:

> The fundamental principle maintained by Mr. Ricardo in this great work, is, that the exchangeable value, or relative worth of commodities, as compared with each other, depends exclusively on *the quantities of labour necessarily required to produce them*. Dr. Smith was of the opinion that this was the principle which determined the exchangeable value of commodities in the earliest stages of society, before land had been appropriated and capital accumulated; but he supposed that, after land had become property and rent began to be paid, and after capital had been amassed and workmen began to be hired by

83. Ricardo, *Principles*, op. cit., pp. 12–13. An important reading principle here is that we consider what was printed on the pages of the first edition of *Principles*, and not read into what is written there imputations about what Ricardo 'really meant' deduced at best from later editions of *Principles*, or from his correspondence.

84. Ibid. pp. 62–63 (in the Appendix to ch. 1, which reproduces the closing section of the text of the first edition). See Peach, *Interpreting Ricardo*, pp. 156–63 for a detailed discussion of the problems in Ricardo's exposition in the first edition.

85. Peach, *Interpreting Ricardo*, op. cit. p. 174. In a letter of 23 August 1818 Ricardo's friend Hutches Trower drew his attention to the confusions in McCulloch's review—cited in *Interpreting Ricardo*, op. cit. p. 175. To point out what might seem obvious, if you are going to eventually write a book about labour and capital and found it upon a 'labour theory of value', Ricardo's 'curious effect' is going to have important ramifications.

> capitalists, the value of commodities would necessarily fluctuate, not only according to the variations in the quantity of labour required to produce and bring them to market, but also according to the rise and fall of rents and wages. But Mr. Ricardo has shown that Dr. Smith erred in making this distinction; and that the same principle which determined the value of commodities in the earliest and rudest stages of society, continue to determine in those that are most cultivated and refined.[86]

This passage gives a clear sense of McCulloch's muscular approach to Ricardo's economics, from which Ricardo must have drawn some comfort given the barrage of criticism that developed over the next few years.[87] His chief critic was Malthus, whose persistent criticism of the detailed working of the model that Ricardo had advanced—in which the movements of wages, profits, and rents were constrained by a labour theory of value, and where the principal interest lay in the long-term trend of the rate of profit—led to the publication of Malthus's own *Principles of Political Economy* in 1820, containing a critique of Ricardo that sought at the same time to revise Adam Smith's treatment of distribution.[88] Ricardo's critics not only pointed out the incoherence of Ricardo's treatment of value, but also the abstract nature of the manner in which he drew conclusions concerning the rate of wages, the price level, and the rate of profit. Among these critics was of course Jean-Baptiste Say, who provided the notes to the edition of Ricardo that Marx read. While not that extensive, they provided Say with the opportunity of 'correcting' Ricardo, introducing yet further complexities for the unwary reader. What, then, did Marx make of Ricardo?[89]

86. McCulloch, 'Notice', in Ricardo, *Principes* (1835) pp. xix–xx, cited as in *Memoir*, op. cit. pp. 17–18. This draws on material also printed in McCulloch's *Discourse on the Rise, Progress, Peculiar Objects, and Importance, of Political Economy*, Archibald Constable, Edinburgh 1824 pp. 66–67.

87. Mark Blaug notes that by the end of the 1820s McCulloch remained Ricardo's only active spokesman, and that 'Among what Mallet called "the great guns of science" there was no no doubt that Ricardo's theory, as he expounded it, was rife with errors'. *Ricardian Economics: A Historical Study*, Yale University Press, New Haven 1958 p. 62, more generally ch. 3, and his concluding ch. 12, 'The Evolution of Ricardian Economics'.

88. See Peach, *Interpreting Ricardo*, op. cit. ch. 5, and also Gilbert Faccarello, 'Sraffa versus Ricardo: The Historical Irrelevance of the "Corn-Profit" Model', *Economy and Society* Vol. 11 (1982) pp. 122–37.

89. This notebook is the same size as the one made up for Say, created from nine folded sheets; it is printed as continuous text in MEGA Bd. I/2 pp. 493–519. The new MEGA editors make no remarks in the Apparat volume about the layout of the notes, but a reproduction of p. 1 in this 12″ by 8″ notebook shows that Marx used the book in 'landscape' rather than 'portrait', and furthermore divided his notes into three columns: Karl Marx, Friedrich Engels, *Gesamtausgabe* Bd. I/2 p. 393. There are no headings to the columns, nor any indication whether the columns run on within the same page, or from page to page.

Marx makes no notes on McCulloch's 'Memoir', but he does pay attention to Say's footnotes. He picks up the differing views of Ricardo and Say on value, based upon the long first clarificatory footnote by Say that made clear his disagreement with Ricardo; as Marx noted, 'In the definition of value Ricardo adheres to cost of production, Say to utility' (MEGA Bd. I/3 p. 493). Although the book he is reading is in French, excerpts, summaries, and comments are overwhelmingly in German, emphasising the manner in which Marx is seeking to think through what he is reading. It should also be emphasised that his notes and excepts are interspersed with substantial comments which do now begin address the substance of the argument; a major development from the way in which he approached Say and Smith, although philosophical 'criticism' does recur. He is very impressed by Ricardo's argument that labour is the source of all value:

> Ricardo develops the way in which labour involves the sum total of the price, since capital is also labour. Say, p. 25 note 1 shows that he has forgotten the profit of capital and of the soil, which does not come free of charge. Proudhon quite rightly concludes from this that where private property exists, a thing *costs* more than it is *worth*, and is a tribute to the owner of private property. (MEGA Bd. I/3 p. 494)

Two things are important here: Marx has not picked up on the issue that exercised Ricardo's early readers and critics, that the inclusion of capital in the value of a commodity introduces an instability in the relationship of value and prices; and second, he here makes the first explicit reference to Proudhon in his writings.[90] Marx does seem to have noticed that something in Ricardo does not quite add up, because he spends the next few pages drafting his own calculations of the relationship between fixed and circulating capital. But the notes and excerpts then proceed onwards as before until the following remark:

> p. 111 Ricardo says that when he speaks of exchange value he always means the natural price, disregarding the accidents of competition, which he calls *quelque cause momentanée ou accidentelle*. Political economy, in order to lend its laws a greater consistency and precision, has to describe reality as accidental and abstraction as real. (MEGA Bd. I/3 p. 502)

90. There is another casual reference to Proudhon a few pages later: MEGA Bd. I/3 p. 501.

Here again we have 'criticism', German philosophical point-scoring rather than attention to the inconsistencies of the text, as in the following:

> Ricardo is only interested in the distinctions of the various classes. The usual circle of political economy. Intellectual freedom as aim. Thus vacuous servitude for the majority. Bodily needs not the sole aim. Hence sole aim of the majority. Or the reverse, Marriage the aim. Hence prostitution for the majority. Property the aim. Hence propertylessness for the majority. (MEGA Bd. I/3 p. 504)

There is however more than this. When Say points out in a footnote that rent cannot be a part of the natural price of a good,[91] but certainly part of the 'prix courant', Marx adds a long aside, beginning with Smith's idea that wages, rent, and profits were all component parts of the natural price, then stating that rent was not a part of necessary production costs; nor was profit—in both cases they were paid by the labour required to maintain land and capital respectively (MEGA Bd. I/3 p. 501). Interest and profit, he went on, lease payments and rent, were formed from '*das plus, das mehr als diese*. So the price of everything is too *expensive*, as Proudhon has already elaborated'.[92] Furthermore, the natural rate of wages, rents, and profit depends upon custom or monopoly, ultimately upon competition, and is not elaborated from the nature of the earth, capital, and labour. 'Production costs themselves are therefore determined by competition, and not by production' (ibid.). Shortly following this there is a long passage in which, again prompted by Say's comments, he compares Smith and Ricardo on the question of natural prices and exchange value, concluding that while production costs made up the natural price, political economy itself dealt more in terms of the *prix courant* (MEGA Bd. I/3 p. 502). Around half-way through his notes he arrives at the chapter on trade, summarised in a few lines; he then continues on through chapters on taxation, noting Ricardo's criticism of Say's determination of value by utility, and noting Say's footnoted response.[93]

There are several extended comments in the later part of his notes, in many cases evaluating what Ricardo writes against Say's objections, concluding provisionally that

> Ricardo's doctrine has only one important thing for present circumstances—that it shows how the competition between capitalists that takes place during

91. Ricardo, *Principes* (1835) t. 1 pp. 83–84.
92. Here we have an allusion to what Marx later called *Mehrwert*, surplus value; it is evident that the original idea came from Proudhon.
93. Ricardo, *Principes* (1835) t. 1 pp. 87ff.; MEGA Bd. I/3 p. 509.

> progressive accumulation and the diminution of their gains, in no way presumes an increase of wages, as Smith supposes. The *number of workers* is now in all industrial countries above the level of demand and can daily recruit from the *workless* proletariat, in the same way that it in turn daily recruits. In contrast, accumulation now has the outcome, with competition, that the wage of labour is reduced ever lower. (MEGA Bd. I/3 p. 511)

We could say that Marx has here moved beyond the naive/philosophical reading that we saw at work in the case of Say and Smith; in his notes on Ricardo's *Principles* we encounter some willingness to engage with the subject matter of political economy. It is also apparent that much of this is prompted by Say's own commentary, through which he is led into a comparison of Smith, Ricardo, and Say. Moreover, running alongside this reading we can also see the continuing influence of Proudhon and Blanc, who read Ricardo as a theorist of immiseration, and not as a theorist of the labour theory of value, free trade, distribution, and a declining rate of profit. Marx does not connect at all with the core technical issues that were matters of such controversy for British critics during the 1820s, and of course McCulloch's bland introductory comments would not have helped him with this. He would only move on from this position in late 1846: in seeking to establish his superior grasp of English political economy from that to be found in Proudhon's new book on the contradictions of political economy, he was finally forced to distance himself from this moralising approach to political economy.[94]

In 1850–51 Marx did come back to re-read Ricardo, and made notes on the English third edition in two separate notebooks. First of all he simply extracted from it various quotations related to money, currency, and trade in Notebook IV.[95] Then it is evident from another Notebook (No. VIII) that in April 1851 he reviewed the entire book, mostly summarising the text in German. While these notes relate to the structure of the text, they do so out of sequence: the notes on chapter 7, 'On Foreign Trade', appear under the heading 'Determination of Exchange Value in Different

94. Proudhon had read the first French edition of Ricardo's *Principles* in October 1841, commenting both on Ricardo and on Say's criticisms of Ricardo, ordering Ricardo to 'The School of Say'. As before, however, Proudhon's notes are more orderly, detailed and reflective than those of Marx. NAF 18259; XXIIIe Cahier in-8 (octobre 1841): pp. 42–48.

95. Karl Marx, Friedrich Engels, *Gesamtausgabe* Bd. IV/7 pp. 316–28, Dietz Verlag, Berlin 1983.

Countries',[96] and are immediately followed by notes on chapter 25. The new chapter 31 on machinery has the heading 'Influence of Machinery on the Wages of Labour', and is followed by notes on chapter 16.[97] Of course, after chapter 6 there is no particular logical structure to Ricardo's book, just a loosely connected series of chapters, but the way in which Marx moves back and forth between chapters in his note-taking strongly suggests that he is seeking material for a line of thought he has already formed, and not seeking to understand the development of Ricardo's argument. The summary he then makes of the new chapter 31 on machinery, and the direct quotations in English that he records, convey no sense at all that this chapter contains arguments that are of any especial significance for him.

After his first reading of Ricardo Marx turned to James Mill's *Elements of Political Economy*, first published in 1821. This was a simplified exposition of Ricardo's ideas, originating in 1819 with the notes written up by a thirteen-year-old John Stuart Mill following lectures on political economy by his father during their daily walk. Marx continues the pattern of note-taking that he had adopted with Ricardo's *Principles*: lengthy excerpts written straight into German, occasional summaries, and little in the way of comment initially, besides one complaint about how tedious the book was.[98] However, not even halfway through the book, having just dealt with Mill's account of the quantity of money,[99] Marx breaks off from his notes and for the first time develops an extended commentary on his reading.[100] And the fact that this occurs in the midst of Mill's discussion of money is significant: for Marx sees money as an 'estranged mediator' in human exchanges:

> Very good in reducing the essence of the thing to a concept when Mill characterises *money* as the *mediator* of exchange. The essence of money is not initially that property is alienated (*entäußert*) in it, but that the *mediating activity* of

96. 'Bestimmung des Tauschwerts in verschiednen Länder'—we can assume that these headings are by Marx and have not been interpolated by the transcriber since they do for the most part correspond to chapters in Ricardo's *Principles*; 'Notizen und Auszüge über Ricardos System März-April 1851', in Karl Marx, *Grundrisse der Kritik der politischen Ökonomie: Rohentwurf 1857–1858*, facsimile of 1939/41 Moscow edition published Berlin 1953, republished by Europäische Verlagsanstalt, Frankfurt am Main 1967 pp. 811–12.

97. 'Einfluß der Maschinerie auf den Arbeitslohn', Marx, *Grundrisse*, op. cit. pp. 822–24.

98. MEGA Bd. I/3 p. 523: 'Siehe p. sqq. die folgende langweilige Brühe'.

99. ch. 3 §8 of *Elements of Political Economy* in James Mill, *Selected Economic Writings*, ed. Donald Winch, Oliver and Boyd, Edinburgh 1966.

100. This section of Marx's notes on Mill has been published separately (Karl Marx, Friedrich Engels, *Werke Ergänzungsband. Schriften, Manuskripte, Briefe bis 1844*, Erster Teil, Dietz Verlag, Berlin 1973 pp. 443–63) with the misleading title

movement, the *human*, social act through which the products of man reciprocally complement each other, is *estranged* and becomes money, the character of a *material thing* external to man. (MEGA Bd. I/3 p. 531)

Here again we can see how Marx, while diligently reading through the text, processes what he reads into the framework that he already developed in 1843 in his two critiques of Hegel's *Philosophy of Right*: the movement of essence, externalisation and domination from which man had to be emancipated, coloured here also by the critique of philosophy and religion which he would be elaborated at length in *The Holy Family*. Marx's comments here quickly become repetitive: 'The metal being of money is only the official plausible expression of money's soul, which is embodied in all elements of the productions and movements of civil society'; '*paper money* . . . is the *more complete* being of *money as money*'; '*Credit* is the judgement of *political economy* on the morality of a person' (MEGA Bd. I/3 pp. 533, 534). And a few pages later: 'One sees how political economy *fixates* the *estranged* form of social intercourse as *essential* and *original*, corresponding to human determination' (MEGA Bd. I/3 pp. 536–37). Quite certainly there is nothing like this in Mill, rather it represents Marx's own ruminations prompted by reading Mill. And these extended musings culminate with the following:

The separation of labour from itself = separation of the labourer from the capitalist = separation of labour and capital, whose original form decomposes into *landed property* and *moveable property* . . . The original determination of private property is monopoly; therefore as soon as there is a political constitution it is one of monopoly. Perfected monopoly is competition. (MEGA Bd. I/3 p. 540)

Marx then resumes his note-taking with Mill's chapter 4, on consumption, breaking off again to comment on Mill's 'cynical acuity and clarity' in treating exchange on the basis of private property (MEGA Bd. I/3 p. 543), and extending this to a consideration of surplus production:

If I produce more than I can directly use of the produced object, then my *surplus* production is *calculated* according to your need, clever. I only *seemingly* produce a surplus of this object. In truth, I produce *another* object, the object

'Auszüge aus James Mills Buch "Élémens d'économie politique"'—this is Marx's own commentary, not his notes). Some writers have treated it as a source for an understanding of Marx's conception of alienation—see for example David Leopold, *The Young Marx: German Philosophy, Modern Politics, and Human Flourishing*, Cambridge University Press, Cambridge 2007 pp. 232–34. Placed back in the context of his notes, these remarks assume a rather different significance.

> of your production which I intend to exchange for this surplus, an exchange which I have already competed in thought. The *social* relationship which I am in with you, my labour for your need, is therefore also mere *appearance*, and our reciprocal complementarity is likewise mere *appearance* which serves mutual plundering. (MEGA Bd. I/3 p. 544)

And so on. Marx then resumes his reading, and he does in fact finish: his final notes relates to taxes on profits, dealt with in the last few pages of Mill's book.

Marx completed his initial foray into political economy by reading McCulloch's *Discourse* in the French translation.[101] Marx would have found here the original 'history of political economy', linking the development of modern economic thinking to earlier writings on commerce and trade. Beginning with a general presentation of political economy, McCulloch then raises the question of why political economy is of comparatively recent origin. His explanation is that in ancient Greece and Rome economic activity was thought ignoble, and so there was little impulse to reflect upon it; this lack of interest continued into the medieval period, with the establishment of universities oriented to classical and theological studies; and he went on to suggest that the real origin of the science could be linked to the extension of commerce during the later fifteenth and sixteenth centuries.[102] There is a distant echo here of Smith's own account of political œconomy in Book IV of *Wealth of Nations*, but McCulloch for the most part presents directly the writings of Mun, Child, Petty, North, and Davenant, rather than the 'mercantile system' of policy that Smith had examined. For the time being, however, Marx appears to have ignored this historical context, his notes on the text focusing on the more general exposition of the science of political economy, and the comments that McCulloch makes on Quesnay, Smith, and Malthus—the direct antecedents of Ricardo, McCulloch, and Mill. McCulloch was a great self-plagiarist, and the summary of Ricardo that can be found in the *Memoir* is lifted straight out of this *Discourse*.[103] Marx copies the passage at length here (MEGA Bd. I/3 pp. 552–53)—so perhaps he had not after all read through the 'Notice' while reading the 1835 French edition of Ricardo's *Principles*.

101. J. R. McCulloch, *Discours sur l'origine, les progrès, les objets particuliers et l'importance de l'économie politique*, trans. Guillaume Prevost, J. J. Paschoud, Geneva 1825. The notebook was made from seven 12″ by 9″ sheets, folded once into 6″ by 9″, making twenty-eight pages, pp. 3–11 and 13–21 of which contain the excerpts from the French McCulloch translation, in two columns landscape: Karl Marx, Friedrich Engels, *Gesamtausgabe* Bd. IV/2 Apparat pp. 781–82.

102. McCulloch, *Discourse*, op. cit. p. 23.

103. Ibid. pp. 66–69.

Nonetheless, it is here in the French translation of McCulloch's *Discourse* that Marx first encounters a short history of political economy and the Ricardian variant thereof. He had doggedly read through Say, Smith, Ricardo, and James Mill, McCulloch's *Discourse* providing a brisk résumé of what he could have found there; but this French edition also came with an appendix by the translator, Guillaume Prévost, who like Constancio was no mere jobbing translator. His father, Pierre, was the brother-in-law of Jane Marcet, whose connection to Ricardo and Malthus was reflected in her very popular book *Conversations on Political Economy* (1816).[104] Guillaume Prévost clearly had an understanding of political economy that was rather more sophisticated than that of McCulloch, and this was reflected in the summary that his appendix provides. By examining the way that Marx responds to this summary, it is possible to gauge rather more exactly what Marx in 1844 understood Ricardian political economy to be.

Prévost noted that 'les Ricardiens'[105] believed that the whole of political economy could be grasped with a small number of principles. He presents six:[106]

1. Rent does not influence price, and the cost of production is composed only of wages plus profits.
2. Variations in wages have a direct impact upon the level of profit.
3. The prices of agricultural products are necessarily regulated by the price which the cultivators of land bearing no rent can pay.
4. The rate of profit in agriculture regulates all other prices.
5. (1) Price is represented by the production cost. (2) The relation of supply and demand has no influence on price and value, except in the case of monopoly or for short periods.
6. The exchange value of a commodity is determined by the quantity of labour employed in its production.

104. See on Jane Marcet my essay 'Economic Manuals in Great Britain and the British Empire 1797–1938', in Massimo M. Augello, Marco E. L. Guidi (eds.) *The Economic Reader*, Routledge, Abingdon 2012 pp. 47–48. For the Prévost family connection to Ricardo, see Alain Béraud, Gilbert Faccarello, 'The Reception of Ricardo in the French Language: Episodes from a Complex History', in Gilbert Faccarello, Masashi Izumo (eds.) *The Reception of David Ricardo in Continental Europe and Japan*, Routledge, Abingdon 2014 pp. 16–17.

105. Guillaume Prevost, 'Réflexions du traducteur sur le système de Ricardo', in McCulloch, *Discours*, op. cit. p. 171. In the transcription provided by MEGA Bd. I/3 it is not clear that the notes Marx makes here are from this translator's appendix to McCulloch, and some recent commentators have assumed that Prévost's text is a separate publication. These excerpts and comments by Marx relate directly to 'Réflexions', pp. 155–204 of McCulloch, *Discours* op. cit.

106. Prevost, 'Réflexions', op. cit. pp. 157–64.

While one might argue with choice of wording or topic, these six points do make quite plain that Ricardo's political economy concerned prices, cost of production, land, labour, and capital, together with rent, wages, and capital. As Ricardo had written to his friend Malthus:

> Political Economy you think is an enquiry into the nature and causes of wealth—I think it should rather be called an enquiry into the laws which determine the division of the produce of industry amongst the classes who concur in its formation. No law can be laid down respecting quantity, but a tolerably correct one can be laid down respecting proportions.[107]

Ricardo's linkage of labour to value, so easily confused with that of Smith, was quite clearly an element that could easily be assimilated to Marx's preoccupation with property, exchange, and exploitation. However, Prévost's bald summary of Ricardo marks out the distance between Smith and Ricardo, proceeding to discuss two 'consequences', and three corollaries:

> First consequence: the abundance of capital has no direct influence on the rate of profit.
> Second consequence: profits diminish with the advance of civilisation.
> First secondary consequence: the decline of profits is a threat to the prosperity of a country.
> Second secondary consequence: the interests to landowners is opposed to that of all other classes of society.
> Third secondary consequence: one means of preventing decline is to establish complete liberty, especially in the grain trade, above all in the most progressive of nations.[108]

Prévost's summary therefore clearly stated Ricardo's central concern to be distribution between the classes, the consequent impact of a long-run declining rate of profit, and the role of trade in counter-acting this decline. What did Marx make of this?

Before making any notes, he commented: 'It is obvious that this concerns the ideas (*Lehren*) that distinguish D. Ricardo from Smith' (MEGA Bd. I/3 p. 553). Prévost's presentation of the Ricardian version of political

107. Ricardo to Malthus, 9 October 1820, *Works and Correspondence* Vol. 8 Letter 392 p. 278.

108. Prevost, 'Réflexions', op. cit. pp. 167–70.

economy drew Marx's attention to the fact that it was organised as a critique of Smithian principles (albeit of a very restricted subset of these principles). He worked through the six points, writing them down in German, and then making excerpts from Prévost's discussion. He then notes down, without comment, the 'consequences' listed above, although the 'Third secondary consequence' is simply noted, passing over Prévost's concluding comment here:

> It is, so say the Ricardians, by giving complete liberty to the grain trade that one can forestall the fall of profits; it is by abolishing the restrictive system that one slows the decline which inheres in the general laws of men's destiny.[109]

The absence of any remark on this by Marx simply confirms something already evident in his reading of Ricardo's *Principles*: in these notebooks he just does not pick up on the economic dynamic underlying Ricardo's arguments. The derivation of a falling general rate of profit from the distribution of incomes arising in the production process, and the role of 'perfect liberty' in forestalling the decline in profit, and hence in investment, is one of the central points separating Smith from Ricardo; and yet Marx, attuned to the fact that there are differences between Smith and Ricardo, apparently just reads on. So what does he think about Prévost's presentation?

First, he criticises Prévost's praise of Ricardian simplicity, arguing that this increasingly abstracts from people, from real life, shifting attention to the abstract movement of material, inhuman property (MEGA Bd. I/3 p. 556). Next he notes that Prévost praises the discovery on the part of the Ricardians that price is represented by costs of production, independently of supply and demand. He objects to the abstraction involved in this, then repeats Say's argument: that the Ricardians assume that to supply a commodity amounts to its sale, whatever the cost or demand might be. Marx argues that free competition determines prices, which, he says, are arbitrary. Of course, no one wants to sell at a price below production costs, 'but wanting to do so, and being able to do so, are different things' (MEGA Bd. I/3 p. 557). Turning then to capital as accumulated labour,

> the more they recognise labour as the sole principle of wealth, the more the worker is degraded, impoverished and labour itself made into a commodity.

109. Ibid. p. 171.

> Besides, given that the expression 'travail accumulée' (*aufgehäufte Arbeit*) expresses the origin of capital, it also means that labour has become increasingly a thing, a commodity, and can only be grasped as *capital*, not as human activity. (loc. cit.)

The Ricardians are only interested in the general law, he goes on; whether thousands are ruined through its operation is not their concern. Indeed, their identification of individual and social interest is necessary for their arguments to have meaning. Once the existence of property is acknowledged this identification is no longer tenable, since inimical interests are formed. Political economy has therefore to assume that interests are not opposed, and property communal. 'In this way they can prove that if I consume everything, and you produce everything, consumption and production are, in relation to society, entirely in order' (MEGA Bd. I/3 p. 558).

> All reasonable principles, such as the unity of different branches of production and interests, of the unity of labour and capital, or production and consumption etc. become in the hands of political economy, on the basis of private property, *infamous* sophistries. (loc. cit.)

And so, despite Prévost's concise presentation of the core distributional agenda of Ricardo's political economy, and the dynamic that links advocacy of free trade to a declining rate of profit, Marx still persists with his moralising evaluation of political economy. Indeed, if Marx really had picked up the point that, unlike Smith, Ricardo was concerned with the *comparative* value of goods in exchange, then we might well have anticipated some kind of comment to the effect that the equality in exchange between men was transposed in political economy to an equality in the exchange of goods. But this is not how his argument about commodity fetishism works, which is purely Smithian in this respect.

This first encounter with political economy would have long-lasting ramifications; Marx would return to these notebooks repeatedly in the years to come, never again reading any of these works so closely as he had in 1844. The foundations of his critique had been laid; and he already began retranscribing some of these notes in the summer of 1844, creating a new set of homemade notebooks that we now know as the 'Economic and Philosophical Manuscripts'.

THE FORMATION OF A PROJECT: 'THE ECONOMIC AND PHILOSOPHICAL MANUSCRIPTS'

Since their publication in 1932, the syntheses Marx wrote during the summer of 1844 have been treated as the first draft of a planned book; and the following year he did sign a contract to write a *Kritik der Politik und Nationalökonomie*.[110] The notebooks were synoptic: they are not new excerpts and comments, but mostly rewrite and reorder notes and excerpts from his previous reading. It is this synthetic form that suggests these particular notebooks are an early draft for a critique of political economy. This practice of synoptic redrafting would however become a significant part of his working method—and given the rather unsystematic way in which he made his original notes and excerpts, a practice fraught with problems. The new MEGA editors have placed these '1844 Manuscripts' in Series I of the *Gesamtausgabe*, reserved for original works; and not therefore in Series IV, which is reserved for notebooks such as the ones reviewed in the previous section. They therefore imply that in composing this material Marx had already begun his 'critique of political economy'. Hence before considering what the contents of these notebooks tell us about Marx's approach to political economy, we need to understand how these notebooks acquired this special status—how they came to be know as the 'Economic and Philosophical Manuscripts', or the '1844 Manuscripts'.

Rojahn has provided a detailed account of their origin and reception, Ryazanov publishing them first in Russian translation in 1927, followed by a French translation in 1929, publication in the original following in 1932.[111] My reference text here is the 1932 MEGA version. However, in the same year Siegfried Landshut and J. P. Mayer published some of this

110. The contract was with the Darmstadt publisher C. W. Leske, signed by both parties and dated 1 February 1845—MEGA Bd. I/3 p. 30.

111. Jürgen Rojahn, 'Marxismus—Marx—Geschichtswissenschaft: Der Fall der sog. "ökonomisch-philosophischen Manuskripte aus dem Jahre 1844"', *International Review of Social History* Vol. 28 (1983) pp. 2–49; for the early publication history see p. 3 fn. 1. Rojahn provides an exemplary, if depressing, account of the reception of 'the' Paris Manuscripts. However, in the course of providing a detailed description of the manuscript material his account loses focus, quickly descending into an exclusive preoccupation with the material form of Marx's writings and an entire neglect of their content. Rojahn does not seem to have looked very closely at the works that Marx took notes on; nor does he consider what Marx's note-taking practice might tell us about how he read these works; nor what this might tell us about how Marx constructed his arguments.

material under the heading 'Nationalökonomie und Philosophie (1844)', and it was this rather different presentation of the notebooks that created their reputation.

The original MEGA version is based on three notebooks (I, II, and III), which are printed in this order, prefaced by some general descriptive remarks:

I. Wage Labour, Profit of Capital, Rent, Alienated Labour (pp. 39–94)[112]
II. The Relation of Private Property (pp. 95–103)[113]
III. Private Property and Labour, Private Property and Communism, Need, Production and the Division of Labour, Money, General Criticism of the Hegelian Dialectic and Philosophy (pp. 105–72)[114]

Sewn into the third notebook there was also a separate folio sheet written on in one column, and not two as with the others. The MEGA editors treated this as a separate notebook (No. IV), and printed it as an appendix (pp. 592–96).

The MEGA editors extracted a 'Preface' from the third notebook on account of the way it provides an overview of Marx's work in 1844, acknowledges Marx's debt to Engels's 'Umrisse', and identifies the analysis of Hegel's philosophy in Notebook IV as the 'closing chapter' (MEGA Bd. I/3 p. 34), strongly suggesting that by later in the summer of 1844 Marx had begun to think of this work as a book. Whether these notebooks were

112. Marx used nine unevenly cut sheets of about 12″ by 16″, five forming the outer leaves and four the inner, which he then folded in half. The clearest, yet still confusing, description of notebook No. I and its presentation is given by Margaret Fay, 'The Influence of Adam Smith on Marx's Theory of Alienation', *Science and Society* Vol. 47 No. 2 (Summer 1983) pp. 149–50; the account given in Karl Marx, Friedrich Engels, *Gesamtausgabe* Bd. I/2 Apparat pp. 703–4, 707–9 is much more difficult to follow. The important point to remember is that, as with some of his other notebooks, Marx wrote across the long axis (i.e., landscape), and divided most of the text into three columns, except for four pages divided into two columns. When the printed transcription comes to 'Alienated Labour' he stops writing in the columns and writes straight across the page; the heading 'Alienated Labour' originates with the editors, while the column headings are from Marx.

113. This manuscript is two loose sheets of different paper, roughly 12″ by 8″, making four pages, written up landscape in two columns, and since it begins in mid-sentence it can be assumed to form the closing section of a lost fragment—Karl Marx, Friedrich Engels, *Gesamtausgabe* Bd. I/2 Apparat p. 704.

114. This manuscript is a thick notebook of seventeen layered sheets, all roughly 12″ by 16″, folded to make sixty-eight pages, the last twenty-three pages of which are unwritten. The original sixteen sheets were divided into two columns before anything was written—Karl Marx, Friedrich Engels, *Gesamtausgabe* Bd. I/2 Apparat p. 705. The 'Preface' printed in MEGA Bd. I/3 pp. 33–35 was originally part of this manuscript, pp. xxix–xl, and preceded the section which the editors entitled 'Money'.

drafts of the book itself, or simply preparatory materials, is not however clear from their contents.

This summary account of the notebooks is based primarily on the brief but precise notes made by the original MEGA editors. But it was the Landshut and Mayer edition that launched the '1844 Manuscripts' as a hitherto hidden key to Marx's mature work, and they provided no such particulars of their sources. Initially intended for separate publication, the original notebooks, at that time held in the SPD archives in Berlin, had been transcribed by J. P. Mayer and Friedrich Salomon. But as the editors explain, the opportunity arose of integrating them within a more extensive collection of early writings.[115] Beginning with Marx's letter to his father of 10 November 1837, the first volume (xli + 414 pp.) included parts of the doctoral dissertation, the 'Critique of Hegel's Philosophy of State' in its entirety, excerpts from Marx's contributions to the *Rheinische Zeitung*, the two pieces on the Jewish Question together with the critique of Hegel's *Rechtsphilosophie*, manuscripts from the summer of 1844 entitled 'Nationalökonomie und Philosophie', and excerpts from the *Holy Family*. The second volume was larger (638 pp.), containing among other short pieces the *German Ideology*[116] in its entirety, excerpts from *Poverty of Philosophy*, concluding with the *Communist Manifesto*.

Landshut argued in his editorial introduction that there was a prevailing idea, shared by Marxists and anti-Marxists alike, that the early writings of Marx were 'still' heavily philosophical, and that in the course of the 1840s Marx had successively freed himself of the influence first of Hegel, then of the Young Hegelians, and finally Feuerbach, breaking out of these ideas into his 'mature', economic interpretation of the world. He suggested that the material presented in the '1844 Manuscripts' undermined this idea that Marx's work was characterised by a movement from philosophy to economics:

> This work ['Nationalökonomie und Philosophie (1844)'] is in a certain sense the most central work of Marx. It forms the nodal point of the entire development of his thinking, in that the principles of his economic analysis derive directly from the idea of the 'genuine reality of man'.[117]

115. Karl Marx, *Der historische Materialismus: Die Frühschriften*, 2 vols., ed. S. Landshut, J. P. Mayer, Alfred Kröner, Lepizig 1932, 'Vorwort', Bd. 1 p. vii.

116. Ironically, also a text of dubious provenance: see Terrell Carver, '*The German Ideology* Never Took Place', *History of Political Thought* Vol. 31 (2010) pp. 121–22.

117. Siegfried Landshut, 'Einleitung: Die Bedeutung der Frühschriften von Marx für ein neues Verständnis', in Marx, *Der historische Materialismus*, op. cit. Bd. 1 p. xiii. Rojahn notes that this introduction was separately published under Landshut's own name in 1932—Rojahn, 'Marxismus', op. cit. p. 4. fn. 8.

Accordingly the '1844 Manuscripts' were placed as the centre-piece of a collection that proposed a reinterpretation of Marx's work, relaunching Marx as a German philosopher who, far from abandoning his philosophical roots with his move to London, continued for the remainder of his life to elaborate the 'genuine reality of man', such that *Das Kapital* should ultimately be read as a work of social philosophy, and not political economy.

This new perspective rapidly caught on. Rojahn documents its diffusion, from articles published by Hendrik de Man and Herbert Marcuse during 1932 in social democratic periodicals,[118] through Kojève's 1933 lectures on Hegel, the publication in American exile of Marcuse's influential *Reason and Revolution* (1942), on through the postwar reception up to Erich Fromm and the broadening reception of Marx as a key social and political thinker during the 1960s.[119] All of this created a distance between an orthodoxy that treated Marx as an economic theorist of capitalism, and an update that presented him as a social philosopher, in which the '1844 Manuscripts' functioned as a key to this reinterpretation.

As Rojahn rightly complains, during the course of this entire reception history, from the 1930s to the 1970s, no interest at all was shown in the provenance of the manuscripts upon which this interpretation was based. In fact, the 'philosophical' Marx originally put into circulation by Landshut and Mayer was in part a product of their own discreet editorial rearrangement of the notebooks. For the version of the '1844 Manuscripts' we find in their collection is not the same as the one we find in MEGA: the notebooks are presented in a different order, and the first notebook is not reproduced at all. In their editorial introduction Landshut and Mayer claim that they print the manuscript without altering its arrangement, preserving the original characteristics of the notebooks apart from placing the 'Preface' from Notebook III at the front of the whole.[120] But in fact their version starts with Notebook III;[121] there is a hiatus where some material is omitted, and then a section discussing Hegel inserted, which in MEGA can be found on pp. 154–55;[122] a similar thing happens on p. 328 of Landshut and Mayer, where an excursus on Hegel appears which in MEGA is printed starting p. 156, resuming then on p. 347 of Landshut and Mayer with MEGA at p. 138. Landshut and Mayer continue on to the end of the section on money (p. 360; MEGA p. 149); then introduce Notebook II, and

118. Michael Maidan provides an interesting summary of the theses of de Man and Marcuse regarding the significance of the 'Manuscripts'—'The *Rezeptionsgeschichte* of the Paris Manuscripts', *History of European Ideas* Vol. 12 (1990) pp. 774–76.

119. Rojahn, 'Marxismus', op. cit. pp. 5–8.

120. 'Vorbemerkung', Marx, *Der historische Materialismus*, op. cit. Bd. 1 p. 285.

121. Ibid. Bd. 1 pp. 287ff.; MEGA Bd. I/3 pp. 108ff.

122. Marx, *Der historische materialismus*, op. cit. Bd. 1 p. 320; MEGA Bd. I/3 p. 133.

at the end of this (Landshut and Mayer p. 368; MEGA p. 103) add on the section separated out by the MEGA editors as Notebook IV (printed on pp. 592–96 of Bd. I/3). And so Landshut and Mayer print III, II, and IV in that order, omit I entirely, and rearrange III with the general effect that Marx's comments on political economy are secondary, and his philosophical ruminations placed centrally. Granted, the MEGA editors had made editorial decisions of their own, but so far as can be judged their reasons for so doing lay with the physical organisation of the notebooks. Landshut and Mayer do preserve the notebooks' page numbers, but provide no further account of their interventions.[123] Landshut and Mayer engaged in editorial rearrangement which determined the way in which the 'notebooks' would be read for decades to come.

The '1844 Manuscripts' do not therefore actually exist as usually understood; instead we have some notebooks that, placed together and in the case of Landshut and Mayer, given a particular slant, can be made to look like the beginning of a project. While they were quickly mobilised for a dubious reinterpretation of Marx's project, this does not however mean that they therefore provide, after all, no evidence at all regarding the development of Marx's vision. For if we examine the structure of Notebook I we can begin to understand how these notebooks were composed.

In the summer of 1844 Marx appears to have suffered a manic episode in which he was reported to be irritable, full of plans and projects, reading voraciously: 'He always wants to write [about] what he has last read'.[124] The first notebook included in the set referred to as the 'Economic and Philosophical Manuscripts' must have been produced around this time, and when Margaret Fay examined it during the 1970s[125] she noticed something important: that it simply contained transcriptions of the earlier excerpts from *Wealth of Nations*.[126] She therefore made a link between this notebook and the notes that Marx had made when he first read Say and Smith. Hence Marx was already, just months after reading these works and making notes on them, recycling these notes. Why would he do this?

123. See Rojahn's scornful comments, 'Marxismus', op. cit. pp. 8–9.

124. Letter from Arnold Ruge to M. Dunker, 29 August 1844, cited in Rojahn, 'Marxismus', op. cit. p. 21.

125. Margaret Fay died in June 1979. Earlier that year Istvan Hont had invited her to present a seminar at King's College Cambridge, and it was Istvan who brought her article to my attention in the mid-1980s. He believed that she was wrong about the importance of Smith to Marx, but that her general argument about the construction of the notebooks was very important.

126. Fay, 'Influence of Adam Smith' op. cit. pp. 133–34. She also noticed the nine sheets of paper were folded to make thirty-six pages after Marx had begun writing on them, and there were four central double pages and five outer, the two sets of pages being originally separate.

As already mentioned, the first notebook was ruled into three columns, headed 'Arbeitslohn', 'Profit des Kapitals', and 'Grundrente'. The version printed in the 1932 MEGA converted each column into continuous text, so that the contents of the first column, on wage labour, are now the first section of the first notebook (pp. 39–51), followed by profits on capital (pp. 52–66), and finally rent (pp. 67–80). The fourth section of this notebook, on alienated labour, represents what Marx wrote from the point where he abandoned writing text into columns and simply wrote straight across the page. Here we find the kind of summary ruminations into which he launched while taking notes on Mill's *Elements*.

Fay's understanding of political economy focused upon Smith's *Wealth of Nations*, and so she argues that the three headings represent categories taken from that work, the material in each column then being copied from the notes Marx had taken on *Wealth of Nations*. In fact, these three categories are generic for early nineteenth-century political economy, and more significant here is the way in which, by organising his previous reading under these heads, Marx aligned his understanding of Smith with the very restricted reading of Smith that is typical of Ricardo. Hence Marx here presents a version of the substance of *Wealth of Nations* as it appeared from the perspective of the 1820s, and this would remain a fixed perspective throughout his life. The first column (or section in the printed version) does not appear to contain much that is taken directly from Smith, but is rather a thematic résumé that seems to owe something to Wilhelm Schulz's *Die Bewegung der Produktion* (1843) and his own treatment of Smith.[127] Fay was however spot on about the second column: this is mostly a rewritten version of the earlier notes on Smith,[128] but also including a direct reference to the French edition of Ricardo:[129] it would be entirely possible to compose a concordance linking the two notebooks.[130] Furthermore, the reference to Ricardo suggests that this is after all being written subsequent to the notes taken on Ricardo's *Principles*. That there is so little Ricardo in this first notebook thus implies not that Marx had not yet read Ricardo, but that Marx did not at that time see *Principles* as a key text, being primarily oriented to *Wealth of Nations*.

127. As noted by the original MEGA editors, see their notes Bd. I/3 pp. 46–47. The analytical listing of passages from Smith in the new MEGA (Karl Marx, Friedrich Engels, *Gesamtausgabe* Bd. I/2 Apparat pp. 870ff.) includes Schulz.

128. Just for one example, see the parallel passages MEGA Bd. I/3 pp. 60 and 473.

129. MEGA Bd. I/3 pp. 63 and 514.

130. Which the new MEGA editors have in fact done (Bd. I/2 Apparat pp. 870–917), but their lack of familiarity with the original texts makes the result very hard to follow.

Fay suggests that this notebook represents

> a consistent attempt to reorganize his source material and to draw conclusions implicit in Smith's work which Smith himself did not draw and which point beyond and contradict the analysis which Smith himself explicitly developed.[131]

This points astutely to what Marx thinks he is doing; but also presumes that this 'symptomatic reading' is a defensible procedure. Marx has read through some political economy, made notes, and now he is synthesising these notes for purposes that remain mostly unclear. It is nevertheless plain that this process of reading, noting, excerpting, and synthesising marks the beginning of a pattern that is part of the construction process of Marx's 'critique of political economy'. Fay argues that it was Marx's critique of Smith's concept of human development that was the source of his own concept of alienation, and not Marx's earlier critique of Hegel. This however gets the relationship back to front: as has been shown above, Marx came to political economy very late, influenced by Engels and French radicals, and assimilated his reading of political economy to a well-established German critical reflex. His 'reading' of Smith's *Wealth of Nations* is moreover entirely conventional for the time, ignoring the system of liberty, the evaluation of economy and government that can be found in Book IV chapter 9, and disregarding entirely Book V—a reading of the text that bears the mark of Garnier's introductory reading guide discussed in chapter 4 above. While Fay's general argument that it was Marx's critique of Smith that led to the formulation of his theory of alienation is unsustainable, by drawing attention to the physical composition of the notebooks Fay sheds a great deal of light on what Marx *thought* he was doing. As suggested already, Smith's notes on Say, Smith, Ricardo, and Mill are best understood as those of a reader of new material having difficulty engaging with its substance. Soon after making these initial notes, Marx set about reordering the material under three headings, according to a logic that is now hard to discern—was one supposed to read across the columns, or down each one?[132] Nonetheless, the fact that Marx transcribed

131. Fay, 'Influence' op. cit., p. 134.

132. The tripartite columnar structure is reproduced in the 1982 Gesamtausgabe edition (I/2 pp. 189ff.), but since the original was written landscape on something similar to A4 (around 12 by 8 inches), and this 1982 version is printed portrait on 6 by 9.5 inches, with a largish typeface, the result is more or less unreadable. Given the new *Gesamtausgabe* editors went to the trouble of printing this twice, once as a continuous flow and once in three columns, it would have made sense to replicate a transcription of the original leaves as an inserted facsimile, since then the reader would be able to appreciate rather better what Marx was doing.

material wholesale into a new arrangement does support the idea that he thought he was doing something profound: creating an immanent critique of political economy which, through the disclosure of its innate contradictions, would make possible their supersession. As is clear from his comments on Proudhon in the *Holy Family*, which he wrote shortly afterwards, he saw this as the difference between them: Proudhon criticised political economy from the standpoint of political economy, while Marx applied his German-sourced 'immanent critique'. This stance is evident in the opening of the fourth section of Notebook I, where he abandoned the columns and wrote straight across the page:

> We began from the presuppositions of political economy. We have accepted its language and its laws. We assumed private property, the separation of labour, capital, and land, also wages of labour, profit of capital, and rent, just like the division of labour, competition, the conception of exchange value, etc. From political economy itself, in its own words, we have shown that the worker descends into a commodity, and the poorest sort of commodity, and that the poverty of the worker is in inverse proportion to the power and extent of his production. (MEGA Bd. I/3 p. 81)

This is therefore the constant ambition of Marx's 'critique of political economy': through the revelation of the contradictions in theory a new, higher synthesis could be achieved, transforming the contradictions of political economy into the contradictions of capitalism, revealing its real laws of motion and preparing the way for its supersession.

One of the problems with this ambition is however the way in which Marx went about it: by constantly recycling older material in new notebooks, eventually forming a mass of material with no discernible structure or argument, besides the constant repetition of very simple formulations regarding wage labour, externalisation, profit, and capital that impose 'German philosophy' upon ideas about exploitation and wage labour already current among French socialists when Marx arrived in Paris in late 1843. This is the chief significance of the '1844 Manuscripts'; and it would some dozen years later be repeated on a much grander scale with the notebooks that we have come to know as the *Grundrisse*.

But these were early days. Expelled from Paris in January 1845, Marx settled in Brussels, where he and Engels drafted a critique of the Young Hegelians that has come down to us as *The German Ideology*. In 1846 Marx came into contact with Proudhon, who was about to publish his *Système des contradictions économiques; ou, philosophie de la misère*. Marx's response to this was a withering critique, which turned out to be the most readable book he would ever write. What was Marx seeking to achieve in writing this book?

MARX THE POLITICAL ECONOMIST

Proudhon announced the imminent appearance of his new book in a letter to Marx written on 17 May 1846, responding to Marx's request that he be a corresponding contributor to discussions among communists and German socialists.[133] While not promising to be able to write very often, or very much, he supported Marx's proposal:

> Let us together search for, if you like, the laws of society; the mode in which they are realised, the manner in which we come to discover them: but, for God's sake, having demolished all *a priori* dogmatisms, let us not in turn dream of indoctrinating the people.[134]

Système was published on 15 October 1846,[135] and by the end of the year Marx was writing a critique of it. He was at least in part prompted to do so because of his failure to complete the work for which he had signed a contract in February 1845 with Leske in Darmstadt. In March 1846 the publisher had written to him seeking assurances of the purely scientific nature of his 'soon to be completed' book; Leske had been threatened with closure by the Prussian authorities if he published any more socialist and communist writings.[136] Marx's response of 18 March has not survived, but clearly the publisher was unconvinced by it and suggested that Marx find another publisher and return the advance that he had been given in 1845.[137] This second letter went unanswered, so the request was repeated in July,[138] producing an immediate response from Marx, who claimed that he had replied straightaway, but actually meaning that he had replied straightaway to the first letter. The reason he had not replied to the second letter, he said, was because he meant to do so when he had found another publisher, as had been requested. Towards the end of this letter he assured Leske that the first volume of the text would be ready by the end of

133. Karl Marx to Pierre-Joseph Proudhon, Brussels 5 May 1846, Karl Marx, Friedrich Engels, *Gesamtausgabe* Bd. III/2 p. 7, Dietz Verlag, Berlin 1979.

134. Letter from Proudhon to Marx, Lyon 17 May 1846, Karl Marx, Friedrich Engels, *Gesamtausgabe* Bd. III/2 p. 205. He later mentions that his book is in production (p. 206).

135. Thierry Menuelle, *Marx, lecteur de Proudhon*, Cahiers de la société P.-J. Proudhon, Paris 1993 p. 99.

136. Carl Friedrich Julius Leske to Karl Marx, Darmstadt 16 March 1846, Karl Marx, Friedrich Engels, *Gesamtausgabe* Bd. III/1 p. 516, Dietz Verlag, Berlin 1975.

137. Carl Friedrich Julius Leske to Karl Marx, Darmstadt 31 March 1846, Karl Marx, Friedrich Engels, *Gesamtausgabe* Bd. III/1 p. 528.

138. Carl Friedrich Julius Leske to Karl Marx, Darmstadt 29 July 1846, Karl Marx, Friedrich Engels, *Gesamtausgabe* Bd. III/2 p. 271.

November, although it had grown by another twenty sheets (i.e. 320 octavo pages) in the meantime.[139] This suggests that by the summer of 1846 Marx should have been well on the way to completing the book, although this is the only indication that any such book ever existed. Leske responded to this in September,[140] and then wrote again more formally in February 1847 noting that the first volume should have been in his hands by November 1846, but that since

> it had not arrived by 2 February 1847, and has quite probably gained a powerful and dangerous competitor in the recently published book by Proudhon, I feel compelled, with great sorrow, to notify you that I *have* to abandon the publication of the work and so expect the *prompt* return of the 1,500 francs honorarium that I sent to you as an advance on 28 June 1845 in the form of a bill of exchange. If you were in November of the last year unable to deliver the promised part of the manuscript, then you owed me a notification and at the same time a definite date of delivery for the manuscript. Instead of that I have heard nothing from you since 1 August of last year.[141]

Nor would he hear from Marx: in September 1847 he wrote again, pleading for the return of at least some of the advance.[142]

From this dispiritingly familiar exchange between a writer and his publisher we can deduce two things. First of all, in the summer of 1846 Marx was at least still thinking of extending the notes and drafts from two years before into a two-volume critique of political economy, although there is no manuscript evidence of any work being done after late 1844, besides some limited note-taking during 1845. Second, we might reasonably conclude that the publication of Proudhon's *Système* galvanised him into writing a shorter work so that he might stake his claim to being Western Europe's foremost 'radical political economist'. *Misère de la philosophie* is primarily a bid for market leadership, and it certainly reads that way.

It was not just the threat of competition from Proudhon that confronted Marx; in May 1847 Leske published *Philosophie der Staatsökonomie oder Notwendigkeit des Elends*, a translation of Proudhon's *Système*. And so

139. Karl Marx to Carl Friedrich Julius Leske, Brussels 1 August 1846, Carl Friedrich Julius Leske to Karl Marx, Darmstadt 16 March 1846, Karl Marx, Friedrich Engels, *Gesamtausgabe* Bd. III/2 pp. 22–24.

140. Carl Friedrich Julius Leske to Karl Marx, Darmstadt 19 September 1846, Karl Marx, Friedrich Engels, *Gesamtausgabe* Bd. III/2 pp. 309–10.

141. Carl Friedrich Julius Leske to Karl Marx, Darmstadt 19 September 1846, Karl Marx, Friedrich Engels, *Gesamtausgabe* Bd. III/2 p. 329.

142. Carl Friedrich Julius Leske to Karl Marx, Darmstadt 2 February 1847, *Karl Marx, Friedrich Engels Gesamtausgabe* Bd. III/2 p. 362.

Leske published a German work on political economy by Proudhon instead of Marx, just before Marx's own critique of Proudhon was published in Brussels; and to crown it all, it had been translated by Karl Grün. Marx thought that he had dealt with this despised 'true socialist' in the manuscripts now known as 'The German Ideology';[143] part of the problem being that Grün was a much more popular figure among Paris workers than Marx. He helpfully told Proudhon in a letter of 5 May 1846 that Grün was 'nothing more than a literary swindler, a species of charlatan, who seeks to traffic in modern ideas'. Proudhon's tactful letter of 17 May 1846 was in part a response to this bluster, suggesting that German socialists would do better not to indulge in such petty polemics. He had in fact already in late 1844 entrusted the translation of his definitive book on political economy to Grün.[144] Distracted by his machinations to place himself at the head of a new communist movement, Marx had been comprehensively upstaged as its oracle by Proudhon, Grün, and Leske.

Why was the content of Proudhon's book such a challenge from Marx's point of view? The 'system of economic contradictions' that Proudhon referred to in the title of his book was French and English political economy: Say, Rossi, Smith, Malthus. Proudhon later decided to follow this critical work up with a book on economics as a positive science, nursing this unrealised ambition through the early 1850s, but nothing came of this, and *Système* remained his major statement.[145] Its aim was to present a critique of political economy as presently constituted, its inability to address those issues of equality and reform that dominated contemporary thinking. For an economist like Malthus, those who came late to 'the grand banquet of nature' were simply superfluous; the system of individual liberty and property that underpinned political economy treated labour like any other commodity, whose price might rise or fall.[146] The second chapter dealt with value, and the general axiom of political economy that 'tout travail doit laisser un excédant' (p. 144), although it was not able to explain how

143. Marx published a hostile review of Grün's *Die soziale Bewegung in Frankreich und Belgien* (Darmstadt 1845) in the August 1847 number of *Westphälisches Dampfboot*; Diana Siclovan, 'The Project of "Vergesellschaftung": German Socialists 1843–1851', M. Phil. dissertation, University of Cambridge 2010 p. 41.

144. Siclovan, 'The Project of "*Vergesellschaftung*"', op. cit. pp. 44–46.

145. See Edward Castleton, 'L'inachèvement de l'oeuvre économique de Pierre-Joseph Proudhon', *Économie et sociétés* (forthcoming).

146. Pierre-Joseph Proudhon, *Système des Contradictions Économique, ou Philosophie de la Misère* t. 1, Guillamin, Paris 1846 p. 25. Proudhon seems to have taken Malthus's characterisation from his reading of Godwin's *Recherches sur la population* (translated by Constancio) during July 1844—NAF 18261; Cahier B in-8°; 'Juillet 1844. Varia variorum': p. 90.

this occurred. The most interesting part of the first volume comes however at the beginning of the third chapter, on economic evolution. Dealing first with the division of labour and its relation to the ongoing resolution of value creation and its proportionality, the 'second era' in chapter 4 belongs to machines. Here there is a lengthy section on the costs associated with machine production, emphasising that machinery would be introduced to the advantage of the capitalist, but to the disadvantage of the worker—and that political economists assumed that the advantage of the capitalist translated into the advantage of all. Instead, Proudhon emphasised 'the subversive influence of machines on social economy' (p. 158), and the emergence of the *salariat* as the necessary corollary of the reducing costs of workshop production.

> With the machine in the workshop, divine right, that is the principle of authority, enters into political economy. Capital, Mastery, Privilege, Monopoly, Partnership, Credit, property etc. these are, in economic language, the various names under which are otherwise called Power, Authority, Sovereignty, Statute Law, Relation, Religion, ultimately God, the cause and the principle of all our poverty and all our crimes which, the more we seek to define it, the more it escapes us. (p. 166)

Sismondi's solution to this was to abandon the division of labour, machinery, and manufacture, but this was impossible; Blanqui proposed worker participation as the solution; but neither of these offered a true resolution of the problem.

This was in part because of the way that competition underwrote the system, the outcome of the machine system, workshops, and the drive for the general reduction of costs: competition

> is the way in which collective activity is manifested and exercised, the expression of social spontaneity, emblem of democracy and equality, the most energetic instrument for the constitution of value, the support for association. . . .
>
> But competition left to itself, and deprived of superior and efficacious direction, is only an empty movement, an aimless fluctuation of industrial power, oscillating between each of its two equally lethal extremes: on one side corporations and patronage, which as we seen were created by workshops; on the other side monopoly. (p. 235)

The 'fourth era' was monopoly, defined as commerce, exploitation, or the enjoyment of a thing, resulting from the introduction of machines and the theory of the general reduction of costs. Later chapters went on to deal with taxation, and in the second volume the balance of commerce, credit, property, communality, and population. Not until the reader is well through the second volume is the title of the book made explicit in the context of the juxtaposition of two forms of poverty, that of primitive peoples, and that of civilised peoples.

> The result of our analysis is that if labour itself possesses the means of creating wealth, these means, by virtue of their inherent antagonism, are likely to become new causes of poverty; and as political economy is nothing other than the affirmation of this antagonism, this demonstrates that political economy is the affirmation and organisation of poverty. The question is no longer one of knowing how labour can expel primitive poverty, it disappeared long ago; but how we can eliminate the pauperism that results from the vice proper to labour, or rather, the false organisation of labour, political economy. (t. 2 p. 419)

As with *Qu'est-ce que la propriété*, Proudhon's criticism of political economy was couched in terms of the civilising process, and the capacity of the contradictions of this process to create harmful outcomes. Marx had maintained in *Die Heilige Familie* that Proudhon's criticism of political economy remained at the level of political economy; and so in criticising Proudhon here we might assume he seeks to adopt a different standpoint. What kind of alternative did he offer?

Engels wrote to Marx on 18 September 1846 that only the day before he had heard about Proudhon's scheme for worker co-operatives: 'I found out that this new nonsense is really a *boundlessly stupid idea*'.[147] The scornful tone in which Engels writes here about Proudhon's scheme for worker co-operatives is suggestive of a shared view—but it was not until the end of December that Marx actually received a copy of Proudhon's new book, which he quickly read. He then wrote a very long letter commenting on sections of the book, rehearsing arguments he would elaborate in his own book, and noting that the only point on which he agreed with Proudhon was in his distaste for the 'socialist sensibility'. His conclusion was, however, that

> M. Proudhon is from head to foot the philosopher, the economist, of the *petite bourgeoisie*. The *petit bourgeois* . . . [is caught between being] dazzled by the magnificence of the *haute bourgeoisie* and sympathy for the sorrows of the people. He is at once bourgeois and people. He brags that in his conscience he seeks to be impartial, to have found the point of equilibrium, which

147. Engels to Marx, 18 September 1846, *Briefe über 'Das Kapital'*, Dietz Verlag, Berlin 1954 p. 15.

> is supposed to be the happy medium. A *petit bourgeois* like this can sense the *contradiction*, for contradiction is the foundation of his being. It is only the social contradiction set in motion.[148]

Having come to this conclusion, Marx immediately set about writing a book rooted in his reading of English political economy.

He finished writing in mid-June 1847; it was published the next month in Brussels with a title that inverted Proudhon's subtitle: *Misère de la philosophie*.

> M. Proudhon has the misfortune to be uniquely misunderstood in Europe. In France he has the right to be a bad economist, since he passes for a good German philosopher. In Germany, he has the right to be a bad philosopher, because he passes as a prominent French economist. Being ourselves both German and economist, we have wished to protest against this dual mistake.[149]

Marx's characterisation of himself here as an 'economist' is significant: he does not identify himself with German philosophy. His notebooks show that he had been doing a fair amount of reading in the English literature of political economy, broadly conceived, and we should also pay attention to his writing style—it is transformed from the turgid, clotted prose of 1844 and before into crisp and clear sentences. And this is more than a superficial rhetorical transformation.

His critique begins with the distinction made by Proudhon between use value and exchange value, the problem of how the former becomes latter. For Proudhon, this is an instance of a contradiction, an opposition of which political economists have been unaware; but instead of endorsing this sentiment, which is what he would have done in 1844, Marx instead cites Sismondi and Lauderdale *making use* of this distinction in their arguments (MEGA Bd. I/6 p. 124). He then launches into an explanation of the nature of exchange value that works entirely in terms of supply and demand, emphasising that these are banal truths, not the 'mysteries' that Proudhon seeks to make of them. Entirely absent here is the language of 'criticism' that he had employed in 1843 and 1844. One could almost say that Marx is in 1847 engaging in a form of autocritique, except that he is lambasting Proudhon for his obscurity and verbosity, rather than his own previous writings. In his initial reading of Ricardo, Marx always sought contradiction and anomaly, all the while ignoring the manner in which

148. Marx to Annenkow, 28 December 1846, ibid. p. 27.

149. Marx, *Misère de la philosophie: Réponse à la philosophie de la misère de M. Proudhon*, MEGA Bd. I/6 p. 119.

Ricardo defined his terms, and structured his argument. In 1847 he makes the following summary judgement:

> The system of Ricardo, which in principle posits that 'the relative value of commodities is exclusively related to the quantity of labour required for their production' goes back to 1817. Ricardo is the head of a school that has reigned in England since the Restauration. Ricardian doctrine encapsulates rigorously, mercilessly, the entirety of the English bourgeoisie, which is itself typical of the modern bourgeoisie. (MEGA Bd. I/6 p. 131).

And in identifying Ricardo as the leading English political economist, Marx adopts the superficial clarity of Ricardo's prose; although we might observe that the principle posited above is still McCulloch's version of Ricardo, not Ricardo himself. This is not the Ricardo of a determinate structure of distribution between rents, profits, and wages; of a theory of trade; of a conception of the price level of a range of commodities being determined by the value of labour. It is a version of Ricardo that borrows the categories, but not the relationships they define.

Nonetheless, this is a definite advance. In aligning himself with Ricardo, Marx has dispensed with the tedious critical habit of 'revealing' contradictions and silences, and is content to deal with the arguments of political economy on its own terms. As he writes:

> We will leave to the reader any comparison between the very precise, very clear, very simple language of Ricardo, and the rhetorical efforts of M. Proudhon, so that we might pass on to the determination of relative value by labour time. (MEGA Bd. I/6 p. 134)

And in drawing attention to Ricardo's 'rather cynical language', he observes that 'the cynicism is in things, and not in the words that express things' (MEGA Bd. I/6 p. 136). There are no new notes on Ricardo in the surviving notebooks for the period 1845–47 published in the new *Gesamtausgabe*,[150]

150. Karl Marx, Friedrich Engels, *Gesamtausgabe* Bde. IV/3, IV/4, IV/6—these do not run entirely chronologically since IV/4 is devoted to the Manchester notebooks completed in July and August 1845, while IV/3 covers notebooks used in Paris and Brussels from late 1844 to 1847, and IV/6 also covers September 1846 to December 1847. This is perhaps the most baffling single volume in the *Gesamtausgabe*: over nine hundred printed pages of excerpts and notes on Gustav von Gülich's five-volume *Geschichtliche Darstellung des Handels, der Gewerbe und des Ackerbaus der bedeutendsten handelstreibenden Staaten unsrer Zeit*, Jena 1830–1845. Bd. 4/5 has not yet (autumn 2012) been published. A useful tabular survey of Marx's economic reading at this time is in Klaus Hennings, 'A Note on Marx's Reading List in His Economic and Philosophical Manuscripts of 1844', *Economy and Society* Vol. 14 (1985) p. 132.

but there is apparent in the wide range of material consulted and excerpted a much greater readiness to engage with their arguments, something that is almost entirely absent in his initial reading of political economy. Having Proudhon as a literary punchbag probably also helped; in demonstrating Proudhon's lack of expertise in political economy, Marx has to demonstrate his superior command of the relevant literature. So, for example, he seeks to show that what might seem novel to Proudhon was well established in English debate:

> After all that we have said, the determination of value by labour time, that is to say, the formula that M. Proudhon presents to us as the regenerating formula of the future, is only the scientific expression of the economic relations of present-day society, and which Ricardo has clearly and precisely well demonstrated before M. Proudhon.
>
> But perhaps at least the 'egalitarian' application of this formula belongs to M. Proudhon? Is he the first to imagine the reform of society through the transformation of all men into direct workers, exchanging quantities of equal labour? . . .
>
> Anyone having some small familiarity with the English political economy movement will not have overlooked that nearly all socialists in this country have, at different times, proposed the egalitarian application of Ricardian theory. We can cite to M. Proudhon: Hodgskin's *Économie politique*, 1822; William Thompson, *An Inquiry into the Principles of the Distribution of Wealth, most Conducive to Human Happiness*, 1824; T. R. Edmonds: *Practical, Moral and Political Economy*, 1828; etc. etc. and four pages of etc. Here we will just let an English *communist* speak, M. Bray. We will introduce some central passages from his remarkable book: *Labour's Wrongs and Labour's Remedy*, Leeds 1839, and we will spend some time here, first of all because M. Bray is little known in France, and second because we believe that we have here found the key to the past, present, and future works of M. Proudhon. (MEGA Bd. I/6 pp. 149–50)

And Marx proceeds for several pages with excerpts from Bray, concluding with criticism of Bray's idealism, which is said to be merely a reflection of the present world, and so 'it is impossible to reconstitute society on a basis which is no more than an inverted shadow' (MEGA Bd. I/6 p. 157).

The second of the two chapters in the book deals with the 'metaphysics of political economy'. Two points can be made here. Marx continues to mock Proudhon's theoretical pretensions, searching for his 'method', and arguing, using a formulation already rehearsed in the *German Ideology*, that while economic categories are mere abstractions from the social relations of production, Proudhon reverses this relationship:

> M. Proudhon the economist has well understood that men make cloth, material, fabric, silks in determinate relations of production. But what he does not understand is that these determinate social relations are also produced by men in the same way as material, fabric, etc. Social relations are intimately linked to productive forces. In acquiring new forces of production men change their mode of production, and in changing their mode of production, the way in which they make their living, they change all their social relationships. The windmill will give you society with a lord; the steam engine society with an industrial capitalist. (MEGA Bd. I/6 p. 179)

Knowledge, argues Marx, is class related, and so progressive knowledge has to be linked to the movement of history:

> Just as *economists* are the scientific representatives of the bourgeois class, *socialists* and *communists* are the theoreticians of the proletarian class. . . . [But due to the lack of development of the latter they are utopian socialists] Inasmuch as they seek science and construct only systems, being at the beginning of the struggle, in poverty they see only poverty, without seeing the revolutionary, subversive side, which will overthrow the old society. From this moment the science produced by the historical movement, and associating itself with complete awareness of the reason why, ceased to be doctrinaire, and became revolutionary. (MEGA Bd. I/6 p. 191)

From this critique of Proudhon's analytical method Marx moves on to Proudhon's account of the division of labour.

Here again, for Proudhon everything has a good side and a bad side, and Marx produces a little table detailing how this works in this particular case (MEGA Bd. I/6 pp. 192–93). Whereas Proudhon sees in the accumulation of machinery the negation of the division of labour, Marx treats it as the condition for development to a future society. And here Proudhon's account of the relationship of the workshop to the division of labour prompts Marx to develop a different argument: that the utility of a workshop lies less in the division of labour as such than in the fact that production takes place on a much greater scale. The relation of machinery to the production process and the worker is elaborated with reference to Babbage, emphasising the development of manufacturing in England as part of the progress of the division of labour, and not its negation as with

Proudhon. When Smith wrote *Wealth of Nations* the 'automatic system' of industrial production was virtually unknown, and to correct Proudhon on this point Marx introduces a lengthy excerpt from Ure's *Philosophy of Manufactures* (MEGA Bd. I/6 pp. 203–4).[151] His reading of Babbage and Ure would prove formative, but the fact that he develops this argument about the division of labour in opposition to Proudhon is also significant. Marx's efforts to rebut on several fronts Proudhon's use of political economy leads him away from the emphasis upon value and prices, and is one of the reasons why the book is an important point in the evolution of his thinking. Marx never freed himself of the problems associated with a labour theory of value, but in turning to the description and analysis of production systems he opened up a new path that would eventually bear fruit in *Das Kapital* Bd. 1.

Marx continues on in this second chapter to examine Proudhon's account of competition, monopoly, property, rent, and labour disputes. He does not in fact deal with any of the material in Proudhon's second volume—trade, commerce, and population—nor even with the chapter on property, which would have previously attracted his attention. Nonetheless, while his exposition of his own political economy of development became increasingly scrappy in the later pages of *Misère de la philosophie*, he soon had the opportunity of presenting it in a more structured manner when, in December 1847, he gave some lectures to the German Workers' Association in Brussels.

'Lohnarbeit und Kapital' was published in the *Neue Rheinische Zeitung* in five parts during April 1849, having been written up from the lectures in early 1848 (MEGA Bd. I/6 p. 450). The didactic context lends this text a commendable clarity, beginning straight away with the question: 'What is a wage? How is it determined?'[152] The answer is that the labourer exchanges his commodity, his labour, against the commodity of the capitalist, money. Labour is a commodity like any other, bought for a particular length of time, but

> The wage is not therefore the worker's share of the commodity that he has produced. The wage is a part of existing commodities with which the capitalist purchases a particular sum of productive labour. . . . Labour is however the worker's own activity, the expression of his own life. And he sells this *activity*

151. For a discussion of Marx's use of Ure and Babbage see my 'De l'atelier au procès de travail: Marx, les machines et la technologie' in F. Jarrige, *Technologies et socialismes: Théories, imaginaires, pratiques au XIXe siècle* (forthcoming).
152. Marx, 'Lohnarbeit und Kapital', MEGA Bd. I/6 p. 472.

> to a third party, to secure the necessary *sustenance*. His activity is for him therefore merely a *means* to exist. He works to live. (MEGA Bd. I/6 p. 475)[153]

But instead of becoming embroiled in this disjunction between the worker's activity and the conditions under which the worker is forced to live, the question is posed: how is the price of a commodity determined? This is the starting point of the second part, and the answer to this question is

> through the competition of buyers and sellers, the relation of demand to supply, of supply to wants. Competition, through which the price of a commodity is determined, is three-sided. (MEGA Bd. I/6 p. 476)

Competition causes the price of labour to rise and fall, fluctuating around the cost of production of labour, the price of maintaining the labourer; attracting capital when the price of the good produced is higher than the price of labour, while capital is withdrawn when the price of labour is higher than the price of the produced commodity.

Having then dealt with the most general laws that regulate wages like the price of any other commodity, Marx turns in Part III to deal with 'our object': capital.

> Capital consists of raw materials, instruments of labour, and food of all kinds which are employed to create new raw materials, instruments of labour and food. All of these components are creations of labour, products of labour, *accumulated labour*. Capital is accumulated labour which serves as the means for new production. That is what the economists say. (MEGA Bd. I/6 p. 482)

The social relationships within which individuals produce, hence the social relations of production, are transformed with the change and development of material means of production, of productive forces. The relations of production as a totality make up what are called social relations, society, and to be precise, a society at a particular historical stage of development, a society with its own distinctive character. Ancient society, feudal society, civil society, these are all totalities of relations of production which describe a specific stage of development in the history of humanity. Capital is also itself a social relation of production.

153. 'According to Proudhon, man does not live just to eat; it is rather the reverse—man exchanges his labour to gain the right to live, not to possess the fruits of his labour'—Castleton, 'Introduction', op. cit. p. 92.

> Capital does not only consist of food, *instruments* of labour, and raw materials, not only of material products: it consists just as much of *exchange values*. All of the products that go to make it up are *commodities*. Capital is therefore not a sum of material products; it is a sum of commodities, of exchange values, of *societal magnitudes*. (MEGA Bd. I/6 p. 483)

The existence of a class possessing nothing but the capacity to work is a necessary condition for the existence of capital.

> The rule of accumulated, past, objectified labour over direct living labour first renders accumulated labour into capital. Capital does not consist of accumulated labour serving living labour as means for new production. It consists in living labour serving accumulated labour as a mean of maintaining and increasing the exchange value of the latter. (MEGA Bd. I/6 p. 484)

The worker in the cotton mill is not only producing cotton cloth; he is producing capital, values that will be used to create other values; and capital can only accumulate through the use of wage labour; they are bound together in a reciprocal relationship.

Part IV takes up this point regarding the accumulation of capital. The exchange value of capital, profit, increases to the same degree that the exchange value of labour, the day wage, falls, and vice versa (MEGA Bd. I/6 p. 489). So here there is a conflict of interest between capital and labour. If capital expands, wages rise, but not so much as profit—for profit and wages are in an inverse relation. And so while workers do benefit from growth of productive capital, this only increases the contradiction between the interests of the workers and those of capitalists. This leads into the final and fifth part, an examination of the impact of the increase of productive capital on wages.

Are in fact the growth of productive capital and the rise of wages so inseparable? The division of labour engenders even greater division, the use of machinery brings more machinery into use, the intensity of work steadily increases. At the same time competition presses down the price of commodities, including labour, to their cost of production. Particular skills become valueless. Work becomes more tedious, hours become longer, and it is less well remunerated. The expansion of production is accompanied by incipient mass unemployment. Marx sums the process up as follows:

> The more that productive capital increases, the greater the division of labour and the greater the use of machinery. The greater the division of labour and

> the use of machinery, the greater the competition among workers, and the smaller their remuneration becomes. (MEGA Bd. I/6 p. 498)

I have summarised *Lohnarbeit und Kapital* at some length because it is a very significant text. It is usually treated as an elementary introduction to the arguments of *Das Kapital*; Engels republished it as a pamphlet in 1884 with precisely this in mind, making some editorial changes to the terminology which supposedly brought it more into line with Marx's 'mature' thinking. However, as presented here it stands revealed as a clear and concise outline of a synthesis of political economy that has taken Marx four years to develop. The juxtaposition with the 1847 critique of Proudhon makes it easier to appreciate the long struggle Marx had in seeking to detach his thinking from the 'critical' reflexes so evident in his 1844 notebooks. *Lohnarbeit und Kapital* is not a summary of the arguments that would be laid out in *Das Kapital*: it is the foundation upon which they were built, being the most coherent statement of his evolving position so far. It should also be evident that it is a brilliant synthesis of much that can be found in Sismondi, Proudhon, Blanc, and Buret: the idea of industrial development as the mark of modernity, and the relative deterioration in the conditions of work and employment that the development of capital brings with it. Through his reading in political economy, and about economic conditions in Britain and France, Marx had created a story about the historical development of industrial society that employed the principal categories of English political economy. It is, nonetheless, just an insightful historical narrative, not a theoretical structure of the kind that Ricardo built, in which the analysis of distribution was linked to a tendency for the rate of profit to fall, so that eventually the economy might arrive at an entropic stationary state, without investment to renew capital, without scope for the increase of population. While this was the reverse of Marx's catastrophist vision for the demise of capitalism, that vision was never linked to an analytical foundation, it would merely come about through 'historical necessity'. Marx made use of Ricardo's terminology, but not of his conceptual structure. Instead, this terminology was used to underpin a historicist critique of industrial society. This was its limit; and Marx arrived at this limit in *Lohnarbeit und Kapital*. It is also for this reason that Marx was never again so clear; in struggling to turn this narrative into a theoretical analysis of the laws of motion of the capitalist mode of production, the product of a 'critique' of political economy, Marx became ensnared in an unrealisable project. *Lohnarbeit und Kapital* was as good a theoretical account of the capitalist mode of production as there was ever going to be.

This brilliant synthesis also came at a turning point in Marx's life. In February 1848 he was expelled from Brussels, and he moved to Paris. In April he returned to Germany, but was in turn expelled from there in May 1849. In July 1849 he was then expelled from Paris, and he travelled to London, arriving in August 1849. This was where he would live for the remainder of his life, in 1851 resuming his economic studies.

THE DEVELOPING CRITIQUE: 1857–1859

It would take Marx seventeen years after his arrival in London before he published the first complete section of his 'Critique of Political Economy'. First came the drafting in 1857–58 of yet another mass of writing lacking any obvious structure or line of argument; in 1859 he actually published *Zur Kritik der politischen Oekonomie*, which remained a torso and was subsequently reworked into the first chapter of *Das Kapital. Kritik der politischen Oekonomie. Erster Band* (1867), which he then revised for a second German edition in 1872, and again for a French edition that appeared between 1873 and 1875. Over this period he had various plans for further volumes that are only partially reconcilable; he applied himself at different times to the development of his work beyond the first volume, leaving behind a large amount of material that Engels sorted through, and from which he composed two further volumes. Quite how Engels went to work has now been studied in some detail,[154] but my interest here is with the book that Marx did publish in 1867, rather than the corpus of work he might have completed if he had ever had the mental and physical capacity to do so.

The first major result of Marx's reading in London was the 1857–58 manuscript which he appears to have considered the 'rough draft' of a critique of political economy, and which when first published in 1939/1941 was given that title, *Grundrisse der Kritik der politischen Ökonomie (Rohentwurf)*. The text has two 'chapters', one on money (pp. 33–148) and one on capital (pp. 149–663), followed by a jumble of notes and plans (pp. 663–980). The book

154. There is now extensive discussion of Engels's editorial practices in putting together volumes 2 and 3 of *Capital*; but all of this literature takes Marx's own 'achievement' as a given, a kind of Marxist *acquis* about which we no longer have to bother—see for example the special issue of *International Journal of Political Economy* Vol. 32 No. 1 (Spring 2002); also Michael Heinrich, 'Engels' Edition of the Third Volume of *Capital* and Marx's Original Manuscript', *Science and Society* Vol. 60 No. 4 (1996–97) pp. 452–66.

opens with some remarks on Alfred Darimon, *De la réforme des banques* (Paris 1856), and contains passages like this:

> The reciprocal and all-sided dependence of individuals who are indifferent to one another forms their social connection. This social connection is expressed in *exchange-value*, through which each individual's activity or his product first becomes an activity and a product for that individual; he must produce a general product—*exchange-value*, or, the latter isolated for itself and individualised, *money*.[155]

Or:

> Circulation is the movement in which the general alienation appears as a general appropriation and general appropriation as general alienation.[156]

Some commentators see in this work important insights and arguments, but after the striking clarity of *Misère de la philosophie* and *Lohnarbeit und Kapital* this looks much more like a throwback to the language of 1844, to no good purpose. Only if we detach this writing from what went before, and read it in terms of what comes after, can one claim any significance for such prose.

As published in 1939/41 the text did come with an 'Introduction' dating from 1857, which presents various remarks upon production, consumption, and distribution, together with a final ten pages on 'method'. Here we can read that

> Civil society is the most developed and diverse historical organisation of production. The categories that express its relations, understanding of its structure, therefore also provide an insight in the structure and relations of production of all past and vanished social formations, whose ruins and elements have been its building-blocks, and partly carrying within it untransformed remnants, mere traces which have assumed an elaborated meaning, etc. In the anatomy of man there lies a key to the anatomy of the ape.[157]

And

> Capital is the all-powerful economic force of civil society. It must be point of departure as well as the point of arrival, and be elaborated before landed

155. Marx, *Grundrisse*, op. cit. p. 74.
156. Ibid., p. 111.
157. Ibid., pp. 25–26.

property. After both have been considered in detail, their mutual relationship must be considered.[158]

But these are general statements of intent unconnected with what Marx actually does in the text to which this is purportedly an introduction. There is a long history of reading Marx's writings in the light of what he said he was going to do, rather than paying attention to what he actually did do; and the *Grundrisse* is both a monument and a challenge to such readings.

What then of the book he *did* publish? Marx started all over again, writing *Zur Kritik der politischen Oekonomie* from August 1858 to January 1859, it being published in Berlin the same year. In retrospect, this is very clearly a less coherent version of the first chapter of the 1867 version of *Das Kapital*. When he came to draft that work, he discarded this 1859 critique in the same way as he had in 1858 discarded the *Grundrisse*, and started yet again. The importance of the 1859 *Kritik* is that it marks a turning point in the project to write a critique of political economy that had begun in 1844, the *Grundrisse* being continuous with those origins. The 1859 book came with a 'Preface', which opens with a listing of the sequence in which he will deal with the system of political economy, for the first time making explicit the plan of work that he had in mind. It is in two main sections, each in three parts:

> Capital, Landed Property, Wage Labour; The State, Foreign Trade, The World Market[159]

He goes on to remark that the first section of the first book has three sections,

(1) The Commodity; (2) Money or Simple Circulation; (3) Capital in General,

and that the present work deals with the first two of these. This tripartite scheme was to become the basis upon which Engels later put together the second and third volumes of *Kapital*. And if only generations of Marx scholars had paid attention to the next comment:

> I exclude a general introduction which I had put together here, because after some reflection it seems that any anticipation of results that had yet to be

158. Ibid., p. 27.
159. Marx, 'Vorwort' to *Zur Kritik der politischen Oekonomie: Erstes Heft*, in Karl Marx, Friedrich Engels, *Gesamtausgabe* Bd. II/2 p. 99, Dietz Verlag, Berlin 1980. As the 'first section', it might be supposed that this text is meant to cover 'Capital'; but actually it does not, as we shall see.

> proved would seem disruptive; and the reader who has any intention of following my argument must resolve to develop from the particular to the general.[160]

But then Marx proceeds for the remainder of the preface to provide a retrospective history of his intellectual development that muddies the significance of this. He begins this badly, by suggesting that his early studies of law were 'however only pursued as a subordinate discipline to philosophy and history', which is of course a complete fiction, given that the significance he gave to property came originally from Savigny and Gans; and the remainder serves anyone seeking an explanation of Marx's intellectual development just as badly. The famous passage in which Marx describes his 'general results'—'in the social production of their life people enter into particular, necessary relations that are independent of their will'[161]—violates the ordinance to which he had just signed up, that the reader should be allowed to follow an argument from the particular to the general. Especially as the 'general result' which Marx announces here was never in fact realised. An entire critique of Marx could be composed around this 'Preface', but would distract us from the task in hand, which is to examine what Marx actually did when he wrote about political economy.

Zur Kritik is itself short (146 pages),[162] and is divided into two chapters. Chapter 1, 'The Commodity', begins like first chapter of the 1867 version of *Das Kapital* Bd. 1, considering the commodity, use value, exchange value, then quickly moving on to labour time. This continues for about thirty pages, when a new section, 'Historical Remarks on the Analysis of the Commodity', begins a review of Petty, Boisguilbert, the Physiocrats, and Sir James Steuart, all of whom, in *Kapital* Bd. 1, appear in the footnotes to the main exposition. Ricardo is here distinguished from Smith by arguing that his conception of value is expressed as labour time, and that he is only interested in the magnitude of value.[163] Marx does not here differentiate between Smith and Ricardo regarding the definition and role of a labour theory of value in their texts; nor that Ricardo is seeking to demonstrate a developmental problem of the rate of profit and distribution, while Smith is elaborating the more general point from which he begins: that the wealth of a nation is the annual produce of its labour. This first chapter takes up forty pages.

160. Loc. cit.
161. Ibid., p. 100.
162. Pages 99–245 in the new *Gesamtausgabe* version.
163. Ibid., p. 137.

Chapter 2 deals with 'Money or Simple Circulation' and is longer than the first, eventually becoming diverted by money forms. Marx here deals with the exchange value of commodities, as a general equivalent and also as the measure of this equivalence in a specific good, expressed as price.

> Price is the transformed form in which exchange value of commodities *appears* in the process of circulation.[164]

The 'real form' in which commodities appear in the process of circulation is as their use value, and they become universal equivalents through their alienation.[165] As we have seen before with his response to James Mill's discussion of money, any broaching of this subject is liable to derail Marx into ruminations on form and appearance, essence and externalisation; this is here kept under control by his turn to an entirely historical account of money forms, organised by the sequence commodity-money-commodity as the typical form of circulation.[166] The text then abruptly finishes, without explanation or conclusion.

The elements of Marx's analysis as presented in the 1859 *Kritik* clearly prefigure the early parts of the first volume of *Kapital* that would be published some eight years later. The substance of the text is far removed from the aspirations expressed in its preface, and it is not entirely clear why Marx published what is clearly a fragment of a much more extensive argument. Certainly he had developed his thinking from where it had been in 1850; and in the succeeding years he would continue to read, draft, and revise his mass of papers. But this examination of Marx's 'critique' of political economy will conclude with a review of the book which has always been taken as his definitive word on the subject.

Das Kapital Bd. 1: The First Edition

The first volume of *Das Kapital* published in 1867 is clearly the outcome of a lengthy period of gestation, but it is not clear what its scope was intended to be: besides the usual subtitle 'critique of political economy', this first volume is also described as 'Book I: The Production Process of Capital'. The availability in print of a great deal of the manuscript material out of which this volume was constructed, plus that which Engels used to put

164. Ibid., p. 141.
165. Ibid. p. 143.
166. Ibid., p. 167. See pp. 237–39 for a recapitulation of his views on Mill.

together volumes II and III, has tended to distract attention from the more limited questions: how is this particular book put together? What might this tell us about the argument it seeks to develop, and is any such argument realised in the text?[167]

The 'Vorwort' gets off to a bad start, the first sentence describing this text as the 'continuation' (*Fortsetzung*) of the 1859 *Kritik*, which it is not: the first chapter represents a complete *rewrite* of that work. It is only a continuation in the sense that it starts again at the same point, revises that text, and then carries on for another five chapters. In the third paragraph Marx states his aphorism: '*Aller Anfang ist schwer, gilt in jeder Wissenschaft*',[168] suggesting that while the analysis of the commodity given in the first chapter is difficult, it is necessarily so, especially the discussion of the form of value, for which he has composed a separate introduction and appended it to the end of the volume. He then turns to describe his intentions:

> My object of study in this work is the *capitalist mode of production* and its corresponding *relations of production and interchange*. So far its historical location has been England. This is the reason that England serves as the prime illustration of my theoretical development. If the German reader were to shrug his shoulders Pharisaically over the conditions of the English factory and agricultural worker, or in so doing optimistically soothe himself with the observation that things were not so bad in Germany, so I have to tell him: *de te fabula narratur*! (p. ix)

Marx's account of the capitalist mode production, his real object of study, is based upon the English case because in England this could be found in its most advanced form. Nonetheless, the capitalist mode of production was not limited by frontiers and seas; it is implicitly represented here as the future for all workers. He proceeds:

> In itself it is not a matter of the higher or lower degree of development of social antagonisms that arise from capitalist production. It is a matter of *these laws themselves*, of these *tendencies* that work with eternal and effective necessity. The more industrially developed country shows to the lesser-developed only the image of its own future! (p. ix)

167. See for a recent example of *Capital* commentary Riccardo Bellofiore, Nicola Taylor (eds.) *The Constitution of Capital: Essays on Volume I of Marx's 'Capital'*, Palgrave, Basingstoke 2004. This has an introduction outlining the history of the text; but the contributors, as usual, assume that '*Das Kapital Bd. 1*' is an unproblematic basis for speculative extrapolation.

168. 'It is true of every science that beginning is difficult'. Marx, *Das Kapital. Kritik der politischen Oekonomie. Erster Band. Buch I: Der Produktionsprocess des Kapitals*, Otto Meissner, Hamburg 1867, p. vii.

And he continues: 'It is the ultimate purpose of this work to reveal the economic laws of motion of modern society'. This as clear a statement of intent as one will find anywhere; the question is whether any of this is realised in the first volume of *Kapital*.[169]

The first edition is divided into six lengthy chapters:

1. The Commodity pp. 1–105
2. The Transformation of Money into Capital pp. 106–40
3. The Production of Absolute Surplus Value pp. 141–290
4. The Production of Relative Surplus Value pp. 291–496
5. Further Studies on the Production of Absolute and Relative Surplus Value pp. 496–550
6. The Accumulation Process of Capital pp. pp. 551–763

The first two chapters are such hard work because they contain Marx's exposition of his conception of value and commodity, linked to his conception of surplus value, that which is 'taken' from the worker and which comes to dominate him in the form of capital. The remainder of the work is chiefly a historico-descriptive account of the extraction of surplus value made possible by the focus upon the role of the production process in the capitalist mode of production.

It is not simply that Marx places the most abstract part of his text at the front, deterring readers through the sheer generality and obscurity of the writing; Marx seems to have made a fundamental expositional error by starting with the commodity, rather than exchange. Just because the nature of the commodity is held to be the elementary form of society's wealth does not mean that it has to be dealt with first. In any case, he first uses the idea of commodity[170] to develop the distinction of use from exchange value; and here I cannot but think of the generations of *Capital* reading groups whose baffled participants must have concluded that this

169. At end of the 'Vorwort' Marx states that the next volume will deal with the 'Circulation Process of Capital', and the third volume with 'The Organisation of the Total Process', the whole being concluded with a fourth volume on the history of theories. This is clearly the warrant for the later work of Engels on the text, and for Kautsky's edition of *Theorien über den Mehrwert* as a 'fourth' volume.

170. Wicksteed made the acute observation in his review of *Capital* Vol. 1 that the German *Ware* should be rendered into English not as 'commodity' but as 'ware', something that is bought and sold, using a term long established in the English language—consider for instance 'warehouse'. Much conceptual difficulty might have been avoided, although in the course of the twentieth century the term gradually fell out of use. Philip H. Wicksteed, review of *Das Kapital*, *Today* October 1884, reprinted as Appendix 2 of C. H. Herford, *Philip Henry Wicksteed: His Life and Work*, J. M. Dent, London 1931 pp. 356–70.

distinction must be particular to Marx, given the laborious way that he goes about 'deriving' something that was at the time quite uncontroversial. Commodities as values are then described as *crystallised labour*;[171] while as values all commodities are only particular quantities of *congealed labour time* (p. 5). Emphasis is then laid upon the phenomenal form of the commodity—the mysterious value equivalence of a coat and its cloth.

> The *value form of the product of labour* is the most abstract, but also most general, *form* of the *bourgeois* mode of production, which is through this characterised as its *special kind of social* mode of production and hence at once *historical*. (fn. 24 p. 34 [on p. 35])

He then talks of the 'mysticism' of the commodity, how individual work becomes social labour:

> The mysticism of the commodity thus comes from the fact that for the private producer, the *social* determinations of their *private* labour appear to be *social natural properties of the product of labour*, that *the social production relations of persons* appear to be *social relations of things* to each other and to persons. (pp. 39–40)

This is of course strongly reminiscent of the kind of rhetoric that Marx indulged in during 1844 in his reading of political economy, presented here as part of a 'scientific' analysis of the capitalist mode of production but, as previously, serving the end of cultural criticism rather than historical or theoretical analysis. This is only underscored by the association of this 'fetishism of commodities' with religion made in the passage immediately following. He then goes on to consider the circulation of commodities in the market, leading into a discussion of money as a commodity which facilitates the circulation process; and with this the first chapter concludes, the following chapter examining the transformation of money into capital.

What is most striking about this second chapter is that the central concept of surplus value—what is extracted from the worker in the production process and then transformed into capital in the circulation process—simply pops ups as an aside—'This increment or excess over the original value I call *Mehrwerth* (surplus value)'.[172] It would have saved a great deal of mystification if Marx had simply begun with this problem,

171. *Kapital* Bd. 1, op. cit. p. 4.
172. Ibid. p. 112. The English 'surplus value' in the brackets is in the original.

rather than eventually produce it, like a rabbit out of a hat, following the laboured presentation in the first chapter of a theoretical variation on what was commonly found in French texts of the 1840s. Of course, it is surplus value which is the purpose of the entire process, and at last the discussion begins to home in on the central issue: how is this realised? For if commodities and money are exchanged as equivalents, no surplus can be extracted:

> The formation of surplus value, and hence the transformation of money into capital, can therefore not be explained either by the *seller* selling commodities *above* their value, nor by the buyer buying them *below* their value.[173]

The problem is how, out of apparently equal exchanges, a surplus can emerge that is then appropriated as capital, so that one party to an equal exchange ends up with 'more than they paid for'. And Marx adds: 'Hic Rhodus, hic salta!'[174]

So we are within a few pages of the end of the second chapter and Marx has only just got to the critical point of the argument. The solution that he offers lies in the idea that what the labourer sells is labour power, which he owns, but none of the means with which it can be constructively employed. The value of this labour power depends on the time necessary for its reproduction—subsistence. But this should remind us of something: Eugène Buret wrote much the same sort of thing in 1840, and for the sake of convenience I will simply repeat the quotation here:

> Labour, in the case where the worker possesses no kind of capital, like day workers or factory workers (*les ouvriers des fabriques*), does not have the economic character of a commodity; the wage does not have the characteristic of a market; for the worker is not in the position of a free seller vis-à-vis the person who employs him. One could say that the capitalist is always free to use labour, and the worker is always forced to sell it. The value of labour is completely destroyed if it is not sold at each instant. Labour can neither be accumulated nor saved, which distinguishes it from genuine commodities. Labour is life, and if life is not exchanged every day for food, it soon enough perishes. For the life of man to be a commodity one would have to restore slavery.

173. Ibid., p. 123. A footnote here quotes from Mercier de la Rivière, *L'ordre naturel*, rather underlining the fact that this general idea is not new. It would be interesting to examine Marx's references in these early chapters, since they tend, by commission or ommission, to obscure the real sources of his argument.

174. A punchline from a tale by Aesop, in which a person boasting of a time he had performed an outstanding jump in Rhodes is given the challenge: this is Rhodes, jump here!

> Capital, the purchaser of labour, is placed in an entirely different position; if it is not employed it ceases only to make a profit, it is not destroyed. . . . In a word, labour is not always demanded, but it is forced to constantly offer itself.[175]

And if this is then juxtaposed to a passage from Proudhon's *Qu'est-ce que la propriété* likewise cited above:

> Every transaction having as its aim an exchange of products or services can be called an *operation of commerce.*
>
> He who says commerce says exchange of equal values; for if the values are not equal, and if the contractor perceives this, he will not consent to exchange, and there will be no commerce.
>
> Commerce exists only between free men; everywhere else transactions may be accomplished through violence and fraud; there is no commerce.[176]

The passages in *Capital* immediately following *Hic Rhodus!* thus simply repeat arguments already made by Buret and Proudhon; and so one could well ask whether the arduous journey through the first hundred-odd pages of *Capital* volume I really gets us much further than the point French radicals had already reached by 1840. There are of course significant differences, but a more temperate form of the same question might instead point back to Marx's own *Lohnarbeit und Kapital.*

Certainly the few references to Proudhon made in *Das Kapital* Bd. 1 suggest that the Marx of the 1860s remained intellectually in the 1840s. He mentions Proudhon a number of times in volume I, all in footnotes, and mostly dismissively.[177] In every case he is referring back to the Proudhon he had criticised in 1847.[178] Only in two instances does he implicitly acknowledge his debt to Proudhon's account of the workshop and machinery: noting Proudhon's insight regarding machinery and the division of labour (p. 413); and observing that Proudhon had referred to the existence of a 'surplus product' (p. 504). That the latter is the germ for his own concept of *Mehrwert*, so laboriously developed through the early pages of his book, suggests that these pages represent a critique of political economy that does not, after all, move far beyond Proudhon—that 'Marxian

175. Eugène Buret, *De la misère des classes laborieuses* Vol. 1, op. cit. pp. 49–50.

176. Proudhon, *Qu'est-ce que la propriété*, op. cit. p. 107.

177. *Kapital* Bd. 1 p. 31 fn. 23, p. 42 fn. 28, p. 45 fn. 33, p. 413 fn. 185, p. 504 fn. 8, and p. 523 fn. 26.

178. After the overbearing polemical onslaught that Proudhon suffered in 1847 he had no more to do with Marx; but of course, it was also true that Marx did little before Proudhon's death in 1862 that might have prompted such attention.

political economy' as represented in *Capital* volume I is a refinement of, and not radically distinct from, the critique of political economy practised by Blanc, Buret, and Proudhon. Furthermore, when Marx moves on to demonstrate how surplus value is realised, appropriated by the capitalist, and thence accumulated as capital, he relies again on Proudhon, whose discussion of factory and workshop in his *Système* had brought Marx back to the notes he had made on Andrew Ure in 1845, but which then seem to have made very little impression upon his thinking.[179]

We also need to consider the manner in which Marx deals with the subsistence of the worker and, therefore, the determination of the value of labour power. This, states Marx, is set by the resources required for the reproduction of labour power, which includes not only food, but also other things, such as clothing and furniture. He then presents a calculation which turns on the assumption that the cost of reproducing a worker in this full sense—the value of labour power—is half of the daily labour time, so that the remaining half forms surplus value.[180] And so for the remainder of the volume the value of labour power and the amount of surplus value to be extracted through the employment of this labour power rests on this simple assumption. There is nothing more to it than that.

However, that is not the end of the story. While the ostensibly theoretical part of *Kapital* turns full circle in this way, the remainder is the truly original part of the work. For Marx's account of exactly how the extraction of surplus value arises introduces his analysis of the labour process, a line of thinking already evident in his use of Babbage and Ure in *Misère de la philosophie*, reinforced in the mid-1860s by his reading of factory inspectors' reports, and quite possibly linked also to the mind-numbing quantity of notes he made from Gülich in 1846 and 1847. For what does Marx actually do in the first volume of *Capital*? The book is based on a dual separation:

1. Worker from means of production
2. Labour power from worker

179. Marx read Ure's *Philosophy of Manufactures* in the 1836 French translation in the spring of 1845. This was in two volumes, unlike the original; and Marx read the second, mainly descriptive, volume *first*, before turning to Tome I, which included the first two parts: 'General Principles of Manufactures'; 'Scientific Economy of the Factory System': *Exzerpte über Arbeitsteilung, Maschinerie und Industrie* (ed. Rainer Winkelmann), Ullstein Verlag, Frankfurt am Main 1982 pp. 73–85, the notes on Pt. I being on pp. 80–85.

180. *Kapital* Bd. 1, op. cit p. 136.

Neither of these is established by the theoretical arguments of the first two chapters. In this sense his search for a theoretical analysis of the 'laws of motion of the capitalist mode of production', a quest initiated in 1844 with his reading of Say, Smith, Ricardo, and Mill, ended in the first two chapters. His efforts to develop from a critique of the categories of political economy his own transformative political economy came to nothing. The same is true with his account of immiseration, and the eventual collapse of capitalism from its alleged contradictions. Even if we assume that the main line of his argument is social—the fact that capitalism drives workers from the countryside into towns, and eventually into factories, within which they can at last recognise their common plight, and so come together as a class capable of changing the social order—this also is a conjecture that lacks theoretical support of the kind usually assumed. It can be said that, as an account of capitalism, *Capital* volume I works at most as a genealogy; it provides a story of how we arrived at this point, but fails to demonstrate the existence of any 'laws of motion' that will carry us further.

The critique of political economy upon which Marx laboured for so many years presupposed that it would be possible, through the work of immanent critique, to arrive at an analysis of the laws of motion of human societies. Instead, he produced something rather different, and more interesting: a text which, while beginning with the laboured presentation of 'theory', eventually broke out into an account of socioeconomic development of a quite novel kind. Well into the twentieth century, works of 'economic history' ceased their narrative in the early 1800s: this was as true of Cunningham's *Growth of English Industry and Commerce* (1882) as it was of Max Weber's final complete course of lectures on 'General Economic History', delivered in Munich during the Winter Semester of 1919–20. This was also the problem with Werner Sombart's *Der moderne Kapitalismus* (1902), which turned out not to be very modern at all. It was for this reason that Alfred Marshall so vigorously denied the relevance of economic history to an understanding of modern economies:

> The study of theory must go hand in hand with that of facts: and for dealing with the most modern problems it is modern facts that are of the greatest use.[181]

One could not understand the structure of the industrial world of the later nineteenth century by examining the history of the English woollen trade.

181. Alfred Marshall, *Principles of Economics* Vol. 1, Macmillan, London 1890 p. 94.

Marx's *Capital* was in this context extremely unusual; it was a compendium of 'modern facts', from the history of bread-making and its adulteration, to the technology of the woollen industry based upon reports by factory inspectors.[182] Although the elements of this practical grasp of the reorganisation of the world that 'capitalism' would bring about can be seen at work in his 1847 critique of Proudhon, the real foundation was laid in his reading during the 1860s—to take just one instance at random, footnote 287 on page 471 cites from a Factory Inspector's Report of 1862. Marx's theoretical sources, by contrast, cited in the first two chapters, date almost entirely from the period before the 1830s; the few references made to contemporary economists, such as John Stuart Mill or Wilhelm Roscher, are uniformly dismissive.

RECEPTION, READING, RESTORATION: THE ENDLESS QUEST FOR AN ABSENT TEXT

However, since Marx's death, it has always been assumed that he had achieved at the very least part of the task he had set himself. In 1883, the same year as his death, the first of many reading guides to *Capital* was published, all of them dedicated to helping the novice reader through the intricacies of Marx's 'theory', as presented in the opening chapters of *Capital*. Gabriel Deville's *Le Capital de Karl Marx* presented first a summary, and then a chapter-by-chapter summary of the text.[183] Karl Kautsky brought out *Karl Marx' Oekonomische Lehren* in 1886, which became a well-used catechism, the reading of which could render the 'theoretical core' of *Capital* accessible.[184] This was also the case with Edward Aveling's *The Students' Marx: An Introduction to the Study of Karl Marx' Capital*,[185] first

182. *Kapital* Bd. 1, op. cit p. 365 fn. 101. From here to the end of ch. 4 on p. 496 Marx provides an account of the English factory system that might have been prefigured by Buret and Sismondi, but which is based on the most recent available sources.

183. Gabriel Deville, *Le Capital de Karl Marx résumé et accompagné d'un Aperçu sur le Socialisme Scientifique*, Henry Oriol, Paris 1883 (n.d. but stamped as received in the British Museum on 1 January 1884) pp. 318. The *Aperçu* covered pp. 9–63, the remainder of the text presenting a summary in twenty-two chapters. This was followed by a *Cours d'économie sociale*, Pts. 1 & 2 Paris 1884, part of which was translated as 'The Genesis of Capital', Modern Press, London 1887.

184. Karl Kautsky, *Karl Marx' Oekonomische Lehren*, 5th edition, Dietz Verlag, Stuttgart 1894 is divided into three main sections: 'Commodity, Money and Capital'; 'Surplus Value'; 'Wage Labour and Capital Income'.

185. The Socialist Labour Press, Glasgow; also Swan Sonnenschein, London 1892 and several later editions.

published in 1891. *The Poverty of Philosophy* was translated into English in 1884 and into German in 1885. Together with the publication of *Wage Labour and Capital*[186] in English in 1886, a small library of texts was quickly assembled whose purpose was to make what Marx had written in the early theoretical sections of *Capital* volume I accessible. Texts such as these provided assistance over the years to generations of *Capital* reading groups, in which committed readers struggled to come to terms with Marx's critique of political economy.

Gareth Stedman Jones has emphasised the role of Engels in laying the foundations for this, beginning with his statement in the Graveside Address that 'Marx is the discoverer of the fundamental law according to which human history moves and develops itself'.[187] Stedman Jones argues that Engels sought, through the selective citation of Marx's occasional statements, to position Marx as the apostle of scientific socialism, in which the 'laws of history' would necessarily bring about the demise of capitalism and the transition to socialism. The 'laws of history' were for Marx economic laws; hence the centrality of *Das Kapital* in demonstrating the inevitability of the demise of capitalism. It was in this way that the famous passage from the 'Vorwort' to the 1859 *Kritik* came to frame readings of Marx, usually treated as a summary of results, rather than a statement of an aspiration:

> In the social production of their life men enter into definite, necessary relations that are independent of their will—relations of production—that correspond to the particular developmental stage of the material productive forces. The totality of these relations of production form the economic structure of society, the real base upon which a legal and political superstructure arises, and to which particular social forms of consciousness correspond. The mode of production of material life determines social, political, and intellectual life in general. It is not the consciousness of men that determines their being, but the reverse: their social being that determines their consciousness. At a particular stage of their development the material productive forces of society come into conflict with the existing relations of production, or, what is only a legal expression of the same thing, with property relations, within which these forces had hitherto moved. These relations switch from being the developmental

186. Trans. J. L. Joynes, The Modern Press, London 1886. Authorised German edition published by Engels in 1891. See also Joynes's own *The Socialist Catechism*, Modern Press, London 1885.

187. Gareth Stedman Jones, 'Marx's *Critique of Political Economy*: A Theory of History or Theory of Communism?', in Chris Wickham (ed.) *Marxist History—Writing for the Twenty-First Century*, Oxford University Press, Oxford 2007 pp. 140–57.

> forms of these productive forces to their fetters. An era of social revolution begins. With the transformation of the economic foundation the whole monstrous superstructure is more or less rapidly overturned.[188]

This passage has often enough served as a key statement of Marx's theory of history, but it lacks all foundation in his 'critique of political economy'. The 1857 introduction also serves in this role, as do other passages selected from his writings. But as Stedman Jones also points out:

> success or failure in Marx's case was not a matter of finishing a book, but of proving a set of propositions which he had assembled between 1845 and 1848. First, it would need to be shown that commercial society or the capitalist mode of production *was* just a particular historical stage in the development of the 'forces of production', that there were limits beyond which it could not further develop. Second, it was necessary to demonstrate that an economy without a market could match the dynamism and creativity of capitalism; that it could sustain and reproduce itself in an ever-expanding world of abundance.[189]

Ultimately, Marx's reputation is based upon the idea that he had identified the 'laws of motion of the capitalist mode of production', laws developed from his critique of political economy. This was however always an aspiration expressed in statements of this kind—in the 1857 introduction, the 1859 preface, the 1867 preface to *Capital*—and not demonstrated in any of his published, or indeed, unpublished writings. In the course of the reception of Marx's writings this unrealised aspiration has been rewritten as the positive achievements of 'Marxist theory', where the writings of Marx figure as rhetorical support, rather than analytical foundation.

In his introductory remarks to *Reading Capital*, Louis Althusser posed the following rhetorical questions:

> is *Capital* merely one ideological product among others, classical economics given a Hegelian form, the imposition of anthropological categories defined in the philosophy of the Early Works on the domain of economic reality; the 'realization' of the idealist aspirations of the *Jewish Question* and the *1844 Manuscripts*? Is *Capital* merely a continuation or even culmination of classical political economy, from which Marx inherited both objects and concepts? And

188. Marx, 'Vorwort' to *Zur Kritik*, in Karl Marx, Friedrich Engels, *Gesamtausgabe* Bd. II/2 pp. 100–101.

189. Stedman Jones, 'Marx's *Critique of Political Economy*', p. 152.

is *Capital* distinguished from classical economics, not by its object, but only by its *method*, the dialectic he borrowed from Hegel?[190]

Althusser of course imagined that the answers to these questions were all resoundingly negative. But like any rhetorical questions, these too present so many hostages to fortune. Posed originally as part of an introduction to a seminar in 1965, Althusser's questions can at last all be clearly answered in the affirmative—insofar as *Capital* volume I is treated as the original work of theory which it was intended to be, rather than as the innovative economic history of capitalism and industrialisation that it always was.

APPENDIX: A VERY SHORT HISTORY OF MARXISM

Friedrich Engels's 'Graveside Address' was a prospectus for a Marxist orthodoxy that quickly became established among the new European socialist parties. The Sozialdemokratische Partei Deutschlands (SPD) was not only the largest such party, but until 1914 regarded by all other socialist parties as the symbolic head of international socialism. However, as early as 1899 the publication of Eduard Bernstein's *Die Voraussetzungen des Sozialismus und die Aufgaben der Sozialdemokratie* inadvertently introduced into Marxism a mechanism for its constant renewal, while at the same time asserting its unchanging rectitude. Bernstein's 'evolutionary socialism' distinguished between an early,[191] philosophical, immature Marx, and a late, economic, mature body of writing best represented by *Capital*. Marxism was therefore primarily a political economy of capitalism, whose materialism was rooted in the natural laws of motion of capitalism which Marx was said to have revealed. The early Marx was consequently not only 'immature', but this immaturity was marked by his struggles to detach himself from an 'idealist' philosophy. Nonetheless, Bernstein went on, while *Capital* analysed the internal contradictions of capitalism, and revealed the inevitability of its collapse, the new mass socialist parties could base their political strategies upon a 'parliamentary' road to socialism through peaceful legislative reform. Bernstein was doing little more here than making explicit the assumptions of the SPD's own Erfurt Programme, but his clear articulation of these assumptions led to his excoriation as a 'revisionist'. And so the dialectic at the heart of 'Marxism' was

190. Louis Althusser, Etienne Balibar, *Reading Capital*, New Left Books, London 1970 p. 15.

191. Notably *The Holy Family* and the *Communist Manifesto*—'The German Ideology' and the '1844 Manuscripts' would remain unpublished until the interwar years.

created: orthodoxy was reproduced as the opposite of revisionism, the critique of various revisionist deviations allowing an orthodoxy to shift its ground while ostensibly remaining the same.[192] In 1899 both Kautsky and Lenin published major treatises on the agrarian question that exemplified this principle: both authors represented themselves as orthodox Marxists, while at the same time 'creatively developing' an account of capitalist development in agriculture that diverged notably from Marx's own writings on the subject.[193]

In 1913 Lenin published an article in the journal *Enlightenment* that robustly articulates the relation of Marx's writing to Marxism as 'scientific socialism':

> The Marxist doctrine is omnipotent because it is true. It is comprehensive and harmonious, and provides men with an integral world outlook irreconcilable with any form of superstition, reaction, or defence of bourgeois oppression. It is the legitimate successor to the best that man produced in the nineteenth century, as represented by German philosophy, English political economy and French socialism.[194]

While Lenin does here identify the 'sources' with some accuracy, the 'truth' of Marxist doctrine existed independently of them: it was true because it was scientific, and it was scientific because it was true. There was consequently no pressing reason why an orthodox Marxist should trouble to examine the sources to which Lenin referred: Marx's achievement had been to transcend them, redoubling the distinction already made by Bernstein between the 'immature' and 'mature' Marx, and so placing the emphasis on Marx as the analyst of capitalism as an economic system.

In 1923 György Lukács published a collection of essays under the title *Geschichte und Klassenbewusstsein* that re-examined Marx's relation to Hegel, and so moved beyond this classic association of Marxism with economic determinism. While Lukács began his book with an essay entitled 'What is Orthodox Marxism?', he went on to develop an account of Marxism that differed significantly from what had gone before, the central section being three essays on reification and the consciousness of the

192. Rather like the Radio Armenia joke: Question: 'Comrade, what is the difference between capitalism and socialism?' Answer: 'They are completely different. Capitalism is based upon the exploitation of man by man; socialism is the exact opposite'.

193. See Athar Hussain, Keith Tribe, *Marxism and the Agrarian Question*, 2nd edition, Macmillan, London 1983 pp. 27, 154 for comments upon the heterodox nature of Kautsky's *Agrarian Question* and Lenin's *Development of Capitalism in Russia*.

194. V. I. Lenin, 'The Three Sources and Three Component Parts of Marxism', *Prosveshcheniye* No. 3, March 1913, in *Collected Works* Vol. 19 pp. 21, 22.

proletariat; this was therefore a 'philosophical Marxism' that reimagined Marx's project as one developing continuously from his earliest philosophical writings, and which saw in *Capital* the realisation of this analysis of human alienation and reification. The subsequent publication of the '1844 Manuscripts' in the version of Landshut and Mayer therefore served to confirm Lukács's approach and dismantle the orthodox emphasis upon a 'mature' Marx; and quite how persistent this emphasis was as an element of orthodox Marxism is still apparent in the *Werke* edition of 1973, in which some of Marx's early writings previously excluded from the *Werke* were published separately, in a supplementary volume.[195]

During the 1930s and 1940s social theorists and philosophers reinforced this alternative reading of Marx as an analyst of capitalism, detaching Marx from his orthodox heritage, questioning his status as a dogmatic, determinist ideologue of communism, and moving the work of Marx away from political debates among socialists into the emerging social sciences of the postwar world. In the process Marx was made *salonfähig*; no longer the wild sectarian firebrand, no longer the ideologue of historical materialism, but a key theorist of the social disorders of capitalism and a consumer society. It was this trend that Louis Althusser confronted in the early 1960s, arguing that the reading of Marx initiated by Landshut and Mayer had turned *Capital* into a work of ethical theory continuous with, developing from, the work of the Young Marx.[196] Althusser therefore sought to detach the Mature Marx from the Young Marx, returning to an emphasis upon the mature Marx; but a Marx reorganised as the true discoverer of the science of history. It was claimed that an 'epistemological break'[197] separated the 'Young' from the 'Mature' Marx, so that this distinction could be rewritten as one between 'ideology' and 'science'. Heated academic exchanges followed on the question of whether any such chronological distinction could be made in Marx's writings, and on what the basis might be for any such distinction. Debate was reinforced by the publication of a collection of papers from a 1965 seminar under the title *Lire le Capital*, in which Althusser, Balibar, Establet, Macherey, and Rancière argued for a re-reading of *Capital* that identified its theoretical achievement in its detachment from the 'early writings'. Their understanding of Hegel and German philosophy relied on the work of French

195. Karl Marx, Friedrich Engels, *Ergänzungsband. Schriften, Manuskripte, Briefe bis 1844 Erster Teil*, Dietz Verlag, Berlin 1973—this includes Marx's doctoral dissertation, an extract from the notes on James Mill, and the 1844 Manuscripts.

196. Louis Althusser, *For Marx*, Allen Lane, London 1969 p. 52 (originally published in French 1965).

197. Althusser, *For Marx*, op. cit. p. 33.

philosophers; they knew little of the radical politics of the 1840s; they knew nothing at all about political economy, French, British, or German. In making a virtue of the fact that they read *Capital* as philosophers,[198] and not economists, they presumed they had no need of guidance on what political economy might be, apart from looking up a definition in a dictionary.[199] In short, this attempt to reboot an orthodox Marxism distinguishing between a Young and a Mature Marx conceived this to be a work for philosophers, reasserting Marx's scientific socialism in much the same way that Lenin had, while at the same time neglecting to consider either the provenance of or sources for Marx's writings, just as the 'humanist Marxism' they so vehemently criticised had failed to do.

Eventually the controversy over a 'Young', 'immature' Marx as opposed to a 'mature' Marx died down, and was succeeded by reconstructions of Marx that sought to bring him more directly into line with the social and political theory of the later twentieth century; prominent contributions to this literature were G. A. Cohen's *Karl Marx's Theory of History: A Defence* (1978), and Jon Elster's *Making Sense of Marx* (1985), both writers seeking to rationalise Marx on the basis of their own academic conceptions and presuppositions. It was assumed that Marx had created a system, and that one only had to reconcile his statements to find the logic of this system; tacitly underwriting the orthodox assumption that there was no need to examine Marx's sources and consider what he had made of them, and that to do so implied revisionist inclinations. At least arguments over the young and the older Marx had been linked in some way to Marx's actual writings, presuming that what Marx wrote had some meaning which we needed to understand, rather than impute to them a consistency and logic that is most apparent where it is actually lacking—extrapolating Marx's statements of intention, rather than examining the execution of this intention, and the means used to do so.

198. Althusser, Balibar, *Reading Capital* op. cit. p. 15.

199. 'I propose only to locate the most general concepts that constitute the *theoretical structure* of the object of Political Economy: in essentials, this analysis concerns the object of classical Political Economy (Smith, Ricardo), but it is not restricted to the classical forms of Political Economy, since the same basic *theoretical* categories still underlie the work of many economists today. With this in mind, I think I can take as my elementary theoretical guide the definitions proposed in A. Lalande's *Dictionnaire Philosophique*'. Althusser in *Reading Capital*, p. 160.

CHAPTER 7

'The Price Is Right': *Le prix juste* and the Algebra of Action

What form of appropriation is good and just? What form of appropriation is endorsed by reason as in conformity with the demands of moral personality? That is the problem of property. Property is equitable and rational appropriation, legitimate appropriation. Appropriation is a fact pure and simple; property, which is a legitimate fact, is a right. Moral theory is placed between fact and right. . . . The fact of appropriation is therefore in essence a moral fact, and the theory of property is therefore in essence a moral science. *Jus est suum cuique tribuere*, justice consists in securing to each his own; if ever science had as its object securing to each his own, if ever science had therefore justice for its principle, then it is most assuredly that which concerns the distribution of social wealth, or, as we shall call it, *social economy*.

—L. Walras, *Éléments d'économie politique pure ou Théorie de la richesse sociale* (1874)[1]

The general equilibrium model of economic exchange which Léon Walras first outlined in the 1870s offers a vision of the economy as a system of economic exchanges which in their reconciliation satisfies all

1. L. Walras, *Éléments d'économie politique pure ou Théorie de la richesse sociale*, Pierre Dockès, Pierre-Henri Goutte, Claude Hébert, Claude Mouchot, Jean-Pierre Potier, Jean-Michel Servet (eds.) Auguste and Léon Walras, *Œuvres économiques complètes*, Economica, 13 vols. Paris 1987–2005; here Vol. VIII pp. 63, 64 (henceforth cited as ŒEC with volume and page number). I would like to thank Edward Castleton for his generosity in bringing to my attention recent work on Proudhon and Léon Walras. I would also like to thank the editors of the *Œuvres économiques complètes* for their exemplary edition of the economic writings of Auguste and Léon Walras, without which it would have been impossible to gain the perspective upon mid-nineteenth-century French political economy that I present here.

agents simultaneously. Whereas Marshall cautiously preferred to express his own partial equilibrium approach in word and image—making iterative changes in states covered by the ruling principle of ceteris paribus, and favouring geometry over algebraic functions—Walras's approach had necessarily to be expressed as rows of equations. For mathematically literate economists of the early twentieth century like his correspondent in the United States, Henry L. Moore,[2] the Walrasian system represented the culmination of three centuries of study: from the observation of the regularities of the planetary system in the seventeenth century, the development in the eighteenth century of the mathematical techniques capable of predicting observed regularities, to the exposure of the regularities of social exchange and the price mechanism in the later nineteenth century. However, pushed to its limit, general equilibrium theory can seem more like a secular theology than a modern foundation for the economic modelling of a human world.

Did Walras share this vision? Did what his work became, the reduction of the 'blooming, buzzing confusion' of the human world to ordered rows of simultaneous equations, coincide with what he set out to do? If it did not, would it matter anyway? I will argue here that it does matter, that understanding the path that Léon Walras took lends us a fresh perspective on the development of twentieth-century neoclassical economics.

There is a paradox at the heart of 'Walrasian economics' that has dogged understanding of his work right up to the present day. Schumpeter built his *History of Economic Analysis* around the emergence of Walrasian general equilibrium, and the neoclassical turn of the 1930s incorporated the idea first into microeconomics, and then in the course of the 1940s into the new macroeconomics. When Walras retired in 1893 he was succeeded by Vilfredo Pareto, and it was only through Pareto that he first gained a wider audience. But this also took time, so that by the 1930s a cumulative detachment from the origins of his work had developed. By the time that the importance of his central ideas was widely acknowledged, the economist Léon Walras had slipped into the obscurity that he had, in his lifetime, already sought to counter through extensive correspondence with his contemporaries. When William Jaffé went to Lausanne in 1930 in search of his letters and papers, he was told (wrongly, it turned out) that

2. See George J. Stigler, 'Henry L. Moore and Statistical Economics', *Econometrica* Vol. 30 (1962) pp. 1–21. Moore's observations of agricultural cycles were related to planetary activity, much as W. S. Jevons had linked economic activity to sunspots—see the citation regarding the eight-year cycle of Venus from Moore's 1923 *Generating Economic Cycles*, p. 11 in Stigler's article. Cf. Mary S. Morgan, *The History of Econometric Ideas*, Cambridge University Press, Cambridge 1990 ch. 1.

there was nothing there. For Jaffé, this was only the beginning of an engagement on behalf of Léon Walras that he pursued right up to his death in 1980, publishing his English translation of *Éléments* in 1954, a three-volume *Correspondence* in 1965, together with a stream of explanatory papers, some of which were then collected in 1983.[3]

However, the Walras that Jaffé progressively revealed to an anglophone audience became increasingly out of sync with the Walras that economists talked about. In particular, Jaffé insisted that Walras had embodied the principle of commutative justice in his general equilibrium system,[4] also pointing out that there was a long tradition, originating with Pareto and Hicks, of ignoring what Schumpeter likewise regarded as 'his questionable philosophies about social justice, his land-nationalization schemes, his projects of monetary management, and other things that have nothing to do with his superb achievement in pure theory'.[5] Donald Walker, who first collected together Jaffé's papers and then assumed his mantle as interpreter of Walras, also baulked at Jaffé's argument. The idea that general equilibrium might have something to do with conceptions of equality and justice was for Walker a 'serious allegation about Walras as a scientist', thus introducing into Walker's account of Walras's work of the 1860s the positivism of the 1960s.[6]

By this time of course Jaffé had been dead for four years and so could not respond as he had done to Morishima in his 1980 *Journal of Economic Literature* essay. But in any case, although Jaffé was aware of the general Saint-Simonian background of Walras's economics, even proposing that Saint-Simon had in essence a dynamic, as opposed to a static, conception of general equilibrium,[7] Jaffé defended the logic of 'Walrasian economics'

3. *Elements of Pure Economics*, George Allen and Unwin, London 1954; *Correspondence of Léon Walras and Related Papers*, ed. William Jaffé, 3 vols. North-Holland, Amsterdam 1965, runs to over 2,000 pages and is a gold-mine for the study of the developing network among economists of the later nineteenth century; see Jaffé's 'Preface' (Vol. 1 pp. vii–xxi) which details the long and arduous history of his engagement with the project, beginning in 1930 (p. xv); and Donald A. Walker (ed.) *William Jaffé's Essays on Walras*, Cambridge University Press, Cambridge 1983.

4. 'The Normative Bias of the Walrasian Model: Walras versus Gossen', *Quarterly Journal of Economics* Vol. 91 (1977) pp. 371–87, reprinted in Walker, *William Jaffé's Essays on Walras*, op. cit. pp. 328–29.

5. Jaffé quoting Schumpeter, *History of Economic Analysis*, George Allen and Unwin, London 1954 pp. 827–28, in his 'Walras's Economics as Others See It', in Walker, *William Jaffé's Essays on Walras*, op. cit. p. 344 (originally published in *Journal of Economic Literature* Vol. 18 (1980) pp. 528–49).

6. Donald A. Walker, 'Is Walras's Theory of General Equilibrium a Normative Scheme?', *History of Political Economy* Vol. 16 (1984) p. 446.

7. 'Reflections on the Importance of Léon Walras', in Walker, *William Jaffé's Essays on Walras*, op. cit. p. 279 (originally published in 1971).

as an economist, and not as a historian. He was generally aware of the importance of Auguste Walras's work to that of his son, but he did not examine what that work was, nor how it might differ from that of their contemporaries. He thus tacitly conceded that evaluation of the economics of Léon Walras is best left to economists, the specialists best equipped to assess the logical consistency of his propositions.

But this is like deferring to the superior judgement of structural engineers in assessing the significance of Stonehenge. There is more to mathematical models of economic action than logical consistency; just as it is beside the point to argue that Gossen's work is fatally compromised by the fact that all his functions are linear.[8] Jaffé's belief that Walras's system of general equilibrium embodies a conception of justice is correct; unfortunately, the manner in which he asserted this left him open to criticism from fellow economists. In this chapter I will try to show that Jaffé was in fact quite right about equality and justice in Walras. To do so I will take a different approach to his work.

Although Walras devised a mathematical economic model of hitherto unprecedented complexity, his background in mathematics was modest. Having gained his baccalaureate in letters on 4 August 1851, he took an elementary mathematics class in 1851–52, and then in 1852–53 a more advanced mathematics class intended to prepare him for the École Polytechnique's entrance examination.[9] It was in this class that he encountered Louis Poinsot's *Éléments de statique* (8th edition 1842), which he later claimed to have read through in two days flat. Jaffé presents strong grounds for treating Poinsot's multi-equational approach to mechanical equilibrium as the source of Walras's own general equilibrium system.[10] However, at the time Walras clearly had some more fundamental problems with mathematical logic: on his own admission, the first time he applied to the École Polytechnique he failed to complete the preparatory exercises and was rejected; then he prepared much more thoroughly,

8. See for the most balanced and thorough assessment of Gossen's arguments and of his mathematics Paola Tubaro, 'Les mathématiques du plaisir et de la peine: La théorie du choix individuel de Hermann Heinrich Gossen', in Alain Alcouffe, Claude Diebolt (eds.) *La pensée économique allemande*, Economica, Paris 2009 pp. 245–67. See also Philippe Steiner's emphasis on the importance of the Creator to Gossen, a sure sign of the influence of *Le Nouveaux Christianisme* expounded by Enfantin and Leroux: 'The Creator, Human Conduct and the Maximisation of Utility in Gossen's Economic Theory', *European Journal of the History of Economic Thought* Vol. 18 (2011) pp. 353–80.

9. 'La vie et l'œuvre économique de Léon Walras', ŒEC Vol. V pp. xxviii–xix.

10. Léon Walras to Melle J. Weill, 23 May 1901, Letter 1483, *Correspondence* Vol. 3 pp. 148–49, note 7. See p. 69 note 1 for details on Weill.

studying among other things the calculus, geometry, and mechanics of Descartes, Newton, and Lagrange, only to be rejected again.[11] He claims to have also read Cournot at this time; but more telling is the judgement of Jaffé, whose examination of an 1860 draft 'Applications des mathématiques à l'économie politique' describes Walras's 'laboured attempt to assign some meaning'[12] to a proposition that Cournot had dismissed.[13] Walras sought to prove Cournot wrong in 1860, and then repeated the exercise in 1869–70, drawing on an analogy from physics.[14] Jaffé elaborates Walras's approach to Cournot in four dense pages of verbal and algebraic argument, concluding that 'This mixed bag of bungled mathematical economics was all L. W. had in pure theory when he offered his services to the Academy of Lausanne'.[15]

Walras did gain his science baccalaureate in 1853, but this was as far as he ever got in his formal education, in striking contrast to the years of work that his father had devoted to gaining advanced certification: Auguste's dissertation on *Le Cid* was only published in the same year that Léon completed his own science baccalaureate.[16] In his extensive and detailed review of Léon's papers, Jaffé comments on a note that his Lausanne colleague Piccard wrote for him in 1872: 'It is even doubtful whether L. W. who arrived in Lausanne with virtually no mathematics beyond elementary analytical geometry, was able to grasp more than the simple algebraic and geometric aspects of Piccard's explanation'. Nor does he seem to have paid any great attention to work by Dupuit and others published around this time.[17] And so the formal underpinnings of Walras's system seem to have been cobbled together very hastily in Lausanne, drawing on the mathematical expertise of his colleagues. Nonetheless, Jaffé goes on to remark that 'it is clear from L. W.'s marginal emendations . . . that he

11. 'Notice autobiographique', in *Correspondence* Vol. 1 p. 2.
12. *Correspondence* Vol. 1 pp. 216–17 note 33.
13. 'The price of things, it is said with near unanimity, is in inverse ratio to the quantity supplied, and is in a positive ratio to the quantity demanded'. A. A. Cournot, *Recherches sur les principes mathématiques de la théorie des richesses*, J. Vrin, Paris 1980 p. 35—this is part of the opening discussion to ch. 4, 'On the Law of Sales'.
14. 'Just as density is defined as the ratio of mass to volume, though mass is not directly measurable, so value in exchange is defined as a magnitude (resulting from the law of supply and demand) directly proportional to the sum of needs (or demand) and inversely proportional to the sum of quantities in existence (or supply), though the sum of needs is not directly measurable'. *Correspondence* Vol. 1 p. 218 note 33.
15. *Correspondence* Vol. 1 p. 221 note 33.
16. Outlined below.
17. Manuela Mosca, 'Jules Dupuit, the French "ingenieurs économistes" and the Société d'Économie Politique', in Gilbert Faccarello (ed.) *Studies in the History of French Political Economy*, Routledge, London 1998 pp. 254–83.

immediately understood the economic implications' of Piccard's note.[18] Hence Walras understood intuitively the argument put to him by Piccard, even if he was not well versed in the formal language in which it was expressed. This suggests that Walras already had a conception of a general system of exchanges with an equilibrium solution before he arrived in Lausanne, and that the mathematical form which this conception was given in Lausanne was an exemplification of this conception, rather than its realisation. When he originally read Poinsot, the only political economy that he knew came from his father, and he soon afterwards ceased any formal engagement with mathematical logic. Put in the starkest terms: Walras was no mathematician, but used mathematics to represent an idea he already had. Why would he do this? And what was the idea?

To answer these questions we need first of all to turn to biography. As with Marx in the previous essay, the context in which Walras developed his thinking about political economy is important for an understanding of what those thoughts were. Marx and Walras were separated by the 1848 Revolution: Marx moved to Paris in 1843, whereas as a young man Walras experienced Paris some ten years later, subsequent to the collapse of the Second Republic and the establishment of the Second Empire in December 1852. He had no formal economic training; his mathematics was limited; he did not have any post-school qualification, so in France would later be disqualified from teaching at a university. Fortunately, he did write an autobiographical essay that indicates the key events in his life between his leaving school and becoming a professor, and the first volume in his complete works is prefaced with a detailed outline of his life and writings.[19] This makes it possible to identify the resources upon which he drew, as well as the pathway which led from a bohemian existence in Paris to a professorship in Lausanne, where he became the originator of a general equilibrium model of economic activity whose importance for economic analysis only became widely acknowledged some fifty years later.

Léon Walras was familiar with the arguments of contemporary political economy from an early age. His father Auguste had sought a career teaching political economy, but eventually was only able to gives some public courses in Paris. Auguste had published two treatises on political economy, *De la nature de la richesse et de l'origine de la valeur* appearing in 1831 and expounding his argument that scarcity, *rareté,* is the source of value; while *Théorie de l'économie sociale*, a much shorter expository work, was published in 1849. In 1831 Auguste was appointed to the municipal

18. *Correspondence* Vol. 1 p. 309.
19. 'Introduction: La vie et l'œuvre économique de Léon Walras', ŒEC V pp. ix–xciv.

college in Evreux; he married there in March 1834, and Léon was born the following December. Following a move to Paris to pursue his studies, he gave a course in political economy at the Athénée during 1836 and 1837, also attending Rossi's lectures at the Collège de France. His academic efforts met with success, being in 1840 appointed professor of philosophy at the Royal College of Caen, and then inspector of the Douai Academy. Auguste had looked to Léon's younger brother Louis to carry on his work in political economy, but in 1858 Louis died, and Auguste turned to Léon, not yet twenty-four, instead. Although lacking at this time any particular knowledge of the subject, Léon agreed, and from then until his death in 1910 continued the work which his father had begun. Naturally enough, this work had been dominated by arguments among French liberals, socialists, and political economists during the 1830s and 1840s over competition, monopoly, protection, distribution, impoverishment, and social wealth. Léon was only thirteen during the June Days of 1848, and not quite seventeen when Louis Napoléon seized power in December 1851. Nonetheless, allegiance to his father's thinking meant that he remained marked by the debates of the 1830s and 1840s, carrying them with him to Lausanne in 1870. And this also brought him closer to Marx: although some fifteen years Marx's junior, through the work of his father Léon shared with Marx a common heritage in the French politics and economics of the 1830s and 1840s.

Léon had done well at school, but subsequently floundered. He failed the entrance examination to the École Polytechnique twice, in 1853 and 1854. Then having gained entrance to the École des Mines he was thrown out within the year, readmitted, and then thrown out again; trying yet again in the autumn of 1856, he came thirty-ninth in a competition for twenty-two places (ŒEC V p. xx).[20] In January 1855 Léon was selected by lot to serve six years in the *Chasseurs alpin*, which he only avoided because his father paid for a substitute. Later that year there are reports of his amorous involvement with a *grisette*, and for the next couple of years he devoted himself to writing a novel, *Francis Sauveur*, which was eventually published in 1858 at his own (presumably his father's) expense. He was unsuccessful the following year in placing an essay on the philosophy of art that he had written in one of the contemporary periodicals. In early 1859 he began living with a young single mother, Célestine-Aline Ferbach,

20. In a letter dated 18 February 1858 Auguste asked how things stood with the École des Mines, clearly not being then aware that any hope of Léon being admitted had ended some eighteen months previously. The editors surmise that it was only during the summer of 1858 that Léon admitted his failure—ŒEC IV pp. 304, 305 note 3.

whom he eventually married in 1869 after the death of his father, a relationship which he concealed from his family until his marriage, and which seems to have directly contributed to a breach with his sister.

Through his early twenties Léon lived the bohemian life. Puccini's 1896 opera *La Bohème* was in fact based upon Henri Murger's *Scènes de la vie de bohème* of 1851, a series of vignettes of life in the Latin Quarter of Paris—and from 1856 Léon Walras did live in the rue de l'Abbaye, on the western fringe of the Latin Quarter (ŒEC V p. xxi). This was exactly his milieu, but his father's request changed his life. Not until November 1870 would Léon be appointed extraordinary professor of political economy in Lausanne, where within a few years he published the work that (eventually) made him famous. The route to Lausanne was slow and indirect, but Léon persisted in his new calling as a political economist, despite ten years of setbacks: through economic journalism, employment in a railway company, involvement in a failed banking venture, and occasional lectures on co-operatives. Critical to his eventual appointment in Lausanne was his presence at a conference on taxation organised by the Vaudois cantonal authorities in 1861. He went as a journalist, but also made several interventions which impressed the organisers. He also made a presentation—hastily put together from some notes by his father. The previous year he had published an essay on social economy and justice, a critique of Proudhon which also relied for the most part upon material given to him by his father. Lacking any formal training in political economy, Léon discharged his father's wish to the letter, working from the notes that his father gave him. And so before we go any further, we need to examine just what Auguste Walras's own views on the nature and scope of political economy were.

THE POLITICAL ECONOMY OF AUGUSTE WALRAS

Auguste was born in Montpellier in 1801 to a family with a Dutch background.[21] In the Montpellier college he excelled at rhetoric, Latin, French, philosophy, and mathematics; interviewed for a place at the École Normale in 1820, he was admitted the same year as a student of 'letters'. Moving to Paris in the autumn of 1820, he remained there more or less continuously until 1831, when he was appointed to the college in Evreux. He passed his baccalaureate in 1821, but in September 1822 the École

21. The following biographical remarks are based upon 'Auguste Walras de 1801 à 1848', ŒEC I pp. cxxi–clxxii.

Normale was closed following political pressure from the Ultras. After two brief spells teaching, at the end of 1823 he became a private tutor, first in the household of the financier Salomon Halphen, and then for maître Sensier, a lawyer. In November 1824 he became a student in the Paris School of Law while continuing his employment as tutor and secretary for the Sensier family.

His studies would be interrupted several times, but it was in this context that he first began to read political economy, having concluded that the theory of property that he was being taught was erroneous. During the years 1824 to 1826 he read works by Say, Destutt de Tracy, Ganilh, and Massias, and his interest gradually shifted from law to political economy, with a marked interest in Saint-Simonian ideas (ŒEC I p. cxxix).

He became a subscriber to *Le Globe*, founded in 1824 as a literary journal by P.-F. Dubois and Pierre Leroux, and whose contributors and readers included many of the scholars and teachers expelled from their posts in 1821. Auguste made notes on several of the articles, and some time in the later 1820s he began writing his first book, *De la Nature de la richesse et de l'origine de la valeur*, the first chapters being published in early 1830 as five articles in *Le Mercure de France au dix-neuvième siècle*. By March 1830 the work was more or less complete as we know it today. Out of Paris during the July Revolution, he first completed final revisions to his book, and then in September began to write his essay on the agrarian law: this proposed the nationalisation of land and the imposition of a single tax in the form of rental payments.

In January 1831 Auguste requested a public teaching appointment, and in March he was appointed as an adjunct teacher of rhetoric in Evreux, some one hundred kilometres from Paris and around sixteen hours by coach. With a secure position and income for the first time, and also the time to pursue his studies, he married in March 1834 into a prominent local family, and in May 1835 was appointed director of the college. His book was finally printed here, part-financed by the local Society for Agriculture, Science, Arts and Belles-lettres, a progressive and influential local society whose board Auguste soon joined, taking responsibility for 'Political Economy and Statistics', and presenting lectures on political economy with the encouragement of the local prefect.[22] But however quickly he had found a provincial niche, he clearly still thought of a wider public. In

22. For details of this Society and its role in Orleanist politics, its split with, and legal proceedings against, Legitimist members who seceded and formed a separate regional society, see ŒEC I pp. cxxxviii–clii. He had forty auditors in 1832–33, and forty-five in 1834–35 (ŒEC I p. cxlix).

October 1835 he took leave from his post so that he might study for the *agrégation* in philosophy; without this he had no hope of advancement. In the spring of 1836 he left Evreux for Paris, together with his wife Aline and their two children.

Things were not easy in Paris: Aline's younger brother lived with them, also a student to whom Auguste gave lessons, and money was tight. For two years he attended Rossi's course at the Collège de France, 'without success and any profit', as he wrote to Léon in January 1860.[23] During the winter and spring of 1836–37 he also gave twenty-three lectures at the Athénée, but his main preoccupation was the study of mathematics, so that he might gain his baccalaureate in physical sciences. In August 1837 he passed the examination with such distinction that he was immediately recommended to the Ministry of Public Instruction. He was less successful in philosophy: he first of all failed in the spring of 1838, gained an honourable mention in September 1839, and then passed in September 1840. He was immediately appointed to teach the subject at the college in Lille, then moving in September the following year to the Royal College of Caen, which at the time had a staff of thirty-four and 614 pupils, 253 of them boarders (ŒEC I p. clxi). In 1846 he was appointed to the Caen Faculty of Letters, responsible for teaching French literature, and by the end of the summer was almost finished with writing his thesis *Le Cid, esquisse littéraire*, which was eventually published in 1853 (ŒEC II p. 9 fn. 1). In January 1848 he was made inspector of the Caen Academy, after some uncertainty about his future. This seems to have been instigated by the rector of the Academy, the abbé Jacques-Louis Daniel, a reactionary cleric who later wrote on 22 March 1849 to the Ministry of Public Instruction that he had 'overlooked his [Auguste's] Saint-Simonian past in the light of the very wise opinions that he held. Unfortunately, his conduct of the past year, the unfortunate role that he has played in clubs, the communist doctrines that he has echoed in a great many circumstances, and the manner in which he performs his functions as inspector has demonstrated to me that I treated him with entirely undeserved favour' (ŒEC II p. 20).

In February 1848 Louis-Philippe suddenly abdicated, taking even Republicans by surprise; and on 2 March 1848 the Calvados provisional government announced that the Republic would be proclaimed on Sunday 12 March, wherever this had not already happened. Even the abbé Daniel expressed his recognition of this new political reality, writing in a letter to the Ministry dated 29 March 1848 that a Republican government was the only viable option under the current circumstances (ŒEC II p. 17 fn. 39).

23. Details of the course Auguste followed are given in ŒEC I p. CLVII fn. 2.

The 'clubs' to which he later referred were formed as part of the preparations for elections to the Constituent Assembly: along with 1,300 others Auguste joined the Association républicaine, and he also gave public lectures on political economy organised by the Club des Travailleurs.[24] Republican and socialist agitation was at this time generally much stronger in provincial centres such as Caen than in Paris. But after the June Days in Paris this surge of support quickly waned; fearing the depredations of imaginary bandits, and with unemployment in Caen during the winter of 1848–49 at 75%, 68% of its inhabitants voted for Louis-Napoleon Bonaparte in the December 1848 presidential election. Nevertheless, as inspector Auguste remained from November 1848 to February 1849 in sole charge of the Caen Academy until, as part of the wave of reaction, Daniel was reappointed rector. He determined on Auguste's removal. In early March Auguste was appointed to an inspectorate in Cahors—well away from Paris, in fact well away from almost anywhere, and especially his influential in-laws in Haute Normandie. Following a personal intercession with the ministry, the appointment was revoked and Auguste was instead given a small pension. He lived in Caen for another year and a half, writing, and visiting Paris, where he was a member of the Société des économistes. In September 1849 he presented his 'Mémoire sur l'origine de la valeur d'échange' at the Académie des Sciences morales et politiques;[25] in the same month Guillamin, the major French publishing house for political economy, brought out his *Théorie de la richesse sociale*. During 1850 the conservative reaction continued apace—power over educational institutions and appointments was shifted to the church, and the franchise restricted to those who could prove three years' continuous residence in the same home, removing the right to vote from some three million individuals, almost half of those previously enfranchised. Finally, in August 1850, Auguste was nominated inspector at the Douai Academy, far from Normandy in northern France.

Henceforth his life was primarily devoted to administration and teaching. He had had a very productive period during 1848–49, not only publishing his second book but also drafting a number of pieces that eventually

24. The abbé Daniel wrote on 5 April 1848 to Lazare Carnot, Minister of Public Instruction, arguing that all such public teaching—in arithmetic, geometry, applied chemistry, so-called republican literature—should be supported, except that in political economy, since the inspector, Auguste Walras, would be fully occupied by his official duties (ŒEC II pp. 15–16). But Daniel was dismissed from his post on 1 May 1848.

25. This had originally been presented at the Caen Academy in July 1844 (ŒEC II p. 24).

remained unpublished: two further chapters of the *Théorie*, two essays on taxation, the much longer 'La Verité sociale par un travailleur', and a long critique of Adolphe Thiers's *De la propriété*, which had been published in September 1848. In contrast to the earlier productive period he had enjoyed in 1830–32, during 1848–49 he did not present his work to a local audience, through public lecture or contributions to periodicals; for this later period, we have to refer to these unpublished papers to establish what his convictions were—convictions which however were later communicated to his son Léon in correspondence that has survived. Having outlined the circumstances in which his interest in political economy developed, we can now consider just what kind of political economy it was upon which Léon drew.

Auguste's work on the book *De la Nature de la richesse et de l'origine de valeur* was completed by early September 1830 at the latest. He had had difficulty finding a publisher for the complete manuscript in Paris, and it was not until he moved to Evreux in March 1831 that he found a solution: the Agricultural Society agreed to subsidise the printing, this was done locally during the early summer of 1831, and then published with new endpapers in Paris. He describes in the 'Avant propos' how he had been led into the study of political economy by his interest in the nature and origin of property, and that his lack of knowledge did not at first seem to him an impediment, since he assumed that the science of wealth was an advanced science whose principles were almost in finished form. He was however quickly disappointed to discover how confused the treatment of wealth and its origin was—one only had to leaf through Say, de Tracy, Ganilh, Massias, and Sismondi to see that they agreed on very little. Nonetheless, while political economy and natural law were not the same science,

> I wish to say here, and have tried to demonstrate in this work, that wealth and property have their common origin in the same fact, which is in my opinion nothing other than the limitation of certain goods, or the scarcity of certain useful objects; that the things that have value and which constitute wealth in the proper sense, or social wealth as it is sometimes called, are exactly the same things that fall into the domain of the personal, and which become the object of property.[26]

The study of wealth and of property therefore went hand in hand; and since property was founded upon the idea of wealth, and it was value that

26. Auguste Walras, *De la nature de la richesse et de l'origine de la valeur*, ŒEC I pp. 47–233, here p. 50.

made possession advantageous, political economy had a logical precedence over natural law.

Organised as a critique of Say and Garnier, the hierarchy of his sources is expressed in the title of chapter 14: 'On the doctrine of M. Say, compared to that of Smith and Ricardo.—Superiority of the first to the second.—Problems of the one and the other'. The book is discursive in style and organised into twenty chapters, and by the third chapter he has exposed his primary criticism of Say: that value derives not from utility, but scarcity. Taking this as his point of departure, Auguste points out that the air we breathe, and the sunlight we enjoy, certainly have utility, but their sheer abundance means that they have no value. It is only scarce objects, those that have *rareté*, which have value, because there are only a certain number of people who can possess them; and even those who have the most only have a fraction of the whole (ŒEC I p. 78). This idea is elaborated much later in chapter 11, in which he distinguishes between the intensity and the extension of utility:

> The needs to which we are subject are not only distinguished by their greater or lesser urgency; they are also distinguished by their extent, or by the number of men who experience them. (ŒEC I p. 137)

Hence value was a relationship between the quantity of a limited good and the number of persons who had need of it: 'scarcity is only the relationship between these two numbers' (loc. cit.). The fact of scarcity was expressed by value, and exchange itself was nothing but a barter between two values:

> and it is the essence of exchange that the objects involved be objects of an equal value. In general, one can only obtain possession of one value that one desires and does not possess by sacrificing an equal value that one possesses; and one cannot sacrifice a value that one possesses, save in the case of alms or charity, without obtaining, by way of indemnification, a value equal to the one that has been sacrificed. (ŒEC I pp. 109–10)

Therefore, he went on to argue, political economy was essentially mathematical in nature: 'one compares values in the same way that one compares lines, angles, surfaces, etc., and the same principles govern all these comparisons' (ŒEC I pp. 207–8).

Auguste's book might have been motivated by his interest in the relation of property and political economy, but in it he confined himself to a critique of contemporary French political economy and the exposition of his idea regarding scarcity as a source of value. However, once he had completed work on the book in the late summer of 1830, he immediately began to draft an essay that was far more revealing of his motivation in studying political economy, and explicitly linked to events surrounding the fall of Charles X that year and the accession of Louis-Philippe. Falling ill during October, it was not until January 1831 that he resumed work, only to be interrupted again by his move to Evreux in March. Here he settled quickly into public employment and an active engagement in provincial culture, and he kept quiet about an essay that proposed the nationalisation of land and the levying of a single tax. He never did resume work on it, but he returned to its arguments again in 1848, in the two unpublished chapters of *Théorie de la richesse sociale*, and in *La Verité sociale*. However, this first unpublished essay provides the most extensive exposition of Auguste's arguments on land nationalisation, the later work drawing upon it in part rather than developing it further.

Originally called simply 'La Loi agraire', the essay was in January 1831 given a more explanatory title: 'De l'Abolition de l'impôt, et de l'établissement de la loi agraire, telle qu'elle peut être conçue et pratiquée aux XIXe siecle' (ŒEC II pp. 7–20). While the July Revolution had seen off Jesuits and emigrés, he argued, there remained a yoke no less oppressive: that of landed property, which had undue influence on the new government. The Chamber of Deputies represented only the landed interest, and was striving to undo what it considered 'concessions made to democracy' (ŒEC I p. 9). There was widespread debate over landed property: weak and murky arguments in its defence, but also irresolution on the part of the 'friends of the revolution' who opposed the rule of a landed nobility, but who would seem to accept a division of power between the new nobility and the 'industrious classes'.[27] Auguste was on the other hand quite clear: he accorded

> all influence and all social importance in modern times to the labouring classes; not content with the weakening of landed proprietors, I maintain that they should be completely eliminated; and rather than narrowly contain their

27. 'les classes savantes et industrielles'—see ŒEC II note 31 p. 466 for an elucidation of this neologism, referring to an article in *Le Producteur* discussing recent changes in the use of language, the word '*industriels* not having existed twenty years ago and which is today on everyone's tongue. . . . *L'industriel* . . . is someone who works freely as a *chef* or worker in agriculture, manufacture, commerce or a bank at something which must be conceived to be of direct use to him, because he remains owner of the fruits of his labour, and indirectly, in that it increases his social importance'—J. Allier, 'Crédit, Discrédit, Industriels, Industrie, Producteur', *Le Producteur* t. 2 (1826) no. 25 pp. 572–73.

privileges, I want to undermine them and completely overturn them: and this will be the outcome of the system I will outline on property and on taxation. (ŒEC II p. 9)

Land, he argued, was a useful and scarce object, which therefore had a value and constituted wealth in the sense of political economy, but was indestructible and eternal, permanent and perpetual. By contrast, man as an individual was ephemeral, mortal, and as such not capable of possessing the land; how could a man possess something that was there before he existed, and would remain after his death? Nor were families eternal; and one could not confer rights over something that was eternal to a being that was not likewise eternal. Hence it was not possible to transmit any such right.

If there were anything durable and human, it was not the individual, but humanity: 'peoples or nations are the sole collective beings who can be considered as durable persons, as durable as the soil that bears them, as the land which feeds them' (ŒEC I p. 10). Property in the soil therefore belonged to the nation, the state as a collection of individuals and a series of generations, and 'the annual product of the land forms the public revenue of each generation called to harvest it' (ibid.). As a corollary to this, Auguste also proposed the abolition of all taxes or whatever kind, public expenditure being covered in future by revenues from the land.

In support of his ideas he invoked Quesnay, although there were several points of difference between a Physiocratic single tax and the one that he was proposing. For one thing, in the Physiocratic system the tax burden fell entirely on the producing class. Second, their emphasis upon land as the sole source of wealth was erroneous: it was land and labour that were the joint source of the satisfaction of human need:

The vegetative force of the soil and the physical force and intellect of man, these are the elements of all property and of all fortune, public and private. Land and labour are the two natural objects which, being limited in their quantity, acquire an exchange value, and in forming the original fund, the indispensable element of all wealth or all public or private fortune. (ŒEC I p. 12)

Man had two means for the exploitation of these utilities, 'these productive forces which combined to satisfy these needs and procure enjoyments' (ŒEC I pp. 12–3): property and community (*communauté*). Property gave to the individual the right of use and disposition over a thing; community attributed this same right to many persons together. It was labour and its fruits that were the true objects of individual property, while land and its products was the object of collective property.

> In other words, physical and intellectual powers (*force*) form the natural patrimony of the individual, while the vegetative powers of the soil form the natural patrimony of the human species, or of a fraction of the human species, that is to say the people of the nation which live on this soil. (ŒEC I p. 13)

This principle ended all argument over property and inequality: that which nature has given to all must be exploited to the profit of all, while that which nature has given to each individual must be exploited to the exclusive advantage of that individual. Land and its products are for the use of everyone; physical and intellectual capacities are given to every individual person, and hence any benefits arising from their legitimate exercise. And since the land and its products were for the benefit of all, it was the nation as a whole that should possess the soil; not simply the present generation, but all future generations to come, just as in medieval times families had possessed the land.

It was the 'industrious' whose efforts supported the whole of society: the annual consumption of what they produced was divided among themselves, capitalists who were paid for the use of their capital, landowners who were paid for the use of the land, and the government that secured the peace in which they could work. However, the revenues that supported the landowners could be diverted without harm to support government expenditure. How would this be achieved? The state could simply confiscate land, but this would be unjust. The state could appropriate land and indemnify its holders; while not as unjust as the first course, the state lacked the financial means to do this. The only feasible course was for the state to declare land public and inalienable property, acquiring it gradually by setting aside each year a sum for its direct purchase.

This was, Auguste went on, a less ambitious plan that that proposed some years before by the Saint-Simonians, who not stopping with landed property, sought the complete abolition of inheritance, the transmission of property by inheritance, the acquisition of wealth by birthright. According to the Saint-Simonians, land and capitals should be put in public hands and then distributed to all citizens according to their capacity, recompensing each individual according to his work.[28] While generally being in favour of the Saint-Simonian system, Auguste had three objections. First of all, where would the capital be found? Such sums as had been

28. See for Saint-Simonian sources on this ŒEC I pp. 472–73 fn. 94.

accumulated were in the hands of individuals who had set money aside for their own future, or for that of their children. By abolishing inheritance the motive for such accumulation would lose all force. Second, this doctrine fragmented, if not entirely destroyed, the family. Third, the Saint-Simonians seemed to have made some errors in their political economy; in this, they went no further than Adam Smith or Ricardo, who had viewed labour as the source of all value, of all wealth.

> The doctrine of Malthus and Ricardo explaining the origin of rent is certainly very ingenious, but it is false. To explain the origin of rent by the inequality of land is like explaining wages by the inequality of capacity among workers. The inequality of workers explains the inequality of wages, just like the inequalities of the soil explains the inequality of rents. But the origin of rent, and the origin of wages, considered in themselves and abstracting from the rate at which they are set, have a different source than the difference one could find, and which really is found, between this or that worker, and this or that land. Land and labour are two forms of wealth, or two values, because they are useful and limited. It is their scarcity that gives them a price. . . . It is for this reason, and this reason only, that they become exchangeable, or values. It is for this reason that they are bought and sold, and that their service obtains a price. (ŒEC I pp. 16–17)

The error of the Saint-Simonians was that they sought to abolish rent, which was a mistake; for so long as land was useful and scarce it had a value, would never cease to produce a revenue—the destination of this revenue might alter, but not its existence. In Auguste's view, it was not rent as such that was a problem, but that it flowed to an idle class, who consumed but did not produce. This rental stream was properly the property of all. Consequently, all rental payments on land should go to the state, providing a single yet adequate source for all government expenditure. This would make possible the abolition of all personal direct taxes, the individual consequently enjoying the entire monetary reward for work that had been done, resulting in a just and equitable system.

Despite the criticism of Saint-Simonians here, his argument about the industrious and the idle classes coincides with a central tenet of Saint-Simonian thinking. And this was not simply a passing phase: when in the spring of 1848 he summarised these ideas his indebtedness was even more marked. 'La vérité sociale par un travailleur' had originally been called 'Organisation du travail: question préliminaire', and begins from the organisation of society into two broad classes: the working and the idle. The former is made up of all those who work the land, directly or indirectly;

industriels who work in factories or manufactories, from entrepreneur to worker; merchants, including those involved in distribution; the liberal professions; and public functionaries. The idle classes were just two: rentiers and landed proprietors.[29] Auguste had nothing against rentiers, living off the revenue from the use of their accumulated capital; but landed proprietors lived off rents that belonged not to them, but to everyone. Land was the property of all humanity; while all that was produced by labour belonged to the individual who produced it (ŒEC II p. 45). He rejected out of hand the idea that land belonged to those who had first enclosed and possessed it; Rousseau's idea that this was the foundation of civil society was simply wrong:

> The first who undertook to enclose some land and said: *this is mine*, did not found *civil society*; he founded *individual landed property*. (ŒEC II p. 47)

As common property, land belonged to all; rental payments properly belonged not to a class of idle landowners, but to the state, for the purpose of public expenditures. Although this is much the longest disquisition on land and labour, including a review of the opinions of political economists (ŒEC II pp. 72–82), it lacks the systematic argument of the 1830/1831 formulation of the problem, not even entering into any discussion of the ways and means of realising the conversion of rental payments into a single tax.

His second book, *Théorie de la richesses sociales, ou résumé des principes fondamentaux de l'économie politique*,[30] was completed after this sketch, and published in 1849 by Guillamin. This was a much shorter book than *De la Nature de la richesse et de l'origine de valeur*, running to just over one hundred pages, and in the first lines of the 'Avant-propos' Auguste emphasised that its purpose was to summarise the principles of political economy, a science that had undergone development since the eighteenth century, but which had never become truly popular, especially among the governing classes. These principles were no less important to a wider society, influenced as it was by a number of competing systems of thought which encouraged the wildest speculations, nourishing quite chimerical aspirations (ŒEC II pp. 113–14). The book is divided into six chapters, beginning with definitions of social wealth and utility, moving to the measure of value and the nature of money, thence to capital and revenue, in chapter 5 broaching the three elements of social wealth: the land, per-

29. 'La vérité sociale par un travailleur', ŒEC II pp. 35–105, here p. 37.
30. Printed in ŒEC II pp. 113–70.

sonal faculties, and artificial capital. The final chapter deals with production and distribution.

Auguste defines utility as 'the faculty that certain things have of satisfying a need of any kind, or procuring any kind of enjoyment' (ŒEC II p. 115)—a broad definition that obviously draws upon Say, but also anticipates the 'value neutrality' that would be embraced almost a century later by Lionel Robbins. This sense is lent emphasis by his qualification that it therefore includes anything which is necessary, agreeable, or superfluous; for political economy is not an ethics, it accepts 'man as he is, with his passions and caprices' (ŒEC II loc. cit.). Wealth and utility were therefore synonymous; however, some things were limited in quantity, while other were limited in duration; and these two qualities were the origin of exchange value and capital respectively. Something which was scarce would become an object of commerce, and hence part of social wealth; and since things that were limited in quantity were appropriable, social wealth was synonymous with property. Consequently, 'the true object of political economy is *social wealth*' (ŒEC II p. 119). From the perspective of political economy, society is a market,

> and human life, as regards the economic relation, is nothing other than a continuing series of exchanges carried on between the proprietors of limited goods. (ŒEC II pp. 134–35)

Chapter 5 outlines the three sources of social wealth—land, labour, and capital, each of which had its own form of revenue: rent, wages, and profit. Land and labour were natural sources of wealth; capital, the result of saving and economy, was artificial (ŒEC II p. 151). Although of course his discussion of rental flows and the idleness of landed proprietors here touches on points raised in his manuscript on the nationalisation of land from 1830–31, Auguste takes this no further. However, some time in the following year or two he drafted two further chapters containing a résumé of his theory of property; from the context it seemed he considered these to be chapters 7 and 8 for a planned second edition of the book.[31] The first of these rehearses arguments about property, possession, and usufruct, drawing a distinction between particular things which by their nature suited themselves to private possession, and others which were more suited to property in common, such as roads—that they were properly the property of the state. Railways could for example be run by companies for

31. 'Mais laissons là toutes ces misères', ŒEC II pp. 609–12, at p. 612. From internal evidence the editors date this from the autumn of 1848 to the spring of 1849.

profit, but they could equally well be run by the state and their revenues used for public purposes (ŒEC II p. 183). The second of these chapters begins exactly like chapter 5, but states clearly that land belongs to the state; land produces a surplus value (*plus-value*) which is diverted to the maintenance of landowners and their families, in effect dividing society into two great classes: a class of landed proprietors on the one hand, and a class of proletarians on the other: 'I call *proletarian* every man who does not possess the land' (ŒEC II pp. 184–85). While taxes on economic activity violate the liberty of private property, applied to the soil private property robs the state of its own resources; consequently, rental payments should be converted into a single tax.

In the fragment from August 1850 in which Auguste had referred to a possible second edition of *De la Nature de la richesse* he made clear his intent:

> Take the socialist theories, of Cabet, of Proudhon, of Louis Blanc and all the rest; and I will clearly show you that the exaggeration and the vice of all these systems rest equally in a false, or incomplete, notion of social wealth or exchange value. The cleverest well understand this. Look at Proudhon. He always comes back to the question: what is value. And it is unarguable that Proudhon's errors derive from what he has taken from political economy as Adam Smith and J.-B. Say left it, and that he has not corrected the error of his masters on this fundamental point. (ŒEC II pp. 609–10)

However, in the early 1850s Auguste finally abandoned his ambition of teaching political economy, and with it the various manuscripts that he had drafted. But he passed these ideas on to Léon, who made them his own. His first book was a critique of Proudhon.

LÉON WALRAS'S PATRIMONY

Léon's younger brother Louis died of complications following typhoid fever on 13 January 1858 (ŒEC IV p. 298). One year later Léon set to work and produced *L'Économie politique et la justice*; two extracts were published in the *Journal des économistes* in February 1860, and then the whole book by Guillamin in March. Its subtitle was 'A critical examination and rejection of the economic doctrines of M. P.-J. Proudhon prefaced by an Introduction to the study of the social question' (ŒEC V pp. 87–313); more particularly, it was a critique of Proudhon's *De la Justice dans la Révolution et dans l'Église*, a book that had made a big splash early in 1858 (ŒEC V

p. 77). As Marx had sought to make his mark in 1847 by lambasting Proudhon's pretensions as a political economist, so Léon followed on in 1859, the thrust of his argument being made easier by the way in which Proudhon represented a position which was the reverse of Auguste's: Proudhon argued that ethics was natural while the economic was social, while Auguste maintained that economic relationships were natural and ethics was social.

Sixty-five hundred copies of Proudhon's book had been printed, and between its publication on 22 April 1858 and its being banned and seized on 28 May all but five hundred copies had been sold. It was a substantial work in four volumes, divided into twelve 'études' covering justice, the state, education, labour, liberty, progress, love and marriage, and moral sanctions. There was material directly relevant to political economy in the third *étude* (goods) and the sixth (labour), the final parts of the first and second volumes respectively. Auguste had got hold of a copy in late October 1858, and had originally been positively impressed; but by December he had changed his mind (ŒEC V pp. 79–80). Evidently he never even got as far as the second volume before this happened, since the commentary that Léon wrote up from his notes was in fact directed to only two chapters from the six in the third *étude*, totalling seventy pages in all. Auguste outlined the plan of the book he wanted Léon to write in a long letter of 6 February,[32] and in a number of other letters conveyed further comments to his son. This process was concluded in June 1858, and then in the autumn Léon wrote his own introduction. The result is a very strange book: polemical in tone throughout, the main sections take the form of quotations from Proudhon followed by ad hoc criticism. There is consequently no argumentative thread, simply a very repetitive pattern that moves, sentence by sentence, paragraph by paragraph, through Proudhon's two chapters.[33] Léon himself never had a copy of the book, underlining his absolute reliance on his father's notes (ŒEC V pp. 87–143).[34]

A sense of how this works can be gained by considering the manner in which Léon represents the nature of equal exchange. As already noted above, Auguste had in his first book argued that exchange was in effect a

32. Auguste to Léon Walras, 6 February 1859, ŒEC IV pp. 324–31 (Letter 122).

33. For example, ŒEC V pp. 220–30 deals with pp. 324–28 of Vol. 1 of the 1870 new edition published by Marpon et Flammarion, Paris, even though the ŒEC has around 30% more words on each page.

34. This also accounts for the monotonous polemical tone that Léon adopts, the 'violence of expression' noted and itemised in Michel Herland's 'Les Walras critiques de *La Justice* de Proudhon', paper presented at the Colloque Walras, Toulouse September 2012.

process of barter in which equal values were exchanged. In section II of *L'Économie politique et la justice* Léon begins by summarising Proudhon's position on exchange as 'equality of conditions and of positions', whereas Léon's is 'equality of conditions, inequality of positions' (ŒEC V p. 179). Proudhon, he argues, persists in running together property and community, equality and inequality, commutative and distributive justice. 'Is it not a pity that he has spent his life arguing against property and against communism, without ever realising that both individualism and communism each have their legitimation and basis?' (ŒEC V p. 180). Now that the discussion has turned to exchange, Léon seeks first to clarify his own position: that some things not being free, they can only be obtained by those who want them through the provision of an equivalent. This implies that

1. Exchange implies appropriation.
2. Exchange implies exchange value.
3. There is an equivalence between the objects exchange, an equality of value.

There follows a long quotation relating to this from Auguste's 1838 article, 'De la richesse sociale' (ŒEC I p. 402). The condition of equivalence is identified as a 'natural law' in the same way that exchange value is a 'natural theory'. The role of 'justice' here is to simply respect the freedom of the market, so that supply and demand might be increasingly reconciled:

> Freedom of exchange! Laissez demander, *laissez offrir. Laissez produire, laissez entrer*; or, to go back to an excellent Physiocratic formula: *Laissez faire; laissez passer.* (ŒEC V p. 182)

The 'economic naturalist' sought to analyse as exactly as possible the diverse manifestations of the fact of exchange, in whatever form they arose; Proudhon, by contrast, sought the origins of exchange in morality. For him, equality resulted from the application of justice, not from the fact of exchange. But, Léon objected, justice was a balance of right and obligation; the 'granite foundation' upon which any social edifice was built. The value of labour, just like the value of a wage, rested upon supply and demand, free competition ruling the market, determining all values, allowing all exchanges to be made between equal values—he quotes from Montesquieu: 'It is competition which places a just price on commodities' (ŒEC V p. 185).[35]

35. Montesquieu, *De l'Esprit des lois* t. 2, Éditions Garniers frères, Paris 1973 pp. 8–9.

The 'Introduction à l'étude de la question sociale' is more interesting, since we do at least know that this is primarily Léon's work. It appears to date from the autumn of 1859, when Léon's knowledge of political economy would still have been very elementary; his criticism of Proudhon's phrase 'property is theft' certainly suggests he had not read very much Proudhon (ŒEC V p. 106). Citing Baudrillart, Bastiat, and Courcelle-Seneuil, he concludes that for a systematic approach to pauperism and the social question one needs a social science, having as its object the free activity of man living in society (ŒEC V p. 93). While men might be unequal from other points of view, as free men they were equal; and if one were to construct a science of society, then one also had to determine what kind of science this might be:

> The theory of society is evidently close to algebra, geometry, and the a priori sciences, in that it pursues the study of a particular rational ideal, independent of all reality. (ŒEC V p. 97)

Social beings were distinguished by the manner in which they engaged in the exchange of objects, which were natural and artificial, material or immaterial, durable or ephemeral; and this in turn presumed *value* and *appropriation*, *utility* and *scarcity*. Exchange value and the activity of exchange were natural facts, like heat. By working one created utility, and diminished scarcity, and 'the study of the means by which a given society could increase its welfare to the greatest extent constituted the art of the production of wealth'.

> The most obvious aspect of society is progress. Faced with an impersonal nature which it has to subject through solidary effort, humanity grasps it with all the force of its faculties. Humanity knows it by science, uses it in labour and industrial arts. Society organises itself from day to day, and more and more approaches the ideal type of a perfect society. (ŒEC V p. 100)

Having established these principles, Léon turned to criticism of Louis Blanc and Proudhon, whose proposals for reform did not rest upon analysis and study, but simply proposed that contemporary practices be replaced by their opposite: competition by monopoly, individualism by the state. The absorption of the individual by the state represented 'the immolation of reality in abstraction' (ŒEC V p. 105).

In April 1860, shortly following the publication of *L'Économie politique et la justice*, Auguste wrote to Léon praising his work, and noting that it would make an impact upon 'intelligent, rather advanced men'. But they would not enjoy it as much as Auguste, given that their judgement would be clouded by prejudice, self-interest, and partisanship.[36] He also congratulated Léon on his appointment to the *Journal des économistes* that month, for with his ideas he was destined 'to carry the sceptre of political economy'. In this context, Auguste commented on contemporary French political economists:

> some, and there are very many, understand absolutely nothing; others, lacking all originality and invention, trot out without comprehension ideas that they have borrowed from their masters. . . . Our doctrine is the only one that is ambitious and complete. We resume the work of the only two great schools that there have ever been: the Physiocrats and Adam Smith. There is no ignorance that we cannot remedy, not one deviation that we cannot correct. (ŒEC IV p. 398)

And Auguste counselled prudence in his new appointment, beginning with light skirmishes, establishing undeniable points and demolishing manifest error, spreading no alarm among the subscribers.

In his letter of 1 April 1860 Auguste remarked that Léon had recently come under the influence of Saint-Simonians, and launched into an itemised summary of the faults that had always prevented his embracing their beliefs: their lack of connection to political economy, their lack of originality, the absence of a clear position on property, preaching the general abolition of inheritance without making any distinction between different goods. 'In my system, the inheritance of landed property is to all intents and purposes abolished, since land becomes the property of the state, and rent on land becomes public revenue' (ŒEC IV p. 399). Capital by contrast was the result of saving and in families the source of solidarity between the generations. They did distinguish between those who worked and those who were idle, but they failed to distinguish between financial proprietors who lived from the interest on capital, and capitalists who lived from profit. Nor had they ever dealt with the issue of taxation. And their maxim 'to each according to his capacity; to each capacity according to his work' had remained quite vague, with no explanation of how capacity and work might be assessed.[37] He went on:

> It is true that I agree that this maxim consecrates the distinction that I make between commutative justice and distributive justice, and that this distinction

36. Letter of 1 April 1860, ŒEC IV p. 397.
37. Ludovic Frobert reviews the modification of the original Saint-Simonian principle from Blanc in 1841 ('the inequality of aptitudes must not lead to the inequality of rights but the inequality of duties', *Organisation du travail* pp. 92–93, 141) to Pecquer in 1849 ('from each according to his forces and aptitudes; to each according

> marks out the domain of equality and of inequality. But all of this is unclear, and I prefer much more my own formulation: equality of conditions, inequality of positions. (ŒEC IV p. 400)

Léon adopted his father's distinction, repeating it explicitly in a public lecture during March 1868, noting that in a race commutative justice gave all competitors the same point of departure, while distributive justice involved the imposition of a differential handicap, according to the order in which they finished (ŒEC IX pp. 139–40).

JUSTICE AND DISTRIBUTION

The introduction to *L'Économie politique et la justice* contains a brief discussion of Louis Blanc's *L'organisation du travail*, noting that it proposed the most complete form of communism, in which the state possessed all capital, distributing this to individuals according to the fraternal formulation: 'from each according to his means; to each according to his needs'. Léon here emphatically rejected this idea, paraphrasing it as 'work as much as you like; eat as much as you can' (ŒEC V p. 104). But he did not simply dismiss the principle.

Early in the 1890s Léon drafted a 'Sketch of an Economic and Social Doctrine' in which he described *L'Économie politique et la justice* as the transcription of principles to be found in Auguste's *Théorie de la richesse sociale*: the laws of the variation of the value of capitals and of financial, personal and landed services in a progressive society:

> but it seemed to me that, phrased in ordinary language, the demonstration of these laws was insufficient, and that to lend them rigour it would be necessary to give them mathematical form to prove that, in general, *value was an increasing function of utility and a decreasing function of quantity.* (ŒEC X p. 418)

He then described how he had in 1860 given a copy of *L'Économie politique et la justice* to Charles Lambert-Bey, a prominent Saint-Simonian and graduate of the École des Mines with whom he was associated at the

---

to his needs' *Le salut du peuple*, 4); to Blanc's 'from each according to his powers and aptitudes, to each according to his needs', *Catechisme des socialistes*, p. 224—'What Is a Just Society? The Answer According to the *Socialistes Fraternitaires* around 1849 (Louis Blanc, Constantin, Pecqueur, François Vidal)', *History of Political Economy* Vol. 46 (2014) pp. 281–306.

time. Visiting Lambert-Bey some time later, the arguments of his book were subjected to vigorous criticism. Lambert-Bey conceded that free competition was a means of relating the quantities of products to their prices; but he did not believe that any economist, nor Walras himself, had shown that these quantities and these prices were unique, nor that they were optimal. Léon defended himself as well as he could; but after he had left, even before he had got all the way downstairs, he had concluded that Lambert-Bey was right. He stood in a reverie outside the building, until he realised:

> Obviously! It has to be proved that *free competition maximises utility*. (ŒEC X p. 419)

He turned to mathematics, and wrote about this insight to his father.[38] Auguste responded that he believed he had succeeded in his second book in clearly distinguishing utility from exchange value, the latter being an appreciable magnitude like length, weight, or speed. Scarcity he had compared to speed, which placed in relation space and time; and so scarcity was a relationship between the sum of needs and the sum of provisions, in other words, of quantity demanded and supplied. Given the heterogeneity of goods, arriving at a unit with which to measure the latter was difficult, but not impossible; the real problem was a unit of need. It was this that made the application of mathematics to the theory of social wealth so troublesome, argued Auguste.[39]

By late 1862 Léon had formulated a project to write a 'Complete Treatise of Political and Social Economy' in four volumes which would deal with this problem by confining the demonstration of the optimality of free competition to an entirely abstract scheme of 'pure economics', conceiving this as the first of four volumes:[40]

Vol. 1 Theory of Social Wealth (Pure Political Economy)
Vol. 2 On the Production, Circulation and Consumption of Social Wealth (Applied Political Economy)
Vol. 3 On Property and Taxation (Social Economy)
Vol. 4 History of Ideas of Economic and Social Theory

38. Since all of Léon's side of this correspondence is lost, we know of the letter only from his father's response.

39. Letter of Auguste to Léon, 18 May 1861 (ŒEC IV pp. 490–92). In this letter Auguste tells Léon that he will find a copy of Cournot among his books on political economy—a book that, he writes, he had never really understood, but which he supposed was a translation into algebra of Ricardo's metaphysics.

40. Detailed in Léon Walras to Jules de Mesnil-Marigny, 23 December 1862, Letter 81 *Correspondence* Vol. 1 pp. 119–24.

He described this tripartite division as turning upon the True, the Useful, and the Just.[41] Only volume IV remained unwritten; and it is clear from the history of his drafts and revisions for the unpublished *Mélanges* that right up to his death he regarded his writings from 1860 onwards as all of a piece, although the *Pure Economics* would not finally appear until the mid-1870s.

However, the path from his critique of Proudhon to an academic post where he would be free to elaborate his project was not straightforward. In the spring of 1860, with his book published and as a member of the editorial board of the *Journal des économistes*, he seemed to have made very rapid progress along the road his father had mapped out for him. That summer another opportunity for Léon suddenly arose. In March 1860 the Vaud Canton announced a prize essay competition, posing the question: 'How, under the present social order, might a system of taxation calculate the most equitable possible distribution of the burden among taxpayers or taxable objects?' (ŒEC V p. 319). As a preliminary, a congress to discuss the issue publicly was staged; Léon went to Lausanne at short notice representing *La Presse*, hoping to make his name as a journalist. Since he had only heard about the essay competition in June, his father once again lent him some notes, which he later worked up and submitted to the organisers as his essay. These notes were organised as a critique of Proudhon's views on taxation; both father and son believed that the solution of the social question ran through the reform of taxation, although the father went no further than a critique of the existing system. Léon Walras by contrast could not see how it might be possible to square the circle presented by the Vaudois council: to reform taxation without changing the social order.

Léon Walras made the most of his presence at the congress through several articulate interventions, impressing the organisers. French liberal economists who attended were less enthusiastic. At a meeting in Paris of the Société d'Économie politique on 5 August 1860 Joseph Garnier summarised Léon Walras's position as advocacy of the appropriation of land by the state and a critique of taxes on capital and income (ŒEC V p. 328). Nonetheless, Walras remained in Lausanne for a few days after the end of the Congress, some members of the educational authorities wishing to offer him a two-year appointment to teach political economy. But this was vetoed by the cantonal council, and the post went to Charles Secrétan. In September 1860 he submitted his entry for the prize competition. As

41. A phrasing he had used to describe the new social science in his 1860 'Introduction' (ŒEC V p. 100).

autumn turned to winter his journalistic career stuttered: seeking a permanent post at *La Presse* he wrote nine articles, of which only two were published. His project in economic journalism was failing; he resigned in February 1861. He still had an editorial post with the *Journal des économistes*, where his proposal to write a series of 'economic paradoxes' was accepted so long as he 'made political economy "amusing", in the manner of Bastiat' (ŒEC VII p. 42 fn. 1).[42] The first piece was duly published in December 1860, but the remainder were rejected and he left the publication in February 1862. Then in May 1861 he had been informed that the organisers of the Lausanne Congress had awarded him only the fourth 'honourable mention' for his essay; while the prize was not awarded outright, Proudhon was granted first place among those so 'mentioned'. Setback and failure would continue for several years until he was recommended by Jules Ferry to Ruchonnet for the new Lausanne chair in political economy; in June 1870 Walras and Ruchonnet met in Paris. On the strength of this meeting Walras handed in his notice at the bank where he worked as a clerk, but it was not until November that he was formally appointed, and not until December that he was able to travel to Switzerland—Paris was under siege and the country at war with Prussia. He gave his first lecture on his thirty-sixth birthday, 16 December 1870, and began serious work on the construction of his system, which at this point was still only an idea.

He first of all presented a series of papers, and then in 1874 published the first part of *Éléments d'économie politique pure*, the second appearing in 1877. Writing in the preface to the fourth (1900) edition of his *Éléments* Walras listed his intellectual debts: he acknowledged Menger's treatment of scarcity, Gossen's priority in respect of the curve of utility, Jevons in respect of the maximum of utility in exchange, Cournot in the use of calculus, and his father with respect to the fundamental principles of his economic doctrine (ŒEC VIII p. 5). He points to that which he shared with his fellow 'marginalists'; and this lends little insight into the feature of his work which clearly separated him off from them: an understanding of the market mechanism as a dynamic equilibrium emerging from the interactions of agents in a freely competitive market, 'groping' their way towards an equilibrium state of supply and demand, in which their utilities might be maximised individually and one with another. This process of *tâtonnement* was introduced by Walras to reconcile the equalities arising in

42. This first paradox was addressed to the proposition: 'Que le sens commun n'est point le critérium de la science en général, ni en particulier celui de l'économie politique'. It is printed in ŒEC VII pp. 42–62.

the theoretical solution of general equilibrium with actual market processes (ŒEC VIII p. 189).

We have already seen that Walras dismissed the definition of value employed by both Smith and Say, adopting instead Auguste's concept of scarcity—social wealth being defined as consisting of material or immaterial objects which have utility and exist in limited quantities, which were available for exchange and were capable of multiplication through the application of human industry (ŒEC VIII pp. 46–48). Hence the extension of social wealth is linked to the application of human industry and is facilitated through the division of labour. Although an abundant supply of goods is secured in this way, there remains the possibility that goods might be produced in inappropriate quantities, there being too much production of some scarce goods and not enough of others. Resolution of this problem was a matter of equity in distribution, the appropriation of social wealth being a human fact originating not in the will of an individual, but in the collective activity of society:

> The fact of appropriation is therefore essentially a moral fact, the theory of property is therefore essentially a moral science. *Jus est suum cuique tribuere*, justice consists in rendering to each that which he is due. (ŒEC VIII pp. 62, 64)

And so Walras's theory of price formation is conditional upon the existence of specific institutions that enable markets to clear in a manner commensurate with commutative justice.

This is plain from the manner in which he introduces his conception of market relations. The model that he takes is that of a bourse populated by individuals seeking to buy and sell stock. This is a regulated market: it has a definite location, transactions are made on the basis of complete knowledge of the goods involved and the conditions attached to them, announced by the shouting out of prices and terms by individual buyers and sellers. There are other markets, Walras goes on, which are less well regulated, but which work well enough, such as fruit and vegetable markets; or streets lined with shops, which are however rather less effective from the standpoint of competition.

> And so the world can be considered as a vast general market composed of a variety of specialised markets where social wealth is bought and sold, and we are concerned with the laws according to which these sales and purchases tend themselves to be made. To do that, we always suppose a perfectly organised market in respect of competition, just as in pure mechanics one at first supposes frictionless machines. (ŒEC VIII p. 71)

This model informs the various market models that Walras goes on to outline, and its importance should not be underestimated: price formation can be treated as a function of the interaction of the demand for and the supply of stock. Since individual agents decide on the prices at which they buy and sell, prices emerge out of the interactions of utility maximising agents, and questions of cost and its components do not arise. This does not however mean that the ex ante and ex post distribution of goods is a matter of indifference—we are dealing, argues Walras, with social wealth, with property, and for such exchanges to function effectively the trading prices must also be just prices.

In 1875, between the publication of the two parts of *Éléments d'économie politique pure,* Walras completed an essay on the state ownership of railways[43] that sheds a great deal of light on the limited applicability of the 'pure' model of competition that he had exposed in terms of a general equilibrium of prices, goods, and utilities. We already know that from the very first he had adopted his father's views about landownership and taxation, views which both sharply limited the remit of pure competition within any real economy, and also liberated the process of competition from any distortion through the taxation of goods or incomes. In this article on railways we encounter clear boundaries to 'market forces' that further limit the extent of markets, and increase the purview of the state.

In the market for private goods, consumers carefully calculate the amount of goods and services they might wish to consume. The consumer compares the intensities of utilities, not only of similar goods or services, but of different quantities of a diversity of services or products:

> Once prices have been shouted out or declared, [the consumer] sees how he must distribute his income between these different commodities to procure the greatest possible effective utility.[44]

The consumer finally demands so much of this or that service or good. For each good or service there is a crowd of consumer/demanders; and facing them a crowd of producer/suppliers who can be sure that what they do not sell to one buyer they can sell to another. Competition functions: order and proportion establish themselves in equilibrium.

However, argues Walras, this does not happen in the market for services and products related to public interest. This is a market in which

43. The article was rejected by the *Journal des économistes* in 1876, used in his teaching from about 1881, and finally published in 1897 in *Revue du droit public et de la science politique en France et à l'étranger* t. 7 in two parts.

44. Léon Walras, 'L'état et les chemins de fer', ŒEC X p. 186.

satisfaction is a matter common to all. The state appears here as a consumer in relation to domestic and external security, justice, education, and communications, operating much as the private consumer does above, seeking to employ its revenue to best effect in maximising its utility. But the similarity stops there. For each public service or product there will be only one consumer/demander, the state; and producers/suppliers know that unless they sell to the state, they will sell to no one.

Economists, suggests Walras, assimilate goods and service related to the public interest to those related to a private interest. But this is an error; there is an absolute difference between the two:

> The need for services or products related to private interest is felt by individuals; the need for services or products related to public interest is only felt to its full extent by the community or the state. (ŒEC X p. 46)

Neither individual nor state always discerns its needs judiciously. In either case this is a mistake to be corrected, but in case of the state this cannot be resolved by transferring the responsibility to private individuals. It is similarly inappropriate for the production of public services to be opened to free competition, since the state has to produce its own services, and for these it is a monopoly provider. Where free competition exists alongside monopoly, the entrepreneur is able to cream off an additional portion of the wealth in circulation. In such circumstances laissez-faire is no longer capable of maximising consumer utility, and it is necessary that the state intervenes: either by exercising the monopoly itself or by organising the monopoly in such a way that there is neither profit nor loss. In this way economic monopolies founded upon social interest take their place alongside moral monopolies founded upon natural law. The services provided by the former for the good of the entire community are free, whereas economic monopolies are exercised for the benefit of individuals and accordingly are charged at cost (ŒEC X p. 189).

Following a discussion of the supply of water and gas and the contribution of Dupuit to the analysis of the impact of tolls, Walras turned to railways. These are distinguished from roads and canals as a form of transportation by the fixed track. Whoever owns this collects both the toll (the fee for the way) and the freightage (the fee for the vehicle and locomotive). Railways, canals, and roads all implied a separation of the costs of maintenance of the way from the cost of freightage. But in the case of railways the limitation of access was an inherent factor, and all fees are paid to a monopolist (ŒEC X pp. 196–97). As an economic monopoly of which the direct beneficiary is an individual, a charge is levied for its use, and Walras duly explores the manner in which rates might be set. Whether the state runs the railway, or it is run for the state, is an open question: in either case pricing is governed by the cost price (ŒEC X p. 208).

As it happened, the development of the European railway system was principally directed by national governments, in part because, as Walras recognised, railways had significant military uses in a century riven by wars within and between states. In conclusion he points out that the British system was one exception to this rule, leading inevitably to overinvestment and major financial losses. Where the state regulated railway development there were neither gains nor losses; where private initiative ruled, there were both: gains for the first comers, and losses for those who followed. In conclusion he returned to his critique of liberal economists:

> The economic school of today, for whom *laisser faire, laisser passer* makes up the entirety of political economy and the whole of social science, will never cease voicing their eternal objection to the construction and exploitation of the railways on the part of the state: the alleged incapacity of the state to do anything. . . . The state has its role, as the individual has his own; one has to be confident in the state within the bounds of its competence in the same way that one has confidence in the competence of the individual. (ŒEC X pp. 211–12)

Couching the argument in terms of the functioning of monopoly and the role of the state enabled Walras to extend this line of argument to other areas where competition was vitiated by monopoly: security for the citizen, justice, and education, where costs were covered by taxation, since no proper price for each service could be formed.

Walras described his principal achievement as follows:

> Exchange according to the mechanism of free competition is an operation in which all exchanging parties obtain the greatest satisfaction of their needs compatible with the condition of giving the good which they sell and receiving the good which they buy in a common and identical proportion. By reuniting the second condition with the first I completed the principle of the mathematical theory of exchange. (ŒEC IX p. 320)

He wrote this in the course of establishing the relationship of his own work to that of Jevons and Gossen, both of whom had published work related to this idea before him. The statement also serves as a summary response to the question posed by Lambert: how exchanges under conditions of free competition might reach an optimal solution. But for Walras it was evident that for a system of exchanges to function in perpetuity, the parties to the exchange had to be satisfied of the propriety, of the 'justness', of the transaction. In any transaction not only are material needs satisfied through the acquisition of goods and services, but the transaction must itself be underwritten by a belief that it is equitable. The problem with which political economy had unsuccessfully wrestled was to explain quite how agents could be consistently induced to part with exactly that amount of an asset they possessed to obtain a desired quantity of one they did not. Conceiving the currency of transactions as ultimately embodiments of labour resolved the problem at one level, but failed to account for the fact that fluctuations in the market price of goods and services bore no clear relationship to variations in the price of their various inputs. It was this problem that Karl Marx thought he had resolved when he sought in the first volume of *Capital* to demonstrate quite how surplus value could be extracted from a process of equal exchange between capital and labour, but failed in his attempt to provide a properly theoretical account of the process.

Walras's great achievement was to demonstrate how this circle might be squared: how the volume of social wealth might be augmented while at the same time the proportion of objects produced was appropriate to the scale of needs on the part of buyers and sellers, of producers and consumers. He endogenised 'fairness' in exchange by relating the emergent market price to the utility schedules of all participating agents. Production is regulated by the fact that the marginal utility of what each consumes is no more than the marginal utility of that which he produces; and consumption is regulated by the reversal of this logic. Adjustments of purchasers' judgements of need and scarcity according to movements in the observed prices offered by sellers lead through mutual adjustments to a prevailing market price which ensures that, in a free market and with many buyers and sellers, each supplies and demands quantities of goods and services such that the marginal utility of the goods and services exchanged is for each party proportional to their price. It is at this point that a purchaser will obtain the greatest possible satisfaction, and it is this quality of each party to the transaction securing a maximum of satisfaction which renders the transaction equitable: each receives 'his own'. As Jevons noted in the 1879 preface to his *Theory of Political Economy*, where marginal utility determines the price of all products, it also determines the prices of all factors of production; and he went on to observe that this insight was the deathknell of a political economy which, instead of deriving factor prices from the prevailing market prices for the product, insisted on deriving the market price of the product from pre-existing factor prices.[45]

45. W. S. Jevons, 'Preface to the Second Edition', *The Theory of Political Economy*, 2nd edition, Macmillan, London 1879 pp. l–lvii.

AFTER *ÉLÉMENTS*

In Lausanne Walras gained no following; no students took an interest in his teaching, and as with Jevons in England, his eventual influence was more indirect. It was through his successor Pareto, with his links to Italian economists, that he first gained some influence; and Joseph Schumpeter was an early convert to the idea of general equilibrium. He long harboured an ambition to gain a chair for political economy in France, but this was always hampered by his early failure to continue formal study past the baccalaureate. During the early 1860s there were only two chairs for political economy in France: at the Collège de France (occupied by Michel Chevalier) and at the École des Ponts et Chaussées (occupied by Joseph Garnier). Then in 1864 the Ministry of Public Instruction and Culture in Paris determined to create a new chair in the Paris Faculty of Law, a significant step since it might be expected to be the first of a series of similar appointments in provincial faculties.[46] The appointee, Anselme-Polycarpe Batbie, was himself a specialist in administrative law, presumably thought suitable for the post, as Walras caustically observed, because the Ministry had been authoritatively advised that political economy was a complete science whose principles had been proved in over a century of debate.[47]

Throughout his tenure of the Lausanne chair he taught three courses, corresponding to the organisation of the subject he had outlined in 1862: pure political economy was taught every year to the first-year students; and applied political economy alternated annually with social economy for the second and third years.[48] He lectured to around twelve students from each year of the Academy, dictating his notes to them—both numbers and style of teaching being quite usual for the period. Owing to the difficulty that the first-year students found in absorbing the elements of general equilibrium theory, Walras also prevailed upon the Department of Public Instruction to purchase copies of the *Éléments* so that he might be able to elaborate his lectures a little, and about one hundred copies were eventually acquired for student use.

46. A decree requiring all Faculties of Law to teach political economy followed in 1877—see L. Levan-Lemesle, *Le Juste ou le Riche. L'enseignement de l'économie politique 1815–1950*, Comité pour l'histoire économique et financière de la France, Paris 2004 ch. 8.

47. L. Walras, 'De l'enseignement de l'économie politique dans les facultés de droit', ŒEC VII p. 350.

48. 'Introduction Générale. L'Enseignement de Léon Walras à Lausanne', ŒEC XII p. 17. From the autumn of 1875 pure political economy was taught for three hours a week in the first semester of sixteen or seventeen weeks, and the other two courses in the second semester for five hours a week over a semester of twelve weeks.

In the later 1870s, in the wake of the decree requiring French faculties of law to teach political economy, Walras entertained hopes of returning to France, and he corresponded with Ferry, now Minister of Public Instruction and culture in Paris, concerning this and other projects, such as the formation of a new faculty of moral and political sciences in Paris. Nothing came of this, nor of later efforts to be considered as a successor to Chevalier at the Collège de France when the latter died in November 1879. His hopes of appointment to the new post in Montpellier, his father's birthplace, were dashed when Charles Gide was appointed in late 1880, but in any case Walras had neither a law degree, nor a doctorate, both of which had by now become necessary for such appointments. The teaching of political economy had moved on from the being the province of dilettantes and ideologues, and was emerging as a regular academic occupation for which acceptable qualifications were required. Having contributed so much to the creation of the new academic economics, Walras now gave up any hope of gaining a suitable post in France.

He resorted, therefore, to revision and refinement of his original vision of the market system of exchanges, corresponding intensively with leading economists, and seeking to establish his legitimate claims to priority in the elaboration of the new economics. Walras had first come across Jevons's *Theory of Political Economy* in May 1874, while drafting the preface to the first part of *Élements d'économie politique pure*. He acknowledged that Jevons's 'equation of exchange' was identical to his own 'condition of maximum satisfaction', an argument which he had first exposed publicly in a paper read to the Académie des sciences morales et politiques in August 1873. Jevons for his part had first aired his new mathematical approach to political economy at a meeting of the British Association in 1862, which knowledge he must have found comforting until Robert Adamson, who succeeded Jevons in 1876 as Manchester's Professor of Political Economy and Mental and Moral Science, showed him in 1878 a copy of Gossen's *Entwickelung der Gesetze des menschlichen Verkehrs*, a work which had been published in Brunswick in 1854.[49]

Walras did not read German; the first copy of Gossen that he had in his hands came from the Staatsbibliothek in Munich, where Charles Secrétan's brother-in-law worked, and it was translated and dictated to him by Secrétan in early 1879. There were plans to publish a French translation, and Walras sought to find out more about Gossen. By the following year Walras

49. Jevons relied upon Adamson as a translator, since his knowledge of German was too slight to permit him to read a book in the language—'Preface to the Second Edition', op. cit. p. xl.

had established contact with relatives, ascertaining that Gossen had died in 1858, and that his nephew, Hermann Kortum, taught mathematics at the University of Bonn. Walras asked Kortum if he might investigate any remaining papers, which he agreed to do; but it was not until July 1881 that Kortum produced the memorandum[50] upon which is based everything that anyone today knows of Gossen, besides what one might surmise from his book. Walras was, on his own admission,[51] by now tiring of his obsessive concern with priority over predecessors, and laid the paper to one side; but then in 1882 Jevons died, and Walras read that Adamson and Foxwell had subscribed to a memorial describing Jevons's *Theory of Political Economy* as the most original work done in economics of its time. What, then, of Gossen, thought Walras? And so he drafted an article on Gossen, which he submitted to the editor of the *Journal des Économistes* in November 1884.

Gossen is important to an understanding of Walras because, in seeking to disentangle the legitimate claims of Jevons, Gossen, and himself, he was driven to clarify what he considered his own innovations to be. Furthermore, Gossen formulated in a more direct manner the problem of the equality of exchanges under conditions of many sellers and many buyers, which Jevons had not done. In the relation of Walras to Gossen, therefore, we can trace the degree to which Walras's new system of economics was in fact novel.

Walras opens his essay on Gossen by reminding his readers of the main points of the paper he had presented in August 1873, and published (twice) the following year.[52] He concludes this section by noting that there are two separate problems to be resolved, the first relating to the current price, and the second to the elements of this price, the latter forming the basis for the former. As he goes on, this

> *theorem of maximal satisfaction* is the cornerstone of the application of mathematics to political economy. (ŒEC IX p. 312)

Having outlined his own understanding of the matter as it stood in the mid-1870s, he then summarised his collaboration with Jevons on his bibliography of mathematical economic writings,[53] following this with an

50. 'Annexe I: La notice d'Hermann Kortum' in ŒEC IX pp. 473–78.
51. 'Un économiste inconnu: Hermann-Henri Gossen', ŒEC IX p. 329—this essay was eventually published in the *Journal des Économistes* in the spring of 1885.
52. In January 1874 in *Séances et travaux de l'Académie des sciences morales et politiques*, and in April 1874 in the *Journal des Économistes*.
53. Published as 'Appendix I. List of Mathematico-Economic Books, Memoirs, and other published writings' in Jevons, *Theory of Political Economy*, 2nd edition, pp. 301–10; and, with additions by Walras, in *Journal des Économistes* 4th series Vol. 4 No. 12 (December 1878) pp. 470–77.

account of Adamson's discovery of Gossen's book drawn from Jevons's preface to the second edition of his *Theory of Political Economy*. Endorsing Jevons's description of Gossen, and noting that the style was 'very German, which is to say rather diffuse and superfluous' (ŒEC IX p. 318), he agreed with Jevons that Gossen's treatment of the basic theorem was both more general and fundamental than that of Jevons. Walras, on the other hand, considered that he had gone beyond Gossen, and he listed the relevant points:

1. Both Gossen and Jevons discovered, before Walras, the mathematical expression of utility, and formulated the condition of a maximum of utility in exchange, for one individual, of one good against another; there was no disputing this.
2. Jevons appeared disposed to concede to Gossen a degree of superiority on the first point and attribute the second to himself. He was right to do so, for Gossen only formulated the condition of an absolute maximum, while it was Jevons who formulated the condition of relative maximum consistent with the equality of supply and demand.
3. Both of them stopped at the point concerning the barter of two goods for one another. Neither Gossen nor Jevons dealt with the question of the current price of these two goods in respect of an indefinite number of agents. But this is exactly one of the issues resolved in Walras's *Principe d'une théorie mathématique de l'échange* (August 1873), from which one can derive the current price from the excess of effective demand over the deficit of effective supply.

It is this last condition which Walras considered necessary to complete a theory of exchange, which he then summarised as follows:

> Exchange according to the mechanism of free competition is an operation in which all exchangers obtain the greatest satisfaction of their needs compatible with the condition of surrendering the good which they sell and accepting the good which they buy in a common and identical proportion. By reuniting the second condition with the first I have completed the principle of the mathematical theory of exchange. In pursuit of this dual condition in the case of the mutual exchange of any number of goods mediated by a *numéraire*, as I showed in my second memoir, entitled *Equations of exchange* (December 1875), I completed the mathematical theory of exchange itself. I stated, besides the law of the determination, that of the variation of prices. That done, I believe that I have not only formulated, but demonstrated, the law of supply and demand. (ŒEC IX p. 320)

He then describes how in a third memoir he had demonstrated the role of an entrepreneur as an agent distinct to the worker, and in a fourth distinguished natural from artificial capitals. Finally, in the closing few pages, he summarises Kortum's memorandum concerning the life and work of Gossen, having therefore devoted the bulk of the essay to an outline of those discoveries which, he believed, he could rightfully call his own. These related to the manner in which, among many agents, each received 'his due' as determined by the utility schedules of all other agents. A 'fair' exchange became equitable once a market price had formed, not before; justice inhered in this market process, not in an allocation determined in advance by some given notion of just rewards, nor even according to the value an individual might attribute to his own faculties and capacities. Instead, it was the utility schedules of all other agents which determined the value of any one agent's services and needs.

What Walras found in Gossen was a clear statement of this idea couched in a form that coincided with his own socialist ideals—that is, critical on the one side of the more reactionary aspects of contemporary economic liberalism, and on the other of socialist and communistic projects which sought to impose ideal forms of distribution upon society. Gossen, like Walras, adhered to the view that the greatest good was achieved at the point where the enjoyment of each was equal, not the amount consumed, nor their revenue:

> In order that the greatest amount of value be created through exchange, it is necessary that after its completion each object be distributed among all individuals in such way that the last atom accruing to each from those objects will create for him pleasure in the same measure as that created by the last atom of the same object for every other individual.[54]

Where this maximum is achieved, Gossen continued, 'each individual receives exactly that share of the total to which he can justly lay claim'.[55] For where each strives to maximise his own pleasure, all will direct their effort to that kind of work most profitable to them, given the prevailing price ratios. Hence each receives a portion of the social product corresponding to the burden he assumes in the productive process. The outcome, argues

54. H. H. Gossen, *Entwicklung der Gesetze des menschlichen Verkehrs und der daraus fließenden Regeln für menschliches Handeln*, 3rd edition, R. L. Prager, Berlin 1927 p. 85.
55. Ibid. p. 90.

Gossen, is to attain the ideals of the communists, without however there being any need of any external intervention:

> What is therefore regarded by socialists and communists as the ultimate aim of their exertions is here realised through the combined action of natural forces in such a degree of perfection that we only experience with respect to the works of the Creator. For it is not here, as socialists and communists would wish, one person, or a majority of persons, who sit in judgement on the merit of an individual—since their limited human knowledge would as a rule bring about an unfitting judgement—instead, mankind in its entirety here passes judgement.[56]

Thanks to the benevolence of the Creator, 'this true paradise'[57] is achieved entirely by our own activities.

Later, writing in the *Revue socialiste* in 1896, Walras contrasted the models of exchange to be found in Jevons and Gossen in terms of simple barter. He describes the first as the author of an 'individualist' model, in which the agent is free to pursue his own interest, but where the inequality of wealth existing before an exchange, in which the individual acquires a quantity of a useful good, is preserved (ŒEC IX p. 180). Gossen's system, argues Walras, abstracts from the property rights of the barterers with respect to the goods; it is

> communistic barter, only occurring with certainty because of the authority of the state, and it will bring about an *equality* which will follow from the equality of needs and their means of satisfaction. It operates upon the terrain of *fraternity*. (ŒEC IX p. 181)

This takes us straight back to his critique of Blanc in the 'Introduction' to *L'Économie politique et la justice* that he wrote more than thirty years previously. He illustrates the problem by a story from his schooldays at Caen College where, every day at 4:00 P.M., the boys were all given a piece of bread. Some of the boys had butter or jam which their parents had sent; and there was a custom that those lacking jam or butter should pass their piece of dry bread along to others, who would return it to them spread with butter or jam. However, argued Walras, although this was a practice that should be encouraged among children, and was acceptable

56. Ibid. p. 99.
57. Ibid. p. 102.

as voluntary behaviour on the part of adults, it was obnoxious if made obligatory, for 'society is not a picnic' (ŒEC IX p. 184).[58]

In 1881 another commentator picked up a problem in Auguste's and Léon's insistence on the equality of initial conditions, echoing in his criticism points already familiar from Blanc's *Organisation du travail.* Raising some criticism of Léon's mathematics, Wilhelm Lexis also observed that

> when L. W. came to derive his theory of the determination of the prices of productive services from the principle of maximum satisfaction under conditions of free competition, he, like Gossen, overlooked the fact that the hunger-driven worker, who has no property, is compelled to offer all his labor-services at whatever price he can get or starve, and is, consequently, in no position to make maximum satisfaction adjustments by withholding part or all of these services for his own use, because he cannot make effective use of his reserved labor services without capital equipment.[59]

This likewise echoes arguments made in the 1840s by French radicals, regarding the inequalities of equal exchange, of what was given and what was received, of the question of the inequality of both conditions and outcomes. As we have seen, these principles of equality and competition remained of central importance to the work of Auguste and Léon Walras; and in creating his mathematical system of general equilibrium in the early 1870s, Léon showed exactly how 'to each according to his contribution' might actually work, improving on the scheme first mapped out by Gossen in 1854, who, in turn, appears to have had the debates of contemporary French and German socialists in mind. For Gossen had studied in Bonn and Berlin, like Marx, completing his studies in 1833, then returning to Cologne, and moving to Bonn in 1841. Between 1844 and 1846 he worked as a government assessor in Magdeburg and Erfurt, retiring in 1846 to Berlin, where he seems to have taken an active part in revolutionary clubs. By 1849 he was back in Cologne, supervising a livestock insurance scheme that he had set up with a partner, and throwing himself enthusiastically into a life insurance scheme, the 'General German Savings Fund'. By 1850 these schemes were failing; he abandoned them, and

58. The phrase which P. Dockès picks up for the title of his book on this issue: *La société n'est pas un pique-nique: Léon Walras et l'économie sociale*, Economica, Paris 1996, espec. pp. 119ff.

59. *Correspondence* Vol. 1, William Jaffé's Editorial Note to Letter 548 of 17 March 1883 to Wilhelm Lexis, p. 747.

began work on the book for which he (eventually) became well known.[60] And so the line from Saint-Simon to Walrasian general equilibrium does not only run through Proudhon, Leroux, and Blanc; Walras recognised in Gossen a clear anticipation of his own construction, and Gossen's inspiration was, it turns out, drawn from the same sources; and he was most likely a reader of the *Neue Rheinische Zeitung* too.

60. Details of Gossen's life are taken from 'La notice d'Hermann Kortum', Annexe I ŒEC IX pp. 473–77.

CHAPTER 8

Sources, Arguments, and Prospect

Im nächsten Leben will ich Philologe werden.
—Wilhelm Hennis, from *Wilhelm Hennis' Politische Wissenschaft* (2013)[1]

The essays brought together here seek to further a particular approach to intellectual history that I now regard as broadly philological—that in studying economics, we should pay attention to the language of economics. After all, the 'history of economic thought' is in fact the history of economic language, since even if it is believed that a worthwhile distinction can be made between thought and language, 'thought' can only be detected here in its expression, rendering the point of making any such distinction moot. The 'reason and speech' which Adam Smith considers to be the likely foundation of the human 'propensity to truck, barter, and exchange one thing for another' can only be evaluated by the language which is used to direct and describe it. Furthermore, by addressing our attention to language, its structure and its use, we can also insist that any argument regarding intentionality, truth, or error be redirected to what is said and what is written.

I want to present some explanation of this stance by way of conclusion; although I should also make clear at the outset that I am not advocating any single method here, nor that the analysis of particular texts is the sole

1. 'In my next life I want to be a philologist'—Wilhelm Hennis's closing remark in an interview with his biographer, Stephan Schlak: '"Die existentielle Dimension des Politischen": Wilhelm Hennis im Gespräch mit Stephan Schlak', in Andreas Anter (ed.) *Wilhelm Hennis' Politische Wissenschaft: Fragestellungen und Diagnosen*, Mohr Siebeck, Tübingen 2013 p. 338.

and proper object of the history of economic discourse. In other work I have proceeded differently: for example, examining the policy context of the 1948 German Currency Reform[2]; using a database of degree results to evaluate the first fifty years of the Cambridge Economics Tripos[3]; or using interviews as a way of reconstructing the history of economics as a university discipline in Britain.[4] Historical work involves the identification of a problem, resolution of which requires methods particular to it. Intellectual fashion too often conspires to reverse this relationship. And while my education as a historian largely took place in Germany during the 1980s, I adopted this orientation to historical problems much earlier, from my reading of Gaston Bachelard in the early 1970s:

> It is precisely this sense of problem which marks the real scientific mind. For a scientific mind, all knowledge (*connaissance*) is a response to a question. If there had been no question, there could be no scientific knowledge. Nothing comes from nothing. Nothing is given. Everything is constructed.[5]

The arguments I have advanced in the foregoing chapters elaborate choices and decisions that I made many years ago. Since then a succession of intellectual fashions might appear to have built upon similar foundations. Given Bachelard's flat assertion that 'everything is constructed', I should perhaps emphasise that I did not set off early down what became the well-worn road of social constructivism, science and technology studies, Actor-Network Theory, postmodernism, or even post-postmodernism, and then somehow lose my way. I remained sceptical of these developments; I had already turned against their social and epistemological assumptions in the early 1970s, and towards the analysis of natural languages. In conclusion, therefore, I wish to renew this attention to the structure and patterns of language use, and identify why it is that I believe that this focus remains a viable and useful way of approaching intellectual history.

Some biography is unavoidable here. While an undergraduate I was of course heavily influenced by the contemporary 'structuralist turn', reading Lévi-Strauss, Barthes, Foucault, and Althusser. Common to all these

2. 'The 1948 Currency Reform: Structure and Purpose' in J. Hölscher (ed.) *50 Years of the German Mark: Essays in Honour of Stephen F. Frowen*, Macmillan, Basingstoke 2001 pp. 15–51.

3. 'The Cambridge Economics Tripos 1903–55 and the Training of Economists', *Manchester School* Vol. 68 (2000) pp. 222–48.

4. *Economic Careers: Economics and Economists in Britain 1930–1970*, Routledge, London 1997.

5. Gaston Bachelard, *La formation de l'esprit scientifique* [1938], J. Vrin, Paris 1970 p. 14.

was a debt to Saussure's emphasis upon the arbitrary nature of the sign, upon the distinction between synchrony and diachrony, of *langue* and *langage*, and on the generation of meaning from structure. In Britain during the 1970s one medium through which this idea was elaborated was film theory, and I developed a lasting interest in documentary film. It could be said that, as a student, rather than read Kant, I watched Vertov and Rosi, but with a rather similar outcome.[6] The 'reality effect' of a documentary film is one constructed by the techniques employed; if it were defined by its relationship to 'reality', we might with some justice argue that *The Lavender Hill Mob* or *Passport to Pimlico* are 'documentary' films 'about' Ealing Studios. Film and photography have always raised interesting general issues about 'reality', and how we come to apprehend it as such. For example, the transformation of photograph into moving image effected by Eadweard Muybridge's Zoopraxiscope—using sequences of photographs of galloping horses or human movement to reproduce what the eye and brain saw—required not only that the photographs be redrawn, but also laterally elongated because of the effect of the device's movement. And so movement that the eye could see and the camera recorded could not be recreated as a moving image without first artificially enhancing the film exposed in the camera.[7]

The context in which I pursued these interests was as a student of sociology at the University of Essex, where I was given a broad foundation in the contemporary social and political sciences in courses ranging from social policy, through the history of sociology, to mathematical sociology, including full courses in both mathematics and computer programming. And so on the one hand I read Lévi-Strauss against a background in set theory, while on the other I came to think that Berger and Luckmann's influential *The Social Construction of Reality* rather demonstrated the real limitations, and not the possibilities, of any 'sociology of knowledge'. An emerging interest in what would now be called intellectual history led me

6. I came to appreciate the importance of film editing from the work of Dai Vaughan, as brilliant a writer as he was an editor. See his *Portrait of an Invisible Man: The Working Life of Stewart McAllister, Film Editor*, British Film Institute, London 1983; and his collection of essays, *For Documentary*, University of California Press, Berkeley 1999. His obituary is in *The Independent*, 3 July 2012; see also Catherine Grant's use of image and word in her own tribute to Dai Vaughan, 'On Cinematic Spontaneity', together with several others tributes on http://filmstudiesforfree.blogspot.co.uk/2012/07/for-documentary-remembering-dai-vaughan.html.

7. See Philip Prodger, *Time Stands Still: Muybridge and the Instantaneous Photography Movement*, Oxford University Press, New York 2003 pp. 142ff; and Simon Cook, '"Our Eyes, Spinning Like Propellers": Wheel of Life, Curve of Velocities, and Dziga Vertov's "Theory of the Interval"', *October* No. 121 (Summer 2007) pp. 79–91.

to Thomas Kuhn's *Structure of Scientific Revolutions*, although initially I took this up in a third-year essay linking Kuhn's ideas to the history of Russian art and design, which also introduced me to Russian Formalism. By the summer of 1971, when I graduated, I was reading widely in the history and philosophy of the sciences, and had already formed the view that Kuhn's approach to the development of scientific knowledge was handicapped by its social reductionism. I argued this in an article published while I was a postgraduate student in Cambridge,[8] where I pursued an interest in the history of economic discourse that turned explicitly against emerging trends in science studies. Fortunately, my postdoctoral work in Germany provided me with a solid foundation in historical study, and also reorganised my understanding of the importance of Max Weber, thanks to Wilhelm Hennis's critique of the post-war reception of his writings and broad emphasis upon Weber as the founding theorist of social and political modernity.[9]

It is however only very recently that Errol Morris's account of his time with Kuhn at Princeton has brought me back to the questions of incommensurability, paradigm shifts, and normal science that had preoccupied me as an undergraduate at Essex. The link that Morris's work makes between documentary film and issues of documentary realism also relates to courses I taught on film and television during the later 1970s and early 1980s, continuing an interest that had first developed at Essex. Added to this was a continuing engagement with Russian Formalist writings on literary devices,[10] an interest which developed with the publication of new translations of, and commentary upon, the work of Bakhtin.[11] The intellectual logic underlying these diverse interests

8. 'On the Production and Structuring of Scientific Knowledges', *Economy and Society* Vol. 2 (1973) pp. 465–78. This was my second published article; the first was devoted to film analysis: 'John Ford's *My Darling Clementine*—an Investigation', *Cambridge Anthropology* Vol. 1 No. 1 (1973) pp. 10–17.

9. My own engagement with the writings of Max Weber began with 'Prussian Agriculture—German Politics: Max Weber 1892–7', *Economy and Society* Vol. 12 (1983) pp. 181–226, and continues with 'What Is Social Economics?', *History of European Ideas* Vol. 40 (2014) pp. 714–33.

10. 'It ought to be obvious by now that "device" was the watchword of Russian Formalism. "Art as a Device", "the device of "making it strange" (*priëm ostranenija*), "a device laid bare" (*obnaženie priëm*), "the literary work is the sum total of the devices employed in it"—in all these crucial formulations *priëm* appears as a key term—the basic unit of poetic form, the agency of "literariness"'. Victor Erlich, *Russian Formalism: History—Doctrine*, 3rd edition, Mouton, The Hague 1969 p. 190.

11. See my 'Introduction to Todorov/Bakhtin', *Economy and Society* Vol. 13 (1984) pp. 20–24, and 'Mikhaïl Bakhtin: Word and Object', *Economy and Society* Vol. 15 (1986) pp. 403–13.

was a commitment to the idea that language is inherently social, but irreducible to social context or structure. Understanding of image and word requires instead a particular approach, which in the current context has resulted in my return to an emphasis upon a philology that was displaced in the early twentieth century by the emergence of literary criticism.[12] I now regard the work of Saussure as a way back to the philological studies with which he started, and not as a resource for the processing of discourse analysis.

Kuhn's reworking of the history of the sciences as long intervals during which the routine practice of 'normal science' prevailed, riven by occasional 'paradigm shifts' that destroyed the obviousness and comprehensibility of what went before, has had a lasting impact.[13] The second edition of the book contained an afterword which reinforced the idea that a 'scientific community' was formed through the sharing a 'paradigm', a term whose slipperiness had been the object of much criticism. Margaret Masterman noted that the term was 'central to Kuhn's whole view of science', but that no attempt had 'been made to elucidate this notion', proceeding to identify twenty-one different senses appearing in Kuhn's book.[14] Kuhn's response to this in the 1969 afterword was, as he recognised, essentially circular: 'A paradigm is what the members of a scientific community share, and, conversely, a scientific community consists of men who share a paradigm'.[15] And he went on:

> If this book were being rewritten, it would therefore open with a discussion of the community structure of science, a topic that has recently become a significant subject of sociological research and that historians of science are also beginning to take seriously.[16]

12. As argued in Haruko Momma, *From Philology to English Studies: Language and Culture in the Nineteenth Century*, Cambridge University Press, Cambridge 2013.

13. His conception of 'paradigm' has passed into the vernacular; see for example Zadie Smith writing about Joni Mitchell: 'I wonder whether it is because I am a perfect fool about music that the paradigm shift in my ability to listen to Joni Mitchell became possible'. 'Some Notes on Attunement', *New Yorker* 17 December 2012 p. 32. Errol Morris reports that *Structure of Scientific Revolutions* has sold over one million copies and been translated into 25 languages—'The Ashtray. 2. Shifting Paradigms', *New York Times* 7 March 2011 fn. 19.

14. Margaret Masterman, 'The Nature of a Paradigm', in Imre Lakatos, Alan Musgrave (eds.) *Criticism and the Growth of Knowledge*, Proceeding of the International Colloquium in the Philosophy of Science, London 1965 Vol. 4, Cambridge University Press, London 1970 pp. 59, 61.

15. Thomas S. Kuhn, 'Postscript—1969', in his *Structure of Scientific Revolutions*, 2nd edition, University of Chicago Press, Chicago 1970 p. 176.

16. Loc. cit.

He also treated the scientific community as a linguistic community which periodically suffered 'communication breakdowns', in which members might use the same words to mean different things.[17] His solution—that 'participants in a communication breakdown can . . . recognize each other as members of different language communities and then become translators'[18]—has the merit of introducing language communities as basic units in the scientific enterprise, although his conception of language is limited to a system capable of naming things, and in which meaning is related to conceptions of veracity, following Quine's *Word and Object*.

The principal argument advanced in my critique of Kuhn was that he posed an epistemological question (what is the nature of a change in scientific thinking?) to which he supplied a sociological answer ('normal science' is socially conformist).[19] At the time I was interested in the early development of economic discourse, especially the shift in the structure of economic argument that David Ricardo initiated. For me, Kuhn was a faulty starting-point, quickly abandoned; of far greater interest was the work of Gaston Bachelard, especially his work on the emergence of new forms of scientific discourse that sought epistemological explanations of new forms of knowledge.

Another obvious source was chapter 6 of Foucault's *Order of Things*, where he criticises retrospective readings of the Classical theory of wealth, and proposes that 'In any given culture and at any given moment, there is always only one *episteme* that defines the conditions of possibility of all knowledge, whether expressed as a theory or silently invested in a practice'.[20] Foucault sought to identify the common epistemological foundations of general grammar, plant physiology, and the analysis of wealth, and the more or less simultaneous transformation of these bodies of knowledge at the end in the later eighteenth century—an idea that has parallels of course with Koselleck's location of the *Sattelzeit*, the period spanning the later eighteenth and early nineteenth centuries during which social, political, philosophical, and economic arguments simultaneously re-formed.[21] In his *Archaeology of Knowledge* Foucault systematised the approach he had taken in *Order of Things*, such that this process of 'simultaneous reformation' was now described as 'the economy of the

17. Ibid. p. 201.
18. Ibid. p. 202.
19. 'On the Production', op. cit. p. 467.
20. Michel Foucault, *The Order of Things: An Archaeology of the Human Sciences*, Tavistock, London 1970 p. 168.
21. The expository axis of my own *Governing Economy: The Reformation of German Economic Discourse 1750–1830*, Cambridge University Press, Cambridge 1988.

discursive constellation'.[22] The conception of 'the one episteme', reformulated in the *Archaeology* as the archive, is

> the first law of what can be said, the system that governs the appearance of statements of unique events. . . . The archive is not that which collects the dust of statements that have become inert once more, and which may make possible the miracle of their resurrection; it is that which defines the mode of occurrence of the statement-thing; it is *the system of its functioning.*[23]

The Archaeology of Knowledge can be read as an extended application of contemporary linguistic theory to the sciences and literature, distinguishing between a universal underlying regularity and the contingencies of expression.[24] It was this aspect of the work that was at the time so seductive when formulating a suitable approach to the shifts and continuities of economic arguments. However, the vision of language and linguistics that Foucault evokes is a very particular one, allied more to the Chomskyian vision of a restricted universal grammar capable of generating all language. In the quotation above, it is precisely this totalising vision that is today disputable, as Chomsky's own work is increasingly criticised by linguistic specialists more aware of the 'blooming, buzzing confusion' of languages. My subsequent education as a historian has likewise led me to adopt a more empirical and contingent conception of social and economic order.

Errol Morris's account of his time in the early 1970s as a graduate student in the History and Philosophy of Science programme at Princeton raises once again the problems presented by the idea of paradigmatic change, focusing not on the problem of how it might be specified, but the nature of the incommensurability that it implies.[25] Kuhn used his metaphor of the gestalt switch, that one can see lines, a duck, or a rabbit, but only ever one at a time, to suggest that one paradigm is strictly incomprehensible from the standpoint of another. In some respects this is a variant

22. Michel Foucault, *The Archaeology of Knowledge*, Tavistock, London 1972 p. 66.

23. Ibid., p. 129.

24. Hence knowledge and science (*connaissance*) is contrasted to discursive practice (*savoir*), the work of archaeology being addressed to the latter, not the former—ibid. p. 183.

25. Paul Feyerabend averred that he 'wholeheartedly' accepted Kuhn's point that 'succeeding paradigms can be evaluated only with difficulty and that they may be altogether incomparable': 'Consolations for the Specialist' in Lakatos and Musgrave, *Criticism* op. cit. p. 219. For a critical review of Feyerabend's curious blend of intellectual brilliance and actual conformity see Terry Counihan, 'Epistemology and Science—Feyerabend and Lecourt', *Economy and Society* Vol. 5 (1976) pp. 74–110.

on the familiar observation that, once one has understood something, it is hard to imagine what it felt like not to understand it. But Morris suggested to Kuhn that the idea of incommensurability entailed the idea that the history of science was impossible, that the past was intellectually inaccessible to us. Morris holds Kuhn to account for the epistemological implications of his argument. He points out that Kuhn is in effect saying: 'once we see the rabbit, all ducks become rabbits', implying that it is impossible to escape the present in seeking to understand semantic systems of the past.[26] But the metaphor he uses, the gestalt switch, implies only that one can see either the past, or the present, but not both at once, since in fact the duck is still there if you care to look for it. Morris rightly sought to emphasise that past events and language were comprehensible, if not immediately so; Kuhn's book, while its argument had a superficial attraction, became murkier, the more one looked at it.

Bachelard introduced the idea that conventional histories of the sciences were retrospective, recurrent, making sense of past arguments and principles through the imposition of a modern discursive order; but also that the sciences themselves proceed by a process of *envelopment*, reordering and containing past ideas in the making of the new.[27] As a way of thinking about changes in scientific language, this metaphor has a great deal more to be said for it than the gestalt switch. Kuhn's usage simply endorsed the idea of recurrence and, having written off the prospect of historical analysis, turned to sociology instead.[28] As he recognised, a 'scientific community' is united by a common language, and it now seems a more fruitful idea to explore the history of the sciences in terms of the history of scientific languages, rather than a history of 'practices'—where 'social analysis' amounts to little more than the classification and description of human activity.

A musical interlude might help elaborate this point. Turning on BBC Radio 3 in the morning, you might hear a snatch of Johann Sebastian Bach, or Mozart, or Haydn, or Beethoven. Even if you had never heard this particular piece of music before, for these were all very prolific composers,

26. 'The Ashtray. 2. Shifting Paradigms'. The 'ashtray' refers to the object that Kuhn threw at Morris when he made the point about incommensurability.

27. Gaston Bachelard, *Le nouvel esprit scientifique* [1934], Presses universitaires de France, Paris 1971 p. 62.

28. An American Science blog on Morris's articles demonstrates how intellectually corrosive this sociological turn has been. Dismissing Morris as outmoded, it was suggested that 'Rather than worry about abstract systems, language, and signifiers, we have become much more concerned with things, practices, and experiences'. http://americanscience.blogspot.se/2011/03/errol-morris-kuhn-ashtray, accessed 26 October 2012.

it would soon be pretty obvious that this must be Bach or Mozart or Haydn or Beethoven.[29] There are some important changes in music-making from the early eighteenth to the early nineteenth centuries—the evolution of musical patronage, the development of the concert hall symphony orchestra from bands of court musicians, the invention of new instruments such as the clarinet, the refinement of existing instruments into the valved horn and trumpet, or the emergence of the modern piano—but, listening to the music, there is a fairly clear evolutionary process. Bach is certainly not Beethoven. While we can describe reasons for this—the *why* we get from Bach to Beethoven, the contingent stages along the way—this gets us no nearer a satisfactory understanding of *what* is aurally different. For this, we need the resources of musical theory: we need to understand the structure of a composition, the tonal resources and sequences employed—and how one composer can write so many different pieces of work that still, at one level, are quite distinctively the work of that composer.

We might conceive such an exercise as the identification of a particular musical language, where most of the components are familiar, but assembled in a way that appears to be novel. To talk coherently about this relationship between familiar components in an unfamiliar structure we cannot rely upon our responses to it; there will always be a range of opinion, but that only identifies popularity, not how that popularity is created. And having followed this musical diversion, we can come back to Kuhn's conceptions of 'paradigm', 'normal science', and 'incommensurability' and see more clearly just what is wrong with the question he posed, the answer he gave to it, and the subsequent development of social constructivism. He asked *what* was different between a and b, and his answer was all about the *why*. Approached in that way, we can only explain Bach in terms of Beethoven—hence recurrently. But from the above, it is also perfectly clear that we can understand that Bach is not Beethoven through the study of their compositions, using a common musicological approach. It is certainly possible to present Bach as a version of a 1950s Beethoven—Herbert von Karajan's recordings of Bach make this point clearly[30]—but the explanation for this relates to fashions in musical taste and the political economy of the music business. These are important matters to understand, but not the same thing as understanding the music, which has to draw on other resources.

29. Even if you have never heard any Bach or Mozart or Haydn or Beethoven, you would see the point of this argument once you had.

30. And explaining the overture to *Die Meistersinger*, set in mid-sixteenth-century Nuremberg, Roger Norrington once remarked that this was Wagner's pastiche of Bach, because he thought of Bach as a late-medieval composer.

It is the same with Alfred Marshall and David Ricardo. They are both recognisably writing about 'the economy', Ricardo employing terminology that recurs in Marshall's writings. Marshall however, and for his own reasons, stretched credibility when he claimed to be elaborating arguments continuous with those of Ricardo. How do we evaluate what unites and separates their writings, and what can we learn from so doing? There are external factors, such as the readers they wrote for, their social and intellectual networks, and Marshall's desire to make economics a modern university discipline. But these contingencies can only tell us why a Ricardo is different from a Marshall, not what this difference is. To do this we have to examine the structure of their writings, consider its terminology, object, and method. A central question then becomes: once we have a clearer image of their differences, how can we conceive the move from Ricardo to Marshall, a move that Marshall himself depicted as one of continuous improvement rather than paradigm shift? And there is certainly a 'paradigm shift' here: from an objective value inherent in a good, to a subjective valuation imputing value to things which, through this imputation, become goods.[31] Economics turns away from the world of goods and re-orients itself to the world of persons using goods.

Given this difference, how can one move from the one to the other? Here it helps to consider John Stuart Mill's *Principles of Political Economy*, the text with which Marshall began his studies. It is often said that Mill represented the limit and completion of political economy—a view that he seems to have shared, given his notorious statement that there was 'nothing in the laws of Value which remains for the present or any future writer to clear up; the theory of the subject is complete: the only difficulty to be overcome is that of so stating it as to solve by anticipation the chief perplexities which occur in applying it'.[32] However, early on in this work Mill had noted that 'What we produce . . . is always, as M. Say rightly terms it, an utility. Labour is not creative of objects, but of utilities',[33] abandoning the firm linkage of value to the objective world of goods common to both Smith and Ricardo, and presenting a means with which one could reconstitute Mill's orthodox political economy as a new subjectivist economics. It is, therefore, possible to identify Mill's *Principles* as a summary of political economy in its conventional structure, while recognising that it contained

31. This is a somewhat Austrian version of Marshall, but a historically accurate one, given that the reception of Austrian economics in the English language was strongest in the early 1890s.

32. John Stuart Mill, *Principles of Political Economy, Collected Works of John Stuart Mill* Vol. 3 (ed. J. M. Robson), University of Toronto Press, Toronto 1965 p. 456.

33. Ibid. p. 46.

elements whose elaboration could result in its supersession. Book I is quite orthodox, presenting Production as a form of 'physical truths'; but in Book II Distribution 'is a matter of human institution solely',[34] a clear shift away from the determinate relationship between production and distribution expounded by Malthus, Ricardo, and James Mill.

So we might identify the substance of this 'paradigm shift' by examining the texts in question, considering how their arguments are constructed, and what the implications might be if some conditions were altered. We can also track changes of this kind over time, demonstrating how, through the course of decades, one form of economic reasoning turns into another. To do so, however, requires close and consistent attention to the use of economic language and the construction of texts; whether texts and arguments became 'influential' at the time, later, or never at all, that is all a different question. The social constructivism that Kuhn's approach to the history of the sciences fostered can answer this latter question, but has nothing to say about the actual organisation of economic language; and so, ultimately, about the way we think. Nor does this 'paradigm shift' between the work of Ricardo and Marshall render Ricardo unintelligible to us; once aware of our tendency to reconstruct the past in the terms of the present, to generate recurrent histories, we are able to read the differences between Ricardo and Marshall, and their specificity. As Errol Morris pointed out, it is simply not true that, once we see the duck, the rabbit is gone forever—Kuhn's own metaphor of the gestalt switch in fact undermines the point he tried to make with it.

To discount what actors talk *about* in favour of describing how they *work*, or even regarding what they talk about as merely a coded way of creating social hierarchies, reduces language to a medium of communication conveying meanings explicable primarily in terms of the social practices of the agents involved. From this perspective the 'social turn' looks more like a new way of dressing up a rather old idea, that language as a social product is inextricably bound up with the interests of the social group using that language: that all language is 'ideological', hence to understand language all we really need do is to identify the (class) position of the user. Paradoxically, therefore, the 'social turn' merely reproduces the idea that meaning is pre-linguistic, is formed intentionally or unintentionally and then conveyed through the (neutral) medium of language. All knowledge thus becomes so many forms of ideology, explicable through social foundations in human activity rather being subjected to any close examination. Obviously these social foundations form an important part

34. Ibid. p. 199.

in arriving at an understanding of what is said or written, and there is a significant part of modern linguistics devoted to exactly this point; but our only access to what anyone 'means' has to begin with an examination of the language they use, and the properties of language can be reduced neither to the structures of social groups, nor to the positions of individuals. We cannot assume that all we need do in seeking to understand language use is to examine the credentials of its users—a new twist on the meaning of the 'language police'.

Linguistic meaning is generated through the repetition and recombination of an ultimately restricted set of linguistic and extra-linguistic units; in the case of the economic writing examined here, through the reworking of a growing corpus of concepts, categories, principles, axioms. Understanding these concepts, categories, principles, and axioms requires that we attend to their use, considering in what way a particular use might simply repeat previous usage, or whether in fact the mode of its use might allow a new meaning to emerge. David Edgerton has remarked that

> We should beware of privileging the novel, in both history and historiography, not out of conservatism, but because we understand the power and influence of claims to novelty to disguise a lack of novelty, and indeed sometimes to suppress it.[35]

Indeed, rather than focus upon novelty, a focus upon the routine regularities of usage presents a rather more promising model for the history of economics. In the world of language, what is new comes from endless repetition, combination, and re-use of what already exists, in the process sometimes creating something that had not before existed; and so for the study of organised economic knowledge we need to begin by examining this kaleidoscopic process of combination and recombination.

The Saussure influential in the 1970s was exclusively the Saussure of the *Course in General Linguistics*, first published in 1916. The emphasis upon the arbitrary and conventional nature of the sign, and the distance separating the signifier from the signified, played a role in encouraging postmodern arguments that emphasised the lability of representation. True, in his work Saussure did move from diachronic, comparative linguistics to a structural approach based upon synchronic analysis, but the 'arbitrary nature of the sign' was not even a novel idea a hundred

35. David Edgerton, 'Innovation, Technology, or History: What is the Historiography of Technology About?', *Technology and Culture* Vol. 51 (2010) p. 697.

years ago. In March 1876, a few months before the nineteen-year-old Saussure went to the University of Leipzig and there encountered Curtius and the *Junggrammatiker*, Charles Dodgson had published *The Hunting of the Snark*. 'Fit the Second' opens with the Bellman presenting to the crew

> a large map representing the sea,
> Without the least vestige of land:
> And the crew were much pleased when they found it to be
> A map they could all understand.
> 'What's the good of Mercator's North Poles and Equators,
> Tropics, Zones and Meridian Lines?'
> So the Bellman would cry: and the crew would reply,
> 'They are merely conventional signs!'
> 'Other maps are such shapes, with their islands and capes!
> But we've got our brave Captain to thank'
> (So the crew would protest) 'that he's bought us the best—
> A perfect and absolute blank!'[36]

Saussure was scrupulous in acknowledging his sources, and the relation of his own work to that of his contemporaries. His *Course in General Linguistics* opens with a rapid survey of the development of comparative linguistics out of comparative philology, a movement from a focus on the written text to analysis of the spoken word.[37] It could be argued that a fresh start could be made today by placing the 'structural' Saussure back in his later nineteenth-century context, in so doing seeking to develop a modern structural philology that can apply the insights of modern linguistics to the study of canonical texts in the history of social, political, and economic discourse.

Jost Trier expressed the post-Saussurean view very cogently when seeking to capture these ideas, suggesting that related concepts

> form among themselves and with the articulated word a structured whole, a framework that one can call lexical field, or linguistic sign field. The lexical field is ordered semiotically to a more or less closed conceptual complex, whose

36. Lewis Carroll, *The Hunting of the Snark*, Macmillan, London 1876 pp. 15–16.
37. Ferdinand de Saussure, *Course in General Linguistics*, ed. Charles Bally and Albert Sechehaye in collaboration with Albert Riedlinger, trans. Wade Baskin, McGraw-Hill, New York 1966 pp. 1–5.

> internal organisation is represented in the structured framework of the sign field which is given for the members of a language community.[38]

Accordingly,

> It is not the individual sign that *says* something; only the totality of the sign system can say something *in respect of* the individual sign. And so the word forms an autonomous whole with the remaining words in the same conceptual field, and acquires from this whole its signifying scope. The meaning of a word is first recognised when it is demarcated from neighbouring and opposing words. It only has a sense as part of a whole; for meaning only exists within the field.[39]

Armed with this conception of the lexical field, one can better understand what Foucault was seeking to do in his *Archaeology of Knowledge*, a leading conception of which is the discursive formation, the underlying structure of language. By identifying and specifying discrete discursive formations, which in Foucault play the role of a kind of historical generative grammar, he was trying to establish how 'ways of doing' things shifted over time—this is after all an archaeology of *savoir*, not of *connaissance*.

This approach also has the advantage of moving beyond argument over authorial intentions, and the problem of recurrent disciplinary histories. Frederick Beiser identifies the prevalence of these problems in castigating postwar anglophone philosophy's approach to German metaphysics and idealism. He suggests that John Rawls saw in Kant 'anticipations' of his own theory of justice, leading students to approach the writings of Kant in the same way. While it is of course legitimate to seek in Kant or Hegel contributions to our own discussions, this slides all too easily into the assumption that the Kants and Hegels constructed in this way are all that we need to know about. But, Beiser argues, these fictional constructs have little to do with any historically existing Kant or Hegel. They are rewritten in our own terms, and so we lose the opportunity of seeing how *different* their thinking is to ours. And to see this, we need to become aware of our

38. Jost Trier, 'Über Wort- und Begriffsfelder' [1931], in his *Aufsätze und Vorträge zur Wortfeldtheorie*, ed. A. van der Lee and O. Reichmann, Mouton, The Hague 1973 p. 40. Lévi-Strauss alludes to a similar idea when he suggests that the 'totemic illusion' arises from a 'distortion of a semantic field to which belong phenomena of the same type'—*Totemism*, Penguin Books, Harmondsworth 1969 p. 86. His construction of the relevant 'semantic field' can be found on p. 84.

39. Trier, 'Über Wort- und Begriffsfelder', op. cit. p. 45.

modern concerns, set them on one side, and struggle to come to terms with unfamiliar artefacts.[40]

Indeed, as became plain in the chapters on Marx and Walras, once one begins to read French and German socialist writing in the mid-nineteenth century about property, possession, and the distribution of rights, one cannot but be struck by the way that Rawls picks up the same issues, more than a century later, but in complete ignorance of the way that these old socialist arguments had fed through into contemporary political thought via the elaboration of 'Marxist theory' and the development of neoclassical general equilibrium theory. Hence, far from Rawls developing a new way of thinking about equality and justice, he simply returned to formulations widely discussed in the mid-nineteenth century, but unfortunately transmitted onward into the twentieth century in progressively garbled form.

By returning to the original arguments we can regain a clarity that has been lost, and which cannot be recovered through a dogged pursuit of critique and counter-critique. For the more that the past is assimilated to the present, the less thinking we have to do in seeking to understand the past. Our task here has been the reconstruction of a past structure of language use. This is not a search for 'origins', much less for 'originality'. Instead, we should seek to disentangle similarity from difference, so that we might be better able to discriminate good from bad arguments in the present. It is worth recalling in this context that Herbert Butterfield's landmark condemnation of 'Whig history', of writing history as the steady emergence of the present, had a specific historical content: as a legitimating ideology of resistance, seventeenth-century Whiggism disguised the new as the re-creation of the old, inventing a conception of liberty that was supposed to have been lost, but which had now been recovered. With the success of the Glorious Revolution, it might have been supposed that this fabricated heritage could have been discarded; but instead, by the nineteenth century, it had transmuted into a myth that confirmed the long history of English liberty.[41] My emphasis upon the contingency of

40. Frederick Beiser, 'Dark Days: Anglophone Scholarship since the 1960s', in Espen Hammer (ed.) *German Idealism: Contemporary Perspectives*, Routledge, London 2007 pp. 69–71. Beiser shows how, following on from Rawls's equivocal reading of Kant, an entire field of inquiry, Kantian ethics, has grown up in the United States based around an imaginary subject: what Kant 'ought to have said if he had been wise enough to leap beyond eighteenth-century Prussian culture to grasp the [Rawlsian] theory of justice' (p. 78).

41. As Istvan Hont argues in his presentation 'Commerce and Politics in 18th. Century Political Thought', International Symposium on 'The Cambridge Moment: Virtue, History and Public Philosophy', Chiba University, Japan 11–13 December 2005 p. 2.

discontinuity and continuity in the preceding essays is a response to this way of legitimating contemporary certainties. But it also facilitates its reverse: exposing claims made for the novelty of current ideas that are merely versions of once-familiar ideas.

Learning how to read canonical texts anew provides a way around the conformity that today's conditions foster. The idea that we can refocus our perspective by a close reading of classic texts has long been a conventional idea in the history of political theory, but one that historians of economics have overlooked through a still-widespread persistence in reading these classical texts from the perspective of a modern economist. My earliest publications were characterised by an assault on this genre of writing, and read as such. But what I then failed to fully appreciate was my own motivation in reading Smith, or Malthus, or Ricardo in the first place. What had brought me to such texts was a strong sense that, during the turbulent years of the early 1970s, as the long postwar boom came to its end with the dollar and the energy crises, the controversies that interested economists were not related to the economic issues which concerned a wider public, while economists appeared to have little worthwhile to say about these issues. What I was then looking for in the political economists was not 'better arguments', but rather arguments over the purpose of economic analysis, and its limits; means for the construction of economic analysis, whether well formed or not. In seeking a way of reading writers that did not assume I already knew what they were talking about, I sought to understand them as economists of their time with new ideas (or not). From this one could learn how to think about the difference between good and bad arguments, and appreciate that this difference could not be read out of a single method, nor from the application of a single instrument, an approach typical of the economic analysis of the time, whether mainstream or heterodox. The point was not to provide an alternative genealogical foundation for economics, but to learn first of all how to read historical texts, and then understand how their arguments were constructed. If one were able to achieve this, it might then be possible to view our contemporary economic arguments in a new light. Historical analysis necessarily involves a sense of dislocation and reconstruction; we must learn to escape the present and read the past. And if we have once learned how to do this, we can turn the insights so gained towards our confrontation with the present. As Gaston Bachelard noted, knowledge proceeds through a process of envelopment, but within this constant movement there is a dialogic relationship between past and present that has to be opened up, and not closed down.

BIBLIOGRAPHY

Akerlof, G. A., Shiller, R. J., *Animal Spirits: How Human Psychology Drives the Economy, and Why It Matters for Global Capitalism*, Princeton University Press, Princeton (NJ) 2009.

Allier, J., *'Crédit, Discrédit, Industriels, Industrie, Producteur'*, *Le Producteur* t. 2 (1826) no. 25 pp. 566–76.

Althusser, L., Balibar, E., *Reading Capital*, trans. Ben Brewster, New Left Books, London 1970.

Aristotle, *Politics*, ed. and trans. Ernest Barker, Oxford University Press, London 1958.

Aristotle, *The Nicomachean Ethics*, trans. D. Ross, revised J. L. Ackrill, Oxford University Press, Oxford 1980.

Aristotle [Pseudo], *Oeconomia*, trans. G. Cyril Armstrong, Harvard University Press, Cambridge MA 1935.

Augello, M. M., Guidi, M. E. L. (eds.) *The Economic Reader: Textbooks, Manuals and the Dissemination of the Economic Sciences during the Nineteenth and Early Twentieth Centuries*, Routledge, London 2012.

Bachelard, G., *La formation de l'esprit scientifique* [1938], J. Vrin, Paris 1970.

Bachelard, G., *Le nouvel esprit scientifique* [1934], Presses universitaires de France, Paris 1971.

Backhouse, R. E., Medema, S. G., 'Defining Economics: The Long Road to Acceptance of the Robbins Definition', *Economica* Vol. 76 (2009) pp. 805–20.

Bagehot, W., 'Adam Smith as a Person', *Fortnightly Review* Vol. 20 New Series (1876) pp. 18–42.

Barone, E., 'Il Ministro della Produzione nello Stato Collettivista', *Giornale degli Economisti* 8 (1908) pp. 267–93, 392–414; translated in Friedrich von Hayek, *Collectivist Economic Planning*, George Routledge and Sons, London 1935 pp. 245–90.

Bastable, C. F., 'Adam Smith's Lectures on "Jurisprudence"', *Hermathena* Vol. X (1899) pp. 200–11.

Beiser, F., 'Dark Days: Anglophone Scholarship since the 1960s', in E. Hammer (ed.) *German Idealism: Contemporary Perspectives*, Routledge, London 2007 pp. 70–90.

Bellofiore, R., Taylor, N. (eds.) *The Constitution of Capital: Essays on Volume I of Marx's 'Capital'*, Palgrave, Basingstoke 2004.

Béraud, A., Faccarello, G., 'The Reception of Ricardo in the French Language: Episodes from a Complex History', in G. Faccarello, M. Izumo (eds.) *The Reception of David Ricardo in Continental Europe and Japan*, Routledge, Abingdon 2014 pp. 10–75.

Blanc, L., *Histoire de la révolution de 1848 t. 1*. C. Marpan and E. Flammarion, Paris 1880.
Blanc, L., *Organisation du travail*, Administration de librairie, Paris 1841.
Blaug, M., *Ricardian Economics: A Historical Study*, Yale University Press, New Haven 1958.
Blecker, R. A., 'The "Unnatural and Retrograde Order": Adam Smith's Theories of Trade and Development Reconsidered', *Economica* Vol. 64 (1997) pp. 527–37.
Bloomfield, A. I., 'Adam Smith and the Theory of International Trade', in A. S. Skinner, T. Wilson (eds.), *Essays on Adam Smith*, Oxford University Press, London 1975 pp. 455–81.
Böhm-Bawerk, E. von, *Kapital und Kapitalzins. Erste Abtheilung: Geschichte und Kritik der Kapitalzins-Theorieen*, Verlag der Wagner'schen Universitäts-Buchhandlung, Innsbruck 1884.
Böhm-Bawerk, E. von, *Positive Theorie des Kapitals (Kapital und Kapitalzins Zweite Abtheilung)*, Verlag der Wagner'schen Universitäts-Buchhandlung, Innsbruck 1889.
Böhm-Bawerk, E. von, *Innsbrucker Vorlesungen über Nationalökonomie*, ed. Shigeki Tomo, Metropolis Verlag, Marburg 1998.
Boldyrev, I., Kirtchik, O., 'General Equilibrium Theory behind the Iron Curtain: The Case of Victor Polterovich', *History of Political Economy* Vol. 46 (2014) pp. 435–61.
Bowley, A. L., 'The Census of Production and the National Dividend', *Economic Journal* Vol. 23 (1913) pp. 53–61.
Bowley, A. L., 'Notes on Index Numbers', *Economic Journal* Vol. 38 (1928) pp. 216–37.
Bowley, A. L., 'Some Constituents of the National Income', *Journal of the Royal Statistical Society* Vol. 103 (1940) pp. 491–518.
Bowley, A. L., *Studies in the National Income 1924–1938*, National Institute of Economic and Social Research, Economic and Social Studies I, Cambridge University Press, Cambridge 1942.
Bowley, A. L., Stamp, J. C., *The National Income, 1924*, Oxford University Press, Oxford 1927.
Brentano, L., *Das Arbeitsverhältniss gemäss dem heutigen Recht*, Duncker und Humblot, Leipzig 1877.
Brunner, O., *Adeliges Landleben und europäisches Geist*, Otto Müller, Salzburg 1949.
Brunner, O., 'Das "Ganze Haus" und die alteuropäische "Ökonomik"' [1958], in his *Neue Wege der Verfassungs- und Sozialgeschichte*, 3rd edition, Vandenhoeck und Ruprecht, Göttingen 1980 pp. 103–27.
Brunner, O., Conze, W., Koselleck, R. (eds.) *Geschichtliche Grundbegriffe* Bd. 7, Klett-Cotta, Stuttgart 1992.
Buckle, H. T., *History of Civilization in England* Vol. 1, John Parker and Son, London 1857.
Buckle, H. T., *Geschichte der Civilisation in England* Bd. 2, C. F. Winter'sche Verlagshandlung, Leipzig 1861.
Buckle, H. T., *History of Civilization in England* Vol. 2, Parker, Son, and Bourn, London 1861.
Buret, E., *De la misère des classes laborieuses en France et Angleterre*, 2 vols., Paulin, Paris 1840.
Cairncross, A., *Planning in Wartime: Aircraft Production in Britain, Germany and the USA*, Macmillan, Houndmills 1991.

Cairncross, A., Watts, N., *The Economic Section 1939–1961: A Study in Economic Advising*, Routledge, London 1989.
Calthrope, C., *The Relation betweene the Lord of a Mannor and the Coppy-holder his Tenant*, London 1635.
Carey, H. C., *Principles of Political Economy*, Pt. 2, Lea & Blanchard, Philadelphia 1838.
Carroll, L., *The Hunting of the Snark*, Macmillan, London 1876.
Carroll, L., *The Annotated Alice*, ed. Martin Gardner, Penguin Books, Harmondsworth 1970.
Carver, T., '*The German Ideology* Never Took Place', *History of Political Thought* Vol. 31 (2010) pp. 107–27.
Castleton, E., 'Introduction. Comment la propriété est devenu le vol, ou l'éducation de Pierre-Joseph Proudhon', in P.-J. Proudhon, *Qu'est-ce que la propriété?*, Livre de poche, Paris 2009 pp. 43–108.
Castleton, E., 'L'inachèvement de l'oeuvre économique de Pierre-Joseph Proudhon', *Économie et sociétés* (forthcoming).
Charles, L., 'The *Tableau Économique* as Rational Recreation', *History of Political Economy* Vol. 36 (2004) pp. 445–74.
Claeys, G., *Machinery, Money and the Millennium. From Moral Economy to Socialism, 1815–60*, Polity Press, Cambridge 1987.
Clark, C., 'Statistical Studies relating to the Current Economic Position of Great Britain', *Economic Journal* Vol. 41 (1931) pp. 343–69.
Clark, C., *The National Income 1924–1931*, Macmillan, London 1932.
Clark, C., 'The National Income and the Net Output of Industry', *Journal of the Royal Statistical Society* Vol. 96 (1933) pp. 651–59.
Clark, C., 'The National Income and the Theory of Production', *Economic Journal* Vol. 43 (1933) pp. 205–16.
Clark, C., 'Further Data on the National Income', *Economic Journal* Vol. 44 (1934) pp. 380–97.
Clark, J. M., et al., *Adam Smith, 1776–1926*, University of Chicago Press, Chicago 1928.
Cliffe Leslie, T. E., 'The History of German Political Economy', in his *Essays in Political and Moral Philosophy*, Hodges, Foster and Figgis, Dublin 1879 pp. 167–78.
Coke, E., *The Compleat Copy-Holder, wherein is contained a Learned Discourse of the Antiquity and Nature of Mannors and Copy-holds*, London 1650.
Colerus, J., 'Vorrede' *Calendarium Perpetuum, et Libri Oeconomici*, Paul Helwig, Wittenberg 1604.
Columella, *Res rustica* 3 vols., Harvard University Press, Cambridge MA 1941 (I–IV trans. Harrison Boyd Ash); 1954 (V–IX trans. E. S. Forster, Edward H. Heffner); 1955 (X–XII trans. Forster and Heffner).
Cook, S. J., '"Our Eyes, Spinning Like Propellers": Wheel of Life, Curve of Velocities, and Dziga Vertov's "Theory of the Interval"', *October* No. 121 (Summer 2007) pp. 79–91.
Cook, S. J., *The Intellectual Foundations of Alfred Marshall's Economic Science: A Rounded Globe of Knowledge*, Cambridge University Press, Cambridge 2009.
Cossa, L., *Guide to the Study of Political Economy*, Macmillan, London 1880.
Counihan, T., 'Epistemology and Science—Feyerabend and Lecourt', *Economy and Society* Vol. 5 (1976) pp. 74–110.
Cournot, A. A., *Recherches sur les principes mathématiques de la théorie des richesses*, J. Vrin, Paris 1980.

Darwin, C., 'Journal of Researches into the Natural History and Geology of the Countries Visited during the Voyage of H.M.S. Beagle Round the World' (1845), in his *Evolutionary Writings*, ed. James A. Secord, Oxford University Press, Oxford 2010 pp. 3–95.

Delatour, A., *Adam Smith, Sa vie, ses travaux, ses doctrines*, Guillaumin, Paris 1886.

Deville, G., *Le Capital de Karl Marx résumé et accompagné d'un Aperçu sur le Socialisme Scientifique*, Henry Oriol, Paris 1883.

Deville, G., *Cours d'économie sociale*, Pts. 1 and 2 Paris 1884.

Devons, E., *Planning in Practice: Essays in Aircraft Planning in War-time*, Cambridge University Press, London 1950.

Dickinson, H. D., 'Price Formation in a Socialist Community', *Economic Journal* Vol. 43 (1933) pp. 237–50.

Dockès, P., *La société n'est pas un pique-nique: Léon Walras et l'économie sociale*, Economica, Paris 1996.

Dodsley, R., *The Oeconomy of Human Life: Translated from an Indian Manuscript written by an ancient Bramin*, London 1751.

Doxiadis, A., Papadatos A., and Di Donna, A., 'Claude Lévi-Strauss (1908–2009)', *FT Magazine* 27 February 2010.

Drechsler, W., 'Herrn Eugen Dühring's Remotion', *Journal of Economic Studies* Vol. 29 Nos. 4/5 (2002) pp. 262–92.

Du Pont de Nemours, P. S., *De l'origine et des progrès d'une science nouvelle*, Paris 1768.

Eckstein, W., 'Adam Smith als Rechtsphilosoph', *Archiv für Rechts- und Wirtschaftsphilosophie* Bd. 20 (1927) pp. 378–95.

Eddy, D. D., 'Dodsley's "Oeconomy of Human Life", 1750–1751', *Modern Philology* Vol. 85 (1988) pp. 460–79.

Edgerton, D., 'Innovation, Technology, or History: What is the Historiography of Technology About?', *Technology and Culture* Vol. 51 (2010) pp. 690–97.

Elmslie, B., James, A. M., 'The Renaissance of Adam Smith in Modern Theories of Trade', in R. F. Hébert (ed.) *Perspectives on the History of Economic Thought* Vol. 9: *Themes on Economic Discourse, Method, Money and Trade*, Edward Elgar, Aldershot 1993 pp. 63–76.

Emerton, W. P., *An Analysis of Adam Smith's Inquiry into the Nature and Causes of the Wealth of Nations Pt. I*, James Thornton, Oxford 1877.

Erlich, V., *Russian Formalism: History—Doctrine*, 3rd edition, Mouton, The Hague 1969.

Evans, M. 'Karl Marx's First Confrontation with Political Economy: The 1844 Manuscripts', *Economy and Society* Vol. 13 (1984) pp. 115–52.

Faccarello, G., 'Sraffa versus Ricardo: The Historical Irrelevance of the "Corn-Profit" Model', *Economy and Society* Vol. 11 (1982) pp. 122–37.

Farrer, J. A., *Adam Smith (1723–1790)*, Sampson, Lowe, Marston, Searle, & Rivington, London 1881.

Fay, M., 'The Influence of Adam Smith on Marx's Theory of Alienation', *Science and Society* Vol. 47 No. 2 (1983) pp. 129–51.

Feavearyear, A. E., 'Spending the National Income', *Economic Journal* Vol. 41 (1931) pp. 51–60.

Feavearyear, A. E., 'The National Expenditure, 1932', *Economic Journal* Vol. 44 (1934) pp. 33–47.

Feyerabend, P. K., 'Consolations for the Specialist', in I. Lakatos, A. Musgrave (eds.) *Criticism and the Growth of Knowledge*, Cambridge University Press, London 1970 pp. 197–230.

Finley, M. I., *The Ancient Economy*, Chatto and Windus, London 1973.
Fitzherbert, *The Book of Husbandry*, ed. W. W. Skeat, Trübner & Co., London 1882.
Flam, H., Flanders, M. J. (eds.) *Heckscher-Ohlin Trade Theory*, MIT Press, Cambridge (MA) 1991.
Fleischer, M. P., 'The First German Agricultural Manuals', *Agricultural History* Vol. 55 (1981) pp. 1–15.
Florinus, *Oeconomus Prudens et Legalis: Oder Allgemeiner Klug- und Rechtsverständiger Haus-Vatter*, Christoph Riegel, Nuremberg 1702.
Flux, A. W., 'Gleanings from the Census of Production', *Journal of the Royal Statistical Society* Vol. 76 (1913) pp. 557–98.
Flux, A. W., 'The Census of Production', *Journal of the Royal Statistical Society* Vol. 87 (1924) pp. 351–90.
Flux, A. W., review of Clark, *The National Income, 1924–31* in *Economic Journal* Vol. 43 (1933) pp. 279–81.
Fogel, R. W., et al., *Political Arithmetic: Simon Kuznets and the Empirical Tradition in Economics*, University of Chicago Press, Chicago 2013.
Force, P., *Self-Interest before Adam Smith: A Genealogy of Economic Science*, Cambridge University Press, Cambridge 2003.
Force, P., 'First Principles in Translation: The Axiom of Self-interest from Adam Smith to Jean-Baptiste Say', *History of Political Economy* Vol. 38 (2006) pp. 319–38.
Fortescue, J., *The Governance of England*, ed. Charles Plummer, Oxford University Press, Oxford 1885.
Foucault, M., *The Order of Things: An Archaeology of the Human Sciences*, Tavistock, London 1970.
Foucault, M., *The Archaeology of Knowledge*, Tavistock, London 1972.
French, D., *British Economic and Strategic Planning 1905–1915*, George Allen and Unwin, London 1982.
Frobert, L., 'What Is a Just Society? The Answer According to the *Socialistes Fraternitaires* around 1849 (Louis Blanc, Constantin, Pecqueur, François Vidal)', *History of Political Economy* Vol. 46 (2014) pp. 281–306.
Garnier, J., 'De l'origine et de la filiation du mot économie politique et des divers autres noms donnés à la science économique', *Journal des Économistes* t. 32 (May–August 1852) pp. 300–16; (September–October) pp. 11–23.
Genovesi, A., *Delle Lezioni di Commercio o sia d'Economia Civile*, 2 vols., Naples 1765, 1767.
Gide, C., Rist, C., *Histoire des doctrines économiques depuis les physiocrates jusqu'à nos jours*, J. B. Sirey, Paris 1909.
Gossen, H. H., *Entwicklung der Gesetze des menschlichen Verkehrs und der daraus fließenden Regeln für menschliches Handeln*, 3rd edition, R. L. Prager, Berlin 1927.
Gregory, D., 'Karl Marx's and Friedrich Engels' Knowledge of French Socialism in 1842–1843', *Historical Reflections* Vol. 10 No. 1 (1983) pp. 143–93.
Grossmann, H., *'Die Änderung des ursprünglichen Aufbauplans des Marxschen Kapital und ihre Ursachen', Archiv für die Geschichte des Sozialismus und der Arbeiterbewegung* Bd. 14 (1929) pp. 305–38.
Haeckel, E., *Generelle Morphologie der Organismen*, Bd. 1: *Allgemeine Anatomie der Organismen*, Georg Reimer, Berlin 1866.
Hagemann, H., Rösch, M., 'German Economists in Parliament (1848–1919)', in M. M. Augello, M. Guidi (eds.) *Economists in Parliament in the Liberal Age (1848–1920)*, Ashgate, Aldershot 2005 pp. 163–89.

Haldane, R. B., *Life of Adam Smith*, Walter Scott, London 1887.

Hasbach, W., *Untersuchungen über Adam Smith und die Entwicklung der politischen Ökonomie*, Duncker und Humblot, Leipzig 1891.

Haushofer, H., 'Das Problem des Florinus', *Zeitschrift für Agrargeschichte und Agrarsoziologie* Jg. 30 (1982) pp. 168–75.

Hecker, R., 'Rjazanovs Editionsprinzipien der ersten MEGA', in Carl-Erich Vollgraf, Richard Sperl, and Rolf Hecker (eds.) *David Borisovič Rjazanov und die erste MEGA*, Argument-Verlag, Berlin 1997 pp. 7–27.

Heckscher, E. F., *Mercantilism*, new edition, 2 vols., Routledge, London 1994.

Heilbroner, R. L., *The Worldly Philosophers*, Simon and Schuster, New York 1953.

Heinrich, M., 'Engels' Edition of the Third Volume of Capital and Marx's Original Manuscript', *Science and Society* Vol. 60 No. 4 (1996–97) pp. 452–66.

Henderson, P. D., 'The Use of Economists in British Administration', *Oxford Economic Papers* (Vol. 13 New Series (1961) pp. 5–26.

Hennings, K., 'A Note on Marx's Reading List in His Economic and Philosophical Manuscripts of 1844', *Economy and Society* Vol. 14 (1985) pp. 128–37.

Herford, C. H., *Philip Henry Wicksteed: His Life and Work*, J. M. Dent, London 1931.

Herland, M., 'Les Walras critiques de La Justice de Proudhon', paper presented at the Colloque Walras, Toulouse September 2012.

Hesiod, *Works and Days*, trans. Glenn W. Most, Harvard University Press, Cambridge (MA) 2006.

Hildebrand, B., *Die Nationalökonomie der Gegenwart und Zukunft*, Literarische Anstalt (J. Rütten), Frankfurt am Main 1848.

Hildebrand, B., 'Die gegenwärtige Aufgabe der Wissenschaft der Nationalökonomie', *Jahrbücher für Nationalökonomie und Statistik* Bd. 1 (1863) pp. 5–26, 137–46.

Hodwala, S. H., *An Analysis of Adam Smith's 'Inquiry into the Nature and Causes of the Wealth of Nations', Books III–V*, Commercial Press, Bombay 1901.

Hohberg, W. H. von, *Georgica Curiosa. Was ist: Umständlicher Bericht und klarer Unterricht von dem Adelichen Land- und Feld-Leben*, Johann Friedrich Endter, Nuremberg 1682.

Hont, I., 'Commerce and Politics in 18th. Century Political Thought', International Symposium on 'The Cambridge Moment: Virtue, History and Public Philosophy', Chiba University, Japan 11–13 December 2005.

Hont, I., *Jealousy of Trade: International Competition and the Nation-State in Historical Perspective*, Harvard University Press, Cambridge (MA) 2005.

Howson, S., 'The Origins of Lionel Robbins's Essay on the Nature and Significance of Economic Science', *History of Political Economy* Vol. 36 (2004) pp. 413–43.

Howson, S., *Lionel Robbins*, Cambridge University Press, Cambridge 2011.

Hufeland, G., *Neue Grundlegung der Staatswirthschaftskunst* Bd. 1 Gießen 1807.

Humphrey, C., *Karl Marx Collective: Economy, Society and Religion in a Siberian Collective Farm*, Cambridge University Press, Cambridge 1983.

Hundert, E. J., *The Enlightenment's 'Fable': Bernard Mandeville and the Discovery of Society*, Cambridge University Press, Cambridge 1994.

Hussain, A., Tribe, K., *Marxism and the Agrarian Question*, 2nd edition, Macmillan, London 1983.

Hutcheson, F., *A Short Introduction to Moral Philosophy, in Three Books; containing the Elements of Ethicks and the Law of Nature* [1747], 2nd edition, Robert and Andrew Foulis, Glasgow 1753.

Hutchison, T. W., 'Some Questions about Ricardo', *Economica* Vol. 19 New Series (1952) pp. 415–32.
Hutchison, T. W., 'Ricardo's Correspondence', *Economica* Vol. 20 New Series (1953) pp. 263–73.
Irwin, D., *Against the Tide: An Intellectual History of Free Trade*, Princeton University Press, Princeton (NJ) 1997.
Jakob, L. H., *Grundsätze der National-Oekonomie oder National-Wirthschaftslehre*, Halle 1805.
Jasny, N., *Soviet Economists of the Twenties: Names to be Remembered*, Cambridge University Press, London 1972.
Jastrow, J., 'Naturrecht und Volkswirtschaft. Erörterungen aus Anlaß der deutschen Ausgabe von Adam Smith Vorlesungen', *Jahrbücher für Nationalökonomie und Statistik* Bd. 126 (1927) pp. 689–730.
Jastrow, J., 'Ein neuer Adam-Smith-Fund und der Aufbau des nationalökonomischen Lehrbgebäudes', *Zeitschrift für Nationalökonomie* Bd. 8 (1937) pp. 338–80.
Jauß, H. R., *Literaturgeschichte als Provokation*, Suhrkamp, Frankfurt am Main 1970.
Jevons, W. S., *The Theory of Political Economy*, Macmillan, London 1871.
Jevons, W. S., *Theory of Political Economy*, 2nd edition, Macmillan, London 1879 pp. 301–10.
Jevons, W. S., 'Preface' to Luigi Cossa, *Guide to the Study of Political Economy*, Macmillan, London 1880 pp. vii–xii.
Jolink, A., *The Evolutionist Economics of Léon Walras*, Routledge, London 1996.
Joyce, J., *Complete Analysis; or, Abridgment of Dr. Adam Smith's Inquiry into the Nature and Causes of the Wealth of Nations*, G & W. B. Whittaker, London 1821.
Joynes, J. L., *The Socialist Catechism*, Modern Press, London 1885.
Kadish, A., *The Oxford Economists in the Late Nineteenth Century*, Oxford University Press, Oxford 1982.
Kadish, A., *Apostle Arnold: The Life and Death of Arnold Toynbee 1852–1883*, Duke University Press, Durham (NC) 1986.
Kaldor, N., 'The White Paper on National Income and Expenditure', *Economic Journal* Vol. 51 (1941) pp. 181–91.
Kautsky, K., *Karl Marx' Oekonomische Lehren*, 5th edition, Dietz Verlag, Stuttgart 1894.
Kelley, D. R., 'The Metaphysics of Law: An Essay on the Very Young Marx', *American Historical Review* Vol. 83 (1978) pp. 350–67.
Kemple, T., *Reading Marx Writing: Melodrama, the Market, and the 'Grundrisse'*, Stanford University Press, Stanford 1995.
Kendrick, J. W., 'The Historical Development of National-Income Accounts', *History of Political Economy* Vol. 2 (1970) pp. 284–315.
Keynes, J. M., *Collected Writings of John Maynard Keynes* Vol. 9: *How to Pay for the War*, Macmillan, London 1972 pp. 367–439.
Keynes, J. M., *Collected Writings of John Maynard Keynes* Vol. 7: *The General Theory of Employment, Interest and Money*, Macmillan, London 1973.
Keynes, J. N., *The Scope and Method of Political Economy*, Macmillan, London 1891.
Knies, K., *Die politische Oekonomie vom Standpunkte der geschichtlichen Methode*, C. A. Schwetschke und Sohn, Brunswick 1853.
Knies, K., *Die politische Oekonomie vom geschichtlichen Standpuncte*, C. A. Schwetschke und Sohn, Brunswick 1883.

Kuhn, T. S., *The Structure of Scientific Revolutions*, 2nd edition, University of Chicago Press, Chicago 1970.
Kuznets, S., 'National Income: A New Version', *Review of Economics and Statistics* Vol. 30 (1948) pp. 151–79.
Landshut, S., 'Der Begriff des Ökonomischen', in his *Kritik der Soziologie und andere Schriften zur Politik*, Luchterhand, Neuwied am Rhein 1969 pp. 131–75.
Leopold, D., *The Young Marx. German Philosophy, Modern Politics, and Human Flourishing*, Cambridge University Press, Cambridge 2007.
Leser, E., *Untersuchungen zur Geschichte der Nationalökonomie*, Gustav Fischer, Jena 1881.
Leshem, D., 'The Ancient Art of Economics', *European Journal of the History of Economic Thought* Vol. 21 (2014) pp. 201–29.
Le Trosne, G. F., *Recueil de plusieurs morceaux economiques*, Desaint, Paris 1768.
Levan-Lemesle, L., *Le Juste ou le Riche: L'enseignement de l'économie politique 1815–1950*, Comité pour l'histoire économique et financière de la France, Paris 2004.
Lévi-Strauss, C., *Totemism*, Penguin Books, Harmondsworth 1969.
Lowry, S. T., 'The Economics and Jurisprudential Ideas of the Ancient Greeks: Our Heritage from Hellenic Thought', in S. Todd Lowry, Barry Gordon (eds.) *Ancient and Medieval Ideas and Concepts of Social Justice*, Brill, Leiden 1998 pp. 11–38.
Macrosty, H. W., 'Proposals for an Economic Survey of the United Kingdom', *Economic Journal* Vol. 19 (1909) pp. 1–12.
Macrosty, H. W., 'Economic Statistics—Retrospect and Prospect', *Journal of the Royal Statistical Society* Vol. 104 (1941) pp. 1–14.
Macrosty, H. W., 'Obituary' (signed M. G.), *Journal of the Royal Statistical Society* Vol. 104 (1941) pp. 85–90.
Maidan M., 'The *Rezeptionsgeschichte* of the Paris Manuscripts', *History of European Ideas* Vol. 12 (1990) pp. 767–81.
Malthus, T. R., *An Investigation of the Cause of the Present High Price of Provisions*, reprinted in E. A. Wrigley, David Souden (eds.) *The Works of Thomas Robert Malthus* Vol. 7, William Pickering, London 1986.
Marshall, A., *Principles of Economics* Vol. 1, Macmillan, London 1890.
Marshall, A., 'A Reply', *Economic Journal* Vol. 2 (1892) pp. 507–19.
Marx, K., *Das Kapital* Bd. 1, Otto Meissner, Hamburg 1867.
Marx, K., *Le Capital* t. 1, Maurice Lachatre, Paris 1872.
Marx, K., *Der historische Materialismus. Die Frühschriften*, 2 vols., ed. S. Landshut, J. P. Mayer. Alfred Kröner, Lepizig 1932.
Marx, K., *Das Kapital* Bd. 1, second edition, ed. Karl Korsch [1932], Anaconda, Cologne 2009.
Marx, K., *Grundrisse der Kritik der politischen Ökonomie. Rohentwurf 1857–1858*, Europäische Verlagsanstalt, Frankfurt am Main 1967.
Marx, K. *Grundrisse: Foundations of the Critique of Political Economy (Rough Draft)*, trans. Martin Nicolaus, Penguin Books, Harmondsworth 1973.
Marx, K., *Exzerpte über Arbeitsteilung, Maschinerie und Industrie*, ed. Rainer Winkelmann, Ullstein Verlag, Frankfurt am Main 1982.
Marx, K., Engels, F., *Historisch-Kritische Gesamtausgabe* [MEGA], Marx-Engels-Verlag, Berlin 1927–35.
Marx, K., Engels, F., *Briefe über 'Das Kapital'*, Dietz Verlag, Berlin 1954.
Marx, K., Engels, F., *Werke*, 43 vols., Dietz Verlag, Berlin 1956–90.

Marx, K., Engels, F., *Gesamtausgabe*, Dietz Verlag/Akademie Verlag, Berlin 1977–.

Masterman, M., 'The Nature of a Paradigm', in I. Lakatos, A. Musgrave (eds.) *Criticism and the Growth of Knowledge*, Cambridge University Press, London 1970 pp. 59–89.

McCulloch, J. R., 'The Opinions of Messrs Say, Sismondi, and Malthus, on the Effects of Machinery and Accumulation, Stated and Examined', *Edinburgh Review* Vol. 35 No. 69 (1821) pp. 102–23.

McCulloch, J. R., *Political Economy*, reprinted from Supplement to the *Encyclopaedia Britannica* Vol. 6 Part 1 (1823), London 1825.

McCulloch, J. R., *A Discourse on the Rise, Progress, Peculiar Objects, and Importance, of Political Economy*, Archibald Constable and Co., Edinburgh 1824.

McCulloch, J. R., *Discours sur l'origine, les progrès, les objets particuliers et l'importance de l'économie politique*, trans. Guillaume Prévost, J. J. Paschoud, Geneva 1825.

McCulloch, J. R. [Anon.], *Memoir of the Life and Writings of David Ricardo, Esq. M.P.*, Richard Taylor, London 1825.

Medick, H., *Naturzustand und Naturgeschichte der bürgerlichen Gesellschaft*, Vandenhoeck und Ruprecht, Göttingen 1973.

Melnik, D., 'The Diffusion of Ricardo's Theories in Russia', in Gilbert Faccarello, Masahi Izumo (eds.) *The Reception of David Ricardo in Continental Europe and Japan*, Routledge, Abingdon 2014 pp. 195–211.

Melon, J. F., *Essai politique sur le commerce*, 2nd edition, n. p. 1736.

Menger, C., *Grundsätze der Volkswirthschaftslehre*, Wilhelm Braumüller, Vienna 1871.

Menger, C., *Untersuchungen über die Methode der Socialwissenschaften, und der Politischen Oekonomie insbesondere* (1883), *Gesammelte Werke* Bd. 1 ed. Friedrich Hayek, J. C. B. Mohr (Paul Siebeck), Tübingen 1969.

Menger, C., *Carl Menger's Zusätze zu den "Grundsätze der Volkswirtschaftslehre"*, Hitotsubashi University Library, Tokyo 1961.

Menuelle, T., *Marx, lecteur de Proudhon*, Cahiers de la société P.-J. Proudhon, Paris 1993.

Meredith, H. O., 'The Finance of War', *Political Quarterly* Vol. 11 (1940) pp. 59–73.

Mill, J., *An Essay on the Impolicy of a Bounty on the Exportation of Grain*, London 1804.

Mill, J., *Selected Economic Writings*, ed. D. Winch, Oliver and Boyd, Edinburgh 1966.

Mill, J. S., *Principles of Political Economy with Some of Their Applications to Social Philosophy*, ed. W. J. Ashley, Longman, Green, London 1909.

Mill, J. S., *Collected Works of John Stuart Mill*, ed. J. M. Robson, University of Toronto Press, Toronto 1963–91.

Miller, P., 'Nazis and Neo-Stoics: Otto Brunner and Gerhard Oestreich before and after the Second World War', *Past and Present* No. 176 (2002) pp. 144–86.

Mirabeau, *L'Ami des hommes ou Traité de la population*, 3 parts, Avignon 1756.

Mirabeau, *Philosophie Rurale, ou Économie générale et politique de l'agriculture*, 3 vols., Amsterdam 1763.

Mitchell, B. R., *British Historical Statistics*, Cambridge University Press, Cambridge 1988.

Momma, H., *From Philology to English Studies: Language and Culture in the Nineteenth Century*, Cambridge University Press, Cambridge 2013.

Montchrétien, A. de, *Traicté de l'économie politique*, ed. Théophile Funck-Brentano, Plon, Paris 1889.

Montesquieu, *De l'Esprit des lois*, Éditions Garniers, Paris 1973.

Morgan, E. V., *Studies in British Financial Policy, 1914–25*, Macmillan, London 1952.

Morgan, M. S., *The History of Econometric Ideas*, Cambridge University Press, Cambridge 1990.
Morris, E., 'The Ashtray. 2. Shifting Paradigms', *New York Times* 7 March 2011.
Mosca, M., 'Jules Dupuit, the French "ingenieurs économistes" and the Société d'Économie Politique', in Gilbert Faccarello (ed.) *Studies in the History of French Political Economy*, Routledge, London 1998 pp. 254–83.
Mossé, C., *The Ancient World at Work*, Chatto and Windus, London 1969.
Müller, H.-P., 'Materialismus und Technologie bei Karl Marx', in Karl Marx, *Die technologisch-historischen Exzerpte*, ed. H.-P. Müller, Ullstein, Frankfurt am Main 1981 pp. i–cxx.
Münchhausen, O. von, *Der Hausvater*, Th. 1, Hanover 1766.
Myint, H., 'Adam Smith's Theory of International Trade in the Perspective of Economic Development', *Economica* Vol. 44 New Series (1977) pp. 231–48.
Natali, C., '*Oikonomia* in Hellenistic Political Thought', in André Laks, Malcolm Schofield (eds.) *Justice and Generosity: Studies in Hellenistic Social and Political Philosophy*, Proceedings of the Sixth Symposium of Hellenisticum, Cambridge University Press, Cambridge 1995 pp. 95–128.
Nathan, R. R., 'GNP and Military Mobilization', *Journal of Evolutionary Economics* Vol. 4 (1994) pp. 1–16.
Newman, P., 'Francis Ysidro Edgeworth (1845–1926)', in *F. Y. Edgeworth: Mathematical Psychics and Further Papers on Political Economy*, ed. Peter Newman, Oxford University Press, Oxford 2003 pp. xiii–xlix.
Nicolaus, M., 'The Unknown Marx', *New Left Review* No. 48 (1968) pp. 41–61.
Nofre, D., Priestley, M., Alberts, G., 'When Technology Became Language: The Origins of the Linguistic Conception of Computer Programming, 1950–1960', *Technology and Culture* Vol. 55 (2014) pp. 41–42.
Norden, J., *The Svrveyors Dialogve, Very profitable for all men to pervse, but especially for Gentlemen, Farmers and Husbandmen, that shall either haue occasion, or be willing to buy, hire or sell Lands: As in the ready and perfect Surueying of them, with the manner and Method of keeping a Court of Suruey with many necessary rules, and familiar Tables to that purpose*, 3rd edition, London 1618.
Oakley, A., *Marx's Critique of Political Economy: Intellectual Sources and Evolution* Vol. 1: *1844 to 1860*, Routledge and Kegan Paul, London 1984.
Oncken, A., *Adam Smith in der Culturgeschichte*, Verlag von Faesy & Frick, Vienna 1874.
Oncken, A., *Adam Smith und Immanuel Kant: Der Einklang und das Wechselverhältniss ihrer Lehren über Sitte, Staat und Wirthschaft*, Duncker und Humblot, Leipzig 1877.
Oncken, A., *Die Maxime laissez faire et laissez passer, ihr Ursprung, ihr Werden*, K. J. Wyß, Bern 1886.
Oncken, A., 'The Consistency of Adam Smith', *Economic Journal* Vol. 7 (1897) pp. 443–20.
Oncken, A., 'Das Adam Smith-Problem', *Zeitschrift für Socialwissenschaft* Jg. 1 (1898) pp. 25–33, 101–8, 276–87.
Oncken, A., 'New Tendencies in German Economics', *Economic Journal* Vol. 9 (1899) pp. 462–69.
Orwell, G., 'Politics and the English Language', in his *Collected Essays*, Secker and Warburg, London 1961 pp. 353–67.
Peach, T., *Interpreting Ricardo*, Cambridge University Press, Cambridge 1993.

Peach, T., 'Introduction' to *David Ricardo: Critical Assessments*, Routledge, London 2003.
Pigou, A. C., 'Review of Marshall, *Principles of Economics* (5th edition)', *Economic Journal* Vol. 17 (1907) pp. 532–35.
Pigou, A. C., *Wealth and Welfare*, Macmillan, London 1912.
Pilbeam, P., *Saint Simonians in Nineteenth-Century France: From Free Love to Algeria*, Palgrave, Basingstoke 2014.
Price, L. L., *A Short History of Political Economy in England from Adam Smith to Arnold Toynbee*, Methuen, London 1891.
Price, L. L., "Adam Smith and His Relation to Recent Economics", *Economic Journal* Vol. 3 (1893) pp. 239–54.
Prodger, P., *Time Stands Still: Muybridge and the Instantaneous Photography Movement*, Oxford University Press, New York 2003.
Proudhon, P.-J., *Qu'est-ce que la propriété? Ou Recherches sur le principe du droit et du gouvernement*, J.-F. Brocard, Paris 1840.
Proudhon, P. J., *Système des Contradictions Économique, ou Philosophie de la Misère*, 2 vols., Guillamin, Paris 1846.
Quesnay, F., *Œuvres économiques complètes et autres textes* t. I, ed. Christine Théré, Loïc Charles, Jean-Claude Perrot, L'institut Nationale d'Études Démographiques, Paris 2005.
Rabe, H., 'Ökonomie', in J. Ritter, K. Gründer (eds.) *Historisches Wörterbuch der Philosophie* Bd. 6, Wissenschaftliche Buchgesellschaft, Darmstadt 1984 cols. 1149–53.
Rau, K. H., *Lehrbuch der politischen Oekonomie* Bd. 1, Heidelberg 1826.
Ricardo, D., *Des principes de l'économie politique, et de l'impot*, 2 vols., trans. Francisco Solano Constancio, notes by Jean-Baptiste Say, J. P. Aillaud, Paris 1819.
Ricardo, D., *Des principes de l'économie politique, et de l'impot*, 2 vols., 2nd edition, trans. Francisco Solano Constancio, notes by Jean-Baptiste Say, J. P. Aillaud, Paris 1835.
Ricardo, D., *Works and Correspondence of David Ricardo*, ed. P. Sraffa with M. H. Dobb, 11 vols., Cambridge University Press, Cambridge 1951.
Richards, I. A., *Practical Criticism: A Study in Literary Judgement*, Kegan Paul, Trench, Trubner, London 1929.
Robbins, L., 'The Economic Works', in C. H. Herford, *Philip Henry Wicksteed: His Life and Work*, J. M. Dent, London 1931 pp. 228–47.
Robbins, L., *The Nature and Significance of Economic Science*, Macmillan, London 1932.
Roesler, H., *Ueber die Grundlehren der von Adam Smith begründeten Volkswirthschaftstheorie*, Verlag von Andreas Deichert, Erlangen 1868.
Rojahn, J., 'Marxismus—Marx—Geschichtswissenschaft. Der Fall der sog. "ökonomisch-philosophischen Manuskripte aus dem Jahre 1844"', *International Review of Social History* Vol. 28 (1983) pp. 2–49.
Rojahn, J., 'The Emergence of a Theory: The Importance of Marx's Notebooks Exemplified by those from 1844', *Rethinking Marxism* Vol. 14 No. 4 (2002) pp. 29–46.
Rollings, N., 'British Budgetary Policy 1945–1954—a "Keynesian Revolution"?', *Economic History Review* Vol. 41 (1988) pp. 283–98.
Roscher, W., *System der Volkswirthschaft* Bd. 1: *Die Grundlagen der Nationalökonomie*, J. G. Cotta, Stuttgart 1854.

Rousseau, J.-J., 'Discours sur l'économie politique', *Oeuvres complètes de Jean-Jacques Rousseau* t. 3, Gallimard, Paris 1964 pp. 239–78.

Ruffin, R. J., 'David Ricardo's Discovery of Comparative Advantage', *History of Political Economy* Vol. 34 (2002) pp. 727–48.

Sartorius, G., *Handbuch der Staatswirthschaft zu Gebrauche bey akademischen Vorlesungen, nach Adam Smith's Grundsätzen ausgearbeitet*, Berlin 1796.

Saussure, F. de, *Course in General Linguistics*, ed. C. Bally and A. Sechehaye, with A. Riedlinger, McGraw-Hill, New York 1966.

Say, J.-B., *Abhandlung über die Nationalökonomie*, 2 vols., trans. L. H. Jakob, Halle 1807.

Say, J.-B., *Traité d'économie politique*, variorum edition, ed. Emmanuel Blanc et al., *Oeuvres Complètes* t. 1, Economica, Paris 2006.

Sayers, R. S., '1941—the First Keynesian Budget', in C. Feinstein (ed.) *The Managed Economy. Essays in British Economic Policy since 1929*, Oxford University Press, Oxford 1983 pp. 107–17.

Schlak, S., '"Die existentielle Dimension des Politischen". Wilhelm Hennis im Gespräch mit Stephan Schlak', in A. Anter (ed.) *Wilhelm Hennis' Politische Wissenschaft. Fragestellungen und Diagnosen*, Mohr Siebeck, Tübingen 2013 pp. 329–38.

Schlözer, C. von, *Anfangsgründe der Staatswirthschaft oder die Lehre von dem Nationalreichthume*, Vol. 1, Riga 1805.

Schumpeter, E. B., *English Overseas Trade Statistics 1697–1808*, Oxford University Press, London 1960.

Schumpeter, J., *History of Economic Analysis*, George Allen and Unwin, London 1954.

Sen, S. R., *The Economics of Sir James Steuart*, G. Bell & Sons, London 1957.

Siclovan, D., 'The Project of "Vergesellschaftung": German Socialists 1843–1851', M. Phil. Dissertation, University of Cambridge 2010.

Sidgwick, H., *The Principles of Political Economy*, 3rd edition, Macmillan, London 1903.

Simonde de Sismondi, J. C.-L., *Principes de l'économie politique, ou de la richesse dans ses rapports avec la population* t. 2, Delauney, Paris 1819.

Singer, K., 'Oikonomia: An Inquiry into Beginnings of Economic Thought and Language', *Kyklos* Vol. 11 (1958) pp. 29–57.

Skarżyński, W. von, 'Pierre de Boisguillebert und seine Beziehungen zur neueren Volkswirthschaftslehre', dissertation, Faculty of Philosophy, University of Berlin 1873.

Skarżyński, W. von, *Adam Smith als Moralphilosoph und Schoepfer der Nationaloekonomie: Ein Beitrag zur Geschichte der Nationaloekonomie*, Verlag von Theobold Grieben, Berlin 1878.

Skinner, Q., *Liberty before Liberalism*, Cambridge University Press, Cambridge 1998.

Smith, A., *Untersuchung über die Natur und Ursachen des Nationalreichthums*, 4 vols., trans. Garve and Dörrien, Breslau 1794–96.

Smith, A., *Recherches sur la nature et les causes de la richesse des nations*, ed. G. Garnier, H. Agasse, Paris An X [1802].

Smith A., *An Inquiry into the Nature and Causes of the Wealth of Nations*, ed. J. Thorold Rogers, Clarendon Press, Oxford 1869.

Smith, A., *Lectures on Justice, Police, Revenue and Arms*, ed. E. Cannan, Oxford University Press, Oxford 1896.

Smith, A., *Theorie der ethischen Gefühle*, trans. and ed. W. Eckstein, Felix Meiner Verlag, Hamburg 1926.

Smith, A., *Vorlesungen über Rechts-, Polizei-, Steuer- u. Heereswesen*, Nach der Ausgabe von Edwin Cannan, intr. J. Jastrow, H. Meyer's Buchdruckerei, Halberstadt 1928.
Smith, A., *Natur und Ursachen des Volkswohlstandes*, trans. and ed. Friedrich Bülow, Alfred Kröner Verlag, Leipzig 1933.
Smith, A., *Die Theorie des Aussenhandels. Inquiry into the Nature and Causes of the Wealth of Nations B. IV. Ch. 1–3 1776*, ed. A. Skalweit, Vittorio Klostermann, Frankfurt am Main 1946.
Smith, A., *Untersuchungen über Natur und Ursprung des Volkswohlstandes*, Georg Westermann Verlag, Braunschweig 1949.
Smith, A., *An Inquiry into the Nature and Causes of the Wealth of Nations*, Oxford University Press, Oxford 1976.
Smith, A., *The Correspondence of Adam Smith*, ed. E. C. Mossner and I. S. Ross, Oxford University Press, Oxford 1977.
Snow, E. C., review of Clark, *The National Income, 1924–31*, *Journal of the Royal Statistical Society* Vol. 96 (1933) pp. 110–14.
Soden, J. H. von, *Die Nazional-Oekonomie*, Vol. 1, Leipzig 1805.
Sommer, A., 'Das Naturrechtskolleg von Adam Smith', *Archiv für Rechts- und Wirtschaftsphilosophie* Bd. 20 (1927) pp. 378–95.
Sonenscher, M., 'Ideology, Social Science and General Facts in Late Eighteenth-Century French Political Thought', *History of European Ideas* Vol. 35 (2009) pp. 24–37.
Sperber, J., *Karl Marx: A Nineteenth-Century Life*, W. W. Norton, New York 2013.
Stamp, J. C., *Wealth and Taxable Capacity*, P.S. King & Son, London 1922.
Stamp, J. C., 'Methods used in Different Countries for Estimating National Income', *Journal of the Royal Statistical Society* Vol. 97 No. 3 (1934) pp. 423–66.
Stedman Jones, G., 'Introduction' to Karl Marx, Friedrich Engels, *The Communist Manifesto*, Penguin Books, London 2002 pp. 1–187.
Stedman Jones, G., 'Marx's Critique of Political Economy: A Theory of History or Theory of Communism?', in Chris Wickham (ed.) *Marxist History—Writing for the Twenty-First Century*, Oxford University Press, Oxford 2007 pp. 140–57.
Stedman Jones, G., 'The Young Hegelians, Marx and Engels', in Gareth Stedman Jones, Gregory Claeys (eds.) *Cambridge History of Nineteenth-Century Political Thought*, Cambridge University Press, Cambridge 2011 pp. 556–600.
Steiner, P., 'Commerce, commerce politique', in Loïc Charles, Frédéric Lefebvre, Christine Théré (eds.) *Le cercle de Vincent de Gournay: Savoirs économique et pratiques administratives en France au milieu du XVIIIe siècle*, Institut National d'Études Démographiques, Paris 2011 pp. 179–200.
Steiner, P., 'The Creator, Human Conduct and the Maximisation of Utility in Gossen's Economic Theory', *European Journal of the History of Economic Thought* Vol. 18 (2011) pp. 353–80.
Steiner, P., 'Administration and Œconomic Government in Quesnay's Political Economy', in Roberto Baranzini, François Allisson (eds.) *Economics and other Branches – In the Shade of the Oak Tree. Essays in Honour of Pascal Bridel*, Pickering and Chatto, London 2014 pp. 123–34.
Stephen, L., 'Adam Smith', *Dictionary of National Biography* Vol. 53, Smith, Elder, London 1898.
Steuart, J., *An Inquiry into the Principles of Political Œconomy: Being an Essay on the Science of Domestic Policy in Free Nations*, 2 vols., A. Millar, T. Cadell, London 1767.

Stewart, D., *Lectures on Political Economy* Vol. 1, Thomas Constable, Edinburgh 1855.

Stewart, D., 'Account of the Life and Writings of Adam Smith, LL.D', in Adam Smith, *Essays on Philosophical Subjects*, Oxford University Press, Oxford 1980 pp. 269–351.

Stigler, G. J., 'Henry L. Moore and Statistical Economics', *Econometrica* Vol. 30 (1962) pp. 1–21.

Stone, R., *Some British Empiricists in the Social Sciences 1650–1900*, Cambridge University Press, Cambridge 1997.

Swain, N., *Collective Farms Which Work?* Cambridge University Press, Cambridge 1985.

Thweatt, W. O., 'James Mill and the Early Development of Comparative Advantage', *History of Political Economy* Vol. 8 (1976) pp. 207–34.

Toews, J. E., *Hegelianism: The Path Toward Dialectical Humanism, 1805–1841*, Cambridge University Press, Cambridge 1980.

Tooze, A., *Statistics and the German State, 1900–1945: The Making of Modern Economic Knowledge*, Cambridge University Press, Cambridge 2001.

Tribe, K., 'John Ford's My Darling Clementine—an Investigation', *Cambridge Anthropology* Vol. 1 No. 1 (1973) pp. 10–17.

Tribe, K., 'On the Production and Structuring of Scientific Knowledges', *Economy and Society* Vol. 2 (1973) pp. 465–78.

Tribe, K., *Land, Labour and Economic Discourse*, Routledge and Kegan Paul, London 1978.

Tribe, K., 'The Structure of Agrarian Capitalism—the "English Model"', in my *Genealogies of Capitalism*, Macmillan, London 1981 pp. 35–100.

Tribe, K., 'Prussian Agriculture—German Politics: Max Weber 1892–7', *Economy and Society* Vol. 12 (1983) pp. 181–226.

Tribe, K., 'Introduction to Todorov/Bakhtin', *Economy and Society* Vol. 13 (1984) pp. 20–24.

Tribe, K., 'Mikhaïl Bakhtin: Word and Object', *Economy and Society* Vol. 15 (1986) pp. 403–13.

Tribe, K., *Governing Economy: The Reformation of German Economic Discourse 1750–1830*, Cambridge University Press, Cambridge 1988.

Tribe, K., 'Locating German Economics: A Biographical Guide to the Study of the History of German Economics', *German History* Vol. 8 (1990) pp. 73–81.

Tribe, K., *Economic Careers: Economics and Economists in Britain 1930–1970*, Routledge, London 1997.

Tribe, K., 'Adam Smith: Critical Theorist?', *Journal of Economic Literature* Vol. 37 (1999) pp. 609–32.

Tribe, K., '*The Cambridge Economics Tripos 1903–55 and the Training of Economists*', *Manchester School* Vol. 68 (2000) pp. 222–48.

Tribe, K., 'The Historicisation of Political Economy?', in B. Stuchtey, P. Wende (eds.) *British and German Historiography 1750–1950*, Oxford University Press, Oxford 2000 pp. 211–28.

Tribe, K., 'Economic Societies in Great Britain and Ireland', in M. Augello, M. Guidi (eds.) *The Spread of Political Economy and the Professionalisation of Economists*, Routledge, London 2001 pp. 32–52.

Tribe. K., 'The 1948 Currency Reform: Structure and Purpose' in J. Hölscher (ed.) *50 Years of the German Mark: Essays in Honour of Stephen F. Frowen*, Macmillan, Basingstoke 2001 pp. 15–51.

Tribe, K., with Mizuta H. (eds.) *A Critical Bibliography of Adam Smith*, Pickering and Chatto, London 2002.
Tribe, K., 'Cameralism and the Sciences of the State', in Mark Goldie, Robert Wokler (eds.) *The Cambridge History of Eighteenth-Century Political Thought*, Cambridge University Press, Cambridge 2006 pp. 525–46.
Tribe, K., '"A Lost Connection": Max Weber and the Economic Sciences', in Karl-Ludwig Ay, Knut Borchardt (eds.) *Das Faszinosum Max Weber: Die Geschichte seiner Geltung*, UVK Verlagsgesellschaft, Konstanz 2006 pp. 313–29.
Tribe, K., 'Economic Manuals and Textbooks in Great Britain and the British Empire 1797–1938' in Massimo M. Augello, Marco E. L. Guidi, (eds.) *The Economic Reader*, Routledge, London 2012 pp. 43–75.
Tribe, K., 'What Is Social Economics?', *History of European Ideas* Vol. 40 (2014) pp. 714–33.
Tribe, K., 'De l'atelier au procès de travail: Marx, les machines et la technologie', in F. Jarrige (ed.) *Technologies et socialismes: Théories, imaginaires, pratiques au XIXe siècle*, (forthcoming).
Tribe, K., 'Jean-Baptiste Say's Footnotes to Ricardo', in press.
Trier, J., 'Über Wort- und Begriffsfelder' [1931], in his *Aufsätze und Vorträge zur Wortfeldtheorie*, ed. A. van der Lee and O. Reichmann, Mouton, The Hague 1973 pp. 40–65.
Tubaro, P., 'Les mathématiques du plaisir et de la peine: La théorie du choix individuel de Hermann Heinrich Gossen', in *La pensée économique allemande*, ed. A. Alcouffe and C. Diebolt, Economica, Paris 2009 pp. 245–67.
Turgot, A. R. J., *Réflexions sur la formation et la distribution des richesses*, n.p. 1788.
United Nations, *Measurement of National Income and the Construction of Social Accounts*, Geneva 1947.
Vatin, F., 'Le travail, la servitude et la vie. La critique de l'économie politique d'Eugène Buret', in his *Trois essais sur la genèse de la pensée sociologique*, Éditions La Découverte, Paris 2005 pp. 23–79.
Vaughan, D., *Portrait of an Invisible Man: The Working Life of Stewart McAllister, Film Editor*, British Film Institute, London 1983.
Vaughan, D., *For Documentary*, University of California Press, Berkeley 1999.
Verri, P. *Meditazioni sulla economia politica*, Livorno 1771.
Walker, D. A. (ed.) *William Jaffé's Essays on Walras*, Cambridge University Press, Cambridge 1983.
Walker, D. A., 'Is Walras's Theory of General Equilibrium a Normative Scheme?', *History of Political Economy* Vol. 16 (1984) pp. 445–69.
Walras, A., Walras, L., *Œuvres économiques complètes*, ed. P. Dockès, P.-H. Goutte, C. Hébert, C. Mouchot, J.-P. Potier, J.-M. Servet, Economica, 13 vols., Paris 1987–2005.
Walras, L., *Elements of Pure Economics*, George Allen and Unwin, London 1954.
Walras, L., *Correspondence of Léon Walras and Related Papers*, 3 vols., ed. W. Jaffé, North-Holland, Amsterdam 1965.
Walter, R., *Critical History of the Economy: On the Birth of the National and International Economies*, Routledge, London 2011.
Watts, J., *The Facts and Fictions of Political Economists: Being a Review of the Principles of the Science, Separating the True from the False*, Abel Heywood, Manchester 1842.
Weber, M., 'Kritische Studien auf dem Gebiet der kulturwissenschaftlichen Logik. 1. Zur Auseinandersetzung mit Eduard Meyer', in *Gesammelte Aufsätze zur*

Wissenschaftslehre, 5th edition, J. C. B. Mohr (Paul Siebeck), Tübingen 1982 pp. 215–65.
Weber, M., *Wirtschaft und Gesellschaft. Soziologie. Unvollendet 1919–1920*, ed. Knut Borchardt, Edith Hanke, Wolfgang Schluchter, *Max Weber Gesamtausgabe* Bd. I/23, J. C. B. Mohr (Paul Siebeck), Tübingen 2013.
Whatmore, R., *Republicanism and the French Revolution: An Intellectual History of Jean-Baptiste Say's Political Economy*, Oxford University Press, Oxford 2000.
Whitaker, J. (ed.) *The Correspondence of Alfred Marshall*, 3 vols., Cambridge University Press, Cambridge 1996.
White, M. V., 'The Moment of Richard Jennings: The Production of Jevons's Marginalist Economic Agent', in Philip Mirowski (ed.) *Natural Images in Economic Thought: 'Markets Read in Tooth and Claw'*, Cambridge University Press, Cambridge 1994 pp. 197–230.
White, M. V., 'In the Lobby of the Energy Hotel: Jevons's Formulation of the Post-classical "Economic Problem"', *History of Political Economy* Vol. 36 (2004) pp. 228–71.
Wicksteed, P. H., *The Alphabet of Economic Science*, Macmillan, London 1888.
Wicksteed, P. H., *The Common Sense of Political Economy*, 2 vols., ed. Lionel Robbins, George Routledge, London 1933.
Wieser, F. von, *Über den Ursprung und die Hauptgesetze des wirthschaftlichen Werthes*, Alfred Hölder, Vienna 1884.
Wootton, B., 'Who Shall Pay for the War?', *Political Quarterly* Vol. 11 (1940) pp. 143–54.
Worlidge, J., *Systema Agriculturae*, 2nd edition, London 1675.
Wrigley, E. A., Schofield, R. S., *The Population History of England 1541–1871: A Reconstruction*, Cambridge University Press, Cambridge 1989.
Xenophon, *Memorabilia and Oeconomicus*, trans. E. C. Marchant, Harvard University Press, Cambridge (MA) 1923.
Yagi, K., *Austrian and German Economic Thought*, Routledge, London 2011.
Zeyss, R., *Adam Smith under der Eigennutz: Eine Untersuchung über die philosophischen Grundlagen der älteren Nationalökonomie*, Verlag der H. Laupp'schen Buchhandlung, Tübingen 1889.

INDEX